Sun™ Cluster Environment

Sun Cluster 2.2

Enrigue Vargas
Joseph Bianco, Ph.D.
David Deeths

Sun microsystems

Sun Microsystems Press
A Prentice Hall Title

The publisher offers discounts on this book when ordered in bulk quantities. For more information, contact: Corporate Sales Department, Phone: 800-382-3419; Fax: 201-236-7141; E-mail: corpsales@prenhall.com; or write: Prentice Hall PTR, Corp. Sales Dept., One Lake Street, Upper Saddle River, NJ 07458.

Editorial/production superviser: *Nicholas Radhuber*
Cover design director: *Jerry Votta*
Cover designer: *Kavish & Kavish Digital Publishing & Design*
Manufacturing manager: *Alexis R. Heydt*
Marketing manager: *Debby vanDijk*
Acquisitions editor: *Gregory G. Doench*

Sun Microsystems Press
Marketing manager: *Michael Llwyd Alread*
Publisher: *Rachel Borden*

10 9 8 7 6 5 4 3 2 1

ISBN 0-13-041870-6

Sun Microsystems Press
A Prentice Hall Title

Table of Contents

Chapter 2: Sun Cluster 2.2 Architecture

Chapter 4: Sun Cluster 2.2 Administration

Chapter 5: Highly Available Databases

Chapter 6: Sun Cluster 2.2 Application Notes

Appendix A: SCSI-Initiator ID

Appendix B: SC2.2 Data Service Templates

Preface

This book is one of an on-going series of books developed by the engineering staff of the Sun BluePrints™ Program. The Sun BluePrints Program is managed by the Enterprise Engineering group, and provides a framework to identify, develop, and distribute best practices information for Sun products.

If you are new to clustering, we discuss how a cluster is built and configured, plus more (a lot more)—we recommend you read the book from cover to cover. For those with cluster experience, the book has been set out in modular fashion—each section covers specific areas that can be quickly identified and referenced.

This book builds a solid foundation by detailing the architecture and configuration of the Sun Cluster software. The information provided in this book extends beyond the Sun Cluster infrastructure and introduces Sun Cluster 2.2 (SC2.2) applications, maintenance, and datacenter best practices to enhance datacenter efficiency and application availability.

The Sun Cluster 2.2 technology has evolved due in part to the involvement and commitment of its customers to achieve a high level of maturity and robustness. Sun Microsystems' participation in the cluster software arena began in the spring of 1995 with the introduction of the SPARCcluster™ 1 product. Table P-1 is a timetable of cluster products released by Sun Microsystems (as of the time of this printing).

Table P-1 Sun Cluster Product Evolution

Year	Product
Spring 1995	SPARCcluster 1 to sustain highly available applications
Summer 1995	SPARCcluster PDB 1.0 support for Oracle Parallel Server (OPS), Informix Extended Parallel Server (XPS), and Sybase Navigation Server
Winter 1995	SPARCcluster HA 1.0
Spring 1996	SPARCcluster PDB 1.1
Summer 1996	SPARCcluster HA 1.1
Fall 1996	SPARCcluster PDB 1.2
Fall 1996	SPARCcluster HA 1.2
Spring 1997	SPARCcluster HA 1.3
Fall 1997	Sun Cluster 2.0 - Initial merge of SPARCcluster PDB and SPARCcluster HA product lines
Spring 1998	Sun Cluster 2.1
Summer 1999	Sun Cluster 2.2 - Final merge of SPARCcluster HA into Sun Cluster

In the summer of 1995, the SPARCcluster PDB (parallel database) 1.0 software was introduced to enable parallel node scalability—this product also supported a highly available application environment. The SPARCcluster PDB software enabled parallel database products such as Oracle Parallel Server (OPS), Informix Extended Parallel System (XPS), and Sybase Navigation Server to be used in a two-node cluster.

After the release of the SPARCcluster PDB software, a separate development group within Sun introduced the SPARCcluster HA (high availability) product in the winter of 1995. The SPARCcluster HA software enabled a highly available environment for mission-critical applications such as databases, NFS, and DNS Servers.

Although the SPARCcluster PDB and SPARCcluster HA software products had different architectures, and different algorithms for data protection, cluster membership, and data management, they shared functional similarities—both environments supported a subset of available Sun servers and storage devices, and used a network interconnect for cluster communications.

A fundamental difference between these cluster products was that SPARCcluster HA required Solstice DiskSuite™ software to support shared disk storage, while SPARCcluster PDB required Veritas Cluster Volume Manager (CVM) software.

To maximize the investment in engineering resources, Sun Microsystems unified its cluster software development program and merged the SPARCcluster HA and SPARCcluster PDB solutions to create the Sun Cluster 2.0 software, which was released in the fall of 1997.

The Sun BluePrints Program

The primary purposes of the Sun BluePrints Program are research, development, and publishing of best practices using Sun products. These BluePrints provide the required building blocks to assist in the creation of high-performance, highly available, and highly reliable datacenters.

To ensure up-to-date information is available to customers, a Web site is provided to compliment the BluePrints Program:

`http://www.sun.com/blueprints`

The mission of the Sun BluePrints Program is to empower Sun customers with the technical knowledge required to implement an expandable, highly available, and secure information system within a datacenter using Sun products. The Sun BluePrints Program is managed by the Enterprise Engineering group. This group provides a framework to identify, develop, and distribute best practice information that can be applied across all Sun products. Subject matter experts in the areas of performance, resource management, security, high-performance computing, networking, and storage write articles that explain the best methods of integrating Sun products into a datacenter.

The Enterprise Engineering group is the primary contributor of technical content for the Sun BluePrints Program, which includes books, guides, and online articles. Through these vehicles, Sun provides down-to-earth guidance, installation tips, real-life implementation experiences, and late-breaking technical information.

Who Should Use this Book

This book is produced for experienced system administrators, system architects, and technologists interested in acquiring or enhancing their Sun cluster expertise. Those who use this book should be familiar with UNIX and the Solaris Operating Environment (Solaris OE).

How this Book Is Organized

This book is divided into two major sections:

Part I, Infrastructure

Describes basic availability concepts and Sun Cluster 2.2 architecture and its components. It contains the following chapters:

Chapter 1, "High Availability Fundamentals" on page 1

High availability is a fundamental component for today's mission-critical applications. Implementation of high availability now spans beyond the hardware and software platforms to include the total system infrastructure. This chapter focuses on the basic concepts and mathematical formulas that define *reliability, availability,* and *serviceability* (RAS). Additionally, we discuss the best practices and elements that play a key role for increasing availability at the single node and datacenter levels.

Chapter 2, "Sun Cluster 2.2 Architecture" on page 31

The Sun Cluster 2.2 framework is a collection of integrated software modules that provides a highly available environment with horizontal scalability. Topics such as cluster topologies, cluster membership, quorum algorithms, failure fencing, and network monitoring are discussed.

Chapter 3, "Sun Cluster 2.2 Components" on page 77

There are many component choices to be made when assembling a cluster. This chapter discusses capacity, performance, and availability features of supported Sun Cluster 2.2 components—servers, disk storage, interconnect, and public networks. This information can help you assemble a cluster to match your requirements.

Part II, Implementation

Discusses the techniques necessary to design, implement, and maintain Sun Clusters.

After a cluster environment has been installed, configured, and is in production, it needs to be correctly maintained to preserve its high availability. This chapter complements existing Sun Cluster 2.2 manuals, and addresses *when*, *why*, and *how* Sun Cluster 2.2 commands should be used to help increase availability.

Databases represent the transactional back-end of a large percentage of mission-critical applications. This chapter presents a general discussion on databases supported by the Sun Cluster 2.2 software—namely, Oracle. This chapter focuses primarily on the Oracle database, and discusses software installation, configuration options, logical host creation, and data service agent monitoring.

This chapter provides the framework for implementing a cluster configuration from scratch. The techniques and issues involved in configuring a low-end, distributed NFS server are discussed.

Sun Cluster 2.2 software is equipped with a standard application programming interface (API) that enables programmers to transform existing applications into highly available applications. This chapter discusses the SC2.2 Data Services API and various routines required to manage an existing application under the SC2.2 infrastructure.

This chapter provides an introduction to the pinnacle of the Sun Cluster technology (Sun Cluster 3.0). Topics discussed include global file services, scalable services, availability, and supported cluster configurations.

"Appendix A: SCSI-Initiator ID" on page 319

This appendix presents an in-depth tutorial for resolving SCSI controller issues when using multiple hosts that share SCSI storage.

"Appendix B: SC2.2 Data Service Templates" on page 339

This appendix is a collection of Bourne shell templates that support *all* data service agent routines.

Related Books

The books in Table P-2 provide additional useful information:

Table P-2 Related Books

Title	Author and Publisher	ISBN Number
Resource Management	Richard McDougall, Adrian Cockcroft, Evert Hoogendoorn, Enrique Vargas, Tom Bialaski; Sun Microsystems Press/Prentice Hall, Inc. (1999)	ISBN 0-13-025855-5
Blueprints for High Availability	Evan Marcus, Hal Stern; John Wiley & Sons Inc. (2000)	ISBN 0471-35601-8
In Search of Clusters	Gregory F. Pfister; Prentice Hall PTR (1998)	ISBN 0-13-899709-8

Typographic Style

Table P-3 describes the typographic styles used in this book:

Table P-3 Typographic Conventions

Typeface or Symbol	Meaning	Example
`AaBbCc123`	Names of commands, files, and directories	Edit your `.login` file. Use `ls -a` to list all files. `machine_name% You have mail.`
`AaBbCc123`	Text entered into the system (**bold**)	**`machine_name% su`** **`Password:`**
`AaBbCc123`	Text displayed on the monitor	`Text varies with output`
AaBbCc123	Command-line placeholder; replace with a real name or value	To delete a file, enter the command: `rm` *filename*.
AaBbCc123	Book titles, new words or terms, or words to be emphasized	Read Chapter 6 in *User's Guide*. These are called *class* options. Example: "You *must* be root user to perform this step".

Shell Prompts in Command Examples

Table P-4 identifies the default system prompt and superuser prompt for the C shell, Bourne shell, and Korn shell:

Table P-4 Shell Prompt Examples

Shell	Prompt
C shell prompt	`machine_name%`
C shell superuser prompt	`machine_name#`
Bourne shell and Korn shell prompt	`$`
Bourne shell and Korn shell superuser prompt	`#`

Acknowledgements

Contributors

Special thanks go to Peter Lees, a Sun Microsystems engineer based in Australia, for providing most of the content for the "Sun Cluster 2.2 Data Services" chapter. Peter also wrote the scripts in Appendix B, "Sun Cluster 2.2 Data Service Templates."

Special thanks also to Ji Zhu and Roy Andrada for providing the underlying core of the "High Availability Fundamentals" chapter—both are members of the Sun Microsystems RAS group.

Thanks to David Gee, our dedicated in-house technical writer/editor for massaging the engineering content into the finished product, and for his constructive writing tips. We also thank his wife, Elizabeth, for her understanding in the midst of the wedding preparation rush.

Thanks to Terry Williams for the edits and proofs, and for building the index and glossary.

General

Writing a book requires much more than just raw material and technical writing. We would also like to thank the following, who helped review, provide technical clarity, and all manner of personal or professional support:

We would like to acknowledge the following cluster experts who helped shape the technical content of this book: Peter Dennis, Tim Read, Geoff Carrier, Paul Mitchell, Walter Tsai, Bela Amade, Angel Camacho, Jim Mauro, Hal Stern, Michael Geldner, and Tom Atkins (and many other experts who contributed through internal Sun Cluster
e-mail aliases).

Additionally, we thank the Sun Cluster marketing and engineering groups for sanitizing our technical claims. We would especially like to thank Yousef Khalidi, Midland Joshi, Sandeep Bhalerao, and Paul Strong.

Thanks to Don Kawahigashi and Don Roach; both of these SUN University cluster instructors helped with the review process. We appreciate the contribution of their own material which enriched the content of the book.

Also, many thanks go to Barbara Jugo for effectively managing our book's publication while caring for an adorable baby daughter.

This book was made possible by the support provided by the Enterprise Engineering team, which generated a synergy that enabled creative and innovative ideas to flow freely in a fun environment.

Finally, thanks to the Sun customers for being our main supporters. We are confident this book will fulfill their expectations and they will benefit from the material presented.

Enrique Vargas

I've been working with cluster technologies for more than eight years; however, writing this book has humbled me into realizing how *little* I knew.

First and foremost, I would like to thank my wife, Michelle, for being a solid wall to lean on, and for the uncounted sacrifices she endured—and to my two daughters, Saralynn and Christine, for the virtual loss of their father during the course of this book.

Also, thanks go to my niece, Pamela, for being a model of courage, and to my great-grandfather, Mariano Zavala, for his strength of character and his qualities as a writer, revolutionary, and poet.

I am grateful to Charles Alexander, creator of the BluePrints Program, for his support of myself and my family. Also thanks to my manager, Bill Sprouse, for freeing up my time to enable my writing activities to flourish.

My personal quest in life is to simplify complexity at every level—in this regard, please feel free to contact me personally at `Enrique.Vargas@Sun.com` with any comments or suggestions.

To all involved, thank you.

Joseph Bianco, Ph.D.

To Scott Woods, thanks for the support, guidance, and resources needed to accomplish this goal.

Thanks to Phil Refano and Darryl Benjamin for their support.

Also, special thanks to Kevin Rabito for his help through the years.

Many thanks to Professor Carl W. Cuttita for everything.

Thanks to Charlie Dugan for giving me my start in the IS field.

A love-filled thanks to my wife, Linda, and daughter, Victoria, for putting up with my antics.

David Deeths

A heart-felt thanks to my family—their unwavering support and encouragement helped me through the arduous task of writing. My parents' dedication to the success of this project fired me with inspiration. I hope that seeing this book will encourage my mother to continue with her writing endeavors. Thanks to my sisters, Christine, Katie, and Elizabeth, and also to "Mother" Gail Gardner.

Thanks to the friends who provided me with a network of caring that was always "highly available"—especially the following (who suffered the brunt of my complaining, book-induced flaking, and stress-filled rambling): Nova Ebbesen, Typhany Farnholtz, Mark Featherstone, Todd Gonsalves, Mary Higgins, Pete Jha, Kristin Johnson, Robin King, Mark Lacuesta, Dave Lubitz, Amy Weinstein, and Janet Wertz.

Thanks to the BluePrints lab manager, Tim Marsh, for scrounging and setting up equipment and machines on short notice.

Special thanks to John Howard, who provided a sounding board for ideas and also for donating technical expertise and guidance.

Also, thanks to my manager, Bill Sprouse, who provided endless support, countless ideas, and insight into producing a well-rounded book.

And finally, thanks to Chuck Alexander for his vision and careful management, which enabled the BluePrints Program to thrive. On a personal level, Chuck has provided guidance and support, which have enabled me to personally and professionally strive to new heights.

List of Figures

Chapter 1: High Availability Fundamentals

Chapter 2: Sun Cluster 2.2 Architecture

Chapter 3: Sun Cluster 2.2 Components

Chapter 5: Highly Available Databases

Chapter 6: Sun Cluster 2.2 Application Notes

Chapter 7: Sun Cluster 2.2 Data Services

Chapter 8: Beyond Sun Cluster 2.2

Appendix A: SCSI Initiator ID

Appendix B: SC2.2 Data Service Templates

List of Tables

Chapter 1: High Availability Fundamentals

Chapter 2: Sun Cluster 2.2 Architecture

Chapter 3: Sun Cluster 2.2 Components

Chapter 4: Sun Cluster 2.2 Administration

Chapter 5: Highly Available Databases

Chapter 6: Sun Cluster 2.2 Application Notes

Chapter 7: Sun Cluster 2.2 Data Services

Appendix A: SCSI Initiator ID

References

Alomari, A., (1999) Oracle & Unix Performance Tuning 2nd Edition. Prentice Hall, Upper Saddle River, NJ.

A Scalable Server Architecture From Department to Enterprise — The SPARCserver 1000E and SPARCcenter 2000E; Sun Microsystems Whitepaper.

Availability Primer: Availability Tuning and Configuration Series for Solaris Servers; Ji Zhu; Sun Microsystems Whitepaper.

Buyya, R., (1999) High Performance Cluster Computing Volume 1 Architectures and Systems. Prentice Hall, Upper Saddle River, NJ.

Campus Clustering with the Sun Enterprise Cluster; Peter Chow, Joe Sanzio, Linda Foglia; Sun Microsystems Whitepaper.

Ensor, D., Stevenson, I., (1997) Oracle Design. O'Reilly & Associates Inc., Sebastopol, CA.

Loney, K., Kock, G., (1997) Oracle 8: The Complete Reference. Osborne McGraw-Hill, New York, NY.

Mahapatra, T., Mishra, S., (2000) Oracle Parallel Processing. O'Reilly & Associates Inc., Sebastopol, CA.

Mauro, J., McDougall, R., (2001) Solaris Internals Core Kernel Architecture. Prentice Hall, Upper Saddle River, NJ.

Membership, Quorum and Failure Fencing in Sun Cluster 2.x; Hossein Moiin, Tim Read; Sun Microsystems Whitepaper.

Netra st A1000 and D1000 Storage Arrays Just the Facts; Sun Microsystems Whitepaper.

Netra t 1120 and 1125 Servers Just the Facts; Sun Microsystems Whitepaper.

Netra t 1400 and 1405 Servers Just the Facts; Sun Microsystems Whitepaper.

Oracle 8 Parallel Server Concepts and Administration Manual. June 1998.

Pfister, G., (1998) In Search of Cluster. Prentice Hall, Upper Saddle River, NJ.

Reliability, Availability, and Serviceability in the SPARCcenter 2000E and the SPARCserver 1000E; Sun Microsystems Whitepaper.

Ryan, N., Smith, D., (1995) Database Systems Engineering. International Thomson Computer Press, Albany, NY.

Stern, H., Marcus, E., (2000) Blueprints for High Availability. John Wiley & Sons, Inc., New York, NY.

SunATM Adapters Just the Facts; Sun Microsystems Whitepaper.

Sun Enterprise 220R Server Just the Facts; Sun Microsystems Whitepaper.

Sun Enterprise 250 Server Just the Facts; Sun Microsystems Whitepaper.

Sun Enterprise 3500-6500 Server Just the Facts; Sun Microsystems Whitepaper.

Sun Enterprise 420R Server Just the Facts; Sun Microsystems Whitepaper.

Sun Enterprise 450 Server Just the Facts; Sun Microsystems Whitepaper.

Sun Enterprise 450 Server Just the Facts; Sun Microsystems Whitepaper.

Sun Enterprise 10000 System Just the Facts; Sun Microsystems Whitepaper.

Sun Fast Ethernet PCI Bus Adapter Just the Facts; Sun Microsystems Whitepaper.

Sun FDDI Adapters Just the Facts; Sun Microsystems Whitepaper.

Sun Gigabit Ethernet PCI Adapter 2.0 Just the Facts; Sun Microsystems Whitepaper.

Sun Quad Fast Ethernet Just the Facts; Sun Microsystems Whitepaper.

Solaris Resource Manager on Sun Cluster 2.2; Sun Microsystems Whitepaper.

Sun StorEdge A1000/D1000 Storage Arrays Just the Facts; Sun Microsystems Whitepaper.

Sun StorEdge A3500 Array Just the Facts; Sun Microsystems Whitepaper.

Sun StorEdge A5x00 Array Family Just the Facts; Sun Microsystems Whitepaper.

Sun StorEdge A7000 Array, Remote Dual Copy, and Sun StorEdge DataShare Just the Facts; Sun Microsystems Whitepaper.

Sun StorEdge MultiPack, FlexiPack, and UniPack Systems Just the Facts; Sun Microsystems Whitepaper.

Sun Ultra Enterprise 150 Just the Facts; Sun Microsystems Whitepaper.

Sun Ultra 2 Workstation Just the Facts; Sun Microsystems Whitepaper.

System Availability Report for Ultra Enterprise X000 Server Family; Sun Microsystems Whitepaper.

The Ultra Enterprise 1 and 2 Server Architecture; Sun Microsystems Whitepaper.

Ultra Enterprise 3000-6000 Just the Facts; Sun Microsystems Whitepaper.

Understanding the Sun Cluster HA API: A Field Guide; Peter Lees; Sun Microsystems Whitepaper.

CHAPTER 1

High Availability Fundamentals

Virtually every aspect of our lives is touched in some way by the computer revolution. We have become highly dependent on computer systems—a good example of this dependence was illustrated by the frenzied preparation for the year 2000 computer bug, Y2K. Apart from the monetary cost, the potential loss of our computer systems caused widespread fears that the world would face various disasters—ranging in severity from failure of the ATM network to planes falling from the sky like ripe plums—or the ultimate bad news story, nuclear Armageddon.

Because our trading systems represent the backbone of our financial stability, users increasingly demand 100 percent availability. Any disruption to service is measured, not only in dollars and cents, but perhaps more importantly, in reputation. We rely on our computer systems for everyday life—e-mail, pager services, pumping gas, and a myriad of other functions.

Availability has long been a critical component for online systems because business processes can quickly come to a halt when a computer system is down. For example, in the world of e-commerce, availability is paramount because of client demand for instant access to a site—if a site is unavailable (for whatever reason), the competitor's site is only a mouse click away.

Sun Microsystems places system availability at the top of its business priority list. Sun has created two organizations for researching high availability in Sun computer systems:

- The RAS (reliability, availability, and serviceability) Engineering group concentrates on statistical analysis of system components to extract availability metrics. The RAS Engineering group develops tools that can assist hardware designers to achieve higher levels of availability in new and existing hardware designs.
- The SunUP organization is part of the SunLabs group, and is responsible for working with customers and third-party partners to develop products and services that enhance availability in Sun computer systems. The Sun BluePrints Program works in alliance with the SunUP program to produce best practice documentation.

Availability is directly affected by computer hardware and software ; however, people and processes can also have a significant impact. This chapter introduces different system categories that can assist in the decision-making process when choosing a server type best suited to your specific business availability requirements. The fundamental concepts of *reliability, availability,* and *serviceability* (RAS) relating to the hardware, operating system, and application elements will be discussed. Although the RAS mathematics may appear tedious to the reader, this information can assist administrators in making decisions when attempting to balance cost against availability.

Note: The statistical concepts and formulas presented in this chapter have been kept basic for the sake of simplicity.

This chapter introduces best practices that can assist in minimizing the impact of people and processes in the datacenter—which may help achieve higher availability goals. The availability model for Sun servers has become increasingly complex due to the increased number of high availability features provided at the hardware, operating environment, and application levels.

Basic System Outage Principles

A system fault can be caused by internal or external factors. Examples of internal factors could include specification or design errors, manufacturing defects, component defects, and component wear-out. Examples of external factors could include radiation, electromagnetic interference, operator error, and natural disasters.

Regardless of how well a system is designed, or how reliable the components are, failures cannot be eliminated completely. However, it is possible to manage failures and thereby minimize impact to the system.

An *error* is the occurrence of a system fault in the form of an incorrect binary output. If an error prevents a system (or subsystem) from performing its intended function, a *failure* has taken place.

For example, a defective DRAM device may cause a data bit to deviate from its correct state and produce an *error* (parity or error correction code [ECC]). If the incorrect data causes a system to crash or reboot, the error becomes a *failure*.

All system outages fall into two major categories:

- Unplanned system outages (failures)

Note: Unplanned outages are the result of uncontrollable, random system failures associated with *faults* affecting hardware or software components. Unplanned outages are the most costly, and can be minimized through component redundancy, enhanced RAS features, and a Sun Cluster environment. Unplanned outages include external influences (for example, network services, power infrastructure, security, naming services, and human error).

- Planned system outages (maintenance)

A planned outage should be scheduled to have a minimum availability impact on a system. Planned outages are the result of a scheduled maintenance event involving repair, backup, or upgrade operations—these outages should be scheduled to minimize impact on availability. Repairs involve replacing faulty components and restoring the system to a functional state. Backing up preserves critical data on a magnetic storage medium (disk or tape) to avoid data loss when a production system experiences a main disk storage failure. Upgrades are implemented to replace current hardware or software with newer (or enhanced) versions.

System Types—Availability Requirements

High availability is often associated with fault-tolerant systems. The term *fault-tolerant* means a system can operate while experiencing hardware component failures. A single component failure in a fault-tolerant system will not cause a system interruption because an alternate component will take over the task transparently.

As the cost of components continues to decrease, and demand for system availability increases, many *non-fault-toleran*t systems have redundancy built-in at the subsystem level. As a result, many *non-fault-tolerant* systems can tolerate hardware faults—consequently, the line between a fault-tolerant system and a non-fault-tolerant system is becoming increasingly blurred.

A service level agreement (SLA) is a written agreement between a system manager and the end-user that details the application requirements of the end-user. It is important to understand the RAS requirements spelled out in an SLA because different RAS levels may require a different design and configuration approach that can impact cost. For example, in a fault-tolerant, highly available environment, any component failure that interrupts system operation may not be acceptable. However, in a general-purpose computing environment, it may be desirable to improve overall system availability by choosing a configuration that has multiple short outages over a configuration that has just one extended outage.

From a traditional availability perspective, computer systems can be grouped into four categories based on their intended applications:

- General-purpose computing

Applications that fall within this category are used in a wide variety of disciplines—including engineering analysis, business purposes, data warehousing, and computational sciences. Failures in general purpose computers are commonplace and users tend to be more forgiving. Occasional, short disruptions to system operation may be tolerable provided the operating system restarts quickly and automatically.

- Highly available systems

Availability is the key metric for applications within this category. Users demand a high probability of receiving service when requested. Although an occasional loss of a localized service may be tolerable, a system-wide outage is unacceptable. Banking and telecommunications systems are typical examples of high availability environments.

- Critical computational systems

These systems have stringent fault tolerance requirements. For some real-time control systems, faulty computations could jeopardize human lives, or have high economic impact. Computations must be highly accurate with minimal fault recovery time. Aircraft flight control systems, military systems, and certain types of industrial controllers are some examples of systems that perform critical computations.

- Long-life systems

In this type of system, reliability is a priority. These include mobile systems that depart from a central facility for extended periods of time, or systems under little supervision that are placed in remote areas. For these types of applications, unscheduled maintenance can be prohibitively expensive. Space flight systems and satellites are examples of long-life systems.

All single-node Sun servers (except the Netra ft series) are typically categorized as general-purpose computers. The Netra ft series is considered highly available because of its fault-tolerant characteristics.

Note: Sun Cluster software assists in the recovery from hardware and software failures, whereas a fault-tolerant system has the operating system and application as a single point of failure. Although Sun servers are not specifically designed for critical computation or long-life applications, there are cases where Sun servers have been placed in remote *lights-out* sites where the performance has resembled that of a long-life system.

Reliability Fundamentals

The academic definition of reliability, *R(t)*, is the probability of a system performing its intended function over a given time period, *t*. For example, a system with a 0.9999 reliability over one year has a 99.99 percent probability of functioning without failures over the time period of a year.

Reliability is only one of many factors that influences availability. For example, 99.99 percent *reliability* does not mean 99.99 percent *availability*. Reliability measures the ability of a system to function without interruptions, while availability measures the ability of a system to provide a specified application service level to clients. Therefore, reliability provides a metric of how often a component is likely to fail, while availability includes the effects of any downtime that failures produce.

Mean Time Between Failures (MTBF)

A commonly used metric for measuring reliability is referred to as the *mean time between failure* (MTBF). The MTBF is the average time interval (usually in hours) between consecutive component failures. Reliability is improved when the time interval spanning separate failures is extended.

The MTBF value does not indicate exactly when a component failure will occur. The MTBF value is a result of statistical analysis—a failure can occur randomly at any point during a component's life cycle (Murphy's law dictates this will usually be at the worst possible time).

The following are typical variations of the MTBF:

Hardware MTBF

This metric refers to the mean time between hardware component failures. Component redundancy and error correction features of the Solaris Operating Environment prevent hardware component failures from becoming system interruptions.

System MTBF

This metric refers to the mean time between system failures. A system failure indicates that users experience an application service level outage that can only be restored by repair. Hardware component redundancy increases the overall system MTBF (although the MTBFs of individual components remain the same). Because a failure of a redundant part does not bring a system down, the overall system MTBF is increased. However, because individual components fail at the same rate, a higher component count increases the probability of component failure. Hardware designers rely on statistical analysis to quantify the reliability gains from introducing component redundancy into a system.

Mean Time Between Interruptions (MTBI)

This metric refers to a temporary system outage where repairs are not required. MTBI is an important concept in the Sun server world because the Solaris Operating Environment includes the Automatic System Recovery (ASR) feature.

Unlike hardware MTBF, system MTBF and MTBI are measurements of events visible to end users. System failures can result in extended periods of application service level outage, while some system interruptions may result in short outages that are addressed by the Solaris ASR feature—this feature automatically isolates faulty hardware components to render a system functional after a component failure reboot.

Failure Rate

Another metric for measuring reliability is the *failure rate*—defined as the inverse of either the hardware or system MTBF as determined by the formula below. If the failure rate is high, the MTBF value is small.

$$\textit{Failure Rate} = \frac{1}{\textit{MTBF}}$$

Where
MTBF = Mean Time Between Failures

Each MTBF definition has a corresponding failure rate. For example, the *hardware failure rate* is the inverse of the *hardware MTBF,* while the *system failure rate* is the inverse of the *system MTBF.*

The hardware MTBF is probably the most frequently cited MTBF metric—even though it does not reflect the typical end-user view of the service level agreement—because hardware component failures in a correctly configured system do not necessarily result in an interruption.

For most electronic components, the MTBF and failure rate change during the life cycle of a component—however, because the variance is small, it is safe to assume the value is constant. The component failure rate curve for a component's life cycle is known as a *Bathtub Curve,* see Figure 1-1.

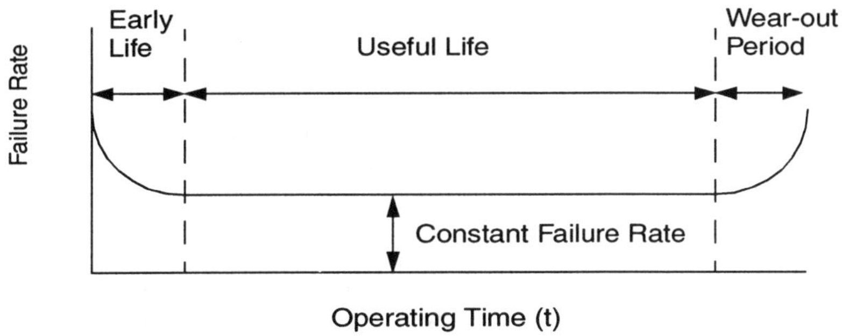

Figure 1-1 Component Failure Rate Bathtub Curve

Figure 1-1 illustrates hardware component failure over time and demonstrates a phenomenon known as *infant mortality*—this is where a component exhibits a high failure rate during the early stage of its life. To help ensure component failures are detected early, manufacturers often subject components to a burn-in process whereby systems are exposed to voltage, temperature, and clock frequency extremes.

The failure rate gradually reduces over time until it approaches a constant value (which is maintained during its *useful life).* Eventually, the component enters the *wear-out* stage of its life—in this stage, failures increase exponentially.

Note: New technologies may also exhibit a similar pattern of failure rate during the *early* and *useful life* time periods.

Common MTBF Misconceptions

MTBF is commonly confused with a component's useful life, even though the two concepts are not related in any way. For example, a battery may have a useful life of four hours and an MTBF of 100,000 hours. These figures indicate that in a population of 100,000 batteries, there will be approximately one battery failure every hour during a single battery's four-hour life span. By contrast, a 64-processor server platform may last 50,000 hours before it enters its wear-out period, while its MTBF value may only be 2,000 hours.

Another common misconception is to assume the MTBF value is higher in a system that implements component redundancy. Although component redundancy can increase the system MTBF, it does quite the opposite for the hardware MTBF—generally, the greater the number of components in a system, the lower the system's hardware MTBF.

Availability Fundamentals

Steady-state availability is a commonly quoted availability metric for most computer systems. Availability is often measured by the *uptime ratio*—this is a close approximation of the steady-state availability value and represents the percentage of time a computer system is available throughout its useful life. Another frequently used availability metric is *downtime per year,* which is calculated using the following formula:

$$\text{Downtime per Year (minutes)} = (1 - \textit{Uptime Ratio}) \times 365 \times 24 \times 60$$

A system is often rated by the number of 9s displayed in its availability classification. Table 1-1 presents the different availability classes and corresponding annual downtime. For example, a system with a five-nine availability rating indicates the system is 99.999 percent available and will have a downtime of 5.26 minutes per year.

Table 1-1 Availability Classes and Downtime per Year

Availability %	Averaged Downtime per Year
99	3.65 days
99.9	8.76 hours
99.99	52.6 minutes
99.999	5.26 minutes
99.9999	30.00 seconds

Availability is commonly defined by the following formula:

$$Availability = \frac{MTBF}{MTBF + MTTR}$$

Where
$MTBF$ = Mean Time Between Failures
$MTTR$ = Mean Time to Repair

This availability formula does not include enhanced RAS features typical of the Solaris Operating Environment. This basic model is illustrated in Figure 1-2 and makes the assumption the system is either available or experiencing a repair cycle. It is important to note a failure must be detected and the system administrator notified before repairs can be scheduled. The time elapsed between a failure occurring and its detection can be reduced (to enhance availability) using sophisticated failure detection systems.

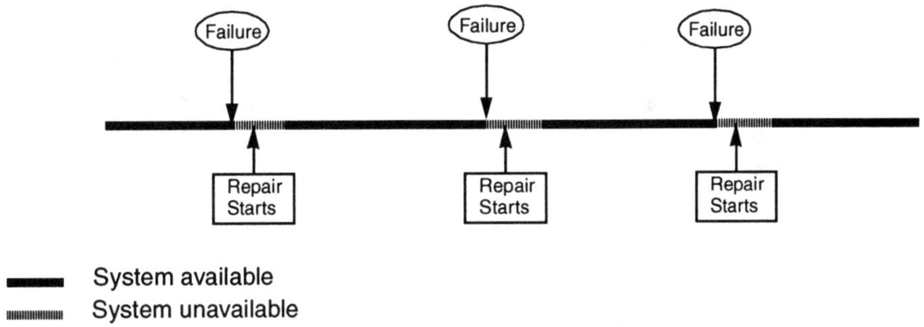

Figure 1-2 Solaris OE Availability Model (without enhanced RAS features)

The Solaris Operating Environment has enhanced RAS features, including online maintenance and ASR. Because some of the failure cycles do not require service intervention, ASR invalidates the old computer systems availability model. The ASR feature enables faulty components to be automatically fenced off after a component-failure reboot—component-failure reboots are invoked by the kernel to prevent data corruption. Hardware component redundancy is critical for system availability because ASR will not grant a system reboot if the remainder of the components cannot guarantee a functioning system.

Note: To enable the ASR feature, the OpenBoot PROM (OBP) `diag-level` environment variable must be set to `max`. The `diag-trigger` OBP environment variable must be set to `error-reset` or `soft-reset` to ensure that diagnostics are executed after a reboot.

The following are potential failure scenarios illustrated by Figure 1-3:

- Failure 1 requires service intervention to bring the system online.
- Failure 2 is detected by ASR, which brings the system online after a reboot. The faulty component can be replaced during routine maintenance.

As an example of the Solaris Operating Environment availability model, a CPU failure on a Sun Enterprise™ 6500 server can be characterized as Failure 2 in Figure 1-3. This failure induces an outage in the form of a component-failure reboot. The second outage occurs when the system board containing the bad CPU module is replaced during maintenance and the system is rebooted.

- Failure 3 does not bring the system down because the faulty component is bypassed using component redundancy. The faulty component can be replaced during routine maintenance.

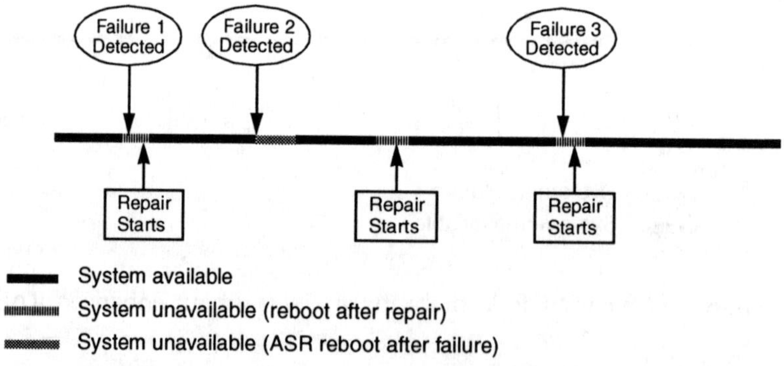

Figure 1-3 Solaris Operating Environment Availability Model (with enhanced RAS features)

The Solaris Operating Environment availability features such as component redundancy, ASR, and online maintenance have made outage scenarios more complex; therefore, it is no longer appropriate to use basic formulas based on MTBF and MTTR figures to calculate availability.

Reliability vs. Availability

There is a difference between *reliability* and *availability*. Depending on a customer's situation, system requirements may favor reliability over availability (or vice versa). For example, reliability will have a higher priority in cases where a system is placed in a remote area where maintenance could be expensive. For additional information, refer to Chapter 3, "Sun Cluster 2.2 Components" to assess the reliability of different hardware component choices for your datacenter needs.

Although availability is a function of reliability and serviceability, it is possible for a system with poor reliability to achieve high availability. For example, assume a system averages four failures a year, and with each failure, the system can be restored with an average outage time of one minute. Using the availability formula discussed in the section "Availability Fundamentals" on page 8, the availability of this system is calculated to be 99.99924 percent—this is 4 minutes of downtime out of a total of 525,600 minutes in a year.

Reliability measures the ability of a system to function continuously without interruptions. A high MTBF for a computer system indicates that on average, the system can operate for extensive periods of time without component failure interruptions. By contrast, *availability*, measures the ability of a system to meet a committed application service level.

The following formula is an approximate conversion of reliability to availability:

$$Availability = \frac{t - (1 - R(t))dt}{t}$$

Where
$R(t)$ = System reliability over a time period, t
dt = Average outage in hours

Note: The formula above is an approximation of a more complex statistical formula and is likely to be inaccurate for an $R(t)$ figure below 90%. This formula was derived by the Sun Microsystems RAS Engineering group.

The reliability, *R(t)*, of a system represents the probability of the system not encountering any failures over a time period, *t*. The value of 1 - R(t) represents the probability of a system encountering failures over a time period *t*. Multiplying 1 - R(t) by *dt* (the average outage time) approximates the total outage time over the same time period (assuming R(t) is close to 1).

The value of t - (1 - R(t)) *x dt* provides the total time a system is working during time period *t* (uptime). Dividing t - (1 - R(t)) *x dt* over the total time period, *t*, yields the total availability figure.

Serviceability Fundamentals

Serviceability, *S(t)*, is the probability of a service action being completed during a given time period, *t*. If a system is said to have a serviceability of 0.95 for three hours, then the probability of a service action being completed within the specified time is 95 percent. Higher *reliability* reduces the frequency of system failures, while higher *serviceability* reduces the duration of each repair incident.

A commonly used serviceability metric is the *mean time to repair* (*MTTR*), which is the average length of time needed to complete a repair action.

Customers do not normally allow for the impact of the logistics time in the MTTR calculation. The *logistics time* is sometimes referred to as the *service response time* (time required for service personnel with the necessary spare parts to arrive at a customer's site). Availability calculations made without including logistics time are referred to as *intrinsic availability* measurements.

Note: Logistics time is often influenced by a service option. We encourage customers to review the available Sun Enterprise service options to find one that suits their availability requirements.

The following sections describe software technology developed by Sun Microsystems that can simplify system serviceability and enhance availability.

Dynamic Reconfiguration

The Solaris Operating Environment supports Dynamic Reconfiguration (DR) software on Sun Enterprise™ 3000 to 6500 and 10000 platforms. The DR software enables the attachment or detachment of hardware resources without incurring system downtime. For further details on dynamic reconfiguration, see the Sun BluePrints book

Resource Management. Dynamic Reconfiguration also enables online maintenance—this feature removes the need for a system reboot when defective hardware components are replaced.

Although DR increases availability, the SC2.2 infrastructure does not support this feature because of the time involved in suspending the operating system during a DR operation. The elapsed time spent in the suspended state by the operating system depends on system resources available during a DR-detach operation. A busy system may stay in the suspended state for long enough to trigger a non-responsive node alarm in the cluster management software.

Alternate Pathing

The Solaris Operating Environment supports *alternate pathing* (AP) software on the Sun Enterprise 3000 to 6500 and 10000 platforms. The AP software enables a *manual failover* of an active network with an *automatic failover* of disk I/O controllers to standby resources after a failure is detected. In the future, AP will provide fully *automated failover* capabilities.

The SC2.2 infrastructure does not support the use of AP because it conflicts with the SC2.2 bundled *network adapter failover* (NAFO) software. NAFO provides automatic failover to alternate network controllers when a network failure is detected.

Single System Availability Tuning

This section discusses the key factors involved in configuring a single system to match availability requirements. The most important considerations before configuring a system for high availability are to fully understand the application RAS requirements and select the appropriate computing platform, see section, "System Types—Availability Requirements" on page 3." *Availability tuning* is similar to performance tuning, and is essentially a process whereby areas that contribute the most to system outages are identified and minimized (or eliminated) to improve overall system availability.

As previously discussed, datacenter processes required to increase the availability level are constrained by the following:

Static Constraints

System configuration, software choices, etc.

Dynamic Constraints

Training, documentation, fire drills, etc.

The following sections address system configuration issues that can help increase system availability.

Configuring to Reduce System Failures

Sun Microsystems servers have been designed with enhanced system availability in mind. This has been accomplished through component count reduction, strict quality control, environmental monitoring, and the removal of active components from critical field replaceable units (FRUs). Memory error correction code (ECC) has been adopted on all servers to minimize system downtime caused by faulty single in-line memory modules (SIMMs) and dual in-line memory modules (DIMMs).

Sun Microsystems servers enable hot-swapping of some components (for example, power supplies and cooling fans). Adding redundancy to subsystem components such as power and cooling modules can provide immediate availability improvement if faulty components can be hot-swapped without interrupting the operating environment.

Production system failures could be caused by a single point of failure (SPOF), or by multiple failures occurring within the same downtime period. Because multiple fault occurrences are rare, SPOFs are the dominant cause of system failures and should be targeted for reduction. SPOFs are unacceptable in a Solaris cluster environment because the fundamental premise of a cluster environment is total component redundancy at all levels of hardware and software.

Eliminating SPOFs can be accomplished by including redundant components in the system. However, having additional components in a system increases the probability of component failure, and could potentially result in further system interruptions.

Component placement is critical for eliminating SPOFs. For example, if disk controller B provides redundancy for disk controller A, both controllers need to be placed on separate system boards to prevent inaccessibility after a system board failure.

Reducing System Interruption Impact

Significant availability improvements can be achieved by reducing system interruptions caused by CPUs, memory, power modules, etc. The basic approaches for increasing availability at the component level are as follows:

Reduce the Number of System Interruptions

System interruptions can be minimized by reducing the number of components whose failure could cause system interruptions. A common approach is to replace a number of low-speed CPU modules with fewer high-speed modules to provide equal processing power with a lower probability of a CPU module failure. Similarly, low-density DIMMs/SIMMs can be replaced with fewer high-density DIMMs/SIMMs—again, to provide equal memory capacity with a lower probability of memory module failure.

Reduce the Duration of System Interruptions

There are several ways to reduce downtime to help increase system availability (see "Datacenter Best Practices" on page 18). File system logging—featured by the Solaris 7 OE, Veritas file system software, and Veritas Volume Manager Dirty Region Logging (DRL) can reduce system downtime by eliminating file system checks during reboot.

Reducing Maintenance Reboots

Most hot-pluggable FRUs in Sun Enterprise servers today can become hot-swappable with the appropriate operating system. The number of maintenance reboots can be reduced by configuring a system for DR. DR software requires considerable front-end planning—especially when adding or removing system boards containing I/O controllers. Although DR software may increase system availability, the SC2.2 infrastructure does not currently support this feature.

Configuring Highly Available Subsystems

A computer system (from an RAS perspective) can be viewed as consisting of multiple subsystems in series, which means that if a subsystem fails, the whole system fails. For example, if the power supply subsystem fails, the whole system will fail. However, computer systems based on RAS principles have redundancy built into each subsystem. For example, a RAS computer system with N+1 redundancy will have more than one power supply module in the subsystem (see Figure 1-4); therefore, the failure of one power supply module will not result in total system failure.

Note: The Sun Enterprise Server 10000 SSP software includes a component blacklisting option that enables the logical removal of intermittent or failed system board components.

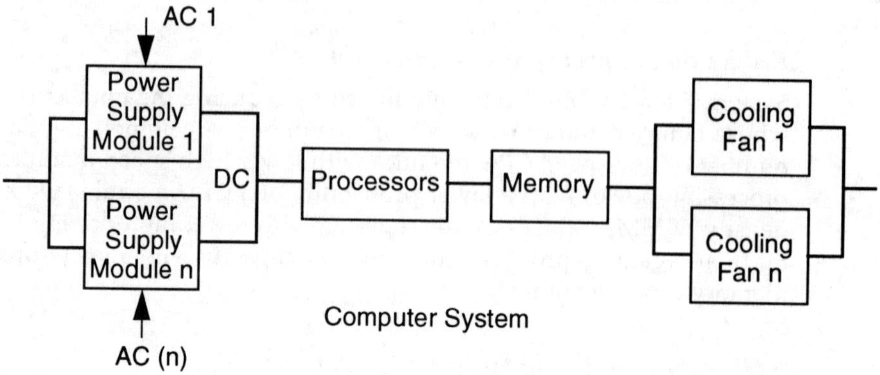

Figure 1-4 Server Subsystems with N+1 Redundancy

The availability of the overall system is only optimized after the individual subsystems are optimized. The following sections highlight subsystem RAS-related issues.

CPU Subsystem

Due to its complexity and high density, the processor module is a component that may have a high failure rate. In most Sun servers, a failed processor will cause the system to invoke a component-failure reboot. However, if the ASR feature is enabled, the failed component will be fenced off after rebooting. There are few configuration choices for processor modules—however, the general rule of reliability applies—the fewer components there are, the less the chance of a failure.

Memory Subsystem

Although memory errors can be single-bit or multiple-bit, the majority of errors are single-bit. A computer system is unaffected by single-bit errors; however, multiple-bit errors cause the system to invoke a component-failure reboot. The general rule of reliability also applies here—the *number* of memory modules should be reduced.

Input/ Output (I/O) Subsystem

There are a large variety of I/O controllers available; consequently, methods of dealing with a failure can vary significantly. Some controllers support redundancy using AP software (see "Alternate Pathing" on page 13), or SC2.2 NAFO software. Some controllers support both redundancy and load sharing using the Sun Trunking™ software, or Veritas VxVM Dynamic Multiple Pathing (DMP).

Note: Neither AP nor Sun Trunking are currently supported by the SC2.2 infrastructure.

Boot Disk Subsystem

Without a boot drive, it would be difficult to bring up the production version of the operating environment. The boot drive can be made highly available by mirroring its contents using a hardware or software volume manager, see Chapter 3, "Sun Cluster 2.2 Components."

Software volume managers such as the Sun Enterprise Volume Manager™ or Solstice DiskSuite™ (SDS) can be used to mirror a boot drive. Additionally, the use of hot-pluggable disk drives could reduce the need to bring the system down to replace a failed mirror.

Power Supply Subsystem

On most Sun servers, a power supply failure will not bring a system down (if it can be hot-swapped transparently). Configuring a power supply is relatively straightforward; however, maintaining the required N+1 redundancy is often overlooked in a rapidly changing environment.

Cooling Fans Subsystem

On most Sun servers, a cooling fan failure will not bring the system down—it can be hot-swapped transparently. Most cooling-related issues are external to the system—such as keeping the computer room temperature stable (below 25°C [75°F]). High temperatures and temperature fluctuations are forms of stress to electronic components.

Disk Storage Arrays Subsystem

Storage array components are almost as complex as computer systems because they have their own power supplies, cooling fans, host interface cards, processors, and memory. By mirroring an array or setting up a redundant array of independent disks (RAID-5) volumes, it is possible to experience a storage array failure without bringing the system down. If hot-pluggable disks are supported by the disk array, failed disks can be replaced transparently, see Chapter 3, "Sun Cluster 2.2 Components."

Sun Cluster Node Subsystem

With an SC2.2 configuration, each of the cluster nodes can be viewed as a subsystem. A node failure (in a correctly configured cluster) should only cause a brief interruption. An interruption induced by this type of failure is generally shorter than a failure incurred in a non-clustered system because the interruption involves only the application failover time with no reboot time.

Datacenter Best Practices

Industry analysts indicate that system hardware accounts for only 20 percent of outages—while people and practices account for 80 percent.[1] For example, a simple change to a system parameter may result in an outage that could have been avoided with appropriate testing, or with a change control process in place.

A lot can be learned from processes that have been developed over the past 20 years by mainframe and UNIX system managers. Processes that affect availability are wide-ranging—careful attention should be paid to analyzing their potential business impact at all levels. The service delivered by an application often requires the availability of connection to storage, client systems, and networks, which all extend beyond the availability of a single system. Any process applied in the datacenter must encompass all components within the system—from the platform and storage, to the network infrastructure that links the business application to users.

The remainder of this section lists best practices that can help improve existing levels of availability in the datacenter.

1. Gartner Group research note, "Tactical Guidelines," 16 March 1999.

Systems Management Principles

Systems should be managed by *highly trained* administrators who can appropriately configure the operating system and applications to fulfill an SLA. Because technology evolves rapidly, a training plan should be in place to keep system administrators' knowledge current.

System resources should be frequently monitored using platform monitors (for example, Sun™ Management Center) and application monitors (for example, BMC Patrol/Best1 and Tivoli) to analyze resource usage trends to ensure existing resources are sufficient. The analysis of resource usage enables a system administrator to predict when resources will be depleted—this enables system resource additions to be scheduled before an application causes an outage.

Note: When using a Sun Cluster environment, it is critical to monitor system resources (kernel memory, CPU, I/O cycles, etc.) to ensure appropriate cluster software behavior.

The Sun Remote Services (SRS) service option can enhance system availability through system event monitoring and service management of critical production systems (via a modem link). Remote monitoring of disk storage subsystems has been adopted by many high-end customers because they appreciate the value of replacing defective hardware and upgrading obsolete firmware before they become a critical issue in the datacenter.

The SRS option is delivered as part of the standardized SunSpectrum Gold℠ and SunSpectrum Platinum℠ service bundles that enable Sun Enterprise Service engineers to monitor production systems on a 24 x 7 basis to assist in reducing service latency after a problem is detected. The SRS feature detects error conditions based on a set of pre-defined thresholds. When errors are detected, a corrective approach is taken in partnership with the customer.

Hardware Platform Stability

System hardware provides the foundation for the operating system and applications. A common source of system problems is loose mechanical connections that may result in intermittent problems manifested through hard-to-track error messages at the operating system and application levels. If the hardware platform is subjected to mechanical vibrations, it could loosen components and change their electrical characteristics.

All components in a system must be correctly fitted and secured to ensure maximum mechanical contact and guarantee that electrical characteristics remain constant. Memory and CPU components must be fully inserted and secured into their sockets. I/O cards must be fully inserted into their SBus or PCI connectors and secured. External cables need to be fully inserted and secured with the correct strain relief in place to ensure the cable weight does not strain internal components.

Consolidating Servers in a Common Rack

Consolidating multiple servers within a single rack can enhance availability through the simplification of system management (and promote efficient use of datacenter floor space). It is recommended that each server within the same rack has independent I/O cabling (correctly labeled) and an independent power source. These measures help minimize SPOFs and can prevent accidental outages.

System Component Identification

When system components need to be replaced, availability is improved if repairs take place swiftly and effectively. Accurate system documentation and component identification provide system administrators with increased control over existing resources. System documentation enables system administrators to plan future system changes without having to repeatedly take an inventory of existing resources.

Each system platform consists of a large combination of components which may be connected to network and storage devices. To prevent a technician from removing a wrong part, each component (including cables) should be uniquely labeled to assist in the identification process.

The Solaris Operating Environment creates controller instances for each device under its control (for example, `hme0`, `qfe1`, `c3`, etc.).

Controller instances should be labeled to identify their physical controller ports.

The Solaris Operating Environment creates soft link entries in the `/dev/dsk` and `/dev/rdsk` directories for hard disk devices. Hard disk devices are also registered as `sd` (SCSI devices) and `ssd` (serial SCSI devices) instances (see the `sd(7D)` and `ssd(7D)` man pages for details). The Solaris Operating Environment displays disk errors using controller instances and `sd/ssd` instances.

Disk devices should be labeled with the controller and `sd/ssd` instances at their replacement point to assist identification.

The Sun StorEdge™ A3500, A3500FC, and A1000 storage array platforms are hardware RAID devices. A single Solaris disk instance may span several physical disks in the same storage array. The `rm6(1M)` utility can identify any physical disk devices needing to be replaced.

The Solaris Operating Environment identifies tape devices by means of soft link entries in the `/dev/rmt` directory (see the `st(7D)` man page for details).

Label each tape device with its `rmt` instances at the replacement point to assist identification.

There should be an interconnection diagram of the system platform showing all external equipment (storage platforms, routers, hubs, client machines, etc.). The diagram should identify each piece of equipment with a unique name and its physical location in the datacenter. Physical locations can be identified by creating a grid diagram of the datacenter, see Figure 1-5. The server location should include an entry to locate a server or peripherals stacked vertically in a rack (for example, a C3F identification maps to a peripheral device located on the sixth layer of a rack at the C3 coordinate). Devices on the same vertical layer *must not* have duplicate port IDs.

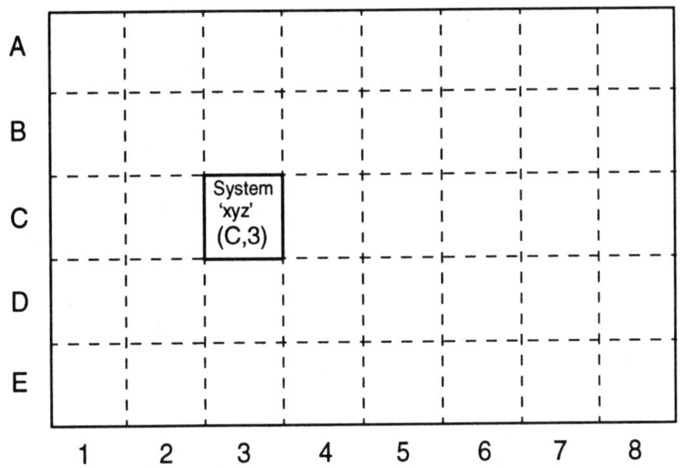

Figure 1-5 Datacenter Floor Plan Grid Diagram

Cables should be uniquely labeled. Using the example in , one of the private interconnect patch cables is labeled *qfe4C3A* on one end to indicate that the qfe4 connector is located on the first vertical level (A) of a rack located at the C3 coordinates. The other end of the cable is labeled *hme0C3B* to indicate that the hme0 connector is located on the second vertical level (B) of a rack located at the C3 coordinates.

To minimize the time required to replace a cable, both ends of a cable should indicate the originating and terminating positions. In our example, one cable end would have a *qfe4C3A- hme0C3B* label, and the other end would have a *hme0C3B-qfe4C3A* label.

AC/DC Power

The AC power supply must conform to the voltage settings established for a specific hardware platform. For example, if the DC power supply subsystem fails, the whole system will fail. To ensure voltages remain constant, they should be continually monitored.

Mission-critical datacenter equipment is commonly equipped with multiple power cords to access alternate sources of AC power. Systems with high availability requirements could have datacenter power that originates from different power grids to remove the potential of a single point of failure.

Power outages are generally brief in nature; therefore, short-term backup power requirements can be met using an uninterruptible power supply (UPS). The UPS battery should provide sufficient power for the system to be kept running for a specific time period. Because a UPS converts a battery source to AC, it has the added advantage of smoothing an erratic power supply (power conditioning).

Systems with higher availability requirements could use a diesel generator to supply power for extended power failures. Because a diesel generator requires time to be fully functional after starting, a UPS is still required to deliver power immediately following a power failure.

Power cords should not be positioned where they are vulnerable to damage. It is also critical that power cords and circuit breakers are secured so that they are not accidentally tripped. Availability can sometimes be enhanced with simple actions such as fitting a cover over any exposed circuit breakers to prevent accidental tripping.

Note: Any covers fitted to circuit breakers should enable clearance for the breaker to trip.

System Cooling

Datacenter equipment should be operated within its specified temperature range. If cooling in the datacenter is not available (for whatever reason), the only option is to shut down all equipment because high temperature can trigger irreversible damage to electronic components.

Newer systems and components generate more heat because they operate at faster clock speeds; therefore, plan for additional air conditioning units to manage the additional heat output.

Systems with higher availability requirements should have standby air conditioning units on hand to avoid an entire datacenter shutdown if the main cooling infrastructure is unavailable.

Network Infrastructure

Network infrastructure is comprised of switches, hubs, routers, and bridges is considered external to the system and is commonly overlooked as being a key component of system availability. The network infrastructure enables communications between peer and client systems at the local and wide area network (LAN/WAN) levels; therefore, network infrastructure scalability and availability directly affect the availability of the total system.

Use the NAFO software provided with the SC2.2 infrastructure to improve availability of the internal network controllers. This is performed by switching all network I/O to an alternate controller when a failure is detected. Most network product vendors are aware of the high availability requirements of network infrastructure, and therefore provide redundancy at the switch and router levels.

To remove the potential of a single point of failure, WAN links for client connections should be duplicated using independent telephone switching stations.

Customers with higher availability requirements can subscribe to the Internet using different ISPs, or at least using separate access points with the same provider, thereby removing another potential single point of failure.

Sun Microsystems Professional Services organization has developed a highly available, scalable, and secure network backbone solution that uses Alteon WebSystems switches in a redundant configuration at the Internet access point to provide scalability and availability.

The solution also provides secure access behind the Internet access point using the switch's firewall function, or by using the SunScreen™ firewall software in a redundant configuration. The remainder of the network services are delivered through Extreme Networks switches configured redundantly to provide high availability without compromising performance and scalability.

Security

In the past, security was mostly required by the government and financial sectors; however, the e-commerce revolution is exposing more businesses to the potential of unauthorized access to confidential data and attacks by hackers and viruses.

Malicious hackers attempt to modify business data to satisfy their own ego, whereas sophisticated hackers steal business data in an attempt to profit financially. Generally, security breaches cause partial outages—however, they have the potential to result in the total demise of a business.

Denial of service (DoS) attacks involve malicious, repetitive requests to a system or application with the intention of depleting resources. DoS attacks are less severe from a security standpoint because they do not interfere with data integrity or privacy. However, because an authorized end-user is not able to access a service during a DoS attack, there is an immediate impact on business costs.

Customers requiring Internet access should secure their external connections with the following:

- A secure application architecture with built-in functionality to resolve DoS attacks
- A secure, hardened operating environment with minimized system builds
- Up-to-date security patches
- Chokepoints and proxies (where chokepoints are filtering routers, flow control devices, and packet-filtering firewalls)

For customers requiring higher levels of security, Sun Microsystems offers the Trusted Solaris™ product, which supplies security features and assurances supported by the National Computer Security Center (NCSC) and Defense Intelligence Agency (DIA). Businesses can use the Trusted Solaris system with their own security levels and options, or they can enable full security to enable users to perform administrative functions in their own workspaces.

Systems Installation and Configuration Documentation

All software applications start with a system platform that can only be accessed through the OBP prompt. After the system platform is connected to tape, disk, network, or printer devices, the system installation is performed through the following steps:

- OBP configuration:
  - Boot and boot mirror devices, device aliases, etc.
  - DR software enabler
  - Power On Self Test (POST) diagnostics level
  - SCSI initiator ID setting
- Operating system installation
- Solaris Operating Environment recommended patches installation
- Operating system (tunable) parameter configuration (`/etc/system`)
- Network, tape, printer, and disk configuration
- Volume manager installation and configuration
- Volume manager recommended patches installation
- System user configuration
- Software application installation and configuration
- Software application recommended patch installation

Note: The Sun Professional Services group produces runbook-style documentation that includes suggested procedures to assist in configuring and managing a system platform.

All steps involved in the application installation should be documented to enable a system to be regenerated from scratch if disaster strikes. Additionally, system documentation can be used to educate other system administrators or provide material for an implementation review. See Chapter 6, "Sun Cluster 2.2 Application Notes" for an example of system documentation.

Backup and disaster recovery plans should be documented for all critical systems. Hardcopy documentation should be provided as a backup to online documentation.

Some system administrators use the `script(1)` utility to capture input and output generated during software installation. However, the `script(1)` approach generates excessive text that can bury important content, and also lacks comments explaining why things must be done in a specific manner. A `script(1)` output could then be edited to create an HTML document (with appropriate comments). User responses can be identified with an alternate font or text style.

Sun Microsystems supplies a software installation tool known as JumpStart™—this product installs system software and application components from an OBP prompt without the risk of errors typically introduced by manual intervention.

Use JumpStart software to automatically re-generate an entire system infrastructure to enable recovery from any local disaster.

Change Control

After a production system platform is stable and all applications are fully functional—it is essential that any proposed system changes undergo peer review to identify any impact and provide a strategy for implementation.

Systems must be rebooted after changes are implemented—it could be difficult to associate a failed reboot to modifications made six months before.

Datacenters with higher availability requirements should have a production system mirrored by a test or staging system (the mirror should be a scaled-down version of the production system) to implement and evaluate any changes prior to adoption. Care should be taken to isolate test operations on the development system from the real production environment. As an example of poor test process, a customer who mirrored an SAP manufacturing environment inadvertently generated a *test* production order that resulted in the building of a $1.5 million piece of equipment (oops!).

In a clustered environment, system modifications should be implemented using guidelines discussed in Chapter 3, "Sun Cluster 2.2 Components."

Production systems should be backed up to tape prior to implementing any changes—this enables the replication of the original system if the proposed modifications prove detrimental.

Maintenance and Patch Strategy

Sun Microsystems continually introduces new software patches. Your local Sun Enterprise Services provider will supply the appropriate e-mail alias subscription to notify you of newly released patches. Additionally, customers can access patches using the PatchPro software available from:

`http://sunsolve.sun.com`

The patch read-me notes should be reviewed to identify which patch is relevant to a specific production installation. For example, some patches might involve I/O interfaces not used by the system, or could involve a locality that does not apply.

All relevant patches should be collected, stored, and applied on a three-or six-month schedule to keep systems current and minimize outage impact. Critical patches that affect the health of a production system should be applied immediately.

Immediately install any required or recommended patches for:

- Solaris kernel updates to Sun Enterprise 10000 System Service Processor (SSP)
- Sun Cluster software
- Volume manager software (Solstice Disk Suite, Veritas Volume Manager, or Raid Manager [rm6])
- Disk controller/disk storage array/disk drive software

Component Spares

Having spare components available in the datacenter can reduce the time to perform repairs. Sun Microsystems emphasizes the importance of producing interchangeable components for use in different system platforms. This strategy enables reduced component inventory.

Previously in this chapter, we discussed the probability of system components having a higher failure rate in their early and late life periods. The strategy used by car rental companies can be applied to this situation—customers with higher availability requirements can take a proactive approach of replacing components prior to them reaching their wear-out stage, see "Failure Rate" on page 6.

Note: Customers may contact a service representative to determine a spare component strategy that matches their datacenter availability needs.

Software Release Upgrade Process

Software products evolve over time—new and enhanced features become available with each version release. Similar to the patch evaluation process, new software product releases should be evaluated by a review process to determine the business impact.

Support Agreement and Associated Response Time

As discussed in the section "Serviceability Fundamentals" on page 12, logistic time can have major impact on a system outage. In general, the impact of logistic time on a system outage can be summarized by the following:

- Logistic time significantly impacts the outage time caused by a SPOF.
- Logistic time minimally impacts the outage time caused by additional system failures occurring within the same downtime period.
- Logistic time has no impact on outage time caused by system interruptions triggered by ASR.
- Logistic time has no impact on outage time caused by maintenance events.

A service contract is a key element of system availability because it determines the maximum time for a service organization to take ownership of a problem. Customers should understand the service options available in their geographic locations to ensure the appropriate service options meet their business requirements.

For mission-critical systems, a specific person should be the contact point for information gathering (in both directions). This reduces the amount of people involved in a service request—which could end up wasting the service engineer's time.

System availability may be enhanced by being aware of the problem escalation process that ensures new bugs and problems are appropriately handled by the service organization. Whenever a problem is discovered with the functionality of a product, a request for enhancement (RFE) document should be filed with the service organization to initiate a review process.

Backup and Restore

Tape backup of critical systems in a datacenter is routine. However, tape restores are not common practice and it is commonly discovered after the fact that an inadequate backup ends in an incomplete restore process.

Routinely schedule tape restore fire drills to familiarize system administrators with the process, and to validate the adequacy of any backup procedure. A tape restore fire drill identifies the time involved to bring mission-critical systems back online—the business impact can be analyzed and reviewed for improvement.

Tape media makes physical contact with the read/write heads on a tape drive, resulting in the tape becoming unreliable after a number of write cycles. It is recommended that the tape media manufacturer be contacted to obtain the best method of retiring unreliable tapes from the backup pool.

Systems with higher availability requirements may benefit from triple mirroring of disk data and making one of the mirrors available to an external system for backups.

Sun Cluster Recovery Procedures

The SC2.2 infrastructure uses a failover server to execute a mission-critical application if an application failure is detected. Although the SC2.2 application failover process is automated, it is important to be familiar with the manual failover process.

Schedule manual failover fire drills to enable staff to become familiar with the process and make informed decisions if a real failover occurs.

Campus Cluster Recovery Procedures

Disaster can take many forms—for example, floods, lightning, earthquakes, and terrorism—any of which could disrupt a production site. The SC2.2 infrastructure enables a campus cluster solution—a failover node can be located up to 10 km (6 miles) from a production node. This distance separation can be an additional layer of protection against a production site disaster.

Campus cluster management is more complex than that of a regular cluster due to the independence of the separate locations. Therefore, staff should engage in fire drills by scheduling routine failovers to help administrators become familiar with the failover process and make informed decisions if a real failover occurs. If the campus cluster is part of an established disaster recovery plan, this plan should also be tested.

Summary

To satisfy operational demands, customers increasingly require data and applications be available around the clock. Commonly, availability is viewed as the single most important metric of overall system performance.

With the increasing reliance on computer systems and wider accessibility of e-commerce, availability is no longer a pre-requisite of just mission-critical applications, but of the whole IT infrastructure.

Availability is affected by hardware and software, and more importantly, by people and processes. Availability can be optimized by implementing a systematic approach to applying best practices in the datacenter, which could assist in minimizing the impact of human error.

CHAPTER 2

Sun Cluster 2.2 Architecture

This chapter discusses the architecture of the Sun Cluster 2.2 (SC2.2) software. To make full use of a Sun Cluster environment, it will be helpful to understand the underlying framework.

We begin by defining the concepts of clustered computing and how they are implemented within the SC2.2 software. The SC2.2 environment has been designed to provide a flexible architecture for high availability and scalability. However, regardless of configuration or cluster topology, the primary function of the product is to provide a highly available computing environment without compromising data integrity.

The SC2.2 software can be configured in many different ways on varying server configurations—from Ultra-2 up to the Sun Enterprise 10000 server. Likewise, it is also possible to use SC2.2 software as a high-performance database computing environment that presents a single database image to clients. A correctly configured SC2.2 cluster can withstand a (single) major failure such as losing a node, disk array, or network connection, or several smaller, less severe errors such as losing a single disk or single interconnect and still continue to provide application services. If a fault is detected, the SC2.2 framework protects all shared data and begins cluster recovery. After recovery is completed, the SC2.2 framework will continue providing access to services. Although rare, multiple failures can occur simultaneously; the cluster framework cannot deal with this situation. If multiple failures do occur, the data service may not be available; however, all shared storage will be protected (because of failure fencing).

What Is a Cluster?

A *cluster* is a collection of computers (heterogeneous or homogeneous) that is connected by a private, high-speed network that enables the cluster to be used as a unified computing resource. Clusters can be designed in a myriad of ways—some cluster architectures are hardware-only, while others are a combination of hardware and software. Sun Cluster technology falls into the hardware/software category. Any approved Sun server, Sun storage device, and supporting hardware coupled with SC2.2 software can be used to create a cluster. Applications such as electronic mail systems, database systems, Web servers, and proprietary systems can take advantage of a clustered environment. One of the economic advantages of clusters is the ability to add resources to the cluster. Therefore, increasing scalability or system availability can provide a greater return on capital investment.

Single System Image

Regardless of implementation, a major feature of a cluster is its ability to provide a single image of the computing environment.

The concept of a *single system image* (*SSI*) can be confusing. This could be due to the fact that an SSI can be implemented at various levels of the computing environment (such as hardware, operating system, or at the application level). Each SSI implementation has a clear and distinct boundary—if the boundary is crossed, the illusion of the SSI disappears. Vendors can implement an SSI within a cluster at various levels.

Examples of SSI levels:

Hardware SSI

At this level, nodes within a cluster share a common address or memory space. For additional information, refer to literature on non-coherent, non-uniform memory access (NC-NUMA) and cache-coherent, non-uniform memory access (CC-NUMA) architectures. SC2.2 software does not offer hardware SSI.

Operating System SSI

A single image of the operating system (OS) runs across all nodes within a cluster at this level. One copy of the OS is used by cluster members. However, for this SSI model to be useful, it requires an API that covers the entire boundary of the OS, thereby enabling programmers to create applications that can scale without having to write complex parallel algorithms. SC2.2 software does not offer an OS SSI. Therefore, each cluster node has its own independent version of the Solaris Operating Environment (Solaris OE) installed on it.

Application Level SSI

With application level SSI, the boundary of the SSI is contained entirely within the application. That is, applications run within each node's own memory space and share the same persistent data with other nodes. Typical applications that offer application level SSI are batch systems, transaction monitors, and database systems. Concurrency and data integrity are typically managed at the application level by means of a low-level lock manager. Of the three levels in which an SSI can be implemented, the application layer is the most important—this is because the end-user operates at this level. Again, it is important to note—an SSI is maintained wholly within the boundaries of the application. Outside the application boundary, an SSI is no longer valid because each cluster node has its own copy of the Solaris Operating Environment (because there is no OS SSI level). Additionally, there is no hardware level SSI. The only commercially available applications that provide an SSI for use with SC2.2 software are parallel databases such as Oracle OPS, Informix XMP, and IBM DB2 EEE.

Note: With Sun Cluster 3.0 software, an SSI is available without using parallel databases, see Chapter 8, "Beyond Sun Cluster 2.2."

High Availability and Scalability

In general, high availability is a metaphor that describes a computing platform that can withstand single or multiple system failures without a prolonged and uncontrolled interruption to service. High availability requires a coalition of process, people, and technology to ensure a revenue-generating or critical application is always available. The level of availability required is usually expressed as a percentage of availability per year. For example, 99.99 percent availability indicates the application downtime would be about one hour over the period of a year.

This figure does not include the number of times the machine went down (or for how long). A machine with a 99.99 percent rating could fail 30 times within a year if each failure was only two minutes' duration, see Chapter 1, "High Availability Fundamentals."

A secondary attribute of a clustered system is its scalability—this can be measured in either of two ways:

Speed up

The speed up concept states that: Increasing the number of nodes in a cluster decreases the workload time. For example, if it takes one hour to perform a complex query, ideally adding a second node will decrease the time to 30 minutes.

Scale up

The scale up concept states that: Adding more nodes enables a greater number of users to perform work. For example, if one node can handle 100 user connections for order entry transactions, ideally adding a second node will enable another 100 users to enter transactions—thereby potentially increasing productivity two-fold.

Application scalability using SC2.2 software can only be achieved using cluster-aware parallel databases such as Oracle OPS, Informix XPS, or IBM DB2 EEE. When using these database products, applications can scale as the number of nodes in the cluster increases. It is also important to note that scalability is not a linear function. It would be unreasonable to assume that by adding two extra nodes to an existing two-node cluster, database performance will increase by 100 percent; however, it is not uncommon for a correctly designed database that has been tuned to achieve 70 to 80 percent scalability.

Note: Adding a node has the potential of *decreasing* performance—this is because vendors have different requirements and guidelines with respect to application design and the tuning of parallel databases. If database guidelines are not followed according to vendor recommendations, performance degradation is likely.

Single Point of Failure (SPOF)

To remove potential SPOFs from a cluster environment, all hardware must be redundant. Creating disk mirrors within a single disk array is a SPOF, and is not recommended (unless a fully redundant Sun StorEdge™ A3500 array is used). If the array loses power or a controller becomes inoperative, data could be lost or corrupted. The cluster software may not be able to recover from data corruption or arrays going offline.

Clustering between two domains within a single Sun Enterprise 10000 server is not recommended because the server has a single backplane which has the (unlikely) potential of being a SPOF. Another disadvantage when using a single machine for high availability is the potential of that single machine becoming unavailable due to a disaster in the building in which it is housed.

Note: Two domains clustered within a single Sun Enterprise 10000 server is a fully viable and supported configuration. However, the trade-off between a SPOF of a single machine and the potential outage that could result becomes a business consideration and not a technical limitation.

Creating a highly available computing environment has a significant dollar cost. The cost is balanced against the value of a data resource, or in keeping a revenue-generating application online. Therefore, any SPOF should be viewed as having the potential of reducing (or stopping) a revenue stream, see Chapter 1, "High Availability Fundamentals" for specific information on SPOFs.

Sun Cluster 2.2 Software Components

Figure 2-1 illustrates the SC2.2 framework layers used to support high availability or parallel databases. Although each box in the diagram represents a major component of the SC2.2 environment, it does not show the relationships between components. For example, each node uses the Cluster Membership Monitor functionality; however, not every node requires (or will have) the Fault Monitor functionality. In subsequent sections, the functionality of each layer will be discussed.

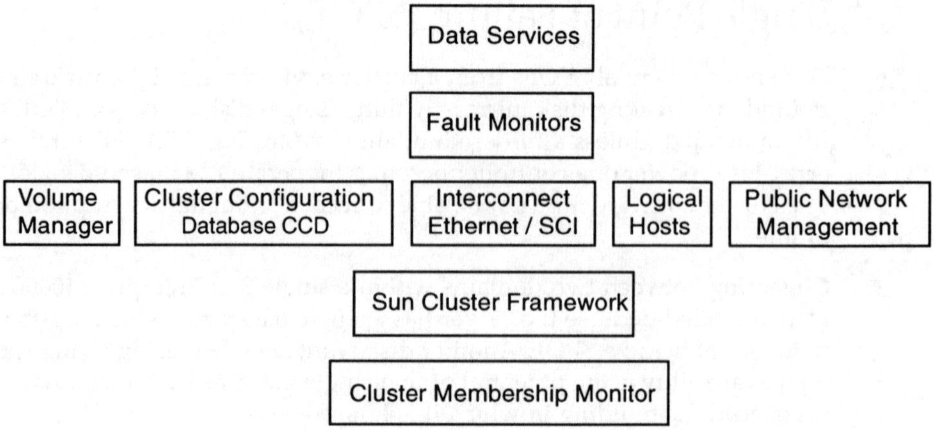

Figure 2-1 Cluster Framework

Cluster Interconnect

Because all cluster communication is performed via the interconnect, it is the focal point of a cluster; therefore, it is essential the interconnect infrastructure is always available. The interconnect supports cluster application data (shared nothing databases), and/or locking semantics (shared disk databases) between cluster nodes.

The interconnect network should not be used for any other purpose except cluster operations. Do not use the interconnect for transporting application data, copying files, or backing up data. Availability of the interconnect is crucial for cluster operation, hence, its redundancy. When a cluster is started, each private network adaptor is configured with a pre-assigned IP address (TCP/IP). The IP addresses used for the interconnect are non-routed and are registered by Sun Microsystems, Inc. Although redundant links are used for availability, only one link is active at any given time. The interconnect is the only component in the cluster that could be considered fault- tolerant—if one link fails, the other is immediately (and transparently) available without affecting cluster operation.

As previously discussed, SC2.2 software can be used for high availability (HA) and parallel database (PDB) configurations. For HA configurations, 100 Base-T can be used for the interconnect transport. The bandwidth and latency of 100 Base-T is sufficient for HA applications because only cluster heartbeat messages use the interconnect. For parallel database applications, Giga Ethernet or SCI should be used as the interconnect transport. Both network topologies offer increased bandwidth for application data or locking semantics. SCI network adapters have a low latency, which is beneficial for shared disk databases such as Oracle Parallel Server (OPS), see Table 2-1.

Table 2-1 Interconnect Hardware for HA and PDB

Topology	High Availability	Parallel Databases
100 Mbit Ethernet	YES	NO
Giga Ethernet	YES	YES
Scalable Coherent Interconnect (SCI)	YES	YES

Switched Management Agent

The Switched Management Agent (SMA) is responsible for monitoring and managing interconnect failures. The cluster interconnect network architecture is designed to broadcast cluster-specific messages such as heartbeats and cluster messages (and in some configurations, application data). The SC2.2 interconnect architecture is not designed for general application traffic and should not be used for this purpose.

The SMA is an important function of the cluster framework because it creates a logical link for the interconnect. Using a logical link rather than a physical link has the advantage of a fast, transparent recovery in the event of interconnect failure. If a fault is detected, the SMA daemon will map the logical link to a new physical link—this mapping of logical to physical is transparent to the cluster framework. In the event of dual interconnect failure (both physical links down), the Cluster Membership Monitor (CMM) is notified and will immediately begin the recovery processes.

Cluster Membership Monitor

The Cluster Membership Monitor (CMM) is also an important function of the SC2.2 framework—it will ensure valid cluster membership under varying conditions and assist in preserving data integrity.

Cluster computing is a form of distributed processing. An essential component of any distributed environment is the ability to determine membership of the participants. Similarly, with clustered computing, it is important to know which nodes are able to join or leave the cluster because resources have to be made available whenever a change in membership occurs. After a cluster is formed, new membership is determined using a consensus of active nodes within the cluster. For a cluster to continue after a membership change (node addition or failure), the CMM will ensure a valid cluster membership. In general, in a three-node cluster, the majority vote is two; therefore, in the event of a failure, two votes must be "available" for the cluster to continue. This concept is discussed in further detail in the failure fencing section, "SC2.2 Failure Fencing/Cluster Membership," on page 58.

Note: "Available" in the preceding paragraph refers to nodes that can communicate with one another via the private interconnect. However, in a multi-node cluster, it is possible to lose the entire interconnect structure and therefore not reach consensus.

The method of determining cluster membership depends on the volume manager used. If Solstice DiskSuite (SDS) is used, a CMM quorum is determined by the majority vote of state database replicas or mediators. When VxVM or CVM is used, a quorum is determined using the cluster framework (by a majority vote of configured nodes). In a two-node cluster, a quorum device is used as a tie-breaker. A quorum device is a disk located within shared storage (accessible to both nodes).

Cluster Configuration Database

After cluster membership has been determined by the CMM and the interconnect has been established by the SMA, a cluster-wide repository is required to ensure each cluster member has access to identical cluster configuration information. The Cluster Configuration Database (CCD) framework is a highly available, distributed database which is used as a repository for cluster-wide configuration information. The primary function of the CCD is to ensure a valid (and consistent) configuration for all nodes.

For example, in a four-node cluster, it is possible for one of the CCDs to become out of synchronization with the other nodes. For example, if node B leaves the cluster and the CCD is updated by node A, when node B rejoins the cluster, its local CCD will be out of synchronization with the other node and it will not be permitted to rejoin the cluster.

Updates to the CCD are only performed when a quorum validation of greater than 50 percent of nodes is present; otherwise, CCD updates are not possible. For example, in a four-node cluster, if node D leaves the cluster, nodes A, B, and C have identical CCDs (which is greater than 50 percent of all cluster members). When node A issues an update to the CCD, it is propagated to nodes B and C. After node D rejoins the cluster, it is provided with a copy of the CCD used by nodes A, B, and C.

CCD Architecture

Not all cluster configuration data is stored and maintained within the CCD. For example, the CCD stores status information on public network management (PNM); however, PNM configuration information is stored in `/etc/pnmconfig` file on each node.

The CCD consists of two components—the initial and dynamic:

- The initial (init) component of the CCD remains static, and is created during the initial cluster configuration by using the `scinstall` command.
- The dynamic component of the CCD is updated by the CCD daemon (`ccdd`) using remote procedure calls (RPCs). Cluster wide `ccdd` communications are performed using TCP/IP (via the cluster interconnect). Valid cluster membership must be reached before a CCD quorum can be achieved. For cluster membership to initiate, each cluster member must have access to the cluster configuration data (stored in the `/etc/opt/SUNWcluster/conf/cluster_name.cdb` file).

Although this file is technically not part of the database structure, it is still considered part of the CCD architecture. For further information on CCD components, see Chapter 4, "Sun Cluster 2.2 Administration."

CCD Components

The CMM configuration data is stored in the

`/etc/opt/SUNWcluster/conf/cluster_name.cdb` file (where `cluster_name` is the name of the cluster).

The `/etc/opt/SUNWcluster/conf/ccd.database.init` file is used to store the init component of the CCD.

The `/etc/opt/SUNWcluster/conf/ccd.database` file is used to store the dynamic component of the CCD.

CCD Updates

Updates to the CCD are performed using a two-phase commit protocol. The ccdd is started on each cluster member. As each node joins the cluster, the ccdd is automatically started. Before updates to the CCD can be performed, three steps must be executed:

- A valid cluster membership must be determined via the CMM.
- The interconnect must be up and running via SMA.
- A valid CCD must be determined.

To ensure consistent replication across clusters nodes, the CCD framework uses two levels of consistency. Each copy of the CCD has a self-contained consistency record—this stores the checksum and length (excluding consistency record) of the CCD, which is used to timestamp the last CCD update. Cluster-wide consistency checks are made through the ccdd by the exchange and comparison of consistency records.

The following are the semantics of the CCD update process:

- The node creates an RPC to its own copy of the ccdd requesting an update.
- The ccdd confirms the CCD is not performing an update. The request is sent to the master node (the master node is determined when the cluster software is installed [has the lowest ID]).
- The master node executes the pre-synchronization phase of the synchronization command.
- If the synchronization command fails, the update is aborted—if the command succeeds, the master CCD server sends an update broadcast to all CCD daemons.
- In the event of a rollback, the CCD daemons on each node make a shadow copy of their CCD. Each node performs the update and acknowledges to the master node that the update is completed.
- The master node manages execution of the post-synchronization phase of the synchronization command. If the update fails, it is rolled back; if the update succeeds, it is committed to the CCD.
- The master node acknowledges the post-synchronization operation. The status of the update operation is forwarded to the node that originated the update request.

Caution: The CCD is a distributed database. ASCII-#(not binary) based files are used to store CCD data. To ensure CCD integrity, modifications should only be performed using the SC2.2 CCD administration tools. Direct modifications of the CCD may cause data corruption.

Shared CCD

The shared CCD option can be used with two-node clusters using the VxVM volume manager. A shared CCD is easier to administer and has higher availability. When using a shared CCD, each node has a local copy of the CCD; however, there is also a copy of the CCD in shared storage. For example, in a two-node cluster with no shared CCD if node B leaves the cluster, node A will perform a CCD update (logical host change, PNM state change etc.). If node B attempts to rejoin the cluster, it will fail—this is because node B has an outdated copy of the CCD.

One way to resolve the issue is to copy the CCD files from node A to B. Although this method works, it can be error-prone and should not be used for mission-critical environments. A better alternative is using a shared CCD instead of a local CCD. This would alleviate the error-prone manual procedure. For example, in a two-node cluster, if node B leaves the cluster and node A makes changes to the CCD, these changes will migrate to the CCD on the shared storage device. When node B rejoins the cluster, it will receive the latest copy of the CCD from the shared storage (without user intervention), thereby increasing uptime and reducing the potential for user error.

A drawback of using a shared CCD is that two disks (primary and mirror) must be allocated for exclusive CCD use, see Chapter 4, "Sun Cluster 2.2 Administration" for configuring and maintaining a shared CCD.

Public Network Management

The Public Network Management (PNM) monitors the network interfaces and subnets of the system. Public network interfaces within an SC2.2 configuration are assigned to a NAFO group(s). The primary and any redundant network interfaces are defined within the NAFO group. Only one interface per NAFO group can be active at the same time. There is no restriction on the number of interfaces per NAFO group; however, redundant interfaces must be identical to the primary adaptor. For example, mismatching Ethernet and token ring interface cards within the same NAFO group will not work—neither will a combination of Giga Ethernet and 100-Mbit Ethernet interface cards. During cluster operation, the PNM daemon for each node will routinely test the subnet by capturing information on each NAFO group(s) within the node.

Note: Latent NAFO interfaces are not automatically tested by the cluster framework.

PNM Fault Detection

After the PNM daemon receives a broadcast, each node writes its results to the CCD. Each node then compares the results with those from other nodes. If nodes are experiencing a problem with network connectivity (hub, switch, cable, or routers), the cluster framework will take no action because all nodes within the cluster are experiencing the same condition. Therefore, a failover of data services to another node will not alleviate this problem. In a situation where the primary interface cannot respond to network requests, its IP addresses (both physical and logical) are migrated to a redundant interface within the assigned group. The IP addresses from the failed adaptor are brought online for the new interface by using the `ifconfig` utility. Although the `ifconfig` utility generates an address resolution protocol (ARP) Ethernet update, the PNM will do several gratuitous ARP updates to ensure the MAC address and IP address are correctly mapped in all ARP tables. If there are no redundant network interfaces defined in the NAFO group, a failover of the data services to another node will be performed.

The following is the basic algorithm used for network adapter testing:

1) In and out packets are gathered for the primary adapter of each NAFO group.

2) The PNM is inactive for a default time of five seconds. This parameter is tunable, see Chapter 4, "Sun Cluster 2.2 Administration."

3) Statistics are gathered again.

4) The current query is compared to the previous query. If the old and new statistics for in and out packets are different, the adapter is considered working. If the statistics indicate no changes, the following is automatically performed:

- Ping the multicast at 224.0.0.2.
- If the ping fails, ping the other multicast at 224.0.0.1.
- If there is no response to either multicasts, perform a general broadcast ping at X.X.X.255.

5) Statistics are gathered again—if they have changed, the adapter is considered working. If the statistics have not changed, a failure has occurred with the adapter or network segment. The PNM daemon will query the status of the CCD to determine adapter status of the other nodes. If the other nodes indicate no problems, a redundant interface will be used. If no redundant interface is present, a failover of the data service will be performed.

Note: The failover of a logical host will only be performed if a fault monitor is associated with the logical host.

See Chapter 4, "Sun Cluster 2.2 Administration" for information on configuring and monitoring NAFO groups.

Cluster Reconfiguration State Machine

Each time a cluster is started (or when a node joins or leaves an existing cluster), the cluster framework performs a reconfiguration. During reconfiguration, cluster membership is determined, the node that masters the logical host(s) is assigned (or re-assigned), and any shared storage is fenced off. The purpose of the reconfiguration is to ensure reliability and consistency in the new cluster.

Reconfiguration of the cluster is a 12-step process (see Figure 2-2). Each step of the reconfiguration process will be completed in lock-step fashion across the cluster—this means every node within the cluster is required to finish the current step of the reconfiguration process before proceeding. The following diagram depicts a state machine used for the reconfiguration algorithm.

The output of each reconfiguration step is sent to each cluster node console (the output is also captured by the SC2.2 log facility). Pay careful attention to the reconfiguration steps—this can assist in troubleshooting and maintenance.

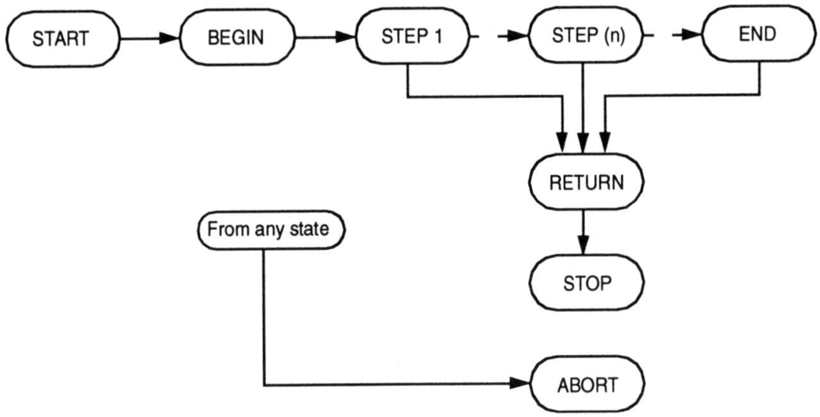

Figure 2-2 Cluster State Transition

The following is a description of the cluster reconfiguration steps (Figure 2-2):

Return Step—Each component prepares for the reconfiguration sequence. All new I/O is disabled and pending I/O is finished. Although the SMA monitors the interconnects, it will not intervene in the event of a failure. At this time, the CCD will drop any network connections.

Begin Step—New cluster membership is established, and faulty nodes are removed from the cluster.

Step 1—The logical interconnect is brought online by the SMA. If a reservation of a quorum device is necessary, it will be acquired at this time.

Step 2—The node lock is acquired.

Step 3—The `ccdd` creates IPC connections (via the interconnect) to the CCD servers. If Oracle OPS is used, the UDLM begins recovery.

Step 4—The CCD elects a valid database. Any running HA fault monitors are stopped.

Step 5—Monitoring of the terminal concentrators begins.

Step 6—Reserved disk groups are released. The CMM updates the Cluster Volume Manager (CVM) with regards to cluster membership. At this time, the CVM creates a list of nodes joining or leaving the cluster.

Step 7—The CVM determines which node is master (*Step 6*). Blocked I/O proceeds, and faulty network interfaces are invalidated via PNM.

Step 8—The CMM will decide which node(s) will become the master or slave. The master node(s) imports the disk groups. The recovery of any faulty node(s) begins (if required).

Step 9—Disk groups (imported in previous step) undergo recovery (if required).

Step 10—Any required shared disk groups are reserved. The logical host(s) is migrated to the standby node as required (tunable parameter).

Step 11—The logical host(s) is mastered (tunable parameter).

Step 12—HA fault monitors are started.

The actions performed in the previous 12 steps appear to be lengthy and time-consuming; however, the most time-consuming part of the process is importing the disk groups and disk recovery (*Step 9*). Reducing the number of disks per disk group or disk set will decrease the time required to complete this step. If file system recovery (*Step 9*) is required using the `fsck` command, it will take longer before the disks are ready. Using a journaling file system can greatly reduce the time required to perform a file system check (if required).

Note: A large storage configuration with hundreds of volumes may take tens of minutes (or longer) to import and check. Ensure the cluster reconfiguration sequence has enough time to perform a full recovery without timing out (*Step 11*). The default timeout value in *Step 11* is five minutes (this value may have to be increased). See Chapter 4, "Sun Cluster 2.2 Administration" for instructions on modifying the timeout values.

Volume Management

Disks and failures are managed using a disk manager. Disk failures are transparent to the SC2.2 framework (providing a disk mirror is available). Disk failures do not affect cluster functionality or membership.

Note: A complete I/O failure is considered a dual failure—this type of failure cannot be tolerated by the SC2.2 architecture.

Logging file systems should be used to decrease recovery time and for file system consistency checks (using the `fsck` command). For journal file logging, SC2.2 supports Solaris OE versions 8.x and 7.x logging, Solstice DiskSuite log devices, and Veritas file systems (VxFS).

The SC2.2 product can be used with the following disk managers:

- Solstice DiskSuite (SDS)
- Veritas Volume Manager (VxVM)
- Cluster Volume Manager (CVM)

Note: Software products change often to keep up with technology; therefore, for specific information on volume managers or logging file systems, consult your Sun Microsystems sales office.

The choice of using the SDS or VxVM volume manager is often based on preference and/or feature sets. Both volume managers can be used with the SC2.2 framework in HA mode, and with shared nothing database systems such as Informix XPS or IBM DB2, see Table 2-2.

Table 2-2 Supported Volume Managers for Various Applications

Disk Manager	High Availability	Shared Nothing	Shared Disk
Solstice DiskSuite (SDS)	YES	YES	NO
Veritas Volume Manager (VxVm)	YES	YES	YES
Cluster Volume Manager (CVM)	YES	YES	YES

The CVM software is based on the VxVM source code (with the added functionality of shared disk groups). Prior to VxVM version 3.0.4, disk groups could only be imported by one host at any time, however; the CVM software enables disk groups to be imported by multiple hosts. The CVM must be used for shared disk databases such as Oracle OPS (and is used in conjunction with the shared disk databases to enable HA configurations).

Note: VxVM version 3.0.4 supports shared disk groups.

After a volume manger has been installed, it can be used for shared and non-shared storage. If VxVM is required for cluster storage management, it must also be used to mirror all disks.

Note: The use of different volume mangers within the same SC2.2 environment is not supported.

Data Service Layer

Sun Cluster 2.2 software provides application monitoring by the data service layer. High availability is achieved at the system level by means of the CMM, SMA, and CCD functions, and also by the data service layer.

The data service layer is integrated into the cluster framework by means of the cluster API. The heart of the data service layer is an API that gives programmers the ability to check cluster parameters (and take appropriate action if the parameters are outside the norm). See Chapter 4, "Sun Cluster 2.2 Administration" and Chapter 7, "Sun Cluster 2.2 Data Services" for additional information on the data service layer.

Data Services

High availability at the application level is handled by a data service agent. Data services are registered with the SC2.2 framework and become an integral part of services the framework provides. The data service layer is responsible for providing the data service methods required to start, stop, or abort an application. Sun Microsystems has data services for common applications such as databases, NFS, DNS, and Web and e-mail servers. If a data service is not available for a specific in-house application, the SC2.2 API can be used to create a custom data service, see Chapter 7, "Sun Cluster 2.2 Data Services."

Fault Probes

Fault probes are data service methods (DSMs) assigned to a data service which probe the application to check its health (or the health of the existing environment). Fault probes cannot exist without a data service; however, a data service does not necessarily require a fault probe, see Chapter 7, "Sun Cluster 2.2 Data Services."

Parallel Databases

Sun Cluster 2.2 software supports two database topologies:

- High availability (HA)
- Parallel database (PDB)

For additional information on both topics, see Chapter 5, "Highly Available Databases."

Clustering for High Availability

There is no value in a stalled mail application on perfectly good hardware—clusters add value by keeping business applications running. End-users (e-commerce, business-to-business, etc.) do not generally know about the hardware or software being used to run their applications; what concerns them is the availability of the service(s) (e-mail access, account status, bill payments, order placing, etc.). To illustrate this point, ask yourself: When was the last time you placed an order for something via a telephone or online and wondered what kind hardware or software was being used? All that should matter to an organization is that its infrastructure is capable and ready to deliver a service to the end-user.

Logical Hosts

Applications using SC2.2 software for high availability exist in an abstraction called a logical host. *Logical host* is the term used to describe the abstraction of storage (disk groups, disk sets), connectivity (IP addresses), and applications (for example, HA-Oracle, HA-Netscape, and HA-NFS).

Logical host parameters (such as IP address) should not be confused with the *physical* IP address of the node—that is, each node within a cluster has a physical IP address *and* a logical IP address (assigned during the OS installation).

Logical IP addresses can migrate across the cluster to different nodes. Therefore, in a simple two-node cluster with one logical host, at any given time (after failover), a node will have two IP addresses—a physical one and a logical one. However, a single node (depending on the number of logical hosts and subnets) can have its physical address *plus* N x S logical IP addresses (where N is the number of logical hosts and S is the number of subnets).

Note: Logical hosts are mastered by one node and must have at least one secondary node assigned to them.

In the event of node failure, the logical host moves from one node to another as a unit (see Figure 2-3). The logical IP address(es) and shared storage (assigned as a disk group or disk set) migrate to the standby node. Application startup is performed by the standby node after the shared storage is imported and the file systems are mounted.

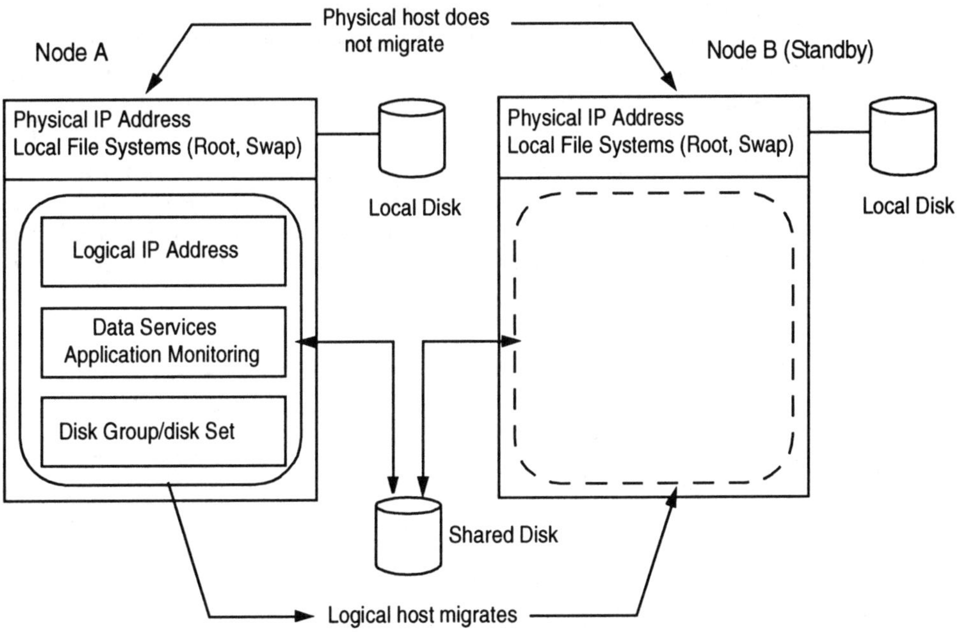

Figure 2-3 Logical Host Abstraction

Cluster Topology

Asymmetric High Availability

Sun Cluster 2.2 software can be configured for high availability in two ways—asymmetric and symmetric. In its most basic configuration, SC2.2 software can be configured as a two-node cluster. One of the nodes will be the primary and the other will be the secondary. If only one database is required to be highly available, one physical server will run the database, with the backup node configured to monitor the primary node (waiting for a problem). The backup node will become active *only* if there is a failover—in this situation, the backup node will master the logical host, start the application(s), and provide access to the application. After the failed node is restored, the logical host can be moved back (manually or automatically) to its original server as required, see Figure 2-4.

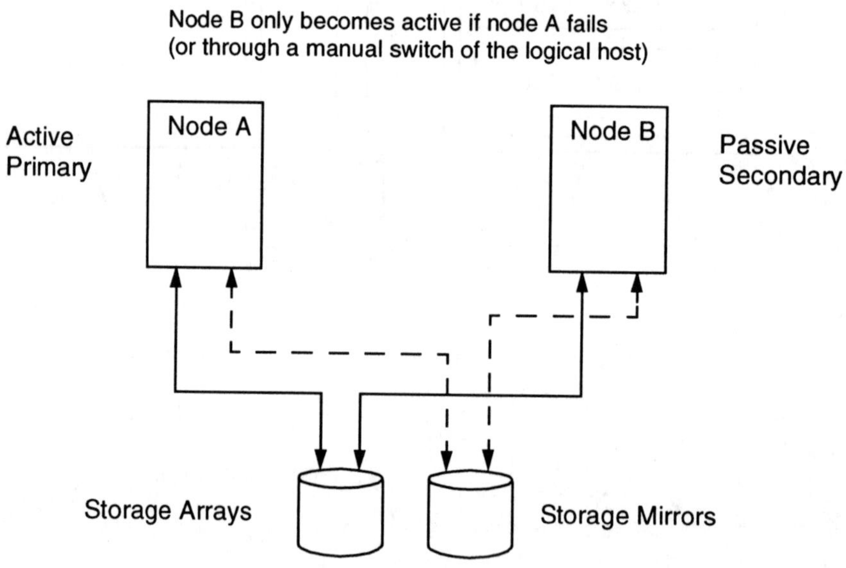

Figure 2-4 Asymmetric HA Configuration

The advantage of an asymmetric configuration is the simplicity of its configuration—which makes administration easier. Asymmetric capacity planning is generally straightforward because all that is required is to replicate the system requirements of the primary server onto the standby (backup) node.

For busy servers (database, e-mail, or Web) where degraded performance would be unacceptable, configuring a cluster for asymmetric high availability will be advantageous.

If downgraded performance after recovery is acceptable, the backup node can be of lower capacity than the primary machine, thereby reducing the cost of redundancy.

Symmetric High Availability

Sun Cluster 2.2 software can be configured for two active nodes hosting more than one database (or a database plus application server in a three-tier architecture). In a symmetric configuration, each server is configured with its own logical host(s), and each provides access to either of the databases hosted by the cluster—for example, node A may host a database for an accounting department, and node B may host a database for a human resources department, see Figure 2-5.

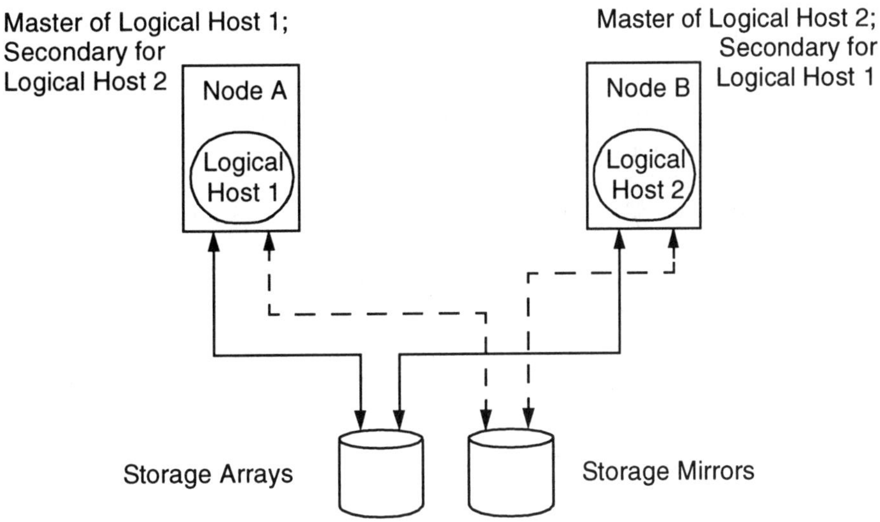

Figure 2-5 Symmetric HA Configuration

Each node is the master of its own logical host, and also acts as a standby for the other node. Therefore, if node A fails, node B continues to support its own services and also takes over the database and services of node A. In this example (Figure 2-5), node B continues hosting the human resources database; however, a second database is started for accounting.

It is important to note that multiple logical hosts can be configured for each node—that is, each node is not limited to one database instance per node. Applying this principle to our example, if five separate databases were used for the human resources department on node A, and three databases were used for the accounting department on node B, in a failure scenario, each node must have the resources and capacity to run all eight databases.

Configuring a symmetric HA configuration can be more challenging than configuring an asymmetric configuration. Application behavior must be fully understood because any node could be required to host multiple applications (thereby pressuring resources). The capacity of each node within a symmetric configuration should be such that it can handle the entire cluster workload—if this is not possible, users will have to settle for reduced levels of service. Decisions of this nature should be driven by business not technical requirements.

Two-Node Clusters and Cluster Pairs

SC2.2 software can be configured to support a variety of hardware topologies. The basic two-node cluster is depicted in Figure 2-6 (this diagram illustrates the physical configuration).

Note: The servers depicted in Figure 2-6 could be two Sun Ultra 2 servers, two Sun Enterprise 10000 servers, or two domains within a single Sun Enterprise 10000 server. The nodes do not have to be identical machine types—it is acceptable to cluster a Sun Enterprise 6500 server with a Sun Enterprise 4500 server.

Each node has its own local boot disk(s) that is not part of the cluster environment, that is, it is not shared among cluster nodes. A boot disk holds the operating system, cluster software, and application software. A boot disk should always be mirrored (not shown in diagram). Failure of a boot disk will force a node to panic (because the OS will no longer be available), and all cluster operations will migrate to the other node.

Note: Although it is a good idea to mirror the boot disk for availability, it is not a technical requirement. Loss of a boot disk that is not mirrored will cause a failover of the data services on that node.

Shared storage is available to both nodes and should be mirrored. A two-node cluster is able to run high availability services in symmetric and asymmetric configurations (and shared disk and shared nothing parallel databases). For parallel databases, Oracle Parallel Server, Informix XPS, or IBM DB2/EEE can be used.

Cluster management and administration are performed using an administrative workstation. Because a cluster node does not have a monitor or keyboard, the network terminal server (terminal concentrator) is used for console access. Connection to the terminal concentrator is performed via serial cables connected to the `ttya` port on each node (including the administrative workstation).

Note: The System Service Processor (SSP) is used for cluster configurations on Sun Enterprise 10000 servers.

Figure 2-6 depicts the use of redundant network interfaces that are connected to different network subnets. Although redundant network interfaces are not a technical requirement, a failure of the primary network interface will lead to cluster failover. Network interface redundancy is managed by the cluster framework, see section, "Public Network Management," on page 41.

Multiple two-node clusters can share the same administrative workstation and terminal concentrator—in this arrangement, the clusters would be independent of each another. Sharing the management framework can make administration easier and reduce costs.

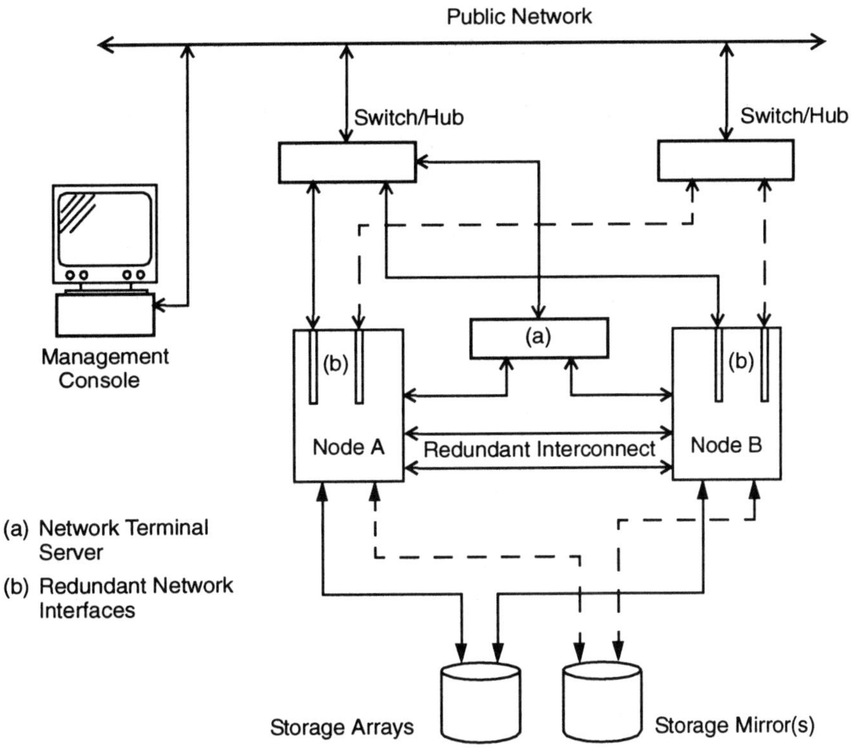

Figure 2-6 Two-Node Cluster and Cluster Pairs

N+1 Topology (Three- and Four-Node Clusters)

Figure 2-7 depicts a four-node N+1 cluster. One difference between an N+1 configuration and a two-node cluster is the interconnects do not use point-to-point connections; with N+1, each node connects to redundant Ethernet or SCI hubs.

In the N+1 configuration, the first three nodes connect to their own storage device(s). The remaining node (node D) connects to all storage devices. The first three nodes are configured to run highly available applications. Node D is assigned to be the standby. If node A fails, node D will take over the services of node A.

A four-node N+1 configuration is ideal for environments where the workload cannot be shared. For example, if the first three nodes are Sun Enterprise 4500 servers hosting Web and database applications, the standby node could be a Sun Enterprise 6500. If the three Sun Enterprise 4500s are running at full capacity, a Sun Enterprise 6500 cannot manage the combined workload of the other three servers. However, when configured correctly, the Sun Enterprise 6500 could handle the workload of *two* Sun Enterprise 4500s (with performance degradation).

The N+1 configuration provides flexibility for cluster configurations where each node requires specific resources for applications (before and after a failure scenario). Additionally, the N+1 configuration has the ability to run highly available services in asymmetric configuration and shared nothing parallel databases. For parallel databases, Informix XPS and IBM DB2/EEE can be used.

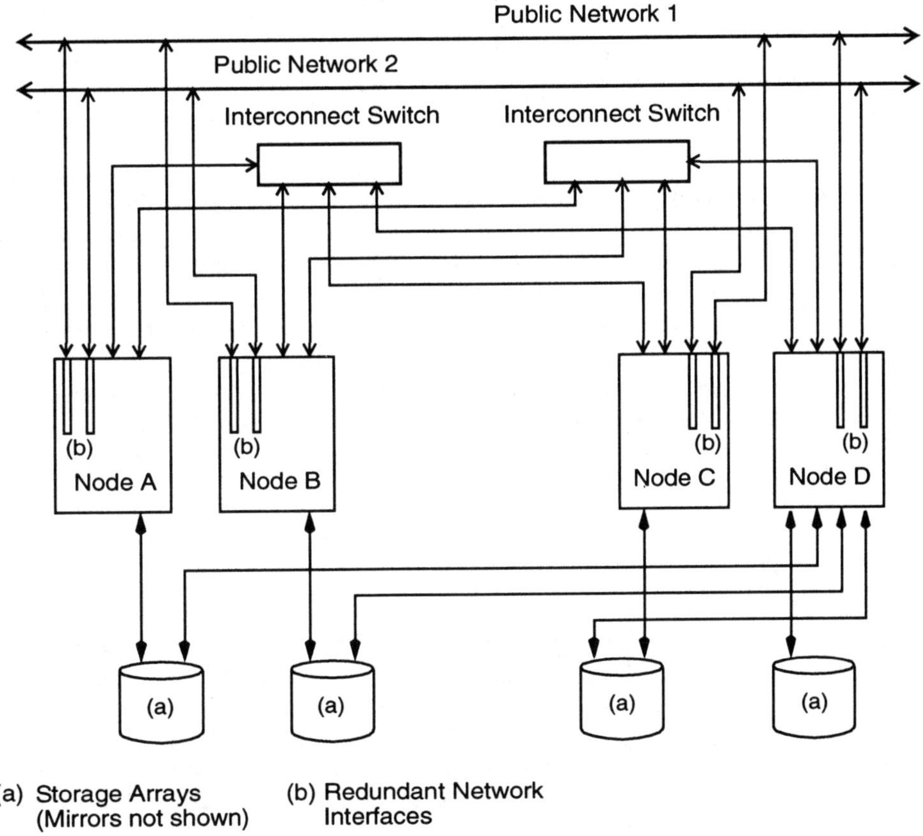

Figure 2-7 N+1 Topology

Note: The configuration depicted in Figure 2-7 requires an administrative workstation and network terminal server (or an SSP when using a Sun Enterprise 10000 server), which are not shown in the diagram.

Ring Topology (Three- and Four-Node Clusters)

Figure 2-8 depicts a four-node ring configuration cluster. A ring topology is a variation of the N+1 configuration; however, there are no dedicated standby nodes. Each node in the cluster is configured to run an application or provide a service.

With a ring configuration, each node is a standby node for its adjacent node. Each node connects to the same shared storage as its adjacent node (including mirrors). For example, if node A fails, node B would takes over its services. Node C is the standby for node B, with node A the standby for node D. This configuration would be a good choice for homogenous workloads, such as Web or e-mail servers, which are subjected to consistent usage patterns (such as intranet environments). Additionally, the N+1 configuration has the ability to run high availability services in both symmetric and asymmetric configurations (and shared nothing parallel databases). For parallel databases, Informix XPS and IBM DB2/EEE can be used.

Note: The configuration depicted in Figure 2-8 requires an administrative workstation and network terminal server (or an SSP when using a Sun Enterprise 10000 server), which are not shown in the diagram.

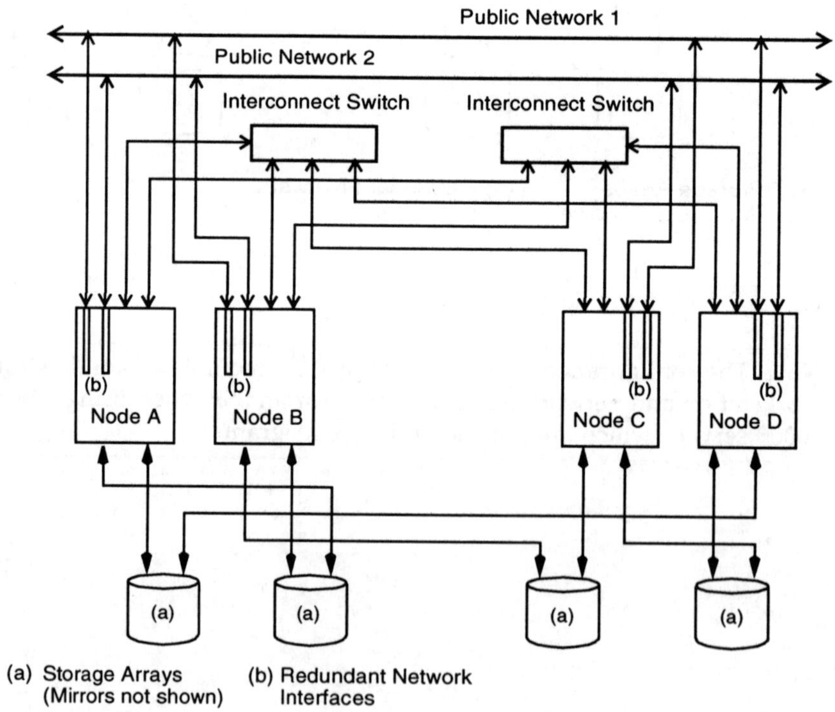

Figure 2-8 Node Ring Topology (three-and four-node clusters)

Scalable Topology

Figure 2-9 depicts a four-node scalable configuration. Each node within this configuration is directly attached to a storage device (Sun StorEdge 5100 or 5200 arrays). This scalable topology offers the greatest flexibility with respect to configurations for high availability and parallel databases. Because each node connects directly to shared storage, there are no restrictions on how nodes can be configured (primary or standby). For example, node A could be a standby for node C, node D could be configured as a standby for nodes A and B, while node C is not configured as a standby.

This cluster configuration has the ability to run highly available services in both symmetric and asymmetric configurations (and also shared and non-shared disk parallel databases). For parallel databases, Oracle Parallel Server, Informix XPS, and IBM DB2/EEE could be used.

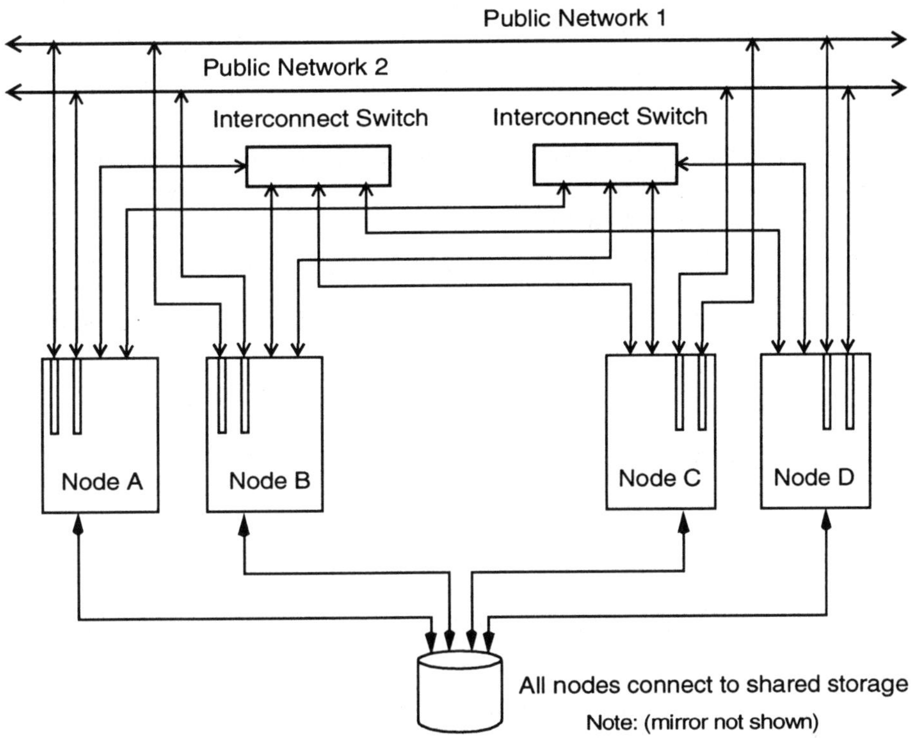

Figure 2-9 Four-Node Scalable Configuration

Note: The configuration depicted in Figure 2-9 requires an administrative workstation and network terminal concentrator (or an SSP when using a Sun Enterprise 10000 server), which are not shown in the diagram.

SC2.2 Failure Fencing/Cluster Membership

Failure fencing is a term used to indicate how shared data is protected in the event of a failure within the cluster. For example, if the interconnect fails or a node leaves the cluster unexpectedly, the cluster framework must ensure that the non-cluster nodes do not have access to shared storage. Locking out non-cluster members from shared storage removes the possibility of data corruption (and also prevents multiple clusters from forming).

Note: This section explains failure fencing scenarios for node failures; however, the same mechanisms are used during routine SC2.2 operations (such as when a node joins or leaves the cluster).

Failure fencing should not be confused with cluster membership because they are different concepts. Because both concepts come into play during cluster reconfiguration, sometimes it can be difficult to distinguish between the two.

The following is an explanation of terms used in this section:

Cluster membership—algorithms to ensure valid cluster membership.

Failure fencing—techniques and algorithms to protect shared data from non-cluster members.

Partition—any node(s) with the potential to form a cluster. If more than two nodes are in a partition, they must communicate exclusively between themselves.

Quorum devices—assigned disk drives (located in shared storage). For a cluster to form, a partition must access a minimum of at least one quorum device. These devices are used as tie-breakers in the event of the cluster degrading into two partitions (of two nodes each). Quorum devices are also used as the basis of failure fencing in two-node, N+1, and ring topologies.

SCSI-2 reservation—a component of the SCSI-2 protocol that enables a host to reserve the disk. Reservations are atomic—that is, only one node can perform and hold the reservation; other nodes attempting to access the device will be denied.

Deterministic policy—process used in clusters with three or four nodes to determine which partition continues in a failure situation. The policy used is determined during cluster installation, and is based on either the high or low node ID.

Ask policy—method used in clusters with three or four nodes to determine which partition continues in the event of a failure. The administrator is asked whether to a *continue* or *abort* for each cluster partition.

Current nodes (cur_nodes)—maximum number of nodes in a cluster at the last successful reconfiguration.

Node lock—used with scalable topologies (three and four nodes only). A cluster node `telnets` into a pre-determined port on the terminal concentrator and holds the session. When a Sun Enterprise 10000 server is used, the functionality of the terminal concentrator is replaced by the SSP.

Fail fast—SC2.2 driver used in two-node clusters to panic a node.

Reset—internal SC2.2 function used to terminate the OS instance on a node—this prevents a node from accessing shared storage.

Exclude timeout (ETO)—minimum time a majority partition must wait before invoking a reset on the minority partition. Used only in a scalable partition. Defined as *ETO* = (X-1) * 40 + 5, (*seconds*), where *X* is the number of nodes.

Scalable timeout (STO)—time out value that a majority partition must wait in addition to the ETO. Defined as *STO* = (X-1) * 40 + 2, where *X* is the number of nodes.

Membership and Failure Fencing

To understand how failure fencing is implemented, a set of rules will be used as a reference. These rules determine the outcome of different failure scenarios using common cluster topologies.

Membership Rules

1. a) If a non scalable partition has less than half of cur_nodes, it will abort out of the cluster.

   b) Scalable topologies wait for ETO+STO, then attempt to reserve the node lock and quorum device. If the partition is successful in reserving the node lock and quorum device, it will become the cluster; otherwise, it will abort.

2. a) If the active partition contains greater than half of cur_nodes (non-scalable partition), all nodes in the active partition will form a cluster.

   b) If the topology is scalable, a node in the majority partition will acquire the node lock. If the node fails to gain the node lock, the partition will abort. The node that acquires the node lock will issue a reset function to terminate all other nodes outside the partition.

3. When a partition has half of cur_nodes, there are three possible outcomes:

   a) In a situation where cur_nodes equals two (when both nodes have access to a common quorum device), if communication is lost between nodes, both nodes will race for the quorum device—whichever node acquires the quorum device will stay in the cluster—the node that does not reserve the quorum will abort out of the cluster.

   b) In a scalable topology, each partition races for the node lock and quorum device after ETO. The successful partition will terminate all other nodes—using Rule 2(b). If the partition fails to acquire the node lock, it will implement the ask policy.

   c) In all other cases (single node partitions not sharing a quorum device or partitions greater than two nodes), the ask or deterministic policy will be implemented.

Failure Fencing Rules

The rules for failure fencing can be applied to either of the following scenarios:

For Valid Nodes Within a Cluster

1. If a node shares a quorum device (or shares data with another node) and is not currently in the cluster, the complement node sharing the quorum device will issue a SCSI reservation for the quorum device (and any shared data).

Note: Nodes with shared data disks must share a quorum device; however, quorum devices can also be used in a configuration where data is not shared.

---

2. After the first node in a scalable cluster starts, it acquires a node lock. If this node leaves the cluster, the node lock will be released and will be acquired by another node.

For Nodes Starting a New Cluster

1. If a node is unable to issue a reservation on one or more shared quorum devices (quorum devices it has been configured to share), the cluster will not start.
2. If any node in a scalable topology cluster cannot acquire the node lock, it will not start the cluster.
3. If a node detects the presence of another cluster on the interconnect, it will not start a cluster.

Note: Solstice Disk Suite ignores Steps 1 and 2 because in these scenarios it uses its own failure fencing algorithms using database replicas.

The following sections describe two failure scenarios for the following cluster topologies:

- Node failure
- Split brain—an interconnect failure resulting in a cluster that divides into one or more partitions

Two-Node Failure

Case 1: Node Failure

The following illustration (Figure 2-10) depicts a two-node cluster in a failure scenario (where node B is unavailable). Node A is notified of node B's failure via the CMM. After notification, node A starts the cluster reconfiguration sequence.

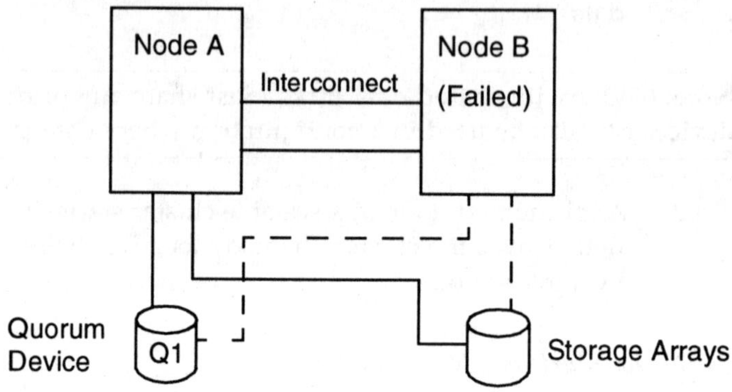

Node B fails; Node A reserves the quorum device

Figure 2-10 Two-Node Cluster (single-node failure)

Cluster Membership

By applying Membership Rule 3(a), it can be seen in Figure 2-10 that node A is half of cur_nodes (and shares quorum device Q1 with node B). After node B fails, node A will acquire the quorum device and will continue as the active partition. If node A was unable to acquire the quorum device, the partition would abort.

Failure Fencing

The failure fencing process begins as soon as node A acquires the quorum device. The scenario depicted in Figure 2-10 uses Rule 1, which states that node A will acquire a SCSI-2 reservation on the quorum device (and all shared disks). The SCSI-2 reservation prevents node B from starting its own cluster (or accessing shared storage), unless it is a cluster member.

Case #2: Two-Node Split Brain (Interconnect Failure)

Two issues need to be addressed to enable the cluster to recover from a split brain situation:

- Protection of shared data
- Recover and provide services

In the following example (Figure 2-11), a dual interconnect failure has occurred. However, unlike Case 1 (node failure), each node is its own active partition and has the potential to continue the cluster.

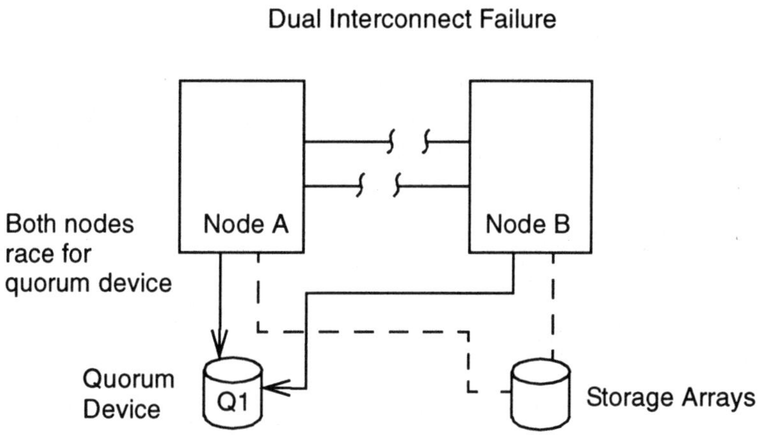

Figure 2-11 Two-Node Interconnect Failure

Cluster Membership

In this example (Figure 2-11), both interconnects failed—the SMA daemon will immediately notify the CMM. The CMM on each node will begin the cluster reconfiguration process. This scenario is covered by Rule 3(a), which states that both nodes will attempt to acquire the quorum device (Q1). The node that succeeds in acquiring the quorum device will be the partition that continues (the remaining node aborts from the cluster). To avoid possible data corruption (pending I/O), the CMM on the node that is not able to reserve the quorum will invoke the fail-fast driver. The fail-fast driver was designed as a safety valve in the event of dual interconnect failure in a two-node cluster. When invoked, the fail-fast driver's function is to bring the node to the boot prompt. After the interconnect is repaired, the node is able rejoin the cluster.

Failure Fencing

The scenario in Figure 2-11 is covered by failure fencing Rule 1. In this example, node B acquires quorum device Q1 and places a SCSI-2 reservation on it (and shared storage devices). The SCSI-2 reservation will prevent node A from reading/writing to shared storage (or starting a cluster). Node B will not release the SCSI-2 reservation until the failed node can rejoin the cluster (after the interconnect is repaired).

N+1 and Ring Topology

Case 1: Node Failure

Figure 2-12 depicts a four-node N+1 cluster configuration where node D can access all shared storage. However, for failure fencing to work, multiple quorum devices are required. In this example, Q1, Q2 and Q3 are quorum devices configured between respective nodes. For example, nodes A and D can access array 1. Quorum device Q1 is configured between the two nodes; likewise for quorum devices Q2 and Q3. In the example, node D fails (in this example there are no other problems).

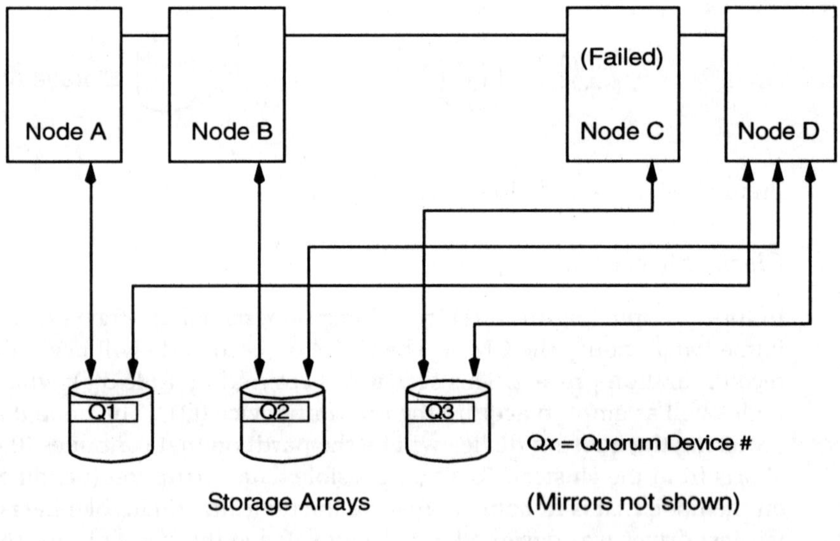

Figure 2-12 Four-Node N+1 (single-node failure)

Cluster Membership

In the example depicted by Figure 2-12, nodes A, B, and D will form a valid partition (Membership Rule 2—greater than half of cur_nodes).

Failure Fencing

In this example, failure fencing is covered by Rule 1. A SCSI-2 reservation will be implemented on Q3 (only) because when two nodes share a quorum, a reservation is implemented on any shared quorum when one of the nodes is not present. SCSI-2 reservations will not be implemented on Q1 or Q2 because the nodes that share those quorum devices are present; therefore, failure fencing is not required. Node D will hold the SCSI-2 reservation for Q3 until node B can rejoin the cluster.

Case 2: Split Brain (Interconnect Failure)

In Figure 2-13, the interconnect has failed between nodes B and C, thereby creating two partitions.

Note: To simplify this concept, the configuration depicted in Figure 2-13 is basic. In practice, two hubs are used for the interconnects—each node is connected to both hubs—making the failure scenario highly unlikely.

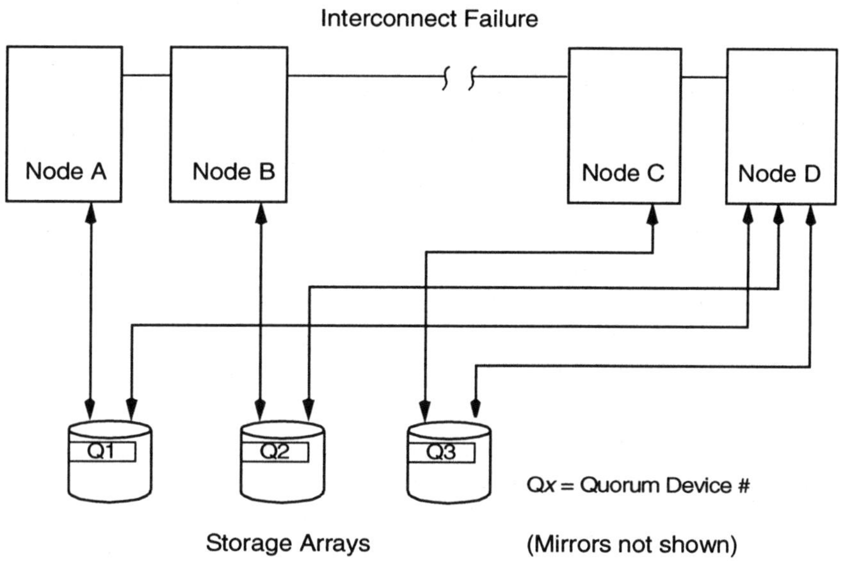

Figure 2-13 Four-Node N+1 (interconnect failure)

Cluster Membership

Using Membership Rule 3(c), a deterministic or ask policy will be implemented. If a deterministic policy is chosen, the partition that has the highest or lowest ID (chosen during install) will be the partition that continues (while the other partition waits for instructions via the ask policy). If the ask policy is chosen, the SC2.2 framework requires user input to determine which partition will continue or abort.

Failure Fencing

Failure fencing is performed using SCSI-2 reservations. If partition 1 (nodes A and B) is the partition that continues, a SCSI-2 reservation will be implemented on Q1 and Q2; however, if partition 2 (nodes C and D) is to remain active, then a SCIS-2 reservation will be implemented on Q3.

Scalable Topology

Scalable topology offers configuration flexibility, which enables it to be used for shared disk databases or HA services. Because of this flexibility, an extra configuration step is required for cluster membership and failure fencing.

For example, if node A starts a scalable cluster, the first function performed during cluster formation is for node A to `telnet` to an unused port (node lock) on the terminal concentrator (the port number is determined at installation). Node A will retain the node lock unless it leaves the cluster. If node A leaves the cluster, the node lock is passed to another node in the partition. If node A is unable to acquire the node lock, it will not start the cluster (failure fencing Rule 2).

Failure fencing and membership rules for scalable topologies are slightly different from other topologies; however, the goals are the same—to protect shared data and (if possible) continue to provide services. Unlike N+1 and ring topologies, it is possible for a multi-node, scalable topology to degrade into a single node and still continue to provide services. Also, with a scalable topology, only a single quorum device is required to be configured (regardless of the number of logical hosts).

With respect to a shared disk database such as OPS, access to shared disks is governed through a Distributed Lock Manager (DLM). The DLM processes require the cluster framework to be functional; therefore, access to shared disks without the presence of a DLM is not possible. For instance, Oracle will not start on a failed node without the DLM being part of the cluster. An additional step performed in an OPS configuration is lock recovery on the failed nodes—this function is performed by the DLM.

Case 1: Node Failure

Figure 2-14 depicts a four-node shared disk configuration cluster. A single quorum device is configured between all nodes. In this example, node C fails and leaves the cluster (leaving nodes A, B, and D in a single partition).

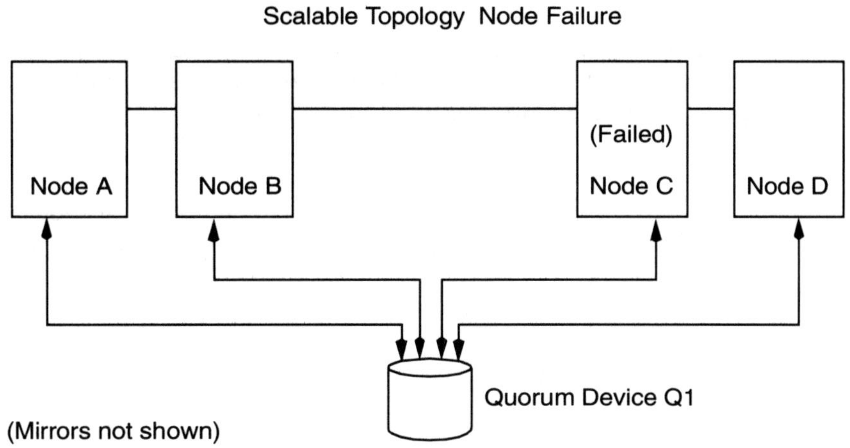

Figure 2-14 Scalable Topology

Membership

In this example, node A acquires and holds the node lock. Because this is the majority partition, all I/O stops, cluster reconfiguration begins, and the isolated node is removed from the cluster membership.

Failure Fencing

Although the failure fencing mechanism used in a two-node cluster is efficient, it is not used with clusters configured in a scalable topology. Because a SCSI-2 reservation is an atomic operation—that is, one node issues and holds a reservation—if performed in a scalable topology, all other nodes will be locked out. Therefore, SCSI-2 is not used. Failure fencing is performed using the node lock on the terminal concentrator (SSP with the Sun Enterprise 10000 server). No other cluster can form without acquiring the node lock—in this example, node A holds the lock for as long as it is a cluster member, thereby ensuring no other cluster can form.

Case 2: Split Brain (Two Active Partitions)

In Figure 2-15, a scalable OPS configuration has experienced an interconnect failure (leaving the cluster with two active partitions). Partition 1 comprises nodes A, B, and C, while partition 2 comprises node D.

Note: To simplify this concept, the configuration depicted in Figure 2-15 is basic. In practice, two hubs are used for the interconnects—each node is connected to both hubs—making the failure scenario highly unlikely.

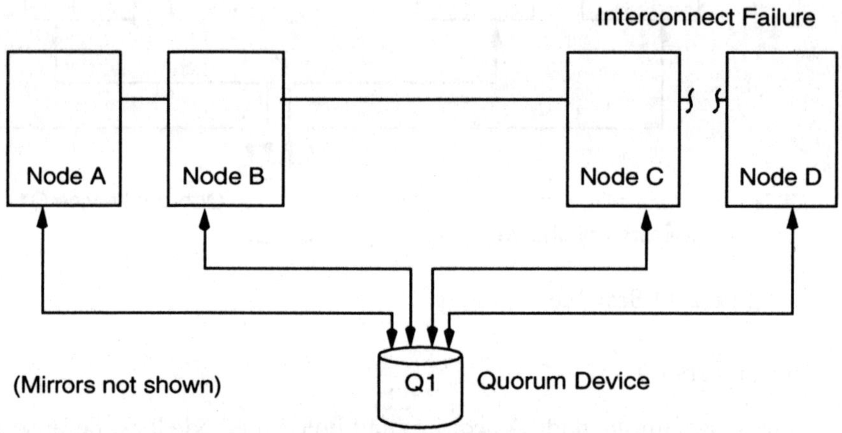

Figure 2-15 Four-Node Scalable Interconnect Failure

Membership

The example in Figure 2-15 is covered by Membership Rule 2(b)—the deterministic or ask policy will be used. The partition containing the single node is covered by Membership Rule 1(c).

If the deterministic policy is chosen, the partition which has the highest or lowest ID will be the partition that continues, while the other partition will implement the ask policy. Assuming the lowest IDs were used, nodes A, B, and C will continue.

A further step is required to ensure node D does not form another cluster. Node A (being part of the majority partition) is able to terminate the boot image of node D (using the reset function). However, node A will not be able to use this function until the ETO has passed (3*40 + 5) seconds, or 2:05 minutes. Node D, being the minority partition, must wait ETO + STO ((3*40 + 5) + (3*40 + 2)) seconds, or 4:07 minutes, before continuing the reconfiguration. Being the minority partition, it cannot use the reset function. Using both timeout functions, ETO and STO, ensures that node D never gets the chance to perform any other steps in the configuration.

Failure Fencing

After the reset function is performed, node A will verify that node D is at the boot prompt—if so, the majority partition will continue; otherwise, the ask policy will be used for both partitions. If the ask policy is used, the SC2.2 framework requires user input to determine which partition continues or aborts. Failure fencing also consists of acquiring the node lock and stopping all I/O until cluster reconfiguration is complete.

Case 3: Split Brain (Even Split)

In Figure 2-16, quorum device Q1 is configured for all nodes. In this example, the interconnect fails, leaving two active partitions consisting of nodes A and B in one partition, and nodes C and D in the other.

Note: To simplify this concept, the configuration depicted in Figure 2-16 is basic. In practice, two hubs are used for the interconnects—each node is connected to both hubs—making the failure scenario highly unlikely.

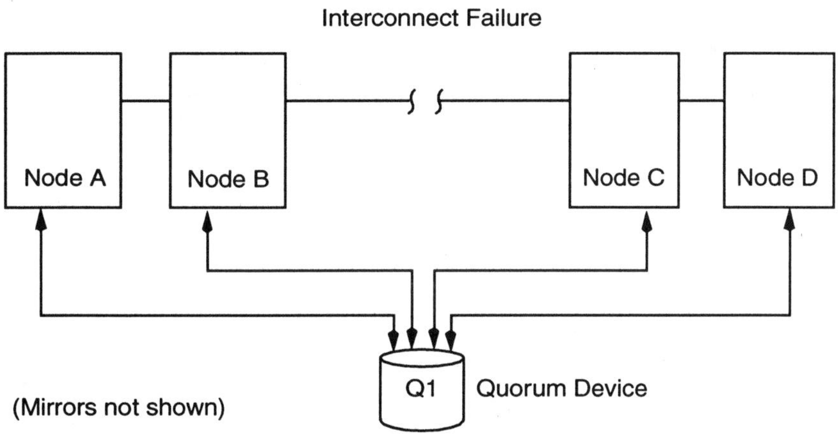

Figure 2-16 Scalable Split Brain

Membership

Because each partition contains half of cur_nodes (membership Rule 3b), both partitions (being scalable) will wait ETO before doing anything; in this case, (3*40+5) seconds, or 2:45 minutes. If the ask policy is used, both partitions will wait for user input (continue or abort) to proceed; however, if the deterministic policy is chosen, both partitions wait until ETO has elapsed (3*40 + 5) seconds, or 2:05 minutes. Because each partition is a minority, the STO timeout will not be used. After ETO has elapsed, both partitions will race for the node lock. Assuming that node A acquires the node lock, it will use the reset function to terminate nodes C and D. If node A can verify that nodes B and C are at the boot prompt, it will proceed; otherwise, the ask policy will be implemented.

Failure Fencing

After the reset function is performed, node A will verify that nodes C and D are at the boot prompt. If so, the partition will continue; otherwise, the ask policy will be used for both partitions. If the ask policy is used, the SC2.2 framework requires user input to determine which partition continues or aborts. Failure fencing also consists of acquiring the node lock and stopping all I/O until cluster reconfiguration is complete.

Case 4: Split Brain (Four-Way Split)

In the example depicted by Figure 2-17, a cluster interconnect completely fails, thereby creating four active partitions. When using ring or N+1 topology, this type of failure cannot be tolerated; however, if using a scalable topology, this type of extreme failure can be tolerated.

Note: To simplify the concept, the configuration depicted in Figure 2-17 is basic. In practice, two hubs are used for the interconnects—each node is connected to both hubs—so both hubs would have to fail for this situation to occur.

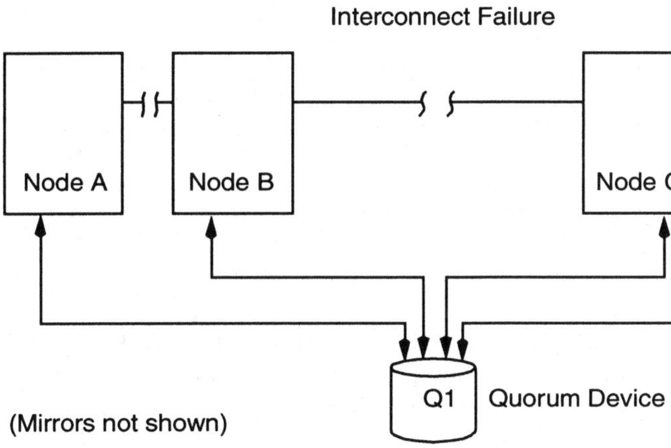

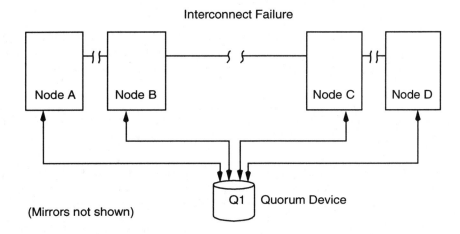

Figure 2-17 Scalable Interconnect Failure (HA)

Membership

In this example (Figure 2-17), each partition is less than cur_nodes—Membership Rule 1(b). In this scenario, each node is a valid partition. Because each node does not know the status of the other nodes, each one will try to become the new cluster. However, every partition will have to wait ETO+STO before proceeding. When these time-outs elapse, each partition will race for the node lock. After the node lock is acquired, the node will then have to acquire the quorum device. The node that is able to reserve both the node lock and quorum device will continue as the sole cluster member.

Failure Fencing

After both the node lock and quorum device have been acquired, the cluster member will use the reset function to terminate the other three nodes' boot images. Once verified that all other nodes are at the boot prompt, the partition will continue; otherwise, the ask policy will be used for all partitions. Failure fencing in this case consists of acquiring the node lock and quorum device and stopping all I/O until cluster reconfiguration is complete.

Cluster Failure Scenarios

Many different types of failure scenarios were covered in the previous section. It is important to remember that the majority of the test cases were extreme and highly unlikely due to the fact that it would require multiple hardware failures for a cluster to degrade to those states.

Note: Again, it is important to stress, SC2.2 software was designed to handle a single failure without a prolonged disruption of services.

It is impressive how the SC2.2 framework is able to protect shared data. In the majority of multiple hardware failures, SC2.2 will continue to provide data services (albeit with degradation), regardless of the failure condition.

Tables 2-3 and 2-4 provide an overview of different scenarios for multi-node clusters configured in N+1, ring, and scalable topologies.

Table 2-3 Three-Node Cluster Failure Scenarios

Failure Scenario	Topology	Quorum Majority	Action
One switch	N+1, ring, scalable	N/A	No action required; cluster continues
Two switches	N+1, ring	No node has quorum majority	Cluster stops
Two switches	Scalable	N/A	First partition that acquires both node lock and quorum device forms new cluster
One node fails	N+1, ring, scalable	Two nodes have quorum majority	Cluster reconfigures and continues without failed node
Two nodes fail	N+1, ring	Single node does not have majority of votes	Cluster stops

Failure Scenario	Topology	Quorum Majority	Action
Two nodes fail	Scalable	N/A	Cluster continues with one node
One node cannot communicate with other cluster members	N+1, ring	Two nodes form majority; single node drops out of cluster	Cluster reconfigures and continues with two nodes
One node cannot communicate with other cluster members	Scalable	Two nodes form majority; reset function is used after ETO elapses	Cluster reconfigures and continues with two nodes

Table 2-4 Four-Node Cluster Failure Scenarios

Failure Scenario	Topology	Quorum Majority	Action
One switch	N+1, ring, scalable	N/A	No action required; cluster continues
Two switches	N+1, ring	No node has quorum majority	Cluster stops
Two switches	Scalable	N/A	First partition that acquires both node lock and quorum device forms new cluster
One node fails	N+1, ring, scalable	Three nodes have majority Quorum	Cluster reconfigures and continues without failed node
Two nodes fail	N+1, ring	Two nodes do not have the majority	Cluster stops
Two nodes fail	Scalable	Two nodes become cluster partition	Cluster continues
One node cannot communicate with other cluster members	N+1, ring	Three nodes form majority; single node drops out of cluster	Cluster continues with three nodes
One node cannot communicate with other cluster members	Scalable	Majority partition waits ETO; minority waits ETO+STO	Majority always wins, it terminates minority partition and continues

Architectural Limitations

Regardless of design, any software or hardware has physical or technical limitations. The SC2.2 environment can be used in varying hardware and software configurations; however, before implementing the SC2.2 software, it is important to understand its product limitations. Failure to use the SC2.2 product within these design parameters could compromise data integrity or have adverse effects on availability.

The following are the SC2.2 limitation considerations:

- Any data services not supplied by Sun Microsystems are not supported; contact third-party supplier for support.
- The Solaris `sendmail` program is not supported.
- For NIS or NIS+ services—cluster nodes can be clients, but not servers or slaves.
- HA boot or installation services.
- HA-rarpd service.
- Do not configure SC2.2 nodes as gateways or routers.
- Do not use the loopback file system (lofs).
- Do not run client applications on SC2.2 nodes.
- Do not run real-time processes on SC2.2 nodes.
- Do not access the `/logicalhost` directories from shells on any nodes—doing so could prevent failover.
- The SC2.2 HA administrative file system cannot be grown using the Solstice DiskSuite `growfs` command.
- File system quotas are not supported.
- Sun Prestoserve and other host-based storage caching is not supported.
- Do not run applications that can access the HA-NFS file system locally—doing so could prevent failover.
- Cross mounting of HA services for NFS is not supported.
- All NFS client mounts for HA-NFS partitions should be hard mounts.
- Do not use hostname aliases for logical hosts—this could cause `statd` lock recovery problems.
- Secure NFS and Kerberos with HA-NFS are not supported.

- Sbus and PCI architectures cannot be used in the same configuration; for example, using a Sun Enterprise 3500 with a Sun Enterprise 450.
- Third-party storage is not supported (DMP, AP, and SANs).

Summary

The SC2.2 architecture is designed to provide high levels of availability for hardware, operating system, and applications without compromising data integrity. The architecture is a flexible, robust computing platform. The SC2.2 framework can be customized using the SC2.2 API to make custom applications highly available.

CHAPTER 3

Sun Cluster 2.2 Components

The task of choosing cluster components from the myriad of available hardware and software can be difficult because administrators are required to adhere to the constraints of supportability, availability, performance, capacity, and cost requirements.

This chapter addresses supported Sun Cluster 2.2 (SC2.2) hardware and software options to highlight the large selection of available choices. This information can assist customers in choosing a cluster configuration that best matches their datacenter capacity, performance, and availability requirements. The hardware components are described to highlight the RAS, performance, and capacity features.

Specific combinations of components supported by the SC2.2 software undergo extensive quality assurance testing using supported cluster topologies to avoid incompatibility issues at customer sites. Contact your local Sun sales office or service representative to obtain the *current* SC2.2 hardware and software support matrix.

This chapter does not address the impact of *component cost*. Although component cost may be a prime factor in determining a customer's cluster component selection, we assume any cost decisions are business driven and will be made at the managerial level.

Server Platform Options

Although symmetrical cluster nodes (servers with the same hardware configuration) are easier to manage, the SC2.2 software enables the use of asymmetric cluster nodes. For example, a Sun Enterprise 10000 server domain can fail over to a Sun Enterprise 6500 server.

Note: Binary compatibility of software applications is guaranteed on all current Sun Microsystems server platforms.

In this section, the term *server platform* refers to the set that comprises the following components:

System Cage

A metal structure that includes a main system board and backplane (or centerplane). The system cage also contains the power supply, power cord(s), and cooling fan(s).

Main System Board / Backplane (or Centerplane)

The Sun main system board/backplane (for single-board machines) contains connectors for I/O cards and also contains on-board controllers such as Ethernet, RS-232/RS-423, and SCSI.

The Sun Enterprise xx00 centerplane accommodates I/O boards and system boards. The system boards contain CPU modules and memory, with I/O boards containing I/O cards. The exception is the Sun Enterprise 10000 centerplane, which provides housing for system boards that may contain CPUs, memory, and I/O cards.

CPU and Memory

Because the CPU and memory components are an integral part of a server, they are not discussed in this chapter.

Power Supply and Cords

Power supplies convert alternating current (AC) voltage into direct current (DC) voltage required by server components. Some servers have hot-swap power supplies and multiple power cords.

Note: All power supplies used in Sun servers are universal (i.e., AC input ranges between 90 to 250 V—this helps make them resilient to AC supply variations.

Cooling Fans

Provides forced air to cool components. Some servers have a hot-swap cooling fan option.

SPARCserver ™ 1000E (SS1000E) and SPARCcenter™ 2000E (SC2000E)

The Sun Microsystems SS1000E and SC2000E servers are legacy servers based on the SuperSPARC™ processor technology. Although the SS1000E and SC2000E servers are no longer manufactured, SC2.2 support is provided for early adopters (those having strict requirements against migrating to a newer platform). The SS1000E and SC2000E servers use early Sun Microsystems technology and include the following RAS features:

- Automatic System Recovery (ASR)

Note: The ASR feature automatically isolates faulty hardware components to make a system functional after a component-failure reboot.

- JTAG (Joint Test Action Group, IEEE Std. 1149.1) ASIC diagnostics
- Dynamic RAM error correction code (ECC)
- System board LED diagnosis
- Redundant packet-switched data/address bus (second XDBus available on the SC2000E only)
- XDBus and CPU cache parity protection

Ultra Enterprise 1 (Ultra-1) and Ultra Enterprise 2 (Ultra-2)

Note: For ease of reading, Sun Microsystems <model number> <product type> will be referred to as model xxxx in the remainder of this chapter (where applicable). Where ambiguity is possible, the model number and product type will be specified.

Sun Microsystems Ultra™-1 and Ultra-2 workgroup servers are based on the 64-bit, SPARC™ Version 9-compliant, UltraSPARC™-I processor technology.

Note: SC2.2 support for the Ultra-1 is restricted to the 170 model. The Ultra-1/170 has the 167 MHz UltraSPARC processor option.

The Ultra-1 and Ultra-2 servers employ a Universal Port Architecture (UPA) interconnect to support internal and external 64-bit SBus (IEEE Std. 1496-1993) peripherals. UPA supports data transfer speeds of 1.3 Gbyte/second on a 167 MHz system and 1.6 Gbyte/second on a 200 MHz system.

System Resources

Sun Ultra Enterprise 1

- Single processor (maximum 167 MHz) with on-chip data and instruction cache (32 Kbytes each), and up to 512 Kbytes of external cache
- Memory capacity of 1 Gbyte (8 x 128 Mbyte SIMMs)

Sun Ultra Enterprise 2

- Two processors (maximum 200 MHz) with on-chip data and instruction cache (32 Kbytes each), and up to 1 Mbyte of external cache available for each processor.
- Memory capacity of 2 Gbytes (16 x 128 Mbyte SIMMs)

On-Board Devices

- One Ethernet IEEE 802.3 RJ45 port (10 Base-T for the Ultra-1 and 100 Base-T for the Ultra-2)
- Two RS-232 or RS-423 serial ports
- One Centronics-compatible parallel port
- One single-ended SCSI-2 connector (8-bit for the Ultra-1 and 16-bit for the Ultra-2)
- One 16-bit, 48 KHz audio device with options for: line-out, line-in, microphone-in, headphone-out, and internal speaker
- Optional drives; SCSI CD-ROM and 3.5″ 1.44 Mbyte floppy drives
- Three SBus slots (Ultra-1) or four SBus slots (Ultra-2)
- Additional UPA connector (Ultra-2)

Note: The SC2.2 software supports the on-board Ethernet standard (IEEE 802.3) for both Ultra-1 and Ultra-2 when configured for private interconnects or public networks.

RAS Features

- Extensive power-on self test (POST)
- ECC bus protection (memory and UPA data)
- Cache RAM parity
- Variable-speed fans with thermal sensors—a thermal fault results in a warning alert and/or shutdown to avoid component damage
- The ability to run SunVTS™ diagnostics to validate system functionality
- Simple clamshell enclosure for easy access to components
- Minimal internal cabling, jumpers, and common fasteners to make servicing easier

Netra t Carrier-Grade Servers

The Netra™ t *carrier-grade* servers (models 1120, 1125, 1400, and 1405) are designed to meet the stringent requirements of the rapidly growing telecommunications and Internet service provider market. The Netra t servers are based on the 64-bit, SPARC Version 9-compliant, UltraSPARC-II processor technology.

System Resources

- Up to four processors (maximum 440 MHz) with on-chip data and instruction cache (32 Kbytes each), and up to 4 Mbytes of external cache available for each processor
- Memory capacity of 4 Gbyte (16 x 256 Mbyte DIMMs)

On-Board Devices

- One Ethernet IEEE 802.3 10/100 Base-T RJ45 port
- Two RS-232 or RS-423 serial ports
- One Centronics-compatible parallel port
- One single-ended fast-wide Ultra SCSI-2 connector
- One 16-bit, 48 KHz audio device with options for: line-out, line-in, microphone-in, headphone-out, and internal speaker
- Four PCI slots (2 at 33 MHz with 5V signalling; 1 at 33 MHz with 5V signalling; and 1 at 33–66 MHz with 3.3V signalling)
- Optional SCSI CD-ROM and DAT drives

Note: The SC2.2 software supports the on-board Ethernet standard (IEEE 802.3) on Netra t servers when configured for private interconnects or public networks.

RAS Features

- Extensive power-on self test (POST)
- ECC bus protection (memory and UPA data)
- Cache RAM parity
- Variable-speed fans with thermal sensors—a thermal fault results in a warning alert and/or shutdown to avoid component damage.
- The ability to run SunVTS diagnostics to validate system functionality.
- Minimal internal cabling, jumpers, and common fasteners to make servicing easier.
- Dual redundant (n+1) hot-swap power supplies (48/60V DC, 110/240V AC options).
- Internal hot-pluggable Ultra-SCSI disks.
- Lights-out management (LOM): telecom RAS management (alarm card with relay output, LED panel, and remote access ports to monitor power inputs and fan failures and control remote reset, programmable watchdog, and user-programmable alarms).
- Ruggedized, rack-mountable chassis capable of operating in hostile environmental conditions (NEBS Level 3-compliant).

Sun Ultra Enterprise Servers x20R/x50

Sun Ultra Enterprise servers (models 150, 220R, 250, 420R, and 450) are workgroup servers with a small physical footprint and multiprocessing power. The Sun Ultra Enterprise 150 server is no longer manufactured; however, SC2.2 support is provided for early adopters (those having strict requirements against migrating to a newer platform). These servers integrate easily into a heterogeneous environment to provide file and print services for Microsoft Windows, Windows NT, Novell NetWare, and Macintosh clients. Sun Ultra Enterprise servers are based on the 64-bit, SPARC Version 9-compliant, UltraSPARC-II processor technology.

System Resources

Model 150

- Supports one processor (maximum 167 MHz) with on-chip data and instruction cache (32 Kbytes each), and up to 512 Kbytes of external cache.
- Memory capacity of 1 Gbyte (8 x 128 Mbyte SIMMs).

Models 220R / 250

- Supports two processors (maximum 450 MHz) with on-chip data and instruction cache (32 Kbytes each), and up to 4 Mbytes external cache available for each processor.
- Memory capacity of 2 Gbyte (16 x 128 Mbyte DIMMs).

Models 420R / 450

- Supports four processors (maximum 450 MHz) with on-chip data and instruction cache (32 Kbytes each), and up to 4 Mbytes of external cache available for each processor.
- Memory capacity of 4 Gbyte (16 x 256 Mbyte DIMMs).

On-Board Devices

- One Ethernet IEEE 802.3 10/100 Base-T RJ45 port.
- Two RS-232 or RS-423 serial ports.
- One Centronics-compatible parallel port.
- One internal and one external single-ended fast-wide Ultra SCSI-2 connectors (except model 150, which allocates one of the three internal SBus slots for a SunSwift™ card to provide 100 Base-T and fast-wide SCSI connectivity).
- One 16-bit, 48 KHz audio device with options for: line-out, line-in, microphone-in, headphone-out, and internal speaker.
- Model 150 supports two 25 MHz, 64-bit SBus slots; models 220R, 250, and 420R support four PCI slots (3 at 33 MHz with 5V signalling and 1 at 33–66 MHz with 3.3V signalling); model 450 supports ten PCI slots (7 at 33 MHz with 5V signalling and 3 at 33–66 MHz with 3.3V signalling).
- Models 220R and 420R support two internal hot-pluggable Ultra-SCSI disks; model 250 supports six internal hot-pluggable Ultra-SCSI disks; model 150 supports 12 fast-wide SCSI disks; model 450 supports 20 internal hot-pluggable Ultra-SCSI disks.
- Optional 1.44 Mbyte drive and 4mm DDS-3 SCSI tape.

Note: The SC2.2 software supports the on-board Ethernet standard (IEEE 802.3) for Sun Ultra Enterprise servers when configured for private interconnects or public networks.

RAS Features

- Extensive power-on self test (POST).
- ECC bus protection (memory and UPA data).
- Cache RAM parity.
- Variable-speed fans with thermal sensors—a thermal fault results in a warning alert and/or shutdown to avoid component damage.
- The ability to run SunVTS diagnostics to validate system functionality.
- Minimal internal cabling, jumpers, and common fasteners to make servicing easier.
- Internal hot-pluggable Ultra-SCSI disks (model 150 supports fast-wide drives only).
- Dual redundant (n+1) hot-swap power supplies with separate power cords (model 150 has a single power supply; model 450 has three).

The Sun Enterprise Server xx00

Sun Enterprise xx00 servers (models 3000, 3500, 4000, 4500, 5000, 5500, 6000, and 6500) are a family of scalable platforms targeted for high-performance computing and commercial applications. These servers are based on the 64-bit, SPARC Version 9-compliant, UltraSPARC-II processor technology.

Enterprise servers share a common centerplane and system board technology—this enables virtually all components within the model x000 and x500 family to be interchangeable. These components include CPU/memory boards, I/O boards, disk boards, UltraSPARC modules, DIMMs, power/cooling modules, clock boards, and peripherals. When upgrading a system, customers can re-use components to preserve their financial investment.

System Resources

Model 3xx0 Servers

- Four centerplane slots—up to 6 processors (maximum 400 MHz) with on-chip data and instruction cache (32 Kbytes each), and up to 8 Mbytes of external cache available for each processor.
- Memory capacity of 12 Gbytes (48 x 256 Mbyte DIMMs).

Model 4xx0 / 5xx0 Servers

- Eight centerplane slots—up to 14 processors (maximum 400 MHz) with on-chip data and instruction cache (32 Kbytes each), and up to 8 Mbytes of external cache available for each processor.
- Memory capacity of 28 Gbytes (112 x 256 Mbyte DIMMs).

Model 6xx0 Servers

- 16 centerplane slots—up to 30 processors (maximum 400 MHz), with on-chip data and instruction cache (32 Kbytes each), and up to 8 Mbytes of external cache available for each processor.
- Memory capacity of up 60 Gbytes (240 x 256 Mbyte DIMMs).

Note: The Sun Enterprise x500 servers have a faster (clock speed) centerplane than the x000 servers.

Each server in the xx00 family can accommodate five types of plug-in boards:

- CPU/memory board
- SBus I/O board
- Graphics I/O board
- PCI I/O board
- Disk board (not available for Sun Enterprise xx00 servers)

On-Board Devices for SBus, PCI, and Graphics I/O Boards

- One Ethernet IEEE 802.3 10/100 Base-T RJ45 port.
- Two RS-232 or RS-423 serial ports.
- One Centronics-compatible parallel port.
- Two (one internal and one external) single-ended fast-wide Ultra SCSI-2 connectors (except for model 150, which allocates one of the three internal SBus slots for a SunSwift card to provide 100 Base-T and fast-wide SCSI connectivity).
- One 16-bit, 48 KHz audio device with options for: line-out, line-in, microphone-in, headphone-out, and internal speaker.
- Model 150 supports two 25 MHz 64-bit SBus slots; models 220R, 250, and 420R support four PCI slots (three at 33 MHz with 5V signalling and one at 33–66 MHz with 3.3V signalling); model 450 supports ten PCI slots (seven at 33 MHz with 5V signalling and three at 33–66 MHz with 3.3V signalling).
- Models 220R and 420R support two internal hot-pluggable Ultra-SCSI disks; model 250 supports six internal hot-pluggable Ultra-SCSI disks; model 150 supports 12 fast-wide SCSI drives; model 450 supports 20 internal hot-pluggable Ultra-SCSI disks.
- Optional 1.44 Mbyte floppy drive and 4mm DDS-3 SCSI tape.

Note: The SC2.2 software supports the on-board Ethernet standard (IEEE 802.3) for model xx00 servers when configured for private interconnects or public networks.

RAS Features

- Extensive power-on self test (POST).
- Variable-speed fans with thermal sensors—a thermal fault results in a warning alert and/or shutdown to avoid component damage.
- ECC bus protection (memory and UPA data).
- Parity protection (cache RAM, interconnect address, and control signals).
- Passive component centerplane.
- N+1 redundancy option available for hot-swap power supplies and cooling fans.
- Remote booting and power cycling.
- Automatic System Recovery.
- Dynamic Reconfiguration enables online maintenance (system boards can be hot-plugged). See, "Dynamic Reconfiguration," on page 12 for additional details.

- Alternate Pathing enables redundant disk and network controller paths to recover from component failures. See, "Alternate Pathing," on page 13 for additional details.

Note: Alternate Pathing and Dynamic Reconfiguration are not currently supported by the SC2.2 software.

Sun Enterprise 10000 Server

The Sun Enterprise 10000 server (also known as Starfire™) is the largest SMP server available from Sun Microsystems. The Starfire server is based on the 64-bit, SPARC Version 9-compliant, UltraSPARC-II processor technology. The Starfire server can be configured with 64 processors, 64 Gbytes of memory, and over 60 Tbytes of online disk storage. Starfire systems offer advanced RAS features ideal for general-purpose applications, and database servers targeted for host-based or client/server applications (online transaction processing (OLTP), decision support systems (DSS), data warehousing, communications services, and multimedia services).

The Starfire server uses the Gigaplane-XB™ interconnect technology to implement the centerplane transport. The centerplane can accommodate 16 system boards (interchangeable within Enterprise 10000 servers only).

System Resources

- 16 centerplane slots—up to 64 processors (maximum 400 MHz), with on-chip data and instruction cache (32 Kbytes each), and up to 8 Mbytes of external cache available for each processor.
- Memory capacity of 64 Gbytes (512 x 128 Mbyte DIMMs).

System Board On-Board Devices

The system boards require an I/O mezzanine (SBus or PCI versions) to accommodate system controllers. Additionally, system boards require a processor mezzanine to support up to four processors and their external caches. Starfire system boards, unlike Sun Enterprise xx00 system boards, do not contain any on-board devices (i.e., serial, SCSI, Ethernet, etc.).

RAS Features

- The System Service Processor (SSP) is the management interface for the Starfire server. The SSP has a dedicated 10 Base-T Ethernet link to emulate JTAG (Joint Test Action Group, IEEE Std. 1149.1) functionality. The JTAG link monitors critical hardware components in the system—component statistics are logged to the SSP file system.
- Second-generation Dynamic Reconfiguration technology enables system boards to be hot-plugged to enable online maintenance and resource management.
- Second-generation Dynamic System Domain technology is exclusive to the Starfire server. This technology enables the Starfire server to be partitioned into 16 (maximum) independent, isolated hardware entities—each running their own instance of the Solaris Operating Environment (Solaris OE).
- Alternate Pathing provides redundant disk and network controllers to sustain continuous network and disk I/O when resources fail or are removed when using Dynamic Reconfiguration.

Note: Alternate Pathing and Dynamic Reconfiguration are not currently supported by the SC2.2 software.

- Redundant control boards provide JTAG, clock, fan, power, serial interface, and SSP Ethernet interface functionality.
- Extensive power-on self-test for all system boards prior to their integration into a domain.
- Variable-speed fans with thermal sensors—a thermal fault results in a warning alert and/or shutdown to avoid component damage.
- ECC bus protection (memory and UPA data).
- Environmental monitoring.
- Parity protection (cache RAM, interconnect address, and control signals).
- Parallel data and address paths provide redundancy for availability and enables load balancing.
- N+1 redundancy available for hot-swap power supplies and cooling fans.
- Redundant AC power cords and circuit breakers.
- Remote booting and system management using SSP.
- Automatic System Recovery (ASR).

Solaris Operating Environment Options

A powerful feature of the Solaris OE is its binary compatibility across all platforms. The SC2.2 software supports Solaris OE versions 2.6, 7, and 8.

Datacenters with high availability requirements are prone to resist changes—especially operating system changes. The downside of running older software versions is the reduced support—including service, trained personnel, and new hardware or software architectures. For example, Sun Cluster customers using version 2.5.1 of Solaris OE are restricted to using version 2.1 of the Sun Cluster software.

Because Sun Microsystems is committed to high availability, each new release of the operating environment provides enhanced functionality, robustness, and RAS features over the previous version.

Although SC2.2 software has 32-bit architecture, it can manage the 64-bit versions of the Solaris OE.

Solaris OE versions 2.6, 7, and 8 support the *live upgrade* feature. This feature enables installation of Solaris OE software (and other applications) on a partition isolated from a production environment. After the software installation is completed, the system should be rebooted to activate the new software. The original partition can be re-activated if problems arise from the software installation.

Solaris OE version 8 RAS enhancements include improved kernel error messaging to clearly identify system anomalies. The newly introduced `syseventd(1M)` command provides a mechanism for user-level applications to receive notification of specific error conditions in the kernel. The system event framework is important in the areas of dynamic reconfiguration, fault management, and resource management, where changes in the kernel must be propagated to user-level management applications.

Another feature introduced by Solaris OE version 8 is the implementation of the Internet Engineering Task Force (IETF) specifications for Internet protocol security architecture (IPSec). IPSec provides out-of-the-box support for smart-card authentication at login.

Note: Sun Cluster 3.0 software only runs on Solaris OE version 8 (and higher), see Chapter 8, "Beyond Sun Cluster 2.2" for additional information.

Public Network Interface Options

Public networks enable client access to the highly available services provided by the SC2.2 software. It is essential to match a controller choice to suit application requirements based on performance, network transport, and availability. The following sections discuss network interface options supported by the SC2.2 software.

Some controllers discussed in this section do not provide redundancy at the controller level; therefore, it is essential to duplicate this type of controller. The controller must be located on a separate system board (or data bus, if possible). Use a volume manager to provide mirrored data access to enable recovery from disk controller failure; use the SC2.2 network adapter failover (NAFO) feature to provide a failover path after experiencing a network controller failure.

Combination of 10/100 Base-T Ethernet and SCSI Adapter Cards

The SC2.2 software supports a combination of Ethernet and SCSI controllers on the same card—this saves I/O slots—which is important with lower-end configurations. The Ethernet/SCSI combination cards support standard 10/100 Base-T Ethernet controllers and contain the following SCSI controller options:

- Fast-wide SCSI-2 single-ended disk controller (SunSwift card)
- Fast SCSI-2 differential (DSBE/S card)
- Fast SCSI-2 single-ended disk controller (FSBE/S card)

Note: A failure of this controller creates a larger availability impact because it brings down the network and disk access functions simultaneously.

Fast Ethernet

Fast Ethernet is an extension of the 10 Base-T Ethernet standard and is capable of supporting a wider range of applications at a higher throughput. The standards for Fast Ethernet are well-defined and accepted throughout the industry (similar to 10-Mbps Ethernet) — a large variety of products use the Fast Ethernet standard.

All Sun servers (except the Sun Enterprise 10000) are equipped with on-board Fast Ethernet cards that have link speeds of 100 Mbps with full-duplex capabilities. Dual-speed Ethernet adapters, 10 Base-T and 100 Base-T, provide compatibility with legacy 10 Base-T devices. Using full-duplex functionality enhances performance by using separate transmit and receive paths capable of full 100 Mbps link speeds (theoretical aggregate of 200 Mbps).

Because dual-speed Ethernet devices negotiate the transport speed with hubs or switches, it is essential to verify the link speed and full-duplex attributes to confirm they are as expected. For example, there may be a problem if a switch configures its link as a single-duplex, 10 Mbps device, when in reality it is attached to a controller capable of supporting full-duplex 100 Mbps.

Quad Fast Ethernet

The quad fast Ethernet controller provides four Fast Ethernet ports with link speeds of 100 Mbps and full-duplex capabilities on the same controller. Each port on this controller has identical attributes as the on-board Fast Ethernet controller (as described above).

The quad fast Ethernet controller introduces quadruple functionality, which saves I/O slots—this is important with lower-end configurations.

Note: Failure of this controller carries a higher availability impact because of the potential of losing four network links simultaneously.

Gigabit Ethernet

The IEEE Gigabit Ethernet 802.3z standard, an extension of the 10- and 100-Mbps IEEE 802.3 Ethernet standard, accommodates larger packet sizes and operates on fiber transport (up to 1 Gbps). Gigabit Ethernet supports full-duplex transmission (aggregate of 2 Gbps) for switch-to-switch and switch-to-end-station connections. Half-duplex transmission for shared connections uses repeaters that implement the carrier sense multiple access with collision detection (CSMA/CD) access method.

The Sun Gigabit Ethernet adapter uses a simplex connector (SC) interface—this cable provides a range of 2 to 220 meters using 62.5 micron multimode fiber cable, or 2 to 550 meters using 50 micron cable.

Token Ring

Token ring is a common transport in the mainframe world. Although token ring supports the TCP/IP protocol, it is generally used to interface with mainframes using IBM's System Network Architecture (SNA) protocol.

Note: The SC2.2 software does not support the SNA protocol.

Token ring supports transport speed options of 4 Mbps or 16 Mbps and adheres to a token-passing bus scheme using IBM type 1 or type 2 STP cabling to make bandwidth allocation predictable.

The Sun Microsystems TRI/S adapter is used in conjunction with the SunLink TRI/S software to provide transparent access to token ring networks without modifying existing applications. The SunLink TRI/S adapter provides IP routing between Ethernet, FDDI, and token ring networks and is compatible with IBM source routing bridges.

Asynchronous Transfer Mode

Asynchronous transfer mode (ATM) is a networking technology capable of supporting WANs. ATM uses small, fixed-sized packets (or cells) to achieve high performance when used in combination with high-bandwidth, low-latency switches. Additionally, ATM supports data rates of 25 Mbps to 2 Gbps, which are ideal for demanding, interactive applications involving voice and video transmission requiring low latency and a specific quality of service.

The SunATM™ controller is a single-wide SBus card that supports high-end users with a technology that addresses increased network bandwidth requirements. The SunATM-155/MFiber and SunATM-155/UTP5 adapters support 155 Mbps transfer rates over multimode fiber or category 5 unshielded twisted-pair (UTP) wire. The SunATM adapters support speeds in excess of 100 Mbps. These adapters also support the *synchronous optical network/synchronous digital hierarchy* (SONET/SDH) and *classical IP* options.

Fiber Data Distributed Interface

The fiber data distributed interface (FDDI) is a legacy fiber transport used in the TCP/IP and SNA worlds that implements a token-passing scheme.

The SunLink™ FDDI supports transport speeds of 100 Mbps and provides single-ring (FDDI/S with a choice of copper transport) or dual-ring (FDDI/D) option. The SunLink FDDI/D controller provides higher availability and performance because the dual rings are used for load balancing. FDDI includes its own hardware protocol to re-route network traffic if one of the rings becomes unavailable.

Private Network Interface Options

The private network cluster interconnect is used to move heartbeat information between cluster nodes. If the SC2.2 cluster is configured with the Oracle Parallel Server (OPS) software (shared everything architecture), the private interconnect is then used to move database information between cluster nodes.

All private network interface options supported by the SC2.2 software provide sufficient minimum latency to deliver heartbeat information on time to avoid unintended failovers. If the private interconnect is used to move data between parallel database cluster nodes, it is essential the private interconnect delivers maximum throughput to avoid performance impact.

The SC2.2 software requires that private interconnects be redundant, and that both interconnects are of the same interface type (i.e., fast Ethernet, Gigabit Ethernet, etc.).

In a two-node cluster configuration, provide point-to-point connectivity (null cable) to minimize the availability impact introduced by hubs or switches.

The following sections provide network interface options supported by the SC2.2 software:

Fast Ethernet

Fast Ethernet is a good choice for a private interconnect when used to move only heartbeat information, see section, "Fast Ethernet" on page 91.

Quad Fast Ethernet

Quad Fast Ethernet controllers enable multiple ethernet functionality to save I/O slots, see section, "Quad Fast Ethernet" on page 91.

Scalable Coherent Interconnect (SCI)

The scalable coherent interconnect (SCI) is the preferred medium for parallel databases because it provides high throughput and low latency.

SCI is a ring-based, token-passing topology that can be configured point-to-point (with two-node clusters), or it can be configured with multiple nodes using an SCI switch. The SCI transport is implemented in copper, not fiber. Because the SCI is implemented in copper, the cluster nodes are required to be in close proximity to one another.

Gigabit Ethernet Interconnect

The Gigabit Ethernet interconnect is a high-throughput, low-latency transport. Because of these features, Gigabit Ethernet can be used as a private interconnect for parallel databases and HA configurations.

Unlike the SCI transport, Gigabit Ethernet is implemented in fiber, which removes the distance limitations between nodes and simplifies cable handling, see section, "Gigabit Ethernet" on page 91.

Disk Storage Options

Disk data is fundamentally important to any computer system because it represents a unique system fingerprint that has taken time and effort to produce. The system data comprises the following elements:

- System hardware configuration: the peripheral environment and accumulated configuration changes.
- Operating system base: kernel patches applied and accumulated configuration modifications.
- Business application: software patches applied and accumulated configuration modifications.
- Business data collected over time and history of transactions that modified the data.

Because data is a valuable commodity, it is important to know which storage devices are supported by the SC2.2 software, and which RAS features are best suited to your requirements. The SC2.2 software supports two classes of storage devices: SCSI (small computer system interface) and fiber channel (FC).

Although an FC device is more expensive than an alternative SCSI device, it is the preferred option for clusters because it minimizes the following limitations:

Distance

FC devices remove the necessity of having disk storage in close proximity to the server—enabling disk storage to be in a physically separated room or building.

Bus Termination

FC devices do not require electrical signal termination and are not affected by electromagnetic interference (EMI).

Multiple Hosts

The FC protocol enables multiple hosts to be connected in the same environment without conflict. By contrast, the SCSI protocol requires multiple hosts sharing the same environment to use unique SCSI-initiator IDs, see "Appendix A: SCSI-Initiator ID."

Note: The SC2.2 software enables SCSI storage to be shared between two nodes. FC storage can be shared between the maximum number of nodes (current maximum is four).

Bandwidth

The FC transport provides a higher aggregate bandwidth than SCSI because the data is transmitted serially (maximum 200 Mbps), whereas SCSI data is transmitted in parallel (maximum 40 Mbps).

Some disk subsystems supported by the SC2.2 software feature a battery-backed cache, which is essential for performance in write-intensive (i.e., OLTP) environments. Either Veritas VxVM or Solstice DiskSuite™ (SDS) can be used to manage volumes across all disk subsystems, including those with hardware RAID capability. It is essential that disk controllers have redundant paths to access mirrored data—alternate controllers should be located on a separate system board or data bus (if possible).

SCSI Storage Devices

The ANSI (American National Standards Institute) SCSI standard uses an I/O bus protocol that provides efficient peer-to-peer connectivity between devices. This standard has evolved over time (from SCSI-1 to the current SCSI-3) to incorporate the following:

- A software protocol that accommodates many types of peripheral device requirements; for example, magnetic and optical disks, tapes, printers, processors, CD-ROMs, scanners, medium changers, communication devices, etc.
- A hardware protocol that supports faster clock speed and has a wider address and data bus to support additional devices with increased bandwidth.

Note: Shared SCSI devices require a unique SCSI-initiator ID on both cluster nodes and limit access to two-node clusters, see "Appendix A: SCSI-Initiator ID."

SCSI storage subsystems have *SCSI-in* and *SCSI-out* ports, see Figure 3-1. In a single-host environment, the SCSI-in connector attaches to the host and the SCSI-out connector is either capped with a terminator (that matches the differential or single-ended bus technology) or connected to the next storage device. In a multi-host environment, the *SCSI-out* connector is attached to the next host sharing the SCSI device.

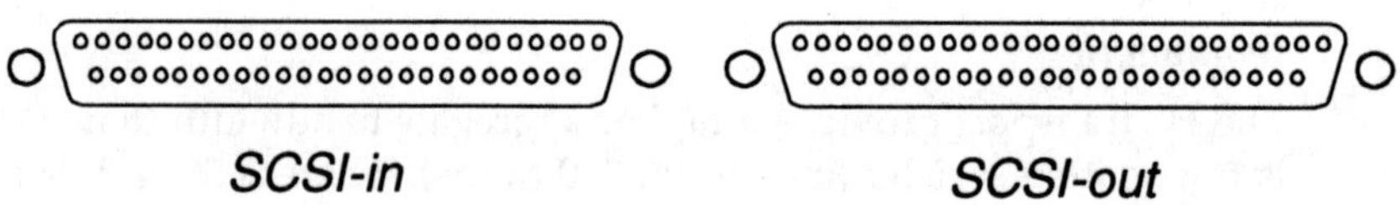

Figure 3-1 SCSI Host Connectors

Sun StorEdge™ MultiPack

The Sun StorEdge MultiPack subsystem supports six single connector attachment (SCA) Ultra-SCSI drives (1-inch drives). This enclosure provides single-ended wide SCSI bus connectivity with automatic termination, and has a switch to select either SCSI-IDs 1 to 6, or 9 to 14.

Sun StorEdge MultiPack RAS Features

- Automatic SCSI ID slot assignment (no jumpering required)
- Automatic SCSI termination
- Single-connector (SCA-2) hot-pluggable drives
- Hardwired (geographical) SCSI addressing
- Locking mechanism to prevent removal of devices

Sun StorEdge A1000 and D1000 Storage Arrays

The Sun StorEdge A1000 and D1000 storage arrays are successors to the SPARCstorage™ 112/114 and 214/219 arrays. The Sun StorEdge A1000 model is a hardware-RAID subsystem, while the D1000 model is a software-RAID JBOD (just a bunch of disks) subsystem. The Sun StorEdge A1000 and D1000 models use the same chassis design and drive technology. These arrays support differential Ultra SCSI connections to hosts and internal hot-pluggable drives. These drives are contained within a disk tray that holds 12 1-inch or 8 1.6-inch drives. The disk tray on the Sun StorEdge D1000 model has two SCSI connectors to access the first half of the drives and two additional connectors to access the other half.

The Sun StorEdge A1000 array has an intelligent controller (based on the 100 MHz Intel Pentium processor) to slice and group internal disk drives into RAID 0, 1, 1+0, 3, and RAID 5 configurations to create the illusion of a single physical disk to an external host. The Sun StorEdge A1000 model supports a maximum of 64 Mbytes of battery-backed read/write cache. The management of logical unit numbers (LUNs), internal cache, and controller firmware requires the use of RAID Manager 6 (rm6) GUI software.

D1000 and A1000 RAS Features

- Automatic SCSI ID slot assignment (no jumpering required)
- Environmental service module board (model A1000 only)
- Redundant hot-swap power supplies with redundant power cords
- Redundant hot-swap fan trays
- Single connector (SCA-2) with hot-pluggable drives
- Hardwired (geographical) SCSI addressing
- Locking mechanism to prevent removal of devices
- Controller module and battery fault status LEDs (model A1000 only)
- Disk fault, temperature, and blower fan fault status LEDs

Sun Netra st D1000 and A1000 Storage Arrays

The Sun Netra st A1000 and D1000 arrays are based on Sun StorEdge A1000 and D1000 array technology. The standard and extended RAS features of the Sun Netra st D1000 and A1000 storage arrays are identical to the features discussed in the previous section, "Sun StorEdge A1000 and D1000 Storage Arrays."

Additional features required by the Telco and Internet environments include:

- 4U rack mount unit
- -48V/-60VDC or AC power options
- Central office and Internet Service Provider (ISP) Post Office Protocol (POP) ruggedization
- Bellcore NEBS-compliant

Sun StorEdge A3000/A3500

The Sun StorEdge A3000 array (originally RSM2000) was the first intelligent SCSI array introduced by Sun Microsystems. Although the A3500 model is based on the same architecture as the A3000 model, it has faster controllers, a larger disk capacity, more disk trays per rack, more disks per disk tray, and a larger battery-backed cache. The Sun StorEdge A3500 model has a maximum of 256 Mbytes of battery-backed read/write cache (128 Mbytes per controller), whereas the A3000 model has a maximum cache of 128 Mbytes.

The Sun StorEdge A3000/A3500 model disk arrays have fully redundant components (no single points of failure). Host connectivity is provided by dual Ultra-SCSCI ports (each port is rated at 40 Mbps). The A3000/A3500 intelligent controllers (redundant dual-active) are housed in a 73.5-inch expansion cabinet (with 19-inch racks) and can be connected to any disk tray within the rack.

The intelligent controllers require RAID Manager 6 (rm6) software to manage the LUNs, internal cache, and controller firmware, and to implement RAID 0, 1, 1+0, 3, and RAID 5 configurations. A RAID disk creates the illusion of a single physical disk to an external host.

Model A3000 and A3500 Controller RAS Features

- Redundant hot-swap controller modules
- Controller module and battery fault status LEDs
- Redundant hot-swap power supplies (with redundant power cords)
- Redundant hot-swap fan trays

Model A3000 and A3500 Disk Tray RAS Features

- Hot-pluggable 3.5-inch disk drives (model A3000)
- Hot-pluggable 1-inch disk drives (model A3500)
- Automatic SCSI ID slot assignment (no jumpering required)
- Environmental service module board
- Single-connector (SCA-2) hot-pluggable drives
- Hardwired (geographical) SCSI addressing
- Locking mechanism to prevent removal of devices
- Disk fault, temperature, and blower fan fault status LEDs

Sun StorEdge A7000

The Sun StorEdge A7000 was the first storage product released by Sun Microsystems that provided dual connectivity to UNIX servers (Solaris, HP/UX) and IBM-compatible mainframes. Although the Sun StorEdge A7000 array is no longer manufactured, SC2.2 support is provided for early adopters (those having strict requirements against migrating to newer platforms).

Fiber Channel Storage Devices

The fiber channel (FC) development was started in 1988 and finalized in 1994, which resulted in the ANSI X3.230-1994 standard. The FC technology supports full-duplex (1 Gbps) fiber link to sustain the high-bandwidth transport requirements of data warehousing, high-performance computing, real-time data, imaging, audio, video, etc. FC can be used as a network and channel transport with the following protocols (currently implemented or under development):

Fiber Channel Protocols

- Small computer system interface (SCSI)
- Intelligent peripheral interface (IPI)
- High-performance parallel interface (HIPPI) framing protocol
- Internet protocol (IP)
- ATM Adaptation Layer for computer data (AAL5)
- Link encapsulation (FC-LE)
- Single-byte command code set mapping (SBCCS)
- IEEE 802.2

Fibre Channel Connectivity Topologies

- Point-to-point connection between two nodes.
- Arbitrated loop connection between n nodes (maximum of 127). Arbitrated loop is not a token-passing scheme and has no limit on how long a device retains control of the loop after winning arbitration.
- A fabric connection involves a node attachment to a FC hub or switch. A fabric connection simplifies cabling connection and prevents a defective node (or broken fiber connection) from affecting other nodes. FC hubs share the same bandwidth between all ports, while switches enable many devices to communicate at the same time.

Fiber channel technology defines various port categories that can simplify management. A server port is defined as an N_Port, while a fabric port is defined as an F_Port. Any port attached to a loop is defined as an L_Port.

Fabric and loop combinations are characterized by the FL_Port and NL_Port definitions. Ports connecting switches are defined as E_Ports. A port that can function as either an E_Port or an F_Port is defined as a G_Port. A G_Port with Loop capabilities is defined a GL_Port.

The SPARCstorage Array

SPARCstorage arrays were the first storage subsystems produced by Sun Microsystems that use fiber channel (FC) storage technology.

SPARCstorage array controllers are based on the MicroSPARC™ or MicroSPARC-II processors. The main function of the SPARCstorage array controller is to provide a disk cache and management functions. The SPARCstorage Array provides dual-ported FC links that sustain a maximum of 50 Mbps full-duplex data transfers (25 Mbps inbound and 25 Mbps outbound).

The following are the available models in the SPARCstorage family:

Models 100/110

Holds 30 drives and have a 4 Mbyte battery-backed NVRAM cache option (Model 110 runs at a higher clock speed).

Models 200/210

Holds 36 drives and have larger disk capacities per drive than the 100/110 models. The battery-backed NVRAM cache option for both models is 16 Mbyte.

Models RSM 214/219

These models introduced hot-swap fans and power supplies for the controller side. The hot-pluggable disk drives were housed separately from the controller in an RSM disk tray.

Sun StorEdge A3500FC Disk Array

The A3500FC disk array is based on the Sun StorEdge A3500 array technology—the A3500 array differs from the A3500FC model in that the controller provides dual fiber channel host connectivity, see section, "Sun StorEdge A3000/A3500," on page 98.

Sun StorEdge A5x00 Disk Array

The Sun StorEdge A5x00 disk array is based on the fiber channel arbitrated loop (FCAL) technology that is capable of 200 Mbps full duplex throughput. The A5x00 model can be used as a fundamental component for building a storage area network (SAN). Although the A5x00 internal drives use FCAL connectivity, they are implemented in copper for connection to the disk tray backplane.

The Sun StorEdge fast write cache option is available for the A5x00 model array to compensate for the lack of an internal cache. The SC2.2 software does not support this option because it uses an NVRAM module (resident on the host), which cannot be failed over.

Model A5x00 disk arrays support four FCAL ports that can be accessed by different hosts. Additionally, FCAL hubs can also be used to provide multiple host connectivity with a single port. Host connectivity is achieved using a Gigabit interface converter (GBIC) transmitter over multi-mode fiber, or a long-wave Gigabit interface converter (LWGBIC) transmitter over single mode-fiber. The LWGBIC option is used to extend the maximum distance limitation (of GBIC) from 500 meters to 10 kilometers (6 miles).

Model A5x00 RAS Features

- Redundant controllers
- Diagnostics console
- Automatic loop failover with load balancing
- Redundant hot-swap power supplies
- Hot-swap cooling fans
- Hot-pluggable disk drives
- Automatic node ID loop resolution (no jumpering required)
- Early failure warning and phone home features using Sun Management Center software

Volume Manager Options

Many Sun customers expand their business capabilities by configuring their production servers with larger disk capacities. For example, Enterprise workgroup servers can be configured to support dozens or hundreds of disks; however, in this situation, the following management problems could be experienced:

- Increased probability of disk failure
- Complex file system partitioning
- Longer reboot times
- Server failure impacts a greater number of users

Volume managers are software tools that provide RAID support to increase availability and disk management capabilities. The three volume managers supported by the SC2.2 software are: Sun Solstice DiskSuite (SDS), Veritas Volume Manager (VxVM), and the Veritas Cluster Volume Manager (CVM).

Solstice DiskSuite Software

The SDS software is supplied with the Solaris OE. This software contains basic disk management and the RAID configuration features necessary to increase the availability of a disk subsystem. The SDS software supports four levels of RAID to provide varying degrees of availability (with corresponding trade-offs in performance and cost). The SDS software includes the following features:

RAID 0: Disk Striping

Disk striping distributes the I/O load over several disk spindles and increases the throughput available to a single process. Although RAID 0 provides more efficient data access, it does not improve disk data availability.

RAID 1: Disk Mirroring

Disk mirroring enables users to access an alternate disk when a disk or controller failure occurs. SDS transparently maintains a mirrored copy of the data and automatically uses the surviving copy in the event of a hardware failure. All mirrored disks have full automatic replication consistency to prevent data corruption when single or compound failures occur.

RAID 0+ 1: Disk Striping Plus Mirroring

This feature provides the performance benefits of RAID 0 while enhancing the disk data availability through the use of RAID 1 (mirroring). If a single stripe fails in a RAID 0+1 configuration, one half of the mirror is unavailable—*all* mirrored disk data must be re-created after repairs are effected.

RAID 5: Striping with Distributed Parity

RAID 5 reconstructs data in the event of a single disk failure. RAID 5 is a less expensive alternative to RAID 0, however, parity computations introduce latency. RAID 5 parity is computed and compared with each *read* cycle, and is computed and stored with each *write* cycle. RAID-5 has less performance impact when hardware RAID is used.

Hot Spares

This feature enhances recovery from a disk failure by automatically replacing a failed mirror or RAID-5 partition with an alternate disk. Hot spares automatically migrate RAID-5 and mirrored data. During this time, users can access surviving partitions.

Journaling File System

When a system reboots, Solaris OE verifies the integrity of all UNIX file systems (UFS) to confirm a stable environment. The journaling file system function is included in the Solstice DiskSuite product and provides a transaction log to eliminate the need for file system checks, thereby enabling fast system recoveries without compromising availability and data integrity. The journaling file system logging feature is fully compatible with the logging feature included in the Solaris 7 OE software.

Increased File System Capacity

Prior to SDS, when a UFS file system ran out of space, a service interruption would be created when moving files into a larger disk space. SDS will append a partition to an existing RAID subsystem and then expand its UFS file system.

Disk Sets

SDS includes host ownership assignment to a group of disks to support the multiple host synchronization required by clusters.

Performance Analysis Tools

SDS includes utilities to monitor the I/O load and gather statistics at the disk partition level.

Veritas Volume Manager (VxVM) Software

The VxVM software provides functionality similar to that of the SDS product (increases availability of a disk subsystem). The VxVM product provides additional functionality when compared to the SDS product. These features include an enhanced naming convention, scalability, and management functions; however, it does not include a journaling file system.

VxVM includes support for RAID 0+1. This feature combines the protection of RAID 1 with the performance benefits of RAID 0. RAID 1+0 manages each stripe as an independent entity and is mirrored separately. If a single stripe fails, only the data associated with the mirrored stripe is required to be re-created after repairs are effected.

A significant difference between VxVM and SDS is the number of supported sub disks within a physical disk—this is limited to seven by Solaris OE. The SDS sub disk limitation may be a significant factor with large-capacity disk drives (9 Gbyte or greater).

Note: The Sun StorEdge Volume Manager™ is the OEM version of the Veritas Volume Manager product.

Veritas CVM Software

The CVM software performs functions similar to the VxVM software; however, CVM provides parallel data access to all cluster nodes by enabling disk groups to be imported by more than one host. The CVM software can only be used in combination with the Oracle Parallel Server (OPS) software. Because each host has read/write access to the same data, OPS uses its own Distributed Lock Manager (DLM) software to ensure data coherency.

Data Storage Options

The method of data access is dependent on the choice of data storage. Disk data can be stored in raw disk format or file system format. The following sections detail available data storage options and their associated issues:

Raw Disk Storage

Raw disk device I/O is supported by the SC2.2 software because it enables database vendors to circumvent file system features such as file buffer cache, inode cache, file access, etc. to enhance performance. Database vendors recommend the use of raw devices to have direct access to data blocks contained within a disk partition; however, such access requires additional proprietary data management software. Choosing raw disk storage can impact an existing backup and restore process because the minimum unit available will be an entire disk partition (as opposed to smaller and more manageable individual files).

File System Storage

File systems provide the infrastructure to store and manage data by using individual files organized under a directory tree. The SC2.2 software supports the UNIX file system (UFS), included with Solaris OE, and the Veritas file system (VxFS).

UNIX File System (UFS)

The UFS is a general-purpose disk-based file system included with Solaris OE. The Solstice DiskSuite 3.x product introduced UFS transaction logging (known as the *journaling file system*). The journaling file system enables faster reboot times by committing the last transactions logged instead of running the exhaustive `fsck(1M)` file system check command.

Note: To enable the journaling file system, the Solstice DiskSuite 3.x product should be used in conjunction with Solaris OE (version 7 or higher).

Veritas File System (VxFS)

The VxFS is an extent-based file system; that is, file system block sizes are variable and automatically adapt to different I/O requirements. VxFS is fully compatible with existing UFS API standards and supports all file system commands.

To assist in file system management, VxFS features a transaction-based journaling log to enable fast recovery from a system crash, as well as enhanced on-line backup capabilities, on-line resizing, and defragmentation.

In addition to these basic file system features, VxFS includes the following:

Discovered Direct I/O

VxFS switches off the file system cache automatically whenever a large read or write operation is performed—this can increase performance by removing unnecessary cache maintenance overhead.

Storage Checkpoint

The VxFS checkpoint feature uses snapshot technology to create a clone of a currently mounted VxFS. A VxFS checkpoint provides a consistent, point-in-time view of the file system by identifying and tracking modified file system blocks. A VxFS checkpoint is required by the *block level incremental backup* and *storage rollback* features.

Block Level Incremental Backup

This feature stores and retrieves only data blocks (not entire files) that have been modified since a previous backup.

Storage Rollback

Storage rollback is a function that promotes faster recovery from problems such as accidentally deleting a file. Because each *storage checkpoint* is a point-in-time image of a file system, the storage rollback feature restores (or rolls back) a file or file system to the storage checkpoint.

Cached Quick I/O

The cached quick I/O feature is useful in a database environment to provide administrative file system flexibility with raw disk performance (i.e., faster sequential file access). Additionally, this feature provides a raw device interface which bypasses file system locking and the file buffer cache.

Data Service Options

Many data services are already available that can match application requirements—these data services can save a long development process. There are many groups within Sun Microsystems, Inc. (Sun Cluster Engineering, Market Development, Engineering, and Sun Professional Services) involved in the development of commercial-grade data services.

This section provides an example of existing data services. Contact your local Sun service provider to obtain the current list of available data services from Sun Microsystems and third-party vendors. See Table 3-1 for descriptions of available data services.

Note: In Table 3-1 the term "Solaris" is used in place of "Solaris Operating Environment."

Table 3-1 Data Services Available from Sun Cluster Engineering

Vendor	Software	Description
Sun	NFS, versions 2 and 3 on Solaris 2.6, 7	Enables an NFS file service to be highly available.
Sun	DNS BIND v4.9 on Solaris 2.6; DNS BIND v8.1.2 on Solaris 7	Enables the DNS named server (primary/secondary) to be highly available
Sun	Sun Internet Mail Server™ (SIMS) 4.0 for Solaris 2.6, 7	Enables SIMS to be highly available—comes bundled with core SIMS 4.0 product and configuration options

Table 3-1 Data Services Available from Sun Cluster Engineering

Vendor	Software	Description
Sun	Solaris PC Netlink 1.2 for Solaris 2.6, 7	Enables PC file services to be highly available. Comes bundled with core PC NetLink product
Oracle	HA 7.3.4, 8.0.4, 8.0.5, 8i/ 8.1.5 (32-bit) for Solaris 2.6, 7	Enables an Oracle (server) database instance to be highly available
Oracle	Parallel Server 7.3.4, 8.0.4, 8.0.5, 8i/8.1.5 (32-bit) for Solaris 2.6	Enables a parallel database to be shared among Oracle instances on nodes with access to a single datastore. In the event of instance failure, surviving instances dynamically take over the load until recovery
Netscape/iPlanet	Netscape Enterprise Server 3.5.1, 3.6, 3.6 HTTPs, and 4.0 for Solaris 2.6	Enables a HTTP (Web) server to be highly available
Netscape/iPlanet	Netscape Messaging Server 3.5, 4.1 for Solaris 2.6	Enables a mail or messaging server to be highly available
Netscape/iPlanet	News/Collabra Server 3.5 for Solaris 2.6	Enables a news server to be highly available
Netscape/iPlanet	Netscape Directory Server 3.5, 4.1 for Solaris 2.6	Enables an LDAP (master) directory server to be highly available
Sybase	Adaptive Server 11.5, 11.9.2 for Solaris 2.6	Enables ASE to be highly available
SAP	R/3 for Solaris 2.6 Oracle: 3.1h, 3.1i, 4.0b, 4.5b	Enables SAP central instance (message and enqueue servers) to be highly available
SAP	R/3 for Solaris 2.6 Informix: 4.5b BIW	Enables central instance (message and enqueue servers) to be highly available
Lotus	Domino 4.6, 4.6.1 for Solaris 2.6	Enables Domino server to be highly available
Informix	Dynamic Server 7.23x, 7.3 for Solaris 2.6	Enables dynamic server to be highly available
Tivoli	3.2, 3.6 for Solaris 2.6	Enables Tivoli management framework to be highly available
Informix	IDS 7.3 for Solaris 2.6	Enables IDS database capability
Informix	XPS IDS 8.11 for Solaris 2.6	Enables XPS parallel database capability

Summary

After deciding to implement a cluster in your datacenter, there are many choices to be made. Component choices (servers, storage, private interconnect, public network interfaces, etc.) should take into account the factors of supportability, availability, performance, capacity, and cost considerations. The detailed SC2.2 component information provided in this chapter will assist in finding a suitable component match for your application requirements with regards to availability and performance.

CHAPTER 4

Sun Cluster 2.2 Administration

Maintaining a clustered system is more complex than maintaining a non-clustered system. Apart from the number of additional components required for redundancy, the cluster software also adds administrative overhead. To get the most out of the cluster software, a sound knowledge of the administrative tools is required.

Understanding the administrative tools thoroughly will enable an administrator to quickly and effectively make any required administrative changes, or replace non-functional components—thereby enhancing system redundancy and high availability.

This chapter discusses the administrative tools supplied with the Sun Cluster 2.2 (SC2.2) software, and demonstrates how to use them effectively. The topics covered are:

- Gathering information about the cluster setup
- Cluster administration
- Administering cluster changes

For new administrators, this chapter provides a generalized understanding of cluster administration practices and commands, and includes pitfalls and mistakes commonly encountered. Additionally, some best practice processes are identified which can assist in the administration of a cluster.

For experienced administrators, this chapter provides a reference for administering and monitoring all aspects of the cluster, along with an overview of the associated best practices.

For an in-depth discussion of cluster administration, refer to the *Sun Cluster 2.2 System Administration Guide*.

This chapter describes commands that are part of the Sun Cluster distribution which are unique to a cluster environment. Commands relating to volume managers, file systems, and third-party software used for monitoring a Sun Cluster environment are not covered—refer to the appropriate manuals.

Chapter Roadmap

This chapter describes cluster administration, including monitoring, managing changes, moving nodes in and out of a cluster, and replacing non-functional components. This chapter has been designed (in part) to be a reference guide—however, an understanding of the cluster components does not in itself demonstrate the larger cluster picture. This section provides a roadmap of the chapter and introduces related chapters.

- Underlying all aspects of cluster administration is monitoring. Monitoring is essential for identifying problems and consequent troubleshooting. Additionally, monitoring provides the current state of the configuration—essential for performing modifications. Although monitoring is covered to some degree in each section, it is important to understand and compare the monitoring tools. Because monitoring is important to all other aspects of cluster administration, it is covered first.
- The commands that output monitoring information are discussed, along with locations of the cluster activity logs. Additionally, the synchronization of time in a clustered environment is discussed because timestamps are essential for comparing cluster logs on different nodes.

An essential part of a highly available cluster is providing a data service; therefore, the core component of this chapter leads into the creation and administration of an HA data service. Chapter 7, "Sun Cluster 2.2 Data Services" delves deeper into HA services and provides insight into the creation of custom HA services. Chapter 1, "High Availability Fundamentals" broadens out the discussion with an explanation of the underlying concepts and implementation of parallel, highly available databases.

The basic aspects of cluster administration are:

Controlling Nodes In and Out of the Cluster

The section, "Cluster Membership Administration" describes how to start and stop a cluster (or cluster nodes).

Configuring a Cluster

The section, "Managing Cluster Configuration" on page 133 describes cluster configuration databases and how to perform changes.

Configuring Public Networks

Network interfaces are links to the outside world. The section, "Administering NAFO Groups" on page 151 describes the Public Network Management (PNM) infrastructure.

Configuring Data Services

The section, "Logical Host and Data Service Administration" on page 158 describes logical hosts and data services and their dependence on all the underlying layers.

Making Changes to the Cluster

The section, "Cluster Topology and Hardware Changes" on page 170 describes updating the cluster to be aware of changes to the underlying hardware. Although the hardware exists as the base level of the cluster infrastructure, an understanding of how the cluster deals with the individual components is necessary because topology or hardware changes could affect cluster membership, PNM, logical hosts, and data services. Additionally, an understanding of the cluster configuration databases is also required because they hold specific configuration information.

Monitoring Sun Cluster Status and Configuration

A fundamental component of administration is the ability to determine the status of whatever it is you are administering. This can be accomplished using logs or informational commands. Both methods are fundamental for avoiding problems and finding solutions to problems that could not be avoided. An understanding of the administrative tools will enable a system administrator to quickly identify and solve cluster problems. Using the appropriate log files is an important step for identifying the root cause of a problem.

Monitoring Tools

There are several commands used for monitoring the status and configuration of a Sun Cluster. Some commands display information on the broader aspects of cluster configuration and current status—others display information about a specific portion of the cluster. A GUI-based monitoring tool is also supplied with the distribution.

Note: The `scconf` command should always use the cluster name as an argument (in addition to an option flag indicating the operation to perform). Throughout this chapter, the cluster name argument is often omitted for ease of readability. For example, where the command `scconf -p` is referred to, the actual command to be used is `scconf` *clustername* `-p`, where *clustername* is the name of the cluster.

Multi-purpose commands are available that display large amounts of information. The `get_node_status`, `scconf -p`, and `hastat` commands are some examples.

The information displayed is not usually set up in a line-by-line form when using multi-purpose commands; therefore, it is difficult to extract a single piece of information using tools like `grep`. However, the information can be easily found if you know which command to use. The output of the `scconf -p` and `hastat` commands can be lengthy; therefore, the `more` utility should be used to display data one page at a time.

Many cluster commands can be grouped together in pairs, whereby one of the commands will display configuration information and its complement command will display the status information. For example, in the case of data services, the `hareg -q` command provides configuration information with the `hareg` command indicating the status.

Table 4-1 provides an overview of cluster monitoring commands. The following summarizes the uses of each command:

`get_node_status`

This command displays the node's status as seen by the Cluster Membership Monitor (CMM). The CMM is responsible for monitoring node status and determining cluster membership, see Chapter 2, "Sun Cluster 2.2 Architecture." The output of the `get_node_status` command includes only information relating to the CMM. Information is listed on whether the node is in the cluster, the status of the interconnects, the volume manager (which affects failure fencing), and the database status (because the database lock manager is related to the CMM).

`scconf -p`

This command displays the configuration parameters set by the `scconf` command. The `scconf -p` command provides information about cluster configuration (but not the current cluster state). The `scconf -p` command is commonly used to verify configuration changes made when using the other `scconf` command options, and for obtaining data service and logical host configuration information.

`hastat`

This command complements the `scconf -p` command by displaying the current state of the cluster—there are no configuration values except for some PNM configuration values. The `hastat` command is a useful way to check the last few `syslog` error messages, or to check the status of data services, logical hosts, or cluster membership. Although the `hastat` command does provide some PNM state information, it is more efficient to use the `pnmstat -l` command because the `hastat` command provides other unrelated information.

`pnmstat -l`

This command displays status information about PNM groups. It lists the configured backup groups, the status of each group (with the currently active adapter in each group), and the time since the last failover. Although the `pnmstat` command can be run without the `-l` option, it may be difficult to interpret the output. The `pnmstat -l` command does not list any configuration information beyond the currently active adapter for each group. To find other adapters in a group, use the `pnmset -pntv` command.

`pnmset -pntv`

This command complements the `pnmstat -l` command because it displays the configuration of each NAFO group. Running this command will list all adapters configured in each NAFO group.

`pnmptor`

This command takes a NAFO group as an argument and outputs the primary (active) interface for the group. The command name indicates a conversion from a pseudo adapter name (a NAFO group) to a real adapter name. The abbreviation *ptor* comes from the expression *pseudo to real.*

`pnmrtop`

This command takes a real adapter name on the command line and outputs the name of the pseudo adapter (NAFO group) it belongs to.

`finddevices`

This command displays the serial numbers for the attached disks. The `finddevices disks` command lists all disks attached to the node and associated serial numbers. Use the `grep` command on this output to determine the serial number of a controller instance (or vice versa) — this can be especially useful for verifying quorum device validity against the configuration displayed using `scconf -p`.

`hareg`

The `hareg` command indicates whether a specific data service is on or off.

`hareg -q`

The `hareg -q` *`servicename`* command lists all command line options used when registering a service.

Sun Cluster Manager

The Sun Cluster Manager is a graphical user interface that may be operated over the Web. This interface displays cluster state information (all of which can be derived using the `hastat` command); however, information provided by the Sun Cluster Manager is a more convenient way of viewing the data. The information displayed by Sun Cluster Manager is not accurate under some circumstances, refer to the *Sun Cluster 2.2 Release Notes.*

Because this information may not be accurate, the `hastat` command should be used in conjunction with other cluster monitoring tools. The Sun Cluster Manager interface provides an easy-to-understand view of a large amount of cluster configuration information. Additionally, because the Sun Cluster Manager interface identifies problems clearly, it may be easier to use than command line tools. However, after a problem is identified, it is often more practical to use the command line tools because each command is specifically focused and does not need to wait for status updates.

The Sun Cluster Manager interface collects log information directly from the `/var/adm/messages` file. Therefore, if messages are redirected to another location, the Sun Cluster Manager will not display the latest logs.

For a summary of the cluster informational commands, refer to Table 4-1.

Table 4-1 Cluster Information Commands

Command	Information Displayed
`get_node_status`	Whether node is in cluster Node ID number Which nodes are in the cluster (by ID, not by name) Interconnect status Volume manager being used Volume manager status Oracle database status (will not display if not using Oracle)
`scconf -p`	Lists all configured cluster nodes (not necessarily active) Lists configured private network interfaces for all nodes Lists quorum devices Lists CMM timeout values (logical host and Step 10 and 11 timeouts) Provides the following information for each logical host: ■ Logical host name ■ Potential masters ■ Logical host disk group ■ Logical address/name ■ Configured network interface ■ Automatic switch-over choice
`hastat`	Lists nodes in cluster Cluster members (by name) Configuration state of each node Uptime, number of users, and load average for each node Logical hosts mastered by each node Logical hosts for which each node is a backup Logical hosts in maintenance mode Private interconnect network status for each node Public network information (same as `pnmstat` -l command) Status of registered data services Status of data services for each node Recent error messages for each node
`pnmstat -l`	Configured backup groups Live adapter in each group Time since last failover for each group Group status
`pnmset -pntv`	Adapters configured into each NAFO group
`pnmptor` *nafoname*	Active interface of NAFO group *nafoname*

Table 4-1 Cluster Information Commands

Command	Information Displayed
`pnmrtop instname`	NAFO group of controller instance *instname*
`finddevices disks`	Lists names and serial numbers for all disks attached to node (Use the `grep` command to identify the controller number for quorum device serial numbers.)
`hareg`	On/off state for all registered data services
`hareg -q`	Command line options used to register data service
Sun Cluster Manager (GUI)	The following general cluster information: ■ Cluster name, state, volume manager, and interconnect type The following information for each logical host: ■ Logical host name or IP address, state, and disk group ■ Default primary, current master, and potential masters ■ Node state ■ Active public network adapter ■ Private network adapters ■ State of private network adapters and public NAFO groups The following information for each HA service: ■ Service type and `hareg -q` information ■ Status ■ List of logical hosts each data service is registered on Cluster events: Latest entries in `/var/adm/messages` file

Cluster Logs

To effectively monitor the status of a cluster, the log files should be frequently reviewed.

Most cluster warnings, errors, and notices are sent to the /var/adm/messages file via syslog. Additionally, error messages displayed to users not logged into the console are terse. For detailed error messages, users should review the logs. Users logged in via telnet or rlogin will only see the message "scadmin: errors encountered" if an error occurs. Because this message could be easily missed or ignored, it is important to confirm cluster health regularly by reviewing the logs.

Note: Most errors described in this chapter display the verbose error messages as displayed to users on the console. The errors displayed to users administering a cluster via a telnet or rlogin window will only display the terse message "scadmin: errors encountered".

Set up the syslog facility to send a copy of all messages to a remote host (such as the administrative workstation) in addition to the copies stored on the local node. Sending the cluster node logs to a remote host enables an administrator to effectively troubleshoot problems (even if the cluster node is down).

Sending the messages to a remote host is performed by appending the following lines in the /etc/syslog.conf file on both nodes:

```
#forwarding cluster messages into a remote host
*.err    @remotehostname
*.notice @remotehostname
*.alert  @remotehostname
```

Note: The *remotehostname* entry is the name of the remote host that will receive the logs. A <TAB> character (not a space) is used as a separator before the *remotehostname* entry. The hostname should be entered into the /etc/hosts file (if not already there).

After the /etc/syslog.conf file has been modified, the syslogd (1M) daemon should be restarted by entering the following commands:

```
# /etc/init.d/syslog stop
# /etc/init.d/syslog start
```

Detailed cluster reconfiguration logs can be found for the CCD and CMM. The logs for the CCD reside in the `/var/opt/SUNWcluster/ccd/ccd.log` file. The logs for the CMM reside in the `/var/opt/SUNWcluster/scadmin.log` file. The CCD and CMM logs can be used to identify problems during reconfiguration. Some quorum device or terminal concentrator warnings could be overlooked by an administrator because they are displayed on a frequently changing console; therefore, it is important to scan these logs on a routine basis.

As described in the following CCD section, CCD reconfiguration occurs in Steps 3 and 4 of the CMM reconfiguration, see Chapter 2, "Sun Cluster 2.2 Architecture."

Managing Time in a Clustered Environment

An essential aspect of managing cluster logs is verifying that timestamps for events on different nodes correspond. Internal server clocks can vary slightly over time due to differences in heat, environmental variables, electrical characteristics, and manufacturing variance within the chips. Over time, these slight differences between node clocks could lead to considerable variation. Any difference in timestamps makes synchronizing events between nodes difficult.

An administrator should not directly change the time on a running node using the `date`, `rdate`, or `ntpdate` (or similar) commands. Changing the time on a cluster node using these types of commands could induce errors.

Note: Confirm that no `crontab(1)` entries use the `ntpdate`, `date`, or `rdate` commands.

Using the network time protocol (NTP) enables synchronized time to be maintained between cluster nodes without administrator intervention. The NTP function corrects time drift by continuously making small changes. Although cluster nodes cannot be configured as NTP servers, they can be NTP clients. To enable cluster nodes to be synchronized (in time), an NTP server using the NTP daemon (`xntpd`) should be set up. In many large datacenters, an NTP server may already be configured; if not, an easy method of setting up an NTP server is to use the administrative workstation. Although this method does not necessarily set the cluster nodes to the actual time, the important thing is to keep the nodes *consistent* with each other.

Note: Keeping the nodes aligned with a time standard, for example, Coordinated Universal Time, could help in situations where cluster problems are caused by external clients or servers.

An NTP server is set up by editing the /etc/inet/ntp.conf file (read by the xntpd daemon during startup). Configuration of the server will depend on your local NTP configuration. Cluster nodes are not supported as NTP servers; therefore, NTP servers must be external to the cluster. The cluster nodes should be configured as clients of the NTP server by including *at least* the following lines in the ntp.conf file:

```
server ntp_server
peer cluster_node
```

In this example, *ntp_server* is the name of the NTP server and *cluster_node* is the name of the other cluster node. Both names should be stored in the /etc/hosts file. For clusters with more than two nodes, peer entries should be included for all other nodes. Changes will be effected after the nodes have been rebooted (or the xntpd daemon has been restarted).

Cluster Membership Administration

The scadmin command has options to enable many high-level administrative cluster functions. These options enable an administrator to start and stop the cluster and deal with cluster partitions (which may occur in some failure scenarios).

Note: Only cluster membership related options of the scadmin command are discussed in this section. The scadmin command also has options to ensure disks can be effectively failure fenced and the logical host can be switched over.

Starting a Cluster or Cluster Node

Building and configuring a cluster is a complex process and is discussed in Chapter 6, "Sun Cluster 2.2 Application Notes." After installation and configuration is completed, the cluster can be started using the following command:

```
# scadmin startcluster localnode clustername
```

In this example, *localnode* will become the first node in the *clustername* cluster. This node (*localnode*) becomes the only cluster member seen by the new instance of the cluster. The time required to start a cluster is dependent on the time taken to start the data services and import the logical host disk groups. During startup, a large number of status messages are displayed on the console.

It is essential that the `scadmin startcluster` command is only run on a single node (with no other nodes in the cluster when run). SC2.2 software takes steps to ensure only one instance of the cluster is alive at any given time, see Chapter 2, "Sun Cluster 2.2 Architecture." However, in some configurations, it is possible (though highly unlikely) for an administrator to accidentally bypass safety features and start the same cluster on two nodes that share storage (but cannot communicate over the private network). This could lead to data corruption, because two different clusters may be in conflict over data ownership. To avoid the potential conflict when a cluster is initially started, confirm no other node is already running the cluster. Cluster status is listed on the first line output by the `get_node_status` command.

Note: Although it may be tempting to use the `-a` option with the `startcluster`, `startnode`, and `stopnode` variations of the `scadmin` command, this option should not be used.

The `-a` option was designed to perform startup asynchronously and return a prompt immediately to the administrator. Two issues make using the -a option a bad idea. The first issue is the fact that problems could occur if other commands are run during startup. The second issue is that important warnings or error messages may be missed because the startup messages are not displayed.

After the cluster is running on the initial node, additional nodes can be added to the cluster using the `scadmin` command.

Contrary to the *Sun Cluster 2.2 Administration Guide*, cluster nodes should be added singularly, as noted in the *Sun Cluster 2.2 Release Notes Addendum*, section 1.4.5. When the following command is run on a single node, it will cause the node to join the cluster:

```
# scadmin startnode clustname
```

Common Errors Starting a Cluster or Adding Cluster Nodes

There are various reasons why a cluster fails to start or is unable to accept new members. All warnings displayed during the startup of a cluster should be investigated. Problems that could occur include issues with quorum devices, shared data disks, private networks, and the CCD. The following sections identify some common problems and ways to troubleshoot them.

Quorum Device

If a configured quorum device is not present, the following message will be displayed during cluster startup:

```
Jun 14 16:55:45 ash unix: WARNING: /sbus@1f,0/SUNW,fas@0,8800000/sd@5,0
(sd20):
Jun 14 16:55:45 ash     disk not responding to selection
Jun 14 16:55:45 ash
Jun 14 16:55:46 ash unix: WARNING: /sbus@1f,0/SUNW,fas@0,8800000/sd@5,0
(sd20):
Jun 14 16:55:46 ash     disk not responding to selection
Jun 14 16:55:46 ash
Jun 14 16:55:46 ash ID[SUNWcluster.reconf.quorumdev.4050]: Quorum
Device 99421Q0722 is not present on the system, Please change quorum
device using scconf -q option.
Jun 14 16:55:46 ash ID[SUNWcluster.reconf.4051]: quorum exited with 1
in startnode
scadmin: errors encountered
```

If this output is displayed, a quorum device should be set using the `scconf -q` command, see section, "Changing the Quorum Device" on page 179.

Logical Host Startup Problems

There are several types of problems that occur with a logical host startup. One problem is caused by a failure to import shared data disks. Problems with shared data disks could create issues at the logical host level and may result in errors or warning messages being displayed. However, these problems do not usually affect cluster membership because logical host problems do not affect the cluster membership monitor.

A reconfiguration involves many changes that make it difficult to determine exactly what the problem is when a logical host fails to start. Generally, the root cause of the problem can be found by looking at the first listed error that occurred during the re-configuration. For example, the following box displays the error messages from a failed mount operation of the administrative file system:

```
Jun 18 16:36:46 ash ID[SUNWcluster.loghost.1030]: Taking over logical
host treefs
Jun 18 16:36:46 ash ID[SUNWcluster.loghost.1170]: importing NFSDISK
Jun 18 16:36:47 ash ID[SUNWcluster.scnfs.3040]: mount -F ufs -o ""
/dev/vx/dsk/FSDISK/NFSDISK-stat /treenfs failed.
Jun 18 16:36:48 ash ID[SUNWcluster.ccd.ccdd.5304]: error freeze cmd =
/opt/SUNWluster/bin/loghost_sync CCDSYNC_POST_ADDU
LOGHOST_CM:treenfs:ash /etc/opt/SUNWcuster/conf/ccd.database 2 "0 1" 0
error code = 1
Jun 18 16:36:48 ash ID[SUNWcluster.ccd.ccdd.5104]: Error
CCD_UNFREEZE_ACK 0x(73658) type = 2007 error = 68: svr error: 2
Jun 18 16:36:48 ash ID[SUNWcluster.scccd.add.4001]: error executing the
freeze cmd - LOGHOST_CM lname:curr_master treenfs:ash
Jun 18 16:36:48 ash ID[SUNWcluster.loghost.1010]: Giving up logical
host treenfs
```

In this example, the problem mounting the administrative file system resulted in the cluster starting without the affected logical host. The problem illustrated here was caused by a busy mount directory. In this case, a local user was using the directory. As discussed in the *Sun Cluster 2.2 Release Notes,* there should be no local access to directories exported by NFS, and users should not access the administrative file system.

While the exact cause of an error may be difficult to ascertain (as in this example), knowing which operation is failing can assist in determining the cause of a problem. An understanding of the reconfiguration steps also assists in identifying the cause of any problems.

Note: The reconfiguration steps for the CMM are discussed in Chapter 2, "Sun Cluster 2.2 Architecture."

A problem can occur if shared disks cannot be imported because, for example, the disks were missing or were not correctly deported.

In the following example, understanding the problem requires considering the errors in the context of the configuration steps, which are being executed as they occur. Notice that the warnings begin after the "`importing NFSDISK`" message. As the reconfiguration progresses, errors become increasingly cryptic. As in the previous example, the first warning ("`importing NFSDISK`") identifies the root cause of the problem.

```
Jun 18 16:48:41 ash ID[SUNWcluster.loghost.1030]: Taking over logical host
treenfs
Jun 18 16:48:41 ash ID[SUNWcluster.loghost.1170]: importing NFSDISK
Jun 18 16:48:43 ash unix: WARNING: /sbus@1f,0/SUNW,fas@0,8800000/sd@1,0 (sd16):
Jun 18 16:48:43 ash     disk not responding to selection
Jun 18 16:49:00 ash ID[SUNWcluster.loghost.4035]: NOTICE: Check disk group
NFSDISK for failed disks or other missing components
Jun 18 16:49:00 ash ID[SUNWcluster.loghost.4030]: Import of disk group NFSDISK
failed
Jun 18 16:49:00 ash ID[SUNWcluster.ccd.ccdd.5304]: error freeze cmd =
/opt/SUNWcluster/bin/loghost_sync CCDSYNC_POST_ADDU LOGHOST_CM:treenfs:ash
/etc/opt/SUNWcluster/conf/ccd.database 2 "0" 0 error code = 1
Jun 18 16:49:00 ash ID[SUNWcluster.ccd.ccdd.5104]: Error CCD_UNFREEZE_ACK
0x(73658) type = 2007 error = 68: svr error: 2
Jun 18 16:49:00 ash ID[SUNWcluster.scccd.add.4001]: error executing the freeze
cmd - LOGHOST_CM lname:curr_master treenfs:ash
Jun 18 16:49:01 ash ID[SUNWcluster.loghost.1010]: Giving up logical host treenfs
```

In this example (as before), the cluster *will start* normally—although the logical host will not be mastered until the problem is fixed. Although the logical host is left unmastered at the end of the reconfiguration, it can be re-mastered using the `haswitch` command after the problem is resolved.

Resolving Cluster Configuration Database Problems

A number of problems can occur when starting a cluster relating to invalid or inconsistant cluster configuration databases—the effects of these problems differ according to the database affected. These problems are discussed in the section, "Resolving Cluster Configuration Database Problems" on page 150.

Stopping a Cluster or Cluster Node

Stopping a cluster on a specific node is performed in a similar manner to starting the cluster. Use the following command:

```
# scadmin stopnode clustname
```

Nodes should be stopped one at a time—no cluster changes should be made while a node is stopping. There is no special command to stop a cluster; therefore, use the `scadmin stopnode` command on the last node in the cluster. It is not necessary to stop the entire cluster to stop the logical hosts—this can be accomplished by putting the logical hosts into maintenance mode (as described in "Managing Logical Hosts" on page 160).

If a cluster node fails during reconfiguration, a situation could occur where nodes are uncertain as to what their reconfiguration state should be—specifically, whether the node is in or out of the cluster. It is important to prevent the condition whereby a node believes it is still part of the cluster, when in fact it is not. This could result in a situation where the confused node attempts to illegally access cluster data. Sun Cluster infrastructure goes to great lengths to ensure this does not happen. When a node is leaving the cluster and an error occurs, the node will either refuse to leave the cluster or be forced to panic using the fail-fast driver. When a node refuses to leave the cluster, it maintains contact with other cluster nodes, thereby coordinating data access (and preventing data corruption). Although panicking may seem extreme, it brings down the OS immediately—thereby preventing access to shared data.

Problems Stopping Cluster Nodes

There are several situations where stopping a node could fail. Although these scenarios are unlikely, a commonly occurring situation is where there has been a configuration change that the cluster is not aware of.

For example, some `scconf` options expect to be out of a cluster when they are run. However, running these options while the node is still in the cluster can lead to a situation where a node is unable to leave the cluster (because of the inconsistency).

Note: If a reconfiguration returns an error because of an unexpected condition, the node will panic.

Another example, is when an administrator changes the interfaces configured for use as the private interconnect on a live node. Here, the affected node will panic when it attempts to leave the cluster, see section, "Changing Private Network Configuration (for Ethernet)."

This is because the scconf command (when used with the -i option) should not be run with the affected node in the cluster.

In the following example, the node is named *pie* and is up and running in a cluster named *pecan*. The node *pie* originally uses hme0 and qfe1 as the private interconnect.

To change the second private interconnect to an unused qfe port on a different card, use the following command:

```
# scconf pecan -i pie hme0 qfe5
```

In this case, a change is made to the configuration files on the node, as opposed to the active configuration. The new interfaces are not plumbed until the node goes through a cluster reconfiguration. The node continues to run as part of the cluster using hme0 and qfe1 as the private interconnect until it leaves the cluster and then rejoins it. An error would be induced if an administrator attempted to remove the node *pie* from the cluster by running the following command (on node *pie*):

```
# scadmin stopnode pecan
```

This command starts the reconfiguration. One of the steps in the process uses the ifconfig command to unplumb the private network interfaces. However, the interfaces in the configuration files (hme0 and qfe5) are the ones that are unplumbed.

The unplumbing of hme0 will proceed normally because it is a legitimate private interconnect; however, when qfe5 is unplumbed, it will return an error because qfe5 was never plumbed.

A failed attempt to unplumb an interface in a non-clustered environment would return a trivial error; however, the Sun Cluster software takes no chances. When the software detects an error of any sort during reconfiguration, it will panic the node (in this case, *pie*). After the node is re-started, if it joins the cluster, it will function normally and use interfaces hme0 and qfe5 for the private interconnect.

There are other conditions that cause problems when stopping a cluster node. One such condition occurs if a logical host disk group cannot be deported from the node during a manual failover. To prevent the cluster from entering an inconsistant state, the CMM prevents the node from leaving the cluster or alternatively forces it out of the cluster.

The code in the following box illustrates a node that failed to leave a cluster because the `vfstab.logicalhost` file for the logical host `treenfs` was incorrectly formatted. In this example, notice how the original node attempts to re-master the logical host and stays in the cluster, rather than entering into an inconsistant state.

```
Jun 18 17:05:37 beech ID[SUNWcluster.loghost.1010]: Giving up logical host
treenfs
Jun 18 17:05:42 beech ID[SUNWcluster.loghost.1050]: fm_stop method of data
service nfs completed successfully.
Jun 18 17:05:43 beech ID[SUNWcluster.loghost.1050]: stop_net method of data
service nfs completed successfully.
Jun 18 17:05:44 beech ID[SUNWcluster.loghost.1050]: stop method of data service
nfs completed successfully.
Jun 18 17:05:44 beech ID[SUNWcluster.loghost.1180]: deporting NFSDISK
Jun 18 17:05:44 beech ID[SUNWcluster.loghost.5020]: Disk group NFSDISK busy.
Deport failed
Jun 18 17:05:44 beech ID[SUNWcluster.loghost.1050]: abort method of data service
nfs completed successfully.
Jun 18 17:05:44 beech ID[SUNWcluster.loghost.1180]: deporting NFSDISK
Jun 18 17:05:44 beech ID[SUNWcluster.loghost.5020]: Disk group NFSDISK busy.
Deport failed
Jun 18 17:05:45 beech ID[SUNWcluster.ccd.ccdd.5304]: error freeze cmd =
/opt/SUNWcluster/bin/loghost_sync CCDSYNC_POST_REMOVE LOGHOST_CM:treenfs:beech
/etc/opt/SUNWcluster/conf/ccd.database 2 "0 1" 1 error code = 1
Jun 18 17:05:45 beech ID[SUNWcluster.ccd.ccdd.5104]: Error CCD_UNFREEZE_ACK
0x(73680) type = 2007 error = 68: svr error: 22
Jun 18 17:05:45 beech ID[SUNWcluster.scccd.remove.4001]: error executing the
freeze cmd - LOGHOST_CM lname treenfs
Jun 18 17:05:45 beech ID[SUNWcluster.reconf.loghost.4010]: Give up of logical
host treenfs failed.
Jun 18 17:05:45 beech ID[SUNWcluster.loghost.1030]: Taking over logical host
treenfs
```

Managing Cluster Partitions

After the appropriate nodes are in the cluster, managing cluster membership becomes largely automated. If a failure occurs, the failed node is automatically configured out of the cluster. Rejoining the node to the cluster is performed using the `scadmin startnode` command.

Another situation that may require manual intervention can occur in a cluster with more than two nodes. In this case, multiple failures of the private interconnects will cause partitioning.

A partition is a group of nodes, each of which can communicate with nodes within the group, but not with nodes outside the group, see Chapter 2, "Sun Cluster 2.2 Architecture." In most cases, the partition that becomes the cluster is automatically determined by the Cluster Membership Monitor (CMM). If the partition does not have a membership quorum, it will shut down. However, if the partition is large enough to represent a majority of the cluster nodes, it will stay up.

In a situation where a partition represents exactly half of the cluster nodes, the partition will be in a state where node majority cannot determine if it should stay up or down. This could occur because of a double failure of the private interconnect, or if two nodes fail at the same time. This type of error, where multiple failures occur simultaneously (or nearly so), is rare. These errors are not an issue in a two-node cluster because the quorum device arbitrates membership.

Although unlikely that the above situation will occur, it is important to understand how this kind of fault can be dealt with.

When the cluster is installed, if there are more than two nodes, the `scinstall` program will prompt the installer on how it should deal with a split brain partition that has exactly half the cluster membership. The two options given are `ask` and `select`. Choosing the `ask` option requires specifying which partition will survive; choosing the `select` option during installation enables an administrator to specify the *preferred* node, which then determines the surviving partition. In a situation where one partition has exactly half the nodes, the partition containing the preferred node will survive, and any partition not containing the preferred node will wait for administrative input. The preferred partition is able to stay up automatically, thereby reducing downtime. However, because the partition without the preferred node waits for administrative input, in some situations, it is possible to lose the logical hosts, even though the cluster remains up. Because of this possibility, the choice of whether to use the `select` or `ask` option depends on the cluster topology and logical host configuration.

In general, if there is a node in the cluster capable of hosting all logical hosts (as with an N+1 topology), make the backup node the preferred node.

With the backup as the preferred node, if a split brain situation results in a partition of half the cluster nodes, the partition containing the backup node stays up to support the logical hosts. This will not resolve situations where the backup node is also down; however, any situation that results in a double network failure and simultaneous node failure will generally bring down the entire cluster. It may be a good idea to use the `select` option even if there are multiple critical nodes, although it depends on the business and architectural requirements.

Another consideration is the `select` option enables only the preferred node to be the highest or lowest ID. Because of this, it is important to initially set up a cluster so that the highest priority node has the highest or lowest ID. Node ID is configured during installation and cannot be changed. Node information is requested by `scinstall` in ID order; therefore, any node can be allocated the lowest node ID by entering its information first during cluster installation.

If the cluster has been set up to prompt an administrator which partition should succeed (the *ask* policy), the administrator should know how to abort or continue partitions in a split brain scenario. If a split brain occurs, an error message is displayed approximately every ten seconds.

Note: The following error is only displayed on the console. Because of this, it is possible that a serious error could be overlooked by an administrator. To be aware of possible partition situations, it is important to monitor the cluster interconnects. All partitioning events result in failed interconnect warnings being logged. These events can be viewed using the Sun Cluster Manager GUI or a log monitor.

The following box provides an example of an abort/continue partition message. The *Proposed cluster partition* and *Unreachable nodes* values depend upon the individual partition and node:

```
*** ISSUE ABORTPARTITION OR CONTINUE PARTITION ***
If the unreachable nodes have formed a cluster, issue ABORTPARTITION.
(scadmin abortpartition <local node> <clustername>)
You may allow the proposed cluster to form by issuing CONTINUEPARTITION.
(scadmin continuepartition <localnode> <clustername>)
Proposed cluster partition:  0  Unreachable nodes: 2
```

If the previous error occurs, the `scadmin` command can be used to nominate a partition. It is important to track which nodes are in which partition.

The first step after a partitioning event occurs is to check if all nodes are up. If only one partition has live nodes, select this partition to continue. A good method of determining which nodes are in which partition is to look at the appropriate error messages (the cluster status commands may be incorrect or not updated immediately). Nodes listed as having the same *Proposed cluster partition* can communicate with each other and form a new cluster together. By mapping which logical hosts are present in each partition, it is possible to determine which partition would be the most advantageous to have up. It can be useful to have a runbook that details which partitions should be continued or aborted for all possible partition situations, see section, "Systems Installation and Configuration Documentation" in Chapter 1, "High Availability Fundamentals."

A partitioning event is likely to be the result of a major problem; therefore, it is important to ensure the integrity of the other cluster components (particularly the shared disks) as soon as possible.

After it has been determined which partition should stay up and which should be aborted, run the appropriate `scadmin` commands.

On the node in the partition that is to be aborted, enter the following command:

```
# scadmin abortpartition nodename clustername
```

Verify that all nodes (supposed to be in the partition) aborted successfully. If any nodes did not abort, run the command on the nodes separately.

After all nodes that should not be cluster members have aborted, entering the following command on a node enables the partition containing that node to become the cluster:

```
# scadmin continuepartition nodename clustername
```

This action will cause the partition to become the new cluster. It is important to verify that all nodes that should be in this partition started correctly. Any nodes that did not should be shut down manually and restarted. The nodes that did not start and any aborted nodes should be checked for problems. After the interconnect is repaired, the nodes should rejoin the cluster in the normal fashion using the `scadmin startnode` command.

Setting and Administering CMM Timeouts

Cluster nodes operate in lock-step fashion during reconfiguration, see Chapter 2, "Sun Cluster 2.2 Architecture." Timeouts are used to prevent a node from waiting for an unsuccessful action to complete. If a timeout occurs, the node will stop its current action and attempt to return to a consistent state. If the node cannot return to a consistent state, it will panic or abort out of the cluster to prevent inconsistencies. Timeout errors are a symptom, not the problem—tracking timeout errors may uncover configuration problems.

In some situations, a configuration may not function correctly with the default timeouts. In this case, the timeouts should be changed. The only CMM timeout values that should be modified are the Step 10 and 11 timeouts and the logical host timeout. There are additional timeouts that can be modified with the assistance of your Sun Enterprise Services representative.

When the values for the Step 10 and 11 timeouts are set, one value is applicable to both Step 10 and Step 11. In earlier versions of Sun Cluster software, the values could be set independently; however, with SC2.2 software, they are always set to the same value. The timeouts involve mastering logical hosts and shared disks, see Chapter 2, "Sun Cluster 2.2 Architecture."

There are a few circumstances where the timeouts may require modification. Having a large number of logical hosts or data services per logical host will increase failover time and may result in timeout values being too small. Additionally, having a large file system that requires running the `fsck` command or a large number of volumes could also cause timeouts to be inadequate.

The Step 10 and 11 timeouts are modified using the `ssconf` *`clustername`* `-T` *`new_timeout_value`* command. This command modifies the number of seconds before a Step 10 and 11 timeout is invoked in cluster *`clustername`* to *`new_timeout_value`*. The *`new_timeout_value`* variable is displayed in seconds (default is 720 seconds).

Note: The Step 10 and 11 timeout values must always be greater than or equal to the logical host timeout.

The logical host timeout value can be set using the `scconf` *`clustername`* `-l` *`new_timeout_value`* command.

The *`new_timeout_value`* specifies the number of seconds before cluster *`clustername`* will give up trying to master a given logical host. Step 10 and 11 timeout values must always be at least as large as the value of the logical host timeout. The default logical host timeout is 180 seconds.

If timeout values are modified, they should be tested under a variety of conditions. Timeout value modifications should be recorded; this can assist in tracking problems. It is necessary to use a significantly longer value than the shortest non-error-causing value. A Sun Enterprise Services representative can provide advice when changing timeouts.

Managing Cluster Configuration

Cluster Configuration Databases

Understanding the cluster configuration databases is an important part of cluster administration, planning for changes, and dealing with any crisis in the clustered environment. There are several files which maintain cluster state and configuration information. The most important of these are the CCD and CDB (cluster database) files. The `/etc/pnmconfig` file (see "Cluster Topology and Hardware Changes" on page 170) is also an important file for managing a cluster configuration because it determines the NAFO group configuration. These cluster configuration databases contain different subsets of cluster configuration information. The content of a cluster database depends on architectural considerations.

Note: The term *cluster configuration databases* (plural) is used as a generic term for all configuration database files involved in tracking cluster configuration and state. This includes the *cluster configuration database* (CCD [singular]) and also several related configuration repositories, including the initial CCD, the `pnmconfig` file, and the CDB (as described in the following section). To avoid confusion, the *cluster configuration database* is referred to by its acronym, CCD.

The CCD

As discussed in Chapter 2, "Sun Cluster 2.2 Architecture," some of the cluster state and configuration information is stored in the CCD.

The CCD is divided into two parts: the *initial CCD* (also called the *init CCD*) and the *dynamic CCD* (or simply the CCD). The dynamic CCD is a distributed database that is kept consistent on all nodes.

The init CCD configuration file is stored in the `/etc/opt/SUNWcluster/conf/ccd.database.init.` file.

The dynamic CCD configuration file is stored in the `/etc/opt/SUNWcluster/conf/ccd.database` file. If a cluster is configured for a shared CCD, the CCD configuration file will be located in the `/etc/opt/SUNWcluster/conf/ccdssa/ccd.database.ssa` file during the time the shared CCD is in use (when one node is out of the cluster).

The init CCD contains data necessary for the dynamic CCD to initialize. For example, the init CCD contains configuration information on the port numbers used for CCD communication over a private network. The information in the init CCD is generally static—few commands can modify it after installation.

The consistency of the init and dynamic CCDs is confirmed when a node joins the cluster because the CCDs are essential for cluster operation. The internal consistency is confirmed by means of checksums. External consistency is confirmed by comparing the databases on each node. A node is not permitted to join if the init CCD on the node is different from other cluster nodes.

If an init CCD is different, an error is returned and the node is not allowed to join the cluster. Because the init CCDs should be the same on all nodes, an init CCD failure can be rectified by copying a (presumably) correct init CCD from another cluster node. If the dynamic CCD differs from the dynamic CCD of the existing cluster, it will be automatically replaced by the CCD from the current cluster nodes when the new node joins. Adding a new node presumes that the CCD on the cluster is valid. The process of electing a valid CCD for a cluster is discussed in Chapter 2, "Sun Cluster 2.2 Architecture."

The CDB

The CCD framework requires stable cluster membership before determining the validity of the CCD database. Configuration information is required to determine cluster membership—the CCD cannot store this information because the CCD has not been elected prior to the time the cluster membership is initially formed. The CDB stores configuration information required by the Cluster Membership Monitor (CMM), and for other related components; for example, Oracle's Distributed Lock Manager (DLM), the Cluster Configuration Monitor (CCM), and for quorum and failure fencing mechanisms (which determine cluster membership).

A non-replicated CDB file exists on each node in the `/etc/opt/SUNWcluster/conf/`*`clustername`*`.cdb` file, where *`clustername`* is the name of the cluster. Because the CDB is not distributed (like the CCD), any commands that modify the CDB only affect the CDB of the node they run on. Therefore, it is important to synchronize the CDBs on all nodes by ensuring that commands to modify the CDB are executed on all nodes.

Modifying the CDB on all nodes requires running commands on each node individually with the cluster control panel, or entering commands directly on each node singularly. Even nodes not currently in the cluster require their CDBs to be updated appropriately. Because it is possible to have different copies of the CDB on different nodes, it is crucial to keep records of cluster changes.

When a node joins a cluster, its CDB is checked for consistency with the CDB of a current cluster node. This, coupled with the fact that the CDB is changed only on the node where the appropriate command was run, makes it easy to accidentally set the CDB on one node different from that of the others. CDB inconsistencies can occur whether a node is in or out of a cluster when changes are made.

If a node is out of the cluster, an inconsistant CDB will prevent it from joining. If the node is in the cluster, it can leave the cluster with an inconsistent CDB; however, it will be unable to rejoin. This scenario can be difficult to troubleshoot because an inconsistent CDB change could be months old before the node leaves the cluster due to failover or maintenance, see section, "Change Control," in Chapter 1, "High Availability Fundamentals." After the node is repaired and attempts to rejoin the cluster, it will fail because of the inconsistency. This will result in an "inconsistent CDB" error as described in section, "Resolving Cluster Configuration Database Problems" on page 125. Tracking down this type of error or even verifying the correct configuration will be increasingly difficult as the time involved increases. This type of error will increase the time the cluster spends in degraded mode.

Table 4-2 Location and Contents of Cluster Configuration Database Files

Database	Location	Contents
Initial CCD	/etc/opt/SUNWcluster/conf/ccd.database.init	■ CCD initialization data ■ CCD location ■ Private network IP addresses ■ Cluster name ■ Number of nodes which are potentially active ■ Node names and ID numbers
Dynamic CCD	When unshared: /etc/opt/SUNWcluster/conf/ccd.database When shared: /etc/opt/SUNWcluster/conf/ccdssa/ccd.database.ssa	■ Logical host state and configuration ■ Data service state and configuration ■ TC/SSP monitoring, status, and IP addresses ■ PNM configuration and status ■ Cluster membership
CDB	/etc/opt/SUNWcluster/conf/clustername.cdb	■ CMM configuration ■ CCM and UDLM configuration ■ Private network addresses and interfaces ■ Cluster name ■ Number of potential nodes (from installation) ■ Node names and IDs ■ Local parts of logical host configuration. ■ Quorum devices ■ TC/SSP monitoring, IP addresses, port #s, type ■ PNM tunables
pnmconfig	/etc/pnmconfig	■ NAFO group configuration

Managing Cluster Configuration Changes

Change control is essential in any environment where availability is paramount; a clustered environment is no exception. There are many reasons for this, including issues previously discussed when changing the CDB. Additionally, there are other issues to be addressed for change control in a clustered environment.

It is important for an administrator to record all changes to a clustered environment regardless of whether they affect the cluster configuration (identifying which commands were used on specific nodes). Additionally, any cluster configuration files touched during a change should be backed up. Table 4-3 provides a partial list of commands and the corresponding databases they modify. It is a good idea to create a directory for storing copies of these files on the cluster nodes prior to backing them up. This enables a local copy of historical configuration files to be accessed quickly for restoring a node to a known state in case of inconsistencies, with a backup copy available in the case of catastrophic failure. In a failure scenario, it is important to know that a file is accurate before reproducing the file. Change records are important because they enable files that may be inconsistent to be compared to a known valid file configuration to confirm the copy is up-to-date and not corrupt.

Table 4-3 Databases Updated by Cluster Commands

Command	Purpose	Database(s) Updated	Applicable Node and Cluster State
`scconf -h`	Changes hostnames	CDB	Do not use
`scconf -i`	Changes internal network interfaces	CDB	See "Changing Private Network Configuration (for Ethernet)" on page 173
`scconf -F`	Configures administrative file system	None	All nodes or all nodes capable of mastering logical host
`scconf -L`	Configures logical host	CCD	One node
`scconf -s`	Associates a data service with a logical host	CCD	One node
`scconf -H`	Changes terminal concentrator to host connection (architecture or port #)	CCD and CDB	Cluster down
`scconf -t`	Changes terminal concentrator public network information	CCD and CDB	Cluster down

Table 4-3 Databases Updated by Cluster Commands

Command	Purpose	Database(s) Updated	Applicable Node and Cluster State
scconf -p	Displays cluster parameters	None (informational command)	One node
scconf -D/+D	Determines if cluster uses direct-attached disks	CDB	All nodes
scconf -q	Changes quorum device	CDB	All nodes
scconf -U	Sets configuration path for DLM	CDB	All nodes
scconf -N	Sets node Ethernet address	CDB	All nodes
scconf -A	Changes active hosts	init CCD	All nodes, cluster down
scconf -S	Switches between shared CCD and unshared CCD	init CCD	All nodes, see "Shared CCD Setup"
scconf -T	Sets Step 10 and 11 timeouts	CDB	All nodes
scconf -l	Logical host timeout value	CDB	All nodes
scconf -R	Removes data service	CCD	One node
pnmset	Sets PNM groups	pnmconfig and CCD	Only the (single) node being modified (which must not be a cluster member when the command is run)
hareg -y/-Y	Turns data services on	CCD	One node
hareg -n/-N	Turns data services off	CCD	One node
hareg -r	Registers data services	CCD	One node
hareg -u	Unregisters data services	CCD	One node

Management for all cluster configuration databases is similar. In general, there are three procedures that should be performed to manage cluster configuration changes:

Implementing and Documenting Changes

The CDB and init CCD are not distributed; therefore, any commands that modify them should be run on all nodes (whether in the cluster or not).

The init CCD holds configuration information for the dynamic CCD; therefore, any changes to the init CCD should *only* be performed when the cluster is stopped.

Commands to modify the dynamic CCD should only be run on one node (because the dynamic CCD is automatically kept consistent). In some cases, a CCD quorum is required to make changes to the dynamic CCD (discussed in the "CCD Quorum" section).

Any changes to cluster databases should be performed using the appropriate commands—administrators should not edit the cluster configuration database files by hand. The only exception to this rule is the editing of the CDB to modify the `rpcbind` monitor tunables (not discussed in this book), and PNM tunables. Whenever possible, changing or reconstructing cluster database files should be performed by a qualified Sun Enterprise Services representative.

Any changes to a cluster configuration should follow established change control procedures—this includes hardware and topology changes (drives added or changed network connectivity), as well as any cluster configuration changes performed with software (`scconf`, `pnmset`) or other Sun Cluster commands.

When documenting changes performed using Sun Cluster commands, it is important to note which node the command was issued on. Logging the use of the `scadmin` command when bringing nodes up or down is not usually necessary because this information does not change the configuration files. Node status can be determined by running the `get_node_status` command.

Using a shared CCD in a two-node cluster eliminates the problem of inconsistent CCDs. In two-node configurations, it is a best practice to use a shared CCD because it reduces the risk of discrepancies. For some low-end configurations, losing the use of these disks may be too costly to justify using a shared CCD (a shared CCD uses two dedicated disks, see section, "Shared CCD," on page 143).

Backing Up Cluster Configuration Databases

Cluster configuration databases should be backed up whenever changes are made. It is unnecessary to routinely back up the CCD, providing that routine consistency checks and checks against the backups are performed regularly.

Consistency checks help ensure the backup copy is current. Additionally, reducing the number of backups by this method prevents the problem of tracking a specific change in a large number of mostly identical backups. Backing up the dynamic CCD is described in the section, "Backing Up and Restoring the CCD" on page 146. Backing up the init CCD and CDB requires an administrator to manually copy the files.

When backing up the cluster configuration files, they should be saved locally using the node name and date. Additionally, the files should be archived to a central location, for example, the administrative workstation—this process can be automated using an appropriate script.

The name of each backup file should indicate the name of the node the file originates from and the date of backup. Keeping old backups remotely enables an easier recovery from a catastrophic failure.

Storing files in a directory where each database is identified with the node name and date makes confirming change history easy.

Verifying Database Consistency with Nodes and Backup Copies

After the cluster configuration files are archived, regularly confirm they are current, and all nodes are consistent with each other.

Confirm that files are current by comparing the current file to the latest archive using the `diff` command.

Node consistency confirmation methods are database-dependent.

For the CDB and init CCD, confirming consistency requires comparing the latest archive copies on all nodes with each other using the `diff` command. This can be performed on the server where the backups are stored.

Inconsistencies in the timestamp line are acceptable, although it may be important to discern the cause of any discrepancy. This procedure is relatively straightforward; therefore, it makes sense to perform it weekly or monthly. Additionally, confirming database consistency should also be performed after any cluster configuration changes to ensure all nodes are consistent. Additionally, these files can be compared against the backup to verify no unregistered changes were made.

The consistency of the database for a dynamic CCD can be checked using the `ccdadm clustername -v` command (where *`clustername`* is the name of the cluster). This command confirms that the current CCDs for all running cluster nodes are consistent with each other.

Change documentation should identify which nodes were in or out of the cluster during a CCD change. It is important to know which nodes were in the cluster during the last change because a node with a current CCD should be brought up first. As with the CDB and init CCD, comparing the CCD against a backup using the `diff`(1) command verifies no unregistered changes were made.

CCD Quorum

The validity of the CCD is important because most of the logical host infrastructure relies on the CCD, see Chapter 2, "Sun Cluster 2.2 Architecture." The CCD must always be consistent and should be backed up often.

Efficient management of the CCD requires:

- Implementing management procedures to ensure consistency of the CCD
- Understanding how to back up and restore the CCD

It is essential to understand how to deal with problems involving the CCD and other cluster configuration databases, see section, "Resolving Cluster Configuration Database Problems," on page 150.

There are several ways to keep the CCD consistent—the CCD is a replicated database; therefore, it ensures all nodes in the cluster are in agreement on the cluster configuration. However, a problem could occur if there are inconsistent CCDs on different nodes because one group of nodes was present in the cluster during a CCD update while the other group was not.

If updated nodes leave the cluster and nodes (which are not updated) restart the cluster, the new cluster would use the CCD that is not updated—this will result in the cluster not using an up-to-date configuration. If the new and old configurations attempt to access the same data, it could lead to data corruption. There are several ways to avoid this problem—these require an understanding of the CCD quorum.

Note: The CCD quorum is not related to the CMM quorum which uses node majority and quorum devices to determine cluster membership.

CCD Quorum in Sun Cluster 2.1

Although this book deals primarily with the SC2.2 environment, many changes have occurred in CCD quorum architecture since version 2.1 of the Sun Cluster software. Administrators who used Sun Cluster 2.1 (SC2.1) software should understand these differences. With SC2.1, the CCD was kept consistent by ensuring a CCD quorum existed prior to making any changes. This meant that any time a CCD change was attempted on a cluster (with N possible nodes), at least (N/2)+1 (rounded down) nodes were required to be in the cluster with valid CCDs (i.e. two nodes in a two- or three-node cluster and three nodes in a four-node cluster).

Because a CCD quorum was required to make changes, in any group of N/2 (rounded up) nodes (i.e., one node in a two-node cluster, two nodes in a three-node cluster, and three nodes in a four-node cluster), at least one node was guaranteed to have the latest version of the CCD. A group of N/2 (rounded up) nodes could elect a valid CCD for the cluster when restarted. Nodes could join the cluster with an incorrect quorum; however, changes to the CCD could only be propagated if a CCD quorum was present.

With the SC2.1 CCD quorum mechanism, starting the cluster with an out-of-date CCD on the cluster nodes was not possible. This ensured the CCD was current; however, it also meant that changes could not be made to a CCD in situations where not enough nodes were up. A common problem encountered was only having one node of a two-node cluster available. If the second node was unavailable, no changes could be made to the CCD until the second node was brought back up. In two-node clusters, quorum restrictions could be dealt with using a shared CCD. However, with SC2.2 software, the CCD quorum requirement has been relaxed. As discussed previously, this does not affect the CMM quorum (which determines cluster membership using a node count and quorum devices).

CCD Quorum in Sun Cluster 2.2

Sun Cluster 2.2 software does not require a CCD quorum to be present to make CCD changes relating to a logical host or a data service. Because a CCD quorum is not required, changes can be made when only one node is in the cluster. However, it also means that a situation called *amnesia* can occur. If a node leaves the cluster and changes are made, the node out of the cluster does not have an up-to-date configuration—the node is said to have amnesia. If the cluster is stopped and restarted using the node with amnesia, the entire cluster will have amnesia because it was started using an incorrect configuration. Because amnesia is not always obvious, it is important to ensure the CCD used is current.

Ensure the CCD is current—the last node to leave the cluster should be the first to join.

Note: Whenever possible, changes should be made to the CCD only when all nodes are in the cluster. If this policy is strictly adhered to, CCD inconsistencies are totally avoided.

Shared CCD

Problems with having a CCD quorum and inconsistent CCDs can be largely overcome in two-node clusters by using a shared CCD. A shared CCD enables two nodes to share a consistent CCD source, even if one of them is unavailable.

Note: Because the CCD is updated during the data service package installation, if a shared CCD is configured, there may be an error if the CCD is updated while the shared CCD volume is in use (when one or more nodes is out of the cluster). This situation can be resolved by disabling the shared CCD before installing the package. If a cluster environment will require adding many new data services after it is put in production, a shared CCD may not make sense.

Shared CCDs can only be used on two-node clusters using Veritas Volume Manager (VxVM) or Cluster Volume Manager (CVM) software as the volume manager. If a shared CCD is used, the CCD functions as a non-shared CCD when both nodes are in the cluster. When a cluster is configured for a shared CCD and a node leaves the cluster, the CCD is copied to the shared CCD volume (which is a dual-ported, mirrored set of two dedicated disks).

Note: A shared CCD cannot be used in a configuration that uses SDS as its volume manager.

Any changes made to the CCD are also made to the shared CCD (but not to the CCDs of the individual nodes). Because the shared CCD volumes are accessible to both cluster nodes, after the second node has left the cluster, the shared CCD can be used by whichever node restarts the cluster. The node that restarts the cluster will use the shared CCD rather than its own CCD copy. When the remaining node joins the cluster, the shared CCD on the disk is copied to both cluster nodes and CCD updates are again performed using the non-shared CCD mechanisms.

A shared CCD requires exclusive use of two disks—the CCD volume will be mirrored across these two disks. Any size disks should be sufficient because the CCD file is relatively small. Each disk should be connected to both cluster nodes (a shared CCD only works on a two-node cluster). Additionally, the disks should have separate controllers (as with any mirrored shared disks). To achieve a higher level of redundancy, the shared CCD must use two disks, each on different arrays.

A straightforward way of implementing this method is to use disks from each of the two arrays containing mirrored halves for the shared data. When the CCD is mirrored across the same arrays as shared data, it is easier to manage the mirrored halves in case of failure or maintenance.

Shared CCD Setup

A shared CCD must be used only with a configuration that uses VxVM or CVM as the volume manager. The disk group can be created by entering the following command onto one node (after the appropriate disks have been initialized):

```
# /usr/sbin/vxdg init sc_dg  sc_dg01=disk1 sc_dg02=disk2
```

In this example, *disk1* and *disk2* are the instance numbers of two disks that use different controllers, for example, `c1t3d0` and `c2t3d0`.

After this command has executed, stop both cluster nodes using the `scadmin stopnode` command. Enter the following command onto both nodes:

```
# scconf clustername -S ccdvol
```

To configure the shared CCD volume, enter the following command onto any node (but only a single node):

```
# confccdssa clustername
```

The following message will be displayed. Answer yes (where indicated).

```
The disk group sc_dg was found and has been imported
on this node. This disk group will be used for the
shared ccd. The ccdvol volume will be recreated to
make certain that no previous shared ccd database
exists.
Do you want to continue (yes/no) ? yes <CR>
```

Then answer yes when asked to verify if a new file system should be constructed.

```
newfs: /dev/vx/rdsk/sc_dg/ccdvol last mounted as /eeweb
newfs: construct a new file system /dev/vx/rdsk/sc_dg/ccdvol: (y/n)? y
<CR>
```

Note: Displayed messages can be ignored if they are only *warnings* (not errors).

Removing a Shared CCD

The procedure for switching from a shared CCD to an unshared CCD requires downtime involving the whole cluster. For the first part of this procedure, one of the nodes should be up, while the other is down.

To stop a node, use the following command:

```
# scadmin stopnode
```

This command causes the remaining node to import the shared CCD disk group (and use the shared CCD volume). This is necessary because access to shared CCD information is required even when the shared CCD is turned off. If the cluster is not running on either node, the shared CCD volume can be manually imported. If this is the case, the paths to the shared CCD could differ from those listed in this section. The paths vary depending on the mount point used; however, the rest of the process is similar.

To safeguard against administrative mishaps, back up the shared CCD before proceeding. The shared CCD file is located in the `/etc/opt/SUNWcluster/conf/ccdssa/ccd.database.ssa` file.

After the shared CCD has been backed up, it can be turned off by entering the following command onto both nodes (nodes in and out of the cluster):

```
# scconf clustername -S none
```

Note: If the command is not run on both nodes, the second node will panic when it tries to rejoin the cluster.

Copy the shared CCD back to the standard CCD location in both nodes. The file should be copied to the correct location on the node that is running the cluster by using the following command:

```
# cp /etc/opt/SUNWcluster/conf/ccdssa/ccd.database.ssa \
/etc/opt/SUNWcluster/conf/ccd.database
```

The CCD should be copied to the other node using FTP and saved to the following file:

```
/etc/opt/SUNWcluster/conf/ccd.database
```

After both nodes have the correct CCD, bring down the cluster on the remaining node. Both nodes should now be out of the cluster with correct CCDs. The shared CCD volume is no longer required and can be unmounted using the following command:

```
# umount /etc/opt/SUNWcluster/conf/ccdssa
```

The shared CCD disk group can now be deported using the following command:

```
# vxdg deport sc_dg
```

Note: The cluster can now be brought up. If the second node panics when entering the cluster, it probably means the "`scconf` *`clustername`* `-S` none" command was not run correctly on both nodes.

If the following message is displayed during the start of reconfiguration Step 4, the CCD was not successfully copied to the first node:

```
Jun 15 15:16:22 beech ID[SUNWcluster.ccd.ccdd.5300]: lack of quorum to
elect a valid dynamic CCD, the dynamic CCD is invalid and needs to be
restored by the Administrator
```

Note that the `sc_dg` disk group still contains CCD information. This enables an administrator to access the data if something has gone wrong with the process. If both nodes join the cluster correctly, files on the shared CCD volume can be deleted safely. However, doing so will require remounting the disk.

Backing Up and Restoring the CCD

Another important task for managing the CCD is backing it up. This will speed cluster recovery in situations where the CCD has become corrupted or unavailable. Because the CCD is a replicated database, it is unlikely that it will need to be recovered. However, as with any database, it is important to have a backup in case of a disaster or an accidental change to the configuration.

Note: The following procedure discusses how to back up the CCD. Procedures for backing up the other cluster configuration databases are discussed in section, "Backing Up Cluster Configuration Databases" on page 140.

The CCD can be backed up using the `ccdadm` *`clustername`* `-c` *`checkpointfile`* command, where *`checkpointfile`* is the name of the file to save to. This command should only be performed with all logical hosts in maintenance mode. Although it is not required for the logical hosts to be in maintenance mode for a checkpoint, it *is* a requirement for CCD restoration. Errors or unpredictable behavior may occur if the state information being restored does not match the state of the cluster at restore time.

To ensure the cluster is in the same state during restoration that it was in during the CCD checkpoint procedure, it is important to have the logical hosts in maintenance mode during a CCD checkpoint.

1) It is necessary to map each logical host to its current physical host to restore the logical host to its correct node. To find the current hosts, use the following command:

```
# hastat | more
```

2) Set the logical hosts to maintenance mode using the following command:

```
# haswitch -m logicalhostname
```

3) Checkpoint the CCD using the following command:

```
# ccdadm clustername -c checkpointfile
```

4) Restart the logical hosts using the following command:

```
# haswitch physical_host logical_host
```

Note: The logical hosts must be in maintenance mode prior to restoring the CCD; therefore, the best time to back up the CCD is during cluster installation or maintenance. Backing up the CCD should always be part of a cluster installation.

Restoring the CCD can be performed using the `ccadm -r` command. The first operation to be performed is disabling the CCD quorum. As described previously, the CCD quorum does not (usually) play an important role in an SC2.2 environment; however, it is necessary to disable the quorum when restoring the CCD. This can be performed by using the following command:

```
# ccdadm clustername -q off
```

Before switching the logical hosts into maintenance mode, determine the current physical host for each logical host so that they can be restored to the correct node. This information can be displayed using the `hastat` command. Use the following command to put one or more logical hosts into maintenance mode:

```
# haswitch -m logicalhost1 logicalhost2
```

After the logical hosts are in maintenance mode, restore the CCD using the following command:

```
# ccdadm clustername -r restore_file
```

In this case, *`clustername`* is the name of the cluster and *`restore_file`* is the file-name of the CCD backup.

The following command can be used to turn the CCD quorum back on:

```
# ccdadm clustername -q on
```

After this command is performed, the logical host(s) can be brought online using the `haswitch` command. For each logical host, use the following command to host *`logicalhost`* on machine *`phys-host`*:

```
# haswitch phys-host logicalhost
```

Cluster Configuration Database Daemon

The cluster configuration database daemon (ccdd) is responsible for managing consistency of the CCD. Each node has a ccdd process running on it—if the daemon dies unexpectedly, the node will panic. The daemon processes (on each node) communicate via the private interconnect using ports 7000 to 7031. The daemon automatically reconfigures when a CCD change occurs (or when the CMM reconfigures). Understanding the states of a CCD is useful when determining errors. The four possible states are as follows:

Idle

In Idle mode, the ccdd is waiting for a trigger to enter the start state.

Start

In the Start mode, the daemon reads and checks the init CCD for the dynamic CCD configuration information. The daemon on each node establishes TCP/IP sockets to communicate with other nodes.

Step 1

The CCD on each node will attempt to communicate with the daemons on all other nodes during the Step 1 state. Each node will parse its local CCD file and verify the internal consistency of its own copy (discarded if inconsistent). The daemons on each node communicate with each other to elect a valid CCD (which requires a CCD quorum—as described previously). With SC2.2 software, the first node in the cluster will have its CCD elected as the valid CCD unless the file has errors or an incorrect checksum.

Return

In Return mode, the daemon closes any connections, discards queued messages, releases resources, and closes any open files.

Step 1 of the CCD reconfiguration begins with Step 3 of the CMM reconfiguration. Any CCD issues are resolved in Steps 3 and 4 of the CMM reconfiguration.

Resolving Cluster Configuration Database Problems

Any problems with the cluster databases are identified and noted during cluster startup. A detailed explanation of cluster databases is provided in the section, "Cluster Configuration Databases" on page 133. A common problem may affect each type of database differently.

The CDB is the first cluster configuration database read—if the CDB does not exist, the cluster cannot verify its name and will not start. If a node attempts to start with a CDB that contains a syntax error, the `startnode` command exits with the following message:

```
syntax error: Starting Sun Cluster software - joining the tree cluster
Jun 14 17:49:24 beech ID[SUNWcluster.clustd.conf.4004]: fatal:
cdbmatch(cmm.osversion,...): syntax error
scadmin: errors encountered.
```

If the CDB (of a joining node) is syntactically correct but differs from other nodes in the cluster (in any way), the following error message will be displayed after the start of the reconfiguration:

```
Jun 15 16:20:24 beech ID[SUNWcluster.reconf.1201]: Reconfiguration
step start completed
Jun 15 16:20:24 beech ID[SUNWcluster.clustd.reconfig.4018]: Aborting-
-received abort request from node 0.
Jun 15 16:20:24 beech ID[SUNWcluster.clustd.signal.4007]: fatal:
received signal 15.
Jun 15 16:20:25 beech ID[SUNWcluster.reconf.1200]: Reconfiguration
step abort started
```

In either case, the CDB can be restored from a backup or copied from another node into the node having problems (via FTP). This will ensure the database is syntactically correct and consistent with the other nodes.

Note: For CDBs to be consistent, they must be identical. Adding a blank space or any comments to one file not reflected in another results in an "`inconsistent CDB`" message.

Note: If the init CCD has an invalid checksum (or differs from a joining node), the joining node will panic.

Note: If the dynamic CCD has an invalid checksum, the node can join the cluster, although a warning will be displayed. In this case, CCD changes cannot be made because a CCD quorum cannot be achieved until a quorum of valid CCDs exists. In a two-node cluster, a quorum is impossible if the first node to join the cluster has an invalid CCD. If this situation occurs, an administrator should restore the CCD on the first node.

Administering NAFO Groups

The Public Network Management (PNM) system is closely associated with the logical host infrastructure. Logical hosts use NAFO groups to refer to network interfaces in an abstract manner, see Chapter 2, "Sun Cluster 2.2 Architecture." Each NAFO group contains one or more physical interfaces (physically connected to the same subnet). If an interface fails, another interface in the group will take over the IP address and connections of the NAFO group. This enables logical hosts with redundant adapters (in a NAFO group) to survive an adapter failure. Although an adapter failure takes time, it generally takes less time than a logical host failover. Therefore, downtime can be reduced (increasing availability) using redundant adapters in NAFO groups.

PNM Daemon

The PNM daemon (`pnmd`) is started at boot unless:

- An error occurs when attempting to start.
- No `/etc/pnmconfig` file exists.
- The `/etc/pnmconfig` file is incorrectly formatted.

The `pnmd` process is important for cluster operation; therefore, if not started at boot time, the problem should be rectified to enable the daemon to be restarted with the `pnmset` command. When the `pnm` daemon starts, its configuration information is read from the `/etc/pnmconfig` file.

Changes can be made to the `/etc/pnmconfig` file by using the `pnmset` command. The `pnmset` command will restart `pnmd` (unless the `-v` flag is used). The `pnmd` daemon is responsible for testing active interfaces in the NAFO group (and performs a failover if the interfaces are not working correctly). The `pnmd` daemon performs fault probing on the active interface within each NAFO group. The frequency of the probes can be set in the cluster database (CDB) file, see section, "PNM Tunables," on page 154.

The PNM daemon plays an important role in fault monitoring of HA services. Each HA service has its own fault monitor; however, if a fault occurs, pnmd determines if the fault was due to an adapter failure (on the node) or a public network failure affecting the entire cluster. If a fault is due to an adapter problem, the cluster framework will switch to another adapter in the same NAFO group (if one exists).

If no other adapters exist in the NAFO group, pnmd will flag the network as down. The cluster will scan the pnmd state for each node and trigger a failover if the network is flagged as down on the master node but is flagged as up on the secondary node. The net_diagnose_comm daemon performs this function for HA-Oracle and some other monitoring frameworks, but is generally managed by the netfmd process. Unless PNM determines the backup node has a preferable network state to the primary node, no failover occurs. Therefore, no failover occurs in the case of a public network failure (because the service would still have the same problem on another node), though a failure on a single node will still trigger a failover.

Setting Up PNM

All NAFO groups are checked during installation; however, after the groups are installed, only active groups are monitored. Because the backup interfaces cannot be monitored while a node is in the cluster, it is a good idea to check the interfaces whenever a node leaves the cluster for maintenance or other reasons. This is performed using the pnmset -nv command when the node is out of the cluster.

Although the pnmset -nv command is the preferred method of checking NAFO interfaces, the ifconfig command may be an alternate method of checking connectivity of the backup interfaces if an error cannot be easily determined from the pnmset -nv output. However the ifconfig command may lead to unpredictable behavior in a running cluster; therefore, this command should only be run when a node is out of the cluster, see Chapter 6, "Sun Cluster 2.2 Application Notes."

Prior to configuring the PNM, each NAFO group requires (exactly) one interface plumbed with an IP address. To automate the plumbing and ensure it is performed correctly, create a hostname.if file for one interface in each group. This interface becomes the default interface for the group—that is, the interface to be the active interface in a NAFO group when the PNM daemon starts.

Each NAFO group is associated with an IP address. This address is initially hosted on the primary interface, but will fail over to a backup interface if the primary fails. For each NAFO group, the primary interface should have an entry in the /etc/hosts file to associate the NAFO group's IP address with the relevant name.

Using the Sun Cluster naming convention is generally a good idea; however, in this case, it might not be the best method. According to the naming convention, the hostname used should be appended with the primary interface (for example, phys-hahost-qfe1). However, because the hostname could fail to another interface, it might be confusing to have phys-hahost-qfe1 hosted on qfe5. In this situation, it may be better to use a different naming convention. A viable option would be to append the hostname with the NAFO group (rather than the interface name). An example /etc/hosts file entry is as follows:

```
129.146.75.200     ha-nfs
129.146.75.201     ha-web
129.146.75.202     phys-hosta-nafo0
129.146.75.203     phys-hostb-nafo0
129.146.75.204     phys-hosta-nafo1
129.146.75.205     phys-hostb-nafo1
```

As can be seen, each physical host has at least one IP address—these are the IP addresses for each NAFO group. Additionally, each logical host needs one or more IP address.

The logical host IP addresses are hosted on whichever physical host currently masters the logical host. The clients will connect to the logical host IP addresses without being aware of the physical host IP addresses.

After the hostnames are correctly configured, the interface database files (hostname.if) can be set up. Each file configures an IP address onto a given interface at boot time. Each NAFO group requires an interface with an active IP address; therefore, one interface in each NAFO group should have an appropriate interface database file.

For the primary interface in each NAFO group, create a file named hostname.if, where hostname is the string "hostname" (not a variable as stated in the *Sun Cluster 2.2 Administration Manual*) and if is the interface instance (hme0, hme1, qfe3, etc.).

The file (hostname.if) should consist of one line containing the hostname for the interface (as reflected in the /etc/hosts file). In the previous configuration example, the node hosta had two interface database files. If hme0 was the primary interface in NAFO group nafo0 and qfe3 was the primary interface in NAFO group nafo1, the files should be as follows:

The file hostname.hme0 should contain the following line:

```
phys-hosta-nafo0
```

The file hostname.qfe3 should contain the following line:

```
phys-hosta-nafo1
```

Because the NAFO infrastructure depends on the preceding files being accurate, the `/etc/nsswitch.conf` file should have files listed as the first source for netmasks and hosts. It is usually a good idea to have files listed as the first source for most other databases in the `nswitch.conf` file to use, see Chapter 6, "Sun Cluster 2.2 Application Notes."

With NAFO groups that use static routing, there is a mechanism that enables failover of static routing information to a new adapter in case of adapter failure. This mechanism can be implemented using special files. For each NAFO group requiring this functionality, a file is created named `staticroutes.nafoX`, where `X` is the NAFO group number. This file should reside in the `opt/SUNWpnm/bin/staticroutes` directory and be executable by the owner (which must be root).

Note: For security reasons, write permissions should be turned off after file creation.

The `staticroutes.nafoX` file should follow the examples in the `staticroutes.nafo.TEMPLATE` file (which can found in the `/opt/SUNWpnm/bin/staticroutes` directory).

Each line in the file represents a static route, with the format being:

```
/usr/sbin/route add net address 0
```

Where *`net`* is the IP address of the network (or host to route to) and *`address`* is the IP address or hostname to route through (the IP address or hostname should be in the `/etc/hosts` file).

PNM Tunables

After the PNM setup is complete, NAFO groups can be configured by running the `pnmset` command. In some cases, it may be advantageous to change the `pnmd` probe values. The default values will be sufficient for most situations; however, some systems may have requirements such as faster detection of a failure or less susceptibility to slow network problems—in these situations, it may be advantageous to modify the PNM tunables.

Modifying PNM tunables requires directly editing the CDB, see section, "Cluster Configuration Databases" on page 133. However, editing the CDB could result in a misformatted CDB that could lead to problems with starting a cluster. Change only the relevant variables—keep the format the same (variable name, spaces, colon, space, and an integer representing the setting).

If the PNM variables are not present in the CDB, it could indicate that the SUNWpnm package did not load correctly, or that there are problems with the CDB. Another consideration when changing the PNM tunables is that changed tunables could lead to a situation where the pnmd daemon does not fault monitor correctly, which could lead to a spurious failover (an unnecessary failover). This type of failover could be caused by setting the PNM parameters too low.

A spurious failover occurring shortly after the settings are changed would indicate the settings are incorrect. However, even if a spurious failover did not occur, it does not necessarily indicate the changed settings are appropriate. The PNM settings may be configured in such a manner that spurious failovers may only occur during periods of heavy network activity (or even randomly). For this reason, editing PNM tunables is generally not a good idea.

Keeping the preceding considerations in mind, there are four tunable parameters for the PNM configuration. There are two additional tunables added by patches 105458 and 109211. These tunable parameters are stored in the CDB. The four standard PNM tunables are:

- pnmd.inactive_time
- pnmd.ping_timeout
- pnmd.repeat_test
- pnmd.slow_network

These parameters are generally the last entries in the CDB file (information on the location of the CDB file can be found in the section, "Cluster Configuration Databases," on page 133). Additionally, details on setting these parameters can be found on the pnmd MAN page.

The PNM tunables and rpcbind monitor tunables should be the only parameters modified directly in the CDB. The rpcbind monitor is responsible for ensuring that rpcbind is running correctly. The associated rpcbind monitor tunables may need to be changed to compensate for heavily loaded systems; however, they are not discussed.

Changing NAFO Group Configurations Using pnmset

Changes to PNM groups are performed using the pnmset command (which saves the configuration to the /etc/pnmconfig file). The /etc/pnmconfig file lists each NAFO group and the interfaces associated with it. Each line begins with the name of a NAFO group followed by a space-separated list of the interfaces within that group.

Note: Although this file is plain-text, users should not edit it directly.

The testing performed by the pnmset command is critical—any errors in the configuration could lead to problems with the functioning of the NAFO groups and fault monitoring of the HA services. Therefore, any changes made to the PNM configuration should be performed using the pnmset command.

The pnmset command affects the entire PNM configuration. It is not possible to reconfigure a single NAFO group. As a result, it is important to ensure all configured NAFO groups are recorded—not just the ones being changed. It is a good idea to use pnmset with the -p option to display the current configuration. Also, verify that all NAFO groups are correct after a change is made.

The pnmset command should not be run on nodes while they are running in the cluster. Adding (or removing) interfaces to an existing NAFO group does not affect other cluster components (provided one interface remains in the group); however, adding or removing a complete NAFO group requires removing any logical host using the NAFO group. In this situation, the logical host should be removed from the cluster configuration, then added again (using the new NAFO group). However, because the relationship between the NAFO group and the logical host is generally only changed when a logical host is created or destroyed, this is not an issue.

The pnmset command first requests confirmation that it is okay to modify the NAFO configuration. The pnmset command next prompts for the number of backup groups that should exist in the new configuration (default is one group). An administrator is then prompted for the number of each NAFO group to be added—for each group, the backup group number and names of the interfaces in the group will be requested.

At the end of the NAFO configuration process, the pnmset command performs a test of the new configuration which can take up to 20 seconds per interface. There are several types of errors detected by the pnmset command.

If an interface is used in more than one NAFO group, the error message "Detected adapter <*adaptername*> in two backup groups" will be displayed. This message indicates that an error occurred during configuration of the NAFO groups. If an interface in a NAFO group cannot communicate with other interfaces in the group, the error message "nafoX test failed" will be displayed, where X is the NAFO group number being tested.

This error message indicates a problem with cabling, hubs, or interfaces. Look for an unplugged cable, a cable plugged into the wrong interface, or a redundant hub that should be on the same subnet but has no network connection.

Note: All NAFO groups should be entered in their default order. This prevents a situation where an administrator accidentally enters a configuration twice. Entering the same group number twice while editing groups could result in a faulty configuration that will not be detected by `pnmset`.

Overview of the `pnmset` Options

There are a number of options for the `pnmset` command. Although these options are discussed fully in the man pages, the following provides a quick overview:

The `-n` option invokes the `pnmset` command in non-interactive mode. In this mode, the `pnmset` command loads the `/etc/pnmconfig` file (instead of prompting the user for the configuration). This option is useful for re-spawning the `pnmd` daemon after testing the (current) configuration.

Adding the `-t` option prevents testing prior to re-spawning the daemon. The `-t` option is only valid with the `-n` option.

The `-p` option displays the current configuration and then proceeds with the standard `pnmset` process.

The `-v` option prevents the daemon from starting.

The `-f` option writes a copy of the current configuration to another file in addition to the copy written to the `/etc/pnmconfig` file. Table 4-4 lists various `pnmset` option sets.

Table 4-4 Common pnmconfig Option Sets

Command	Results
pnmset -ntvp	Prints the current PNM configuration (without doing anything else)
pnmset -pf /backups/pnmconfig.bak	Provides the current configuration (performs the standard interactive pnmset, then saves a backup copy)
pnmset -n	Restarts the daemon
pnmset -nt	Fast restarts the daemon (with no testing)
pnmset -nv	Tests the PNM configuration in /etc/pnmconfig

Logical Host and Data Service Administration

Logical Hosts and Data Services

Logical hosts are the basis of HA data services. The logical host is the mechanism by which a data service can fail over from one node to another, see Chapter 2, "Sun Cluster 2.2 Architecture." A logical host consists of data services, a shared IP address, and shared data disks. The logical host provides a mechanism to hide the details of failover from the data services. After a failover, a data service is still accessible to the network using the same IP address and can access the shared data in the same manner. Failover is managed by means of the logical host framework, and is transparent to the data service, with the exception of the interruption to service.

A highly available data service is an application that uses the cluster data services API to interact with the logical host framework. This interaction enables the application to fail over using the logical host framework. The API creates a wrapper for the application, which includes data service methods (DSMs) to enable the application to be started, stopped, and fault monitored through the SC2.2 framework, see Chapter 7, "Sun Cluster 2.2 Data Services."

Note: While the data service fault monitors detect some sorts of faults, performance problems are often not detected. Depending on the fault monitor, the data service fault monitors may not detect application performance problems as the result of memory exhaustion or other conditions which could enable an unhealthy application to stay up. It is important to monitor such issues on a cluster node, just as you would on a non-clustered system.

Any given data service runs normally, except if a fault is detected in the service or the cluster node the service is hosted on; in this situation, the service will fail over to an alternate node (by means of the logical host).

The logical host controls the data service's interface to:

- The outside world (logical host IP address)
- The data (shared data disks are under the logical host's control)

When the data service restarts on a new node, the configuration will be identical (because all functions are performed through the logical host).

A useful metaphor in this situation could be that the logical host is like a box, and a data service is like an object that can be put into the box.

Note: Recall that multiple data services can coexist in a logical host, and a simple dependency model can control the order in which the services start or shut down.

A single data service can be registered with multiple logical hosts. In these situations, each logical host would have its own instance of the data service. However, instances cannot be controlled independently (registering, unregistering, turning on, or turning off the service affects all instances of the service). It is not possible to unconfigure or stop a single instance of a data service—this introduces a dependency between instances of the same data service on different logical hosts.

Because of this dependency, there are some considerations to be aware of. Removing or performing changes involving the relationship of the logical host to its IP address(es) or shared disk(s) requires unconfiguring any currently configured data services on the logical host. If other logical hosts are running instances of the same data service, they may also have to be brought down during the change—this could lead to unexpected downtime during maintenance.

For example, if logical host A has data services for HA-NFS and logical host B has data services for HA-NFS plus a custom service, if a major change needs to be made to logical host A, HA-NFS needs to be turned off and unconfigured. However, performing this action will also turn off and unconfigure the HA-NFS instance on logical host B, making the service unavailable, and may impact the custom service (if dependent on the HA-NFS instance).

It is important to consider the ramifications of having a single data service on multiple logical hosts (especially if there are data service dependencies involved). Generally, you should avoid having the same data service run on more than one logical host. Although some architectural constraints may require breaking this guideline, if it is followed, independence between hosts will be promoted (which could increase availability).

Another consideration for data service configuration is limiting the number of data services in a logical host. This will prevent instances of *upgrade interference*, where upgrading one application may be difficult or impossible due to support issues for versions of other applications on the cluster.

For example, upgrading a Web server may only be supported with an upgraded OS. However, the upgraded OS may not support the database you use. Although such situations are rare with single applications, the odds of having a support issue increases exponentially with the number of applications. This situation can be exacerbated because support for applications is conservative in a clustered environment and because quality assurance is essential for an HA environment.

The data service instance dependency and upgrade interference issues provide good reasons to limit the number of applications on a cluster, and to keep the logical hosts abstracted. If the logical hosts are abstracted correctly, it is generally possible to migrate different logical hosts into separate clusters. This is useful if there is no upgrade path that enables the desired version upgrades of all data services to be simultaneously supported by the service contract. It is important to consider these issues when planning a cluster.

Managing Logical Hosts

Adding Logical Hosts

Logical hosts can be added by using either the `scinstall` command or the `scconf -L` command. The `scinstall` command enables an interactive configuration, while the `scconf -L` command enables the configuration of the logical hosts from the command line.

Note: It is acceptable to set up the appropriate disk groups or NAFO groups before *or* after the logical host is set up.

Adding Logical Hosts with `scinstall`

Setting up logical hosts using the `scinstall` command is a straightforward procedure because the command has a menu-driven interface for configuring the logical hosts (and many other cluster functions). Although primarily used during cluster install, it can be used after the installation to modify some configuration parameters. Menu options vary according to whether the cluster is up or down.

To add a logical host using the `scinstall` command, first select *change* from the main menu of the `scinstall` interface, then select *logical hosts*, then select *add*.

The `scinstall` program will prompt for the following information regarding the cluster:

- Primary public network controller on each node
- Secondary network controllers on each node (as necessary)
- Logical hostname
- Default master for the logical host
- Whether or not the logical host should automatically fail back
- Name of the disk group for the logical host

After the appropriate information is entered, create an administrative file system for the logical host. Instructions for creating the file system are provided at the end of this section.

Adding Logical Hosts with `scconf`

Adding a logical host using the `scconf` command requires the same information discussed in this section; however, the format is not intuitive, so therefore the `scconf -L` command takes the form:

```
scconf clust_name -L name_of_host_to_add -n nodelist \
-g dg_list -i logical_addr_info [-m]
```

Where *`clust_name`* is the name of the cluster, *`name_of_host_to_add`* is the name of the logical host, *`nodelist`* is a comma-separated list of nodes that are potential masters for the logical host (the first node listed is the preferred master), and *`dg_list`* is a comma-separated list of the disk groups for the shared data of the logical host.

The shared disks within the logical host disk groups should be mirrored across different controllers, see Chapter 3, "Sun Cluster 2.2 Components."

Using the `-m` option indicates that a manual (as opposed to automatic) failback is required. A manual failback means that if the logical host fails over to a new node, it will stay there unless it is manually switched back to the original node. An automatic failback means that the logical host will automatically switch back to a specified node when that node is in working condition in the cluster. The node specified for this behavior is called the *preferred master* for that logical host.

Because a failback causes an additional failover when the preferred master re-enters the cluster, it reduces availability and therefore is not usually a good idea. However, there are some situations where using the failback feature is a good idea—including a situation where the backup node has less capacity than the primary.

The *`logical_addr_info`* entry is more complex. This entry is a comma-separated list of network interfaces, followed by an IP address or resolvable name associated with an IP address in the `/etc/hosts` file.

Register logical hosts with a resolvable name rather than with an IP address. This enables changing the IP address by modifying the `/etc/hosts` file rather than by removing the logical host and re-creating it with a new address.

One network interface should be listed for each node (with the interface order corresponding to the node order specified using the `-n` flag). The network interfaces should be those network interfaces to be used first (not NAFO groups). The selected adapter automatically fails over to another adapter within its NAFO group. If there are multiple hostnames and addresses associated with a logical host, the `-i` flag can be used more than once with the information for the additional hostname provided in the same format.

For example, in the following configuration:

```
# scconf trees -L treeweb -n ash,beech,cyprus -g TREEWEBDISK \
-i hme0,qfe0,hme1,website1 -i hme1,qfe3,hme2,website2
```

The logical host named `treeweb` is configured on the `trees` cluster. It uses the disk group `TREEWEBDISK`, which can be mastered by the nodes `ash`, `beech`, and `cyprus`. Because the `-m` flag is not present, an automatic failback will occur. Therefore, whenever the host *`ash`* (primary host) enters the cluster, the logical host will fail over to be hosted on *`ash`*. The logical host has two network hostnames. The network hostname `website1` can be hosted by the NAFO groups containing the interface `hme0` on the host *`ash`*, `qfe0` on the host *`beech`*, and `hme1` on the host `cyprus`. The network hostname `website2` can be hosted by the NAFO groups containing the interface `hme1` on the host `ash`, `qfe3` on the host *`beech`*, and `hme2` on the host *`cyprus`*.

As previously discussed, after a logical host is added, an administrative file system should be created.

Adding an Administrative File System to a Logical Host

The administrative file system is used by the logical host infrastructure to store administrative messages. The administrative file system should be created on a volume that is at least 2 Mbyte in size (this file system should be mirrored onto two disks using different controllers). For systems using VxVM, the `scconf -F` command can be used to automate the volume creation, file system creation, and file creation. However, because this does not guarantee maximum independence of mirrored halves, it is a best practice to manually create the appropriate volume and then use the `scconf -F` command to create the file system (and appropriate files). If using an SDS configuration, all steps are performed manually.

In a configuration using Veritas Volume Manager, use the following commands to create the required volume:

```
# vxassist -g DG_NAME make DG_NAME-stat 2M layout=nolog DISK01
# vxassist -g DG_NAME mirror DG_NAME-stat layout=nostripe DISK02
```

Where *DG_NAME* is the name of the disk group; *DISK01* and *DISK02* are the Veritas disk names for two disks on different controllers. The volume name should be the name of the disk group appended with the string `-stat`. Therefore, if the disk group is named `NFSDISK`, the volume name for the administrative volume would be `NFSDISK-stat`.

After the volume is created, use the `scconf -F` command to create the appropriate file system and files.

The `scconf -F` command performs the following:

- Creates the *DG_NAME*-`stat` volume (if not already existing).

Note: Manually create the *DG_NAME*-`stat` volume prior to running the `scconf -F` command.

- Creates a UFS file system on the volume. This occurs only on the host with the volume currently imported.
- Creates a directory under the root with an identical name as the logical host. This directory will be used to mount the file system (in the previous step).
- Creates the `/etc/opt/SUNWcluster/hanfs` directory (if not already existing). The files `vfstab.`*`logicalhost`* and `dfstab.`*`logicalhost`* are created under the directory (where *`logicalhost`* is the logical hostname). These files are associated with the HA-NFS data service; however, logical hosts require these files even if not configured with the HA-NFS data service. When the

vfstab.logicalhost file is created, it will include a line for mounting the appropriate administrative file system in the directory that has an identical name to the logical host.

The code in the following box identifies the contents of the vfstab.logicalhost file, where the logical hostname is *logicalhost* and the disk group name is *DG*:

```
/dev/vx/dsk/DG/DG-stat /dev/vx/rdsk/DG/DG-stat /logicalhost ufs 1 no -
```

Note: The previous line for mounting the administrative file system *must* appear before any other volumes to be mounted.

If the configuration uses the SDS product, all steps should be performed manually.

The scconf command should be run using the following syntax:

```
scconf clustname -F logicalhost DG_NAME
```

[*clustname* is the name of the cluster, *logicalhost* is the name of the logical host that the administrative file system is being created for, and *DG_NAME* is the name of the disk group on which to create the administrative file system].

Note: If the scconf -F command has been run with the wrong logical hostname, manually remove the files created.

Adding and Configuring a Data Service

Starting a data service is a two-step process. A data service first needs to be registered. Although this enters the data service into the cluster configuration, it does not start the data service. The data service can be turned on after being registered. Turning on the data service turns on all instances of the service and associated fault monitors.

Data services cannot be unregistered until turned off. There is no mechanism that enables turning on or off specific instances of a data service associated with multiple logical hosts. When a data service is turned off or unregistered, all instances of that data service are affected.

Registering a data service can be performed using the hareg command. The syntax used to start a Sun-supplied data service is as follows:

```
# hareg -s -r service_name [-h logical_hosts]
```

Where *service_name* is the name of the service to be registered and *logical_hosts* is a comma separated list of logical hosts that will use the service.

In the general availability release of the SC2.2 product, it is not possible to set dependencies or timeouts for Sun-supplied services. However, the patches listed in Table 4-5 enable this functionality. Setting a Sun-supplied service to be dependent on a custom HA service links the behavior of the Sun-supplied service to the custom service. This means the Sun-supplied service may have reduced availability if there are problems with the custom service (or implementation of the custom service). Although this may be acceptable, keep in mind that with a chain of dependencies, the availability level achieved is limited by the weakest link—that is, the service with the least reliability.

Table 4-5 Patches to Enable Setting Dependencies and Timeouts

OS Version	Patch Numbers
Solaris 2.6	108518 and 108519
Solaris 7	109207 and 108519

Using the `-h` flag to specify logical hosts is optional. If not used, the data service will be configured on all logical hosts. It is a good idea to only configure data services on the logical hosts that will use them. Data services can be associated with new logical hosts later using the following command:

```
# scconf clustername -s DS_name LH_name
```

Where *DS_name* is the name of the data service to be associated with the logical host *LH_name* in the cluster *clustername*.

Similarly, a service can be disassociated with a logical host using the following command:

```
# scconf clustname -s -r DS_name LH_name
```

This command disassociates a data service from a logical host, but does not unregister it. Unregistering a service will automatically disassociate it with all logical hosts. Changing the data service to a logical host association works the same for Sun-supplied services and custom services.

Note: The `hareg -s -r` command and `scconf -s -r` command are partial opposites. The `hareg -s -r` command registers a service (associates it with logical hosts). The `ssconf -s -r` command disassociates a data service with a logical host, although it does not unregister it.

Associating or disassociating a custom data service with a logical host is performed using the `scconf` command. Registering a non-Sun-supplied data service is similar, but slightly more complex. In this case, the `-s` option (which would indicate a Sun-supplied data service) is not used. And, because the configuration information for the service has not been pre-supplied with the cluster release, it needs to be specified. The information to be supplied includes:

- Data service name
- Names of the data service methods (DSMs) used by the data service to communicate with the data services API, and therefore the cluster infrastructure, see Chapter 7, "Sun Cluster 2.2 Data Services"
- The directory where the DSMs reside
- Timeouts for starting, stopping, and fault monitoring the service
- Dependencies on other HA services in the same logical host
- Logical hosts the service is associated with
- Version number of the service
- Packages making up the service

The exact syntax for registering a non Sun-supplied data service is discussed in the `hareg` man pages, see Chapter 7, "Sun Cluster 2.2 Data Services."

As discussed previously, a data service can be associated or disassociated with logical hosts using the `scconf -s` or `scconf -s -r` options.

After a data service is registered, it can be turned on using the `hareg -y` command. This command expects a comma-separated list of services to turn on. The syntax to turn on the services *service1* and *service2* is as follows:

```
# hareg -y service1,service2
```

The `hareg -y` (lowercase *y*) command turns on the individual services or list of services. The `hareg -Y` (uppercase *Y*) command turns on all registered data services.

Depending on the data service used, there may be additional configuration requirements during the process. Any additional configuration requirements for a given service will be provided in the documentation supplied with the service. The configuration instructions for Sun-supplied data services are found in the *Sun Cluster 2.2 Software Installation Guide.*

Administering Logical Hosts

After the data services are configured into a logical host, they will fail over with the logical host they are registered to. Failover occurs automatically due to network problems on a node, a node failure, disk access problems, private interconnect failure, or detection of a data service fault. A switchover (a manual failover) is performed using the `haswitch` and `scadmin` switch commands. The functionality of these commands is duplicated—as shown in Table 4-6:

Table 4-6 The `scadmin` Functionality

The `scadmin` **Switch Command**	**Equivalent** `haswitch` **Command**	**Effect**
`scadmin switch` *`clustname dest_host logical_hosts`**	`haswitch` *`dest_host logical_hosts`**	Switches *`logical_hosts`* mastered on *`dest_host`*
`scadmin switch` *`clustname`* `-r`	`haswitch -r`	Performs a cluster reconfiguration
`scadmin switch` *`clustname`* `-m` *`logical_hosts`**	`haswitch -m` *`logical_hosts`**	Puts the specified logical hosts into maintenance mode

* *`logical_hosts`* can be one logical hostname or a space-separated list of logical hostnames.

The concept of logical hosts is straightforward—the logical host can be hosted on any node in the cluster that is connected to the logical host's shared storage and appropriately configured to host it.

During a cluster reconfiguration, the logical host moves in a specific pattern from one node to the next. At this time, the HA services configured into the logical host are stopped or aborted. By the time the reconfiguration has completed, the shared disks are deported from the old host. The new host imports the shared disks and performs a startup sequence based on the configured data services. The steps of this reconfiguration are performed in lock-step fashion—that is, the next step will be performed *only* if the previous step has completed on all nodes.

Note: It is important to ensure that the node a logical host is moving to has enough resources to host the data services associated with the logical host. Sizing appropriate capacity monitoring of backup nodes is necessary to ensure a failover can be performed as required.

Because the coherency of the logical host data is important, the cluster will not permit the logical host to be in an indeterminate state. If a logical host move fails and the logical host is able to remain hosted on its original host, the cluster framework will keep the logical host where it is (to ensure the state remains determinant). If neither node is able to master the logical host, it will configure the logical host down.

Switchovers are performed using the `haswitch` command:

```
# haswitch dest_host logical_host1 logical_host2 ...
```

This command will switch logical hosts *logical_host1* and *logical_host2* over to physical host *dest_host*.

In some situations, it may be desirable not to have the logical host mastered by any physical hosts. This situation is called maintenance mode and results in the logical host deporting its disks and stopping data services (on all nodes). This is the first part of the switchover process. The host leaves its current master and is not remastered. Maintenance mode can be useful when making some types of logical host changes (and for backing up or restoring the CCD). A logical host can be switched into maintenance mode using the following command:

```
# haswitch -m logical_hosts
```

This command will switch one or more logical hosts into maintenance mode (*logical_hosts* can be a single logical host name or a space-separated list of logical hostnames). Logical hosts can be switched out of maintenance mode using the `haswitch` command to host them to a new physical host.

There is no way of making on-the-fly changes to the logical host configuration. However, to modify values set by the `scconf` command line options or `scinstall` prompts, remove the logical host and re-introduce it into the cluster with the new information.

The following are the logical host configuration parameters that cannot be modified on-the-fly:

- Primary public network controller on each node (determines the NAFO group to use)
- Secondary network controllers on each node (if used)
- Logical hostname
- Default master for logical host
- Whether the logical host should automatically fail back
- Name of disk group for logical host

In most situations, this information will not need to be changed. However, some options (such as automatic failback) may need to be changed as the cluster evolves. When performing such changes, the logical host will need to be removed and re-added.

Removing Logical Hosts and Data Services

Logical hosts can be removed using the `scinstall` or `scconf -L -r` commands. However, prior to using these commands, all data services configured into the logical host should be unregistered.

Recall that stopping or unregistering a data service will stop or unregister all instances of the data service—this could affect other logical hosts using these data services.

All instances of the data service can be stopped by using the following command:

```
# hareg -n dataservice
```

After the data service has been stopped, it can be unregistered by using the following command:

```
# hareg -u dataservice
```

This command unregisters all instances of the data service. If the `hareg -u` command fails, it will leave the cluster in an inconsistent state.

Note: If the `hareg -u` command fails, run the `scconf -R` command. This command forcibly removes the data service instances (performing a similar function to the `hareg -u` command).

If all data services present in a logical host have been stopped, the logical host can be removed using the `scinstall` command (or the following command):

```
# scconf clusname -L -r logical_host
```

The available options for removing a logical host using the `scinstall` command are: *change* (main menu), *logical hosts* (change menu), and *remove* (logical hosts configuration menu).

After the logical host is removed, delete the `/etc/opt/SUNWcluster/conf/hanfs/vfstab.logicalhost` file. If you are not planning to use the disks again in a logical host, you could remove the `stat` volume. Alternatively, it may be a good idea to keep the `stat` volume because it takes up little space and provides the flexibility to re-introduce shared data into a cluster in the future.

Because all instances of the affected data services were unregistered and turned off previously, it may be necessary to re-register the services and turn them on to enable other logical hosts to use them again.

Note: This will only be required if the services were configured into other logical hosts in addition to the removed one.

Cluster Topology and Hardware Changes

Administering Hardware and Topology Changes

Clusters are commonly used to increase availability by making node failures more transparent. However, maintaining this high level of availability increases the complexity of changes (even minor hardware changes). For example, changes involving the cluster topology can be difficult or restricted because of failure fencing concerns. Although the SC2.2 software enables a smooth transition between different service demands, efficient planning and processes are essential to minimize difficulties.

This section discusses methods for making hardware and topology changes to existing clusters.

Note: One meaning of the term *cluster topology* refers only to the number of nodes and the topological relationships among them. However, in this discussion, the term *topology* denotes both the topological relationships among nodes and their connections (including networking and shared storage).

There are many types of changes that can be performed on a cluster. The fundamental goal of a cluster is to keep the application available. Although this goal can be attained when implementing some topology changes, it is not possible in others.

Interruptions to a service caused by topology changes can vary depending on the type of change. Interruption can be classified according to the amount of downtime (no downtime, the time to perform a switchover, or even the time required to reinstall the cluster).

Non-invasive changes may cause no interruption at the application level. However, complex changes may require failing over a service. If a node does not master any logical hosts, the node can be taken out of service, modified, then re-introduced into the cluster without interrupting service. If a node does master a logical host, some downtime occurs during the time it takes the logical host to fail over to a backup node (in preparation for bringing the node down).

Note: Some types of highly invasive changes to cluster topology may involve bringing the entire cluster down. This includes changes that affect the init CCD.

Any topology changes should be applied carefully because they are potentially disruptive. Disruptions can occur as a result of misconfiguration problems or reduced redundancy while a backup component is out of service.

During the time a backup node is down, availability of the primary node is reduced to its base availability rating. Because the backup node is not available during this time, if the primary node fails, the failure results in an extended downtime. Additionally, while running in degraded mode, the failure of a node will generally have a longer downtime because errors that usually result in a failover may result in a reboot.

The basic method of a topology change involves putting the cluster in the correct state, implementing the change, then making the necessary changes to the cluster configuration so that the change is recognized. Implementation of (almost) all changes are the same as for a non-clustered environment—in other words, it involves the same basic changes to the hardware, OS, or volume manager. However, there are additional steps required to enable the cluster to recognize changes.

Before making cluster changes, it is important to understand the current cluster state. If the cluster is in the correct state, appropriate cluster commands can be run. The following section discusses these considerations without discussing the lower level changes for the hardware, OS, and volume manager.

Changing the Node Hardware

There are various changes that can be made to the node hardware. Changes internal to a node that do not affect the network or disk interfaces do not affect cluster topology. Therefore, these changes do not cause topology restrictions. For example, adding or removing memory or CPU modules can be done with no effects on the cluster beyond the effects of taking out the node.

Note: Because a node may not be able to respond to heartbeats during Dynamic Reconfiguration (DR), the DR features of Sun servers are not supported in an SC2.2 environment.

If a change to a node affects the network or disk interfaces, it may affect the logical hosts or other cluster functionality. As a result, additional steps may be required to ensure the cluster correctly deals with the change. This is because the cluster will be unaware of changes to the underlying hardware (with the exception of components it is actively monitoring).

Network or storage interfaces that are not used by the logical host framework or the cluster itself do not require additional configuration. In these cases, the node can simply be taken down and the appropriate interface can be added or replaced. If the logical host or cluster framework are affected, the card can be added in the standard manner; however, additional actions may be required before the node can rejoin the cluster with the new component. The following sections detail the procedures involved in updating the cluster configuration appropriately when different components are added or changed.

It is important to keep in mind that the standard Solaris OE actions for adding the appropriate interface still apply. Cluster configuration changes are in addition to any changes normally required to use the interface. For example, when adding a network interface, an administrator needs to perform a reconfiguration reboot, create an `/etc/hostname.if` file (if required), run `ifconfig`, etc. After the changes are accomplished, the configuration steps outlined in the following sections should be performed to make the cluster aware of the change.

If a new controller is replacing a failed controller, the replacement can be performed without stopping the cluster. If the replacement card is identical to the existing card, the change is transparent to the cluster. This is because the cluster uses instance numbers to communicate with hardware interfaces. Providing the instance number of the new interface has not changed, the cluster uses the new interface as if it were the original interface.

Another consideration related to instance numbers is the order in which the cards are added—the order may determine the instance numbers associated with the cards. Because of this, if the Solaris OE is reinstalled on the node, the instance numbers should be confirmed as matching (or retain the same instance numbers by using the same `/etc/path_to_inst` file). An alternative method is to use new instance numbers—in this case, the cluster configuration needs to be updated on all cluster nodes.

Changing Private Network Configuration (for Ethernet)

Changing which network interfaces are used for the private interconnect on a node requires taking the node out of the cluster (and switching over any logical hosts being hosted). Removing the node from the cluster is required because the new interface cannot be plumbed while the cluster is running on the node. After the node is brought down, it is possible to switch to a different interface for the internal network or perform a hardware swap to substitute a new card (of the same type). In most situations, changing or replacing the interface will only need to be performed due to hardware failure.

If a hardware failure occurs, replace the failed card with a new card of the same type (same part number). This reduces the chance of a misconfiguration, because the instance numbers remain the same.

At some time, an interface may need to be permanently moved or replaced with an upgraded card of a different type. For example, to support additional logical hosts, a card that enables only one Ethernet port (currently used for the private interconnect) may need to be replaced with a quad fast Ethernet card. The hardware portion for changing interfaces follows the standard Solaris OE procedure for interface additions. However, because the card was previously involved with the cluster framework (as part of the interconnect), the cluster configuration requires updating. In this example, the private network interconnect that was hosted on the old interface should be changed to enable the cluster to communicate using the new card. The cluster configuration should be updated—this is performed using the `scconf` command in association with the `-i` option on all cluster nodes (whether they are currently running the cluster or not). This should be performed while the node with the new interface is out of the cluster.

The `-i` option modifies the private network interfaces for a specified host. Private interface data is not stored in the CCD; therefore, it will not be dynamically updated to all cluster nodes.

Note: When interfaces are changed, run the `scconf -i` command on all nodes, including any node being upgraded (even though not currently in the cluster membership)—a good method of doing this is to use the cluster console.

Make a record of the current configuration. A list of cluster information will be displayed using the `scconf` *`clustername`* `-p` command. Also, note which interfaces are being used for the private network. After the configuration is recorded, the `scconf -i` command can be used to change interfaces using the following command:

```
# scconf clustername -i hostname interface1 interface2
```

This command updates the configuration for host *`hostname`* of cluster *`clustername`* to enable the private interconnect used by *`hostname`* to connect to cluster *`clustername`*. Interfaces are *`interface1`* and *`interface2`*.

The interface parameters for *`interface1`* and *`interface2`*, should be interface instance names, for example, `qfe0`, `qfe3`, or `hme1`. The two private network interfaces should be located on different cards.

Note: The listed order of *`interface1`* and *`interface2`* is important.

The first interface listed should correspond to the interconnect on the first private network; the second interface listed should correspond to the interconnect on the second private network. For example, if *`interface2`* has not been upgraded, it will still be the second entry listed. If the interface order is reversed, the node will be unable to communicate over the private network and will be prevented from rejoining the cluster.

Switching to a new internal network interface only causes downtime in the logical hosts that are hosted on the node to be upgraded. These logical hosts should be failed over while the node is out of the cluster.

Changing Private Network Configuration (for SCI)

A Scalable Coherent Interconnect (SCI) is a high-speed low-latency network used as an interconnect for clusters. Because of its low latency and high bandwidth, SCI is the preferred interconnect medium for parallel databases; however, it works equally well for large HA configurations. When a cluster is installed, if SCI is chosen for the interconnect, the appropriate drivers will be installed and the adapters automatically configured. SCI adapters require hardware and software configuration changes when replaced.

SCI is a ring-based, token-passing topology that operates point-to-point between two cluster nodes, or it can be used with more than two nodes by using SCI switches. In addition to cabling, SCI adapters have a physical hardware jumper that must be set. This jumper is called a scrubber, which can be set to on or off. Setting the jumper requires removing the adapter card from its slot or I/O board and either removing or shunting the two scrubber pins.

SCI Configuring: Two-Node Point-to-Point Cluster (no SCI switch)

A *single node* in the cluster must have the SCI adapter scrubber jumpers set to *ON* (as shown in Table 4-7).

Table 4-7 SCI Scrubber Settings for Two-Node Cluster

SCI Adapter	Scrubber Setting
Node0, SCI0	ON
Node0, SCI1	ON
Node1, SCI0	OFF
Node1, SCI1	OFF

After the scrubbers are set, reinstall the cards and connect the cables. The corresponding SCI cards on each node should connect to each other; for example, SCI0 on Node0 attaches to SCI0 on Node1, and SCI1 on Node0 attaches to SCI1 on Node1.

Note: SCI cables are heavy—ensure they have adequate support to prevent damaging connectors.

Three- and Four-Node Clusters

For those customers using SCI switches, the adapter cards on all hosts must have their scrubbers set to the ON position.

For redundancy, two SCI switches are required. Each SCI adapter must connect to the same port on each SCI switch, see Table 4-8.

Table 4-8 Connectivity to SCI Switches in Three- or Four-Node Clusters

Node ID Number	Port on Switch 0	Port on Switch 1
0	0	0
1	1	1
2	2	2
3	3	3

Setting SCI Node ID

After the scrubber jumpers have been set, the SCI adapters require a corresponding node ID to be programmed. This function is performed using SCI `admin` commands (located in the `/opt/SUNWsci/bin` directory).

The `/opt/SUNWsci/bin/Examples/template.sc` file contains a template for using SCI with SC2.2 software. This file should be copied to a new location and edited as required (as described in the `sm_config(1m)` man pages). Specifically, the host ID section requires modifying to reflect the correct cluster configuration and correct node names. If the cluster has potential nodes which will not be used in the initial configuration, the non-active node names should be commented out in the `sm_config` file by entering a "`_%`" string in front of the relevant line. This procedure is described in the *Sun Cluster Administration Manual.*

After the `sm_config` file has been edited, use the following command on one node only:

```
# /opt/SUNWsci/bin/sm_config -f sci.config
```

Where *`sci.config`* is the configuration file that has been modified from the template as described above.

The nodes can now be rebooted—after they come up, any configuration changes should be updated in the cluster configuration database, see section, "Changing Private Network Configuration (for Ethernet)" on page 173. To update the changes, use the following command:

```
# scconf clustername -i hostname interface1 interface2
```

Where *hostname* is the name of the host having its interfaces updated in the configuration of the cluster *clustername*. The interface *interface1* will be used for the first private network, and the interface *interface2* will be used for the second private network. Interface parameters *interface1* and *interface2* should be interface instance names, for example, scid0 and scid2.

Checking SCI Scrubber Jumper Setting

To confirm the ID and scrubber setting of a node, use the sciinfo command. The output should be similar to the following:

```
#/opt/SUNWsci/bin/sciinfo -a
sciinfo $Revision: 2.10 $
There are 2 ASbus adapters found in this machine
------------------------------------------------
Adapter number :                              0
Node id        :                              4
Serial Number  :                           5035
Scrubber       :                             ON
------------------------------------------------
Adapter number :                              1
Node id        :                              8
Serial Number  :                           5027
Scrubber       :                            OFF
```

Note: If the SCI cable is connected incorrectly, the scrubber status cannot be determined.

Note: No SCI adapters should have the same node ID.

Changing Terminal Concentrator/SSP Connectivity

Changes to terminal concentrator connectivity are more invasive because the terminal concentrator is involved in failure fencing in some topologies. Changing terminal concentrator connectivity can also be performed using the `scconf` command.

The `scconf` command enables replacing a terminal concentrator or changing connectivity between nodes and the terminal concentrator. In a two-node cluster, or a cluster running the SDS volume manager, modifying the terminal concentrator setup is straightforward because the terminal concentrator is not part of the cluster framework in these cases. Therefore, it is not necessary (or useful) to update the cluster with the terminal concentrator configuration information. For clusters where the terminal concentrator is not used for failure fencing, the terminal concentrator can be physically replaced with no impact on failure fencing or the availability of the cluster. The only problem that may be encountered while changing a terminal concentrator is there is no console access while performing the change.

It is a good practice to plan ahead to ensure all nodes are accessible while changing the terminal concentrator. Ensure correct privileges are set for the administrator.

For clusters with three or more nodes using Veritas Volume Manager, the above problem is compounded because the terminal concentrator *is* involved with failure fencing.

As previously discussed, the terminal concentrator is involved in failure fencing in two ways. It has *lock port* functionality, which signals partitions that a cluster is already running (preventing multiple clusters from becoming active and attempting to access data). The terminal concentrator also has direct connections to the consoles of the cluster nodes to enable the chosen partition to forcibly terminate a non-chosen partition in some failure scenarios.

Note: In clusters where the terminal concentrator plays a role in failure fencing, any changes to the terminal concentrator configuration should only be performed when the cluster is stopped.

Two commands modify terminal concentrator settings. The following command should be run on all nodes in tandem—this requires the cluster to be down on all nodes:

```
# scconf clustername -H hostname -d node_architecture -p port_number_of_host
```

This command is used to modify information regarding connections from a terminal concentrator to a host. In the preceding box, `clustername` is the name of the cluster, *`hostname`* is the name of the host, *`node_architecture`* specifies the architecture of the node, and *`port_number_of_host`* specifies which SSP or terminal concentrator port connects to the specified host *`hostname`*.

The `-d` option is not needed if the node architecture will remain the same.

Although the node architecture type may need to be changed in the case of a misconfiguration, there are other considerations when changing the architecture type of a node. In most situations, a reinstallation of the cluster will be necessary. The previous command modifies information regarding how the terminal concentrator is connected to nodes. The following command is used to modify configuration information required for accessing the terminal concentrator from a public network:

```
# scconf clustername -t old_IP_or_name -i new_IP -P new_pass -l new_port
```

Where *`old_IP_or_name`* is the name or IP address of the terminal concentrator, *`new_IP`* is the new IP address, *`new_pass`* is the new password for the terminal concentrator, and *`new_port`* is the port to be used for the node lock.

Changing the Quorum Device

Administration of quorum devices is performed using the `scconf` command with the `-q` option. In this situation, the `scconf` command should be run simultaneously on all nodes (currently in the cluster or not). This is performed by means of the cluster control panel. Use the command `scconf -q` *`hostname1 hostname2`* to enable the new quorum device to interactively select between nodes *`hostname1`* and *`hostname2`*. This command sets up the `/.rhosts` file to temporarily enable root user access on *`hostname1`* from *`hostname2`* (and on *`hostname2`* from *`hostname1`*). The `/.rhosts` files will be returned to their original state after the command is finished.

This arrangement enables nodes to execute commands on each other and compare devices (even while one or more nodes are not cluster members). However, when using this method, it is necessary to run the commands simultaneously (if possible) to ensure nodes can run remote commands on each other and disks can be successfully compared.

The `-D` option is used to specify a change to a directly attached quorum device.

Another way to change a quorum device between two nodes is to use the `-m` option with the `scconf -q` command. This enables selecting a quorum device as a command option rather than using the method described above.

Note: This method is described in detail in the `scconf` man pages.

Quorum devices are essential for failure fencing when using VxVM configurations; therefore, manually selecting a device is generally not a good practice. Using the interactive selection verifies both nodes can see the quorum device (and the device name is correct).

Physically mark the disks that are used as quorum devices to clearly identify them. Because the cluster expects a certain disk ID for the quorum devices, if the quorum disk is replaced with a new disk, it cannot perform as a quorum device unless the cluster configuration is updated. It is important that data center staff never replace a quorum device without notifying cluster administrators to update the configuration.

In cases where a quorum device already exists between two nodes, the `scconf` *`clustername`* `-q` command can be run while the cluster is up (so there will be no downtime)—this enables switching quorum devices for maintenance. The `scconf -q` command can also be used to add a new quorum device between two nodes that did not previously share a quorum device (changing the quorum topology). When such quorum topology changes are implemented, the cluster should be down. Quorum topology changes may be necessary if the maximum number of nodes permitted in the cluster is increased, or the topology is changed so that two nodes are configured to share data they did not previously share.

Changing Shared Data Disks

Disk groups are an extremely flexible component of the SC2.2 architecture. Because the disks in a disk group are abstracted away from the cluster, modifications within a disk group are transparent to the cluster. Disk groups can be added or removed transparently (provided they are not used by a logical host).

Dealing with disk groups connected to a logical host may require bringing the entire cluster down.

A consideration to be addressed is when making failure fencing changes to disk groups. Because cluster infrastructure is abstracted away from the disks in a disk group, new disks will not be recognized as being failure fenced. The exact mechanics of configuring disks for failure fencing is dependent on the volume manager used.

If using the VxVM, when changes are made to shared disks, use the following command:

```
# scadmin resdisks
```

Executing this command identifies all shared disks and configures them to enable failure fencing.

For configurations that use Solstice DiskSuite, the disks should be configured for failure fencing *individually.* Use the following command to configure the disk `instance_num` for failure fencing:

```
# scadmin reserve instance_num
```

Where *`instance_num`* is the instance number of the disk (in the form `cXtYdZ`).

Changing Node Topology

During cluster installation, additional potential nodes can be specified (beyond those initially set). The number of nodes chosen as *potential* during the initial cluster installation determines the maximum number of nodes permitted in a given cluster. If the desired number of nodes to be in the cluster is greater than the maximum permissible number of nodes, it will be necessary to reinstall the software from scratch. The number of nodes chosen as *active* during cluster installation determines the number of nodes expected to be running in the short term. Nodes that fall within the active total can be added or removed using the `scadmin` command. Changing active nodes to potential nodes requires modifying the cluster configuration using the `scconf` command—this requires downtime. A method for performing this is described later in this section.

All nodes (regardless of whether they are set as active or potential) require configuration information (such as node name, primary interface, and Ethernet address). For example, if administering a parallel database that eventually scales to twice its original size, it make sense to have two nodes chosen as active and four nodes as the potential number of nodes. Two nodes can be up and running immediately, with provision for adding two more nodes later.

During installation, specify node names, primary network interfaces, private network interfaces, and Ethernet addresses for all four nodes. Ethernet addresses and private network interfaces can be changed at a later date (primary network interfaces are only for NAFO initialization). This information will be automatically updated in all nodes if a NAFO change occurs.

It is difficult to change cluster node hostnames due to a (documented) bug. The procedure supplied by the *Sun Cluster 2.2 Administration Manual* does not address all the issues required for changing a node name. In most situations, a hostname is merely a matter of convenience; therefore, it is appropriate to choose hostnames at cluster installation and retain them. Because cluster nodes (usually) follow a naming scheme or numbering scheme, this is generally not a restrictive requirement.

Adding a node that was previously identified as a *potential* node is not as difficult as reinstalling the cluster. However, there is still a downside: Node names are relatively difficult to change; therefore, it is important to choose appropriate names during installation. Also, the appropriate Ethernet addresses and interfaces for non-active nodes will probably not be known at installation time—these may require changing manually. The public and private network interfaces may not be known in advance; however, these can be modified later.

All procedures in this section should be performed while the cluster is not running on any nodes.

Note: Some of the following directions below use `scconf` command variations. These commands should be run on all nodes in the cluster, including old nodes and any new nodes to be added to the cluster.

When adding a new node to the cluster, the installation should be performed on the new node using the `scinstall` program. When this program is run on the new node, the requested information about the existing nodes should reflect the existing nodes' current configuration. The information requested for the new node should match the desired end state of the cluster (regardless of the answers provided during the initial cluster installation). Because the cluster does not permit a node to join if there is an inconsistency between its configuration files and the configuration files of the remaining nodes, a problem is relatively easy to spot (although not necessarily easy to diagnose).

Cluster configurations on the original cluster nodes will not contain the same configuration information as the new nodes (their configuration information will not include the new node). To synchronize configurations, it is necessary to perform additional administrative tasks.

As previously discussed, it is unlikely that the correct Ethernet address of the new node will match the Ethernet address configured during the initial installation.

The Ethernet address of the node can be changed using the following command:

```
# scconf clustname -N nodenum Ethernet_address
```

Where *`clustname`* is the name of the cluster, *`nodenum`* is the node number of the node to change the Ethernet address of, and *`Ethernet_address`* is the Ethernet address of the node. The node number can be obtained using the `get_node_status` command.

After the previous command has executed, the quorum devices should be updated to failure fence the new node. This is performed using the `scconf -q` command on all cluster nodes for each possible quorum device combination, see section, "Changing the Quorum Device" on page 179.

After the process is complete, confirm the quorum configuration using the `scconf -p` command to list serial numbers and the `find_devices` command to map serial numbers to controller instances.

Note: It is essential to configure quorum devices correctly because they are a fundamental component of the failure fencing architecture. The configuration should be confirmed after any quorum device change.

After the configuration has been performed, the new node(s) can be added to the cluster using the `scconf -A` command to modify the number of permitted nodes. The argument is the new number of nodes in the cluster. Nodes can only be added to the cluster in node ID order; a cluster with three nodes can only contain node IDs 0, 1, and 2 (ID 3 is not permitted—node ID 3 can only be used in a four-node cluster).

For example, the following command configures the first three nodes so they can join the cluster—if there were a fourth potential node, it would not be able to join:

```
# scconf clustername -A 3
```

Note: A node is also able to be removed using the `scconf -A` command; however, the nodes with the highest node numbers will always be removed from the cluster first.

Another important component of failure fencing is the terminal concentrator. The terminal concentrator (or SSP with Sun Enterprise 10000) should be configured on each node using the `scconf -t` and `scconf -H` commands, see section, "Changing Terminal Concentrator/SSP Connectivity" on page 178. Using these commands will only be necessary if the terminal concentrator was configured incorrectly during the initial installation. In many situations, it will be necessary to change which terminal concentrator port the new node is connected to.

The configuration of the private interconnects may need to be updated as well. This is discussed in section, "Changing Private Network Configuration (for Ethernet)," on page 173. Configurations that use SCI require additional configuration input, see the *Sun Cluster 2.2 System Administration Guide*. Additionally, some other changes may need to be made; for example, setting up the cluster to use direct-attached disks and node lock ports—see the *Sun Cluster 2.2 Administration Guide*.

If the old configuration used a shared CCD, the shared CCD should be removed (a shared CCD can only be used with two node clusters). The procedure for removing a shared CCD was discussed, see the *Sun Cluster 2.2 Administration Guide."*

Recall that appropriate `hostname.if` files should be created for the new node to use its public network, see section, "Setting Up PNM," on page 152. Additionally, all nodes should have the new physical hostnames added to their `/etc/hosts` files. After this is performed, the new node should be rebooted. The `pnmset` command can then be run to set up the necessary public network interfaces.

The *Sun Cluster 2.2 Administration Guide* directs an administrator to use FTP to copy an existing CDB file to a new node. In most cases, this will be unnecessary if the `scinstall` and any subsequent configuration was performed correctly. Because the CDB of any node joining a cluster will be verified with the CDBs of existing cluster nodes, any problems will be discovered when the cluster starts. Regardless of whether FTP is used or not, identical copies of the CDB must exist to enable the new node to join.

Because all cluster nodes should be updated to the same configuration (in the previous steps), the CDBs should be identical, even without having to FTP them. If the CDBs are not copied to the new node, problems are easily detected because the CDB identifies any differences.

The cluster can now be restarted. Because the new node has the highest probability of being misconfigured, it should be started last to ensure the correct databases on the old nodes provide a consistency check.

Summary

This chapter described administrative tools and the essential tasks of cluster administration and maintenance. It dealt with information gathering for cluster setup, administering a cluster, and how to perform cluster hardware topology changes.

Monitoring a cluster is an important task for cluster maintenance. This function can be performed using log monitors, cluster logs, and the monitoring commands. Monitoring is especially critical when a cluster is running, see section, "Monitoring Sun Cluster Status and Configuration," on page 113.

Starting or stopping a cluster requires the use of the `scadmin` command. This command is used to start nodes, stop nodes, and to solve problems with cluster partitions, see section, "Cluster Membership Administration," on page 121.

Managing the cluster configuration databases is an important element of cluster management. There are three processes required to successfully manage cluster configuration databases:

- Perform and document all cluster changes correctly (change control)
- Back up the databases/confirm database consistency
- Two-node clusters should use a shared CCD

For information on these processes, see section, "Managing Cluster Configuration Changes" on page 137.

The most important time to be aware of cluster configuration database issues is during a cluster change. The section, "Cluster Topology and Hardware Changes," on page 170, describes how to change the cluster configuration.

CHAPTER 5

Highly Available Databases

Relational database systems make up the majority of information systems (IS) applications and have become the preferred method of data storage for various applications, including e-commerce, decision support systems (DSS), online transaction processing (OLTP), and management information systems (MIS). An unavailable database generally has a negative impact on business revenue—this problem can be alleviated by having the database highly available in a clustered environment.

High Availability for Business

High availability (HA) means different things to different people. For a database system, high availability can be viewed from two different perspectives: business and technical. We have already discussed the attributes of HA from a technical perspective; however, from a business perspective, database HA can be viewed as a strategy to minimize loss of revenue.

The purpose of HA is to reduce lost revenue due to system failures; however, any resulting loss of revenue from a system outage must be higher than the associated costs of hardware and software required to implement high availability.

The potential loss of revenue can be derived by performing an analysis on a business unit to determine the dollar amount generated per unit of time. After the dollar amount is calculated, it is straightforward to determine how much revenue could be lost due to a system failure.

Because of its large installed user base, the Oracle Relational Database Management System (RDBMS) will be used in this chapter as the example database when discussing parallel and highly available databases. For other database systems, the reader should refer to the Sun Cluster 2.2 (SC2.2) documentation.

To enable high availability for applications, SC2.2 software supplies fault probes for some of the most popular databases available today: Oracle, Sybase, and Informix. See Table 5-1 for a list of currently supported database versions for which Sun Microsystems provides high availability for. Other database modules are available (for example, IBM DB2 EEE) which are provided by their respective vendors.

Table 5-1 Sun-Supplied Database Agents for High Availability on Sun Cluster 2.2 Software

Vendor	Versions	Parallel Database (Cluster Aware)	OS Version
Oracle	7.3.x, 8.0.x, 8.1.x	Oracle Parallel Server OPS (7.3.4, 8.0.x, 8.1.5)	Solaris 2.6, 2.7 for OPS 2.6
Sybase	11.5.x, 11.9.2	None available	Solaris 2.6, 2.7
Informix	7.3.x	Informix XMP 8.2.1	Solaris 2.6, 2.7

Parallel Databases

Although SC2.2 software is capable of running parallel databases (PDBs), the subject is only discussed briefly here. PDB functionality within the SC2.2 software provides database vendors a computing platform which enables all nodes within the cluster to act as a single system—thereby offering scalability and high availability. Vendors currently using SC2.2 software with PDB functionality are: Oracle (Oracle Parallel Server), Informix (XMP), and IBM (DB2 EEE).

Although the underlying SC2.2 software for PDB uses the same hardware and software as an HA solution, PDBs use a fundamentally different approach to system redundancy and concurrency.

The basic goal of a clustered database is to use multiple servers with a single data store. One approach is called *shared nothing*—this is used by Informix XPS and IBM DB2/EEE. Each node within the shared nothing cluster only has access to its own array. If data on another array is required, it must be accessed through the node that owns the storage; the data is transported between nodes via the interconnect.

The benefit of a shared nothing database system is its excellent application scalability (for specific classes of workload); for example, where there is little data sharing—as with OLTP workloads and large reporting-centric decision support applications. A noticeable characteristic of these application workloads is that data access is predictable and highly controlled.

Note: Distribution of data across the interconnects may present scaling liabilities.

By contrast, Oracle Parallel Server (OPS) software uses shared disk topology—that is, every node within the cluster has access to the same set of disks (with a single shared data store). Unlike the shared nothing approach, shared disk databases access data directly from storage; therefore, data transport speed is only constrained by the disk I/O system (not the interconnect). This approach is extremely flexible and enables the interconnect to be used to communicate instance locking activities between nodes.

The shared disk environment offers excellent robustness, and because each server connects directly to the shared disks, administration becomes easier. However, performance could become vulnerable because excessive lock contention could significantly slow a system.

The best means of scalability (availability notwithstanding) may not be by clustering additional servers through Oracle Parallel Servers. The simplest way to solve a scaling problem is by upgrading CPUs, I/O, and memory on the same server. The Sun Enterprise Server line makes this process straightforward because a single-architecture (SPARC/Solaris) server scales from 1 CPU to 64 CPUs (Enterprise 10000 server).

System capacity may be increased by adding a new server; however, creating a larger single instance does not guarantee improved availability. Moreover, beyond machines with 64 CPUs, clustering is the only option for increased scalability.

Note: At the time of this writing, there are few commercial workloads that can keep so large a population of CPUs continually busy within a single database instance.

Parallel Databases Using Sun Cluster 2.2 Software

The following diagram illustrates a typical two-node Oracle OPS cluster using SC2.2 software. Each node in the cluster runs its own Oracle instance (illustrated as ORA-A and ORA-B). Each instance has simultaneous access to the same data store—that is, both ORA-A and ORA-B can read and write to the database as required.

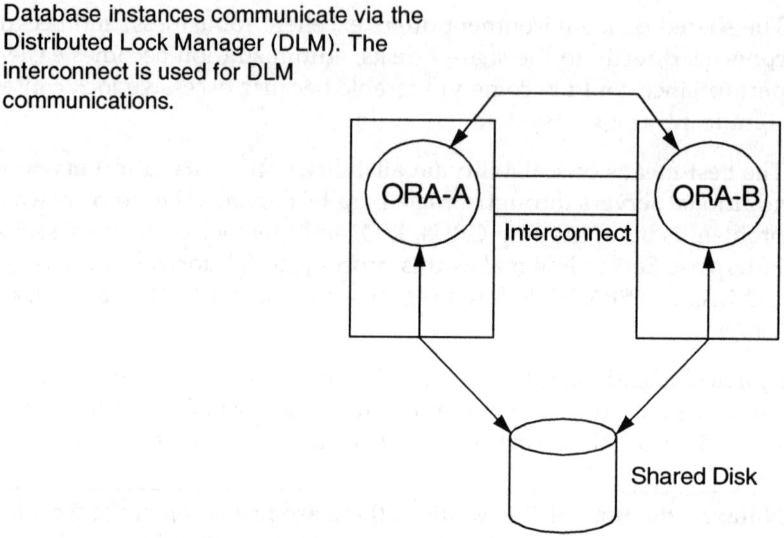
Database instances communicate via the Distributed Lock Manager (DLM). The interconnect is used for DLM communications.
ORA-A
ORA-B
Interconnect
Shared Disk

Figure 5-1 Typical Two-Node Oracle OPS Cluster Using Sun Cluster 2.2 Software

Configuring SC2.2 software for OPS uses a different setup procedure than that of HA-Oracle. HA-Oracle and OPS also differ in their use of volume managers and configuration of the cluster software (given the shared disk architecture of the OPS system).

The Sun Enterprise™ Volume Manager (SEVM) controls storage devices such as disk arrays, which adds the capabilities of disk mirroring and striping. After the disks are controlled by the volume manager, they are grouped together in diskgroups. Diskgroups are extremely flexible, and can be assigned to one or multiple servers.

Disks within diskgroups are created into logical partitions called volumes. These volumes can be parts of stripes or mirrors and have the flexibility to be raw devices or file system-based volumes. Applications access data by means of volumes—because volumes are logical units, they offer excellent flexibility for I/O layouts, disk, and recovery management.

SC2.2 software includes a Cluster Volume Manager™ (CVM). The CVM is similar to the SEVM product but has the added benefit of enabling diskgroups to be imported by more than one host. It is within these shared diskgroups that volumes are created for data. Additionally, these volumes (as shared devices) must be accessed by the database as a raw device because OPS does not currently support file system-based volumes. This is an important consideration if making a choice between OPS or HA-Oracle.

Each Oracle instance is able to perform database functions (read, write, update, and if necessary, recover) within the OPS environment (because each instance has its own rollback segments and online redo logs). This makes instance recovery possible without affecting the overall cluster. Nodes share control files, data dictionary, and tablespaces for data.

For example, if instance A needs to roll back a transaction, it will not affect transactions processed by instance B.

Because data processing is managed across multiple Oracle instances, a significant challenge for Oracle OPS software is cache coherency. Oracle OPS uses a distributed lock manager (DLM) to manage caches and presents a single system image (SSI) within a clustered environment. The DLM controls logical resources, but does not control access to tables or specific objects within the database—instead, any database activity that requires shared resources is managed by the DLM.

Oracle uses a variety of lock types (row locks, transaction locks, enqueues, and latches); however, the DLM manages what are known as instance locks or distributed locks. Instance locks come in two varieties: parallel cache management (PCM) locks and non-parallel cache management (non-PCM) locks.

The main function of PCM locks is to protect data file blocks. After a row-level lock has been acquired, it will not be released until a commit or roll back operation is performed. Transaction-level locks only affect the instance that issues the lock, and have no effect on other instances. PCM locks and transaction locks are autonomous.

Transaction congruencies (which require row-level locks) are not dependent on PCM locks. In contrast, non-PCM locks provide locking mechanisms for different types of access to resources, and to perform various types of communications functions between instances. The following list describes how the lock management process functions when a single instance needs resources:

1. Node A gets data from the database and brings it into its system global area (SGA).

2. Depending on the request type for the data (update, read, or write), Oracle will allocate the appropriate lock on all blocks that correspond to the data.

3. Work is performed against the data.

4. The lock is changed to reflect current read/write policy.

5. When data is written back to the disk, the lock is released.

In a situation where two instances require access to the same blocks, the DLM will coordinate access. For example, if instance A requests data for a read, the DLM would mark that block with a lock and enable other instances to read the block (only). However, if another instance acquires the block and updates it, all other instances would have to flush their data block(s) and re-read the data block with the new lock values. Although the DLM algorithms work well to protect data, they can be detrimental to performance.

Here lies the main challenge in taking advantage of OPS. Constant updating and flushing of cache buffers can take a significant toll on performance. High lock activity will cause each instance to use additional CPU cycles when maintaining DLM locks.

A comprehensive understanding of the application is required to effectively determine if it is a potential candidate for OPS, and to choose a locking strategy best suited to the application.

Parallel Database/Highly Available Database Comparison

Whether HA-Oracle has an advantage over an OPS configuration depends on several factors:

- How fast does the system need to recover in the event of failure? For example, is up to 20 minutes acceptable for recovery time in a failover situation? — or does the business impact of downtime warrant the instantaneous availability of a standby system?
- Is long-term scalability a real issue? Is the database size or user population growing at a linear rate every 6 to 12 months? If the application is suitable for partitioning with OPS, it can enable significant incremental scalability and/or speed up.

Are there business or operational factors that dictate a specific configuration? For example, if the system cannot or will not use raw devices, or if an application has to use file system-based tablespaces, OPS would not currently be a viable option because OPS requires the use of raw devices for volumes. Therefore, using SC2.2 software for high availability would restrict the choice to HA-Oracle.

Failover Latency

The amount of time a system is unavailable during a recovery process—the failover latency—is the basic difference between a standard Oracle database and an OPS configuration. With OPS, each node has access to the same database; therefore, there is no requirement to start a second database if a failover occurs.

SC2.2 software configured with OPS does not fail over. Although HA-Oracle has no special handicaps in recovery time, the speed is dependant on many factors, some fixed and others variable.

For parameters that have a fixed recovery time—for example, the time required to start an Oracle instance, allocate memory, check, mounting, and open the database if fixed—the process cannot be tuned to go faster than the underlying hardware. Table 5-2 lists functions in which the recovery time can be modified to achieve finer-grained control.

Table 5-2 Factors Affecting Failover Time

Factor	Impact	Function of
File system check consumes time	VARIABLE	Journal logging can reduce this time. Use raw devices for data.
Resynchronization time for disks	VARIABLE	Use dirty region to log on volumes.
I/O throughput	VARIABLE	Use smaller disks. Add controllers. Stripe data across disks and controllers.
Database performance	VARIABLE	System memory, database block buffers, database block size, and many other performance-related parameters.
Time taken to start database instance	FIXED	Use faster disks or CPUs.
Time taken to start all database instances in a symmetric configuration	VARIABLE	Reduce number of logical hosts.
Failure detection time	FIXED	Data service layer.
Database recovery	VARIABLE	Reduce Oracle checkpoint intervals. Use the parallel recovery option in Oracle 8.1.x (8i).

Failover times vary widely due to system and workload characteristics. Technical implications are secondary and any business choices made should be driven by cost benefit analysis. For example, increasing checkpoint frequency causes Oracle to flush data from redo logs to disks faster (but decreases transaction throughput). This decrease in throughput could make the difference between a system that delivers application-level requirements and one that does not. Therefore, understanding exactly what factors you have control over is an important consideration when determining uptime and recovery time.

A second major difference between the two approaches is in scalability. HA-Oracle (in itself) offers no added benefits of scalability other than that provided by the hardware platform it is running on. Therefore, if a database appears to be growing at a rate that will surpass the existing level of servers being used, implementing an HA-Oracle environment would not help with respect to scalability or speed up. Therefore, it is crucial to understand what your current and future requirements are.

Configuration Issues

This section discusses configuration of the Sun Cluster framework and HA-Oracle or OPS. Table 5-3 lists the differences between HA-Oracle and OPS:

Table 5-3 HA-Oracle/OPS Differences

ISSUE	HA-Oracle	Oracle Parallel Server (OPS)
Data storage	Choice of file system or raw devices. Compatible with SDS and VxVM.	Raw devices only. Cannot use file system-based tablespaces. Must use CVM.
Management issues	Cluster and Oracle DBA issues.	Complex Oracle DBA issues with respect to DLM locking and application partitioning.
Disk	More disks are required when multiple logical hosts are used.	No more disks required than normally used for standard Oracle instance (unless multiple instances are used).
Failover latency	Could be high. Highly dependent on configuration.	Failover latency is much lower than HA-Oracle (subject to workload dependencies).
Packaged applications	Any Oracle database can be created or used, including, SAP, ERP, and Financials.	Any Oracle database except SAP and Financials. Database(s) may have to be redesigned to take full advantage of OPS.
Enterprise 10000 domains	No issues. No support for IDN, AP/DR.	No issues. No support for IDN, AP/DR.
System resources	No issues outside of standard OS, database, or cluster requirements.	Uses slightly more memory resources due to DLM activity.

Highly Available Databases

The basic premise of database high availability is to ensure that any designated database instances will be available for use in the event of hardware or software failure. Although the SC2.2 framework controls monitoring of the hardware and operating system, application software monitoring is performed by means of a data service agent.

The primary function of a data service agent is to log into the database system, query the internal structure, and determine if the database is functioning correctly. If the probe determines that the database is functioning correctly, no further action is taken. This process is repeated N times per time interval. If the agent determines no useful work is being performed, it will query the database again, analyze the response, and again determine if the situation is normal.

Each data service agent has one or more software probes. Sun Microsystems database data service modules feature a command line interface configurator, which is used to configure database instances for monitoring (and perform system administration tasks). Each configurator has two (configuration) files associated with it.

Configuration files are distinguished by the `ha` prefix, followed by the database vendor name, for example, `ha-oracle`.

These configuration files (discussed later) instruct the SC2.2 framework as to which database version can be monitored. The `ha_config_V1` file specifies database error codes the fault monitor may encounter (and the appropriate action to take for each error condition). The configurator application is used to update the cluster configuration database (CCD) on a per instance basis. The configurator application is used for adding, deleting, and modifying database entries, starting and stopping the fault probe, and acquiring the current status of all database instances.

Minimum Configurations for Highly Available Databases

Configuring a database for high availability is a time-consuming but straightforward process. Different cluster topologies require setup procedures in relation to the following components:

- Volume managers
- Disk stripes
- Disk layout
- Database binary placement
- File systems, or raw device database storage

There are additional considerations when configuring a database to be a highly available with the SC2.2 software, such as:

- Operating system version
- Hardware requirements (a minimum of two supported servers, an administrative workstation, and a terminal concentrator)
- Boot disk mirroring (recommended)
- Shared storage allocation
- Data service agent configuration
- Database software version

Cluster Configuration Issues Prior to Installation

Consider the following:

- Type of HA configuration: symmetric or asymmetric
- Number of database instances per node
- Number of logical hosts per node
- Type of volume manager: Solstice DiskSuite (SDS), Veritas Volume Manager (VxVM), or Cluster Volume Manager (CVM)

Note: The CVM product is required for shared disk database architectures such as OPS.

- Disk striping and layout

- Number of public networks required (and redundancy level)
- Client failover strategy (not supported by SC2.2 software)
- Logical host failover method after node recovery (automatic or manual)

Note: Manual failover of a logical host after node recovery is recommended (to avoid unscheduled downtime).

- Shared or non-shared CCD for two-node cluster
- Clusters with greater than two nodes should use a deterministic policy or node ID to determine valid cluster in the event of cluster partitioning
- Naming convention for cluster, host identification, disk label, volume, logical host, disk groups, meta sets, mount points, etc.
- Backup and recovery procedures

Database Software Package Placement

When using SC2.2 software, database software can be installed in either of two locations:

- Logical host(s)
- Local disk node

The advantage of installing the software package on the logical host becomes evident when upgrading or applying software fixes to the database. Only one set of programs per logical host needs to be upgraded. However, if the programs reside on a local disk, database upgrades or software fixes have to be performed on each node in the cluster. The cluster configuration should determine where to install database programs. If the cluster configuration is asymmetric with only one logical host, locating the database programs on the logical host has its advantages—upgrades can be applied to the entire cluster. However, if more than one logical host is to be serviced by the same set of programs (or the cluster configuration is symmetric), locating database programs on the logical host is not recommended for the following reason: If the migration of a logical host is required because of a failover scenario or manual intervention, the database programs will migrate with the logical host; therefore, other database instances that were started with those programs will not be able to use them again (because they moved with the logical host).

This situation leaves an administrator (and clients) without tools to access the database to start or stop database instances (and other database processes).

The following illustrations demonstrate advantages and disadvantages of asymmetric and symmetric cluster configurations.

In following diagram (Figure 5-2), data and database programs reside on the logical host. Only one database instance resides on node A. Node B is always ready to take over the logical host (standby mode).

The database programs reside on the logical host; therefore, they migrate with the logical host—ensuring database programs are available in the event of a logical host failover.

A symmetric configuration can be the most expensive to implement because of the cost of the additional hardware; however, it is easier to administer and configure. This type of configuration offers the best *potential* performance characteristics—this is because the master node can be tuned specifically for one or more database instances.

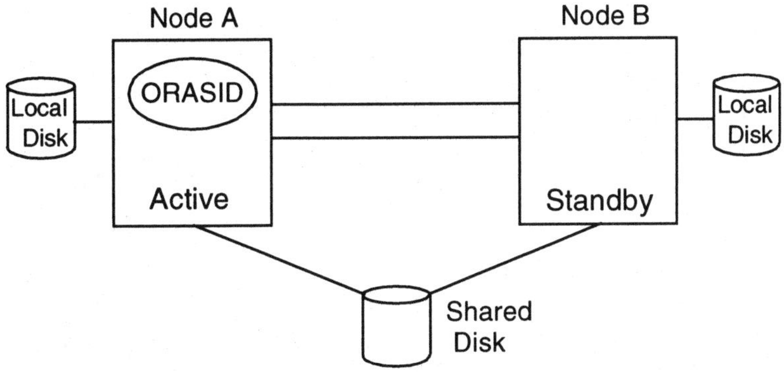


```
/logicalhost/u01/orahome/bin (Oracle RDBMS programs)
/logicalhost/u02/data1
/logicalhost/u03/data2
```

Figure 5-2 Asymmetric Configuration with Database Programs on a Logical Host

In this configuration, the data and database programs reside on the logical host. There is only one database instance residing on node A. Node B is always on standby—waiting to take over the logical host. Because database programs reside on the logical host, they always migrate with the logical host, thereby ensuring the database programs are available in the advent of a logical host failover.

An asymmetric configuration offers the best potential performance characteristics because the master node can be tuned specifically for one or more database instances.

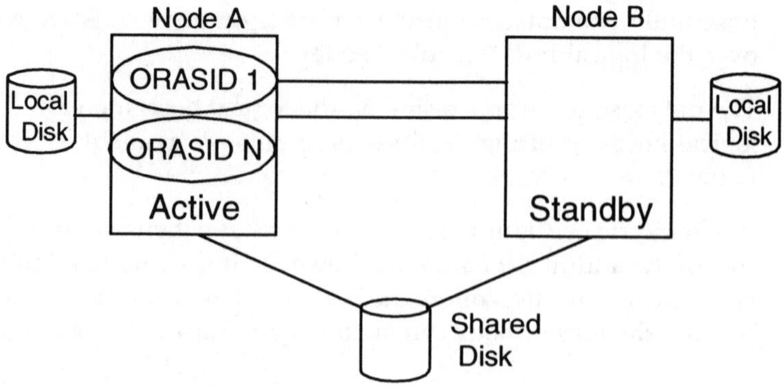

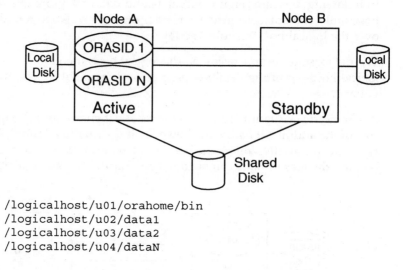

```
/logicalhost/u01/orahome/bin
/logicalhost/u02/data1
/logicalhost/u03/data2
/logicalhost/u04/dataN
```

Figure 5-3 Asymmetric Configuration with Database Programs on a Logical Host (multiple database instances)

The configuration illustrated in Figure 5-3 is physically identical to Figure 5-2 with the exception of multiple database instances running on node A. If node A had a physical failure, all instances would migrate to node B (along with the logical host). However, a problem could arise with a logical failure of a database which is not physical.

For example, assume ORASID 1 had a problem that froze the database. If after an unsuccessful attempt to correct the situation, the cluster framework determined it should send the logical host over to node B—the switch over would be performed. However, if an instance ORASID N was still active on node A, and because ORASID N is bound to the logical host, it must also fail over (even though there was no problem with the instance). All uncommitted transactions on ORASID N would be lost and clients would have to reconnect to ORASID N after the failover was completed.

A logical host could be created for each database instance. In this situation, ORASID 1 would switch over without affecting ORASID N; however, because the software is on the first logical host, ORASID N would not have access to those binaries. If ORASID N had to be stopped, an administrator would not be able to do so because the Oracle software would only be accessible to node B.

The way to ensure each instance is unaffected by any other instances (in the event of a logical host migration) is to assign an instance to its own logical host and place the database binaries on the node of each local disk. Then, a problem arose (physical or logical), only the logical hosts required to be migrated would do so (without affecting other instances).

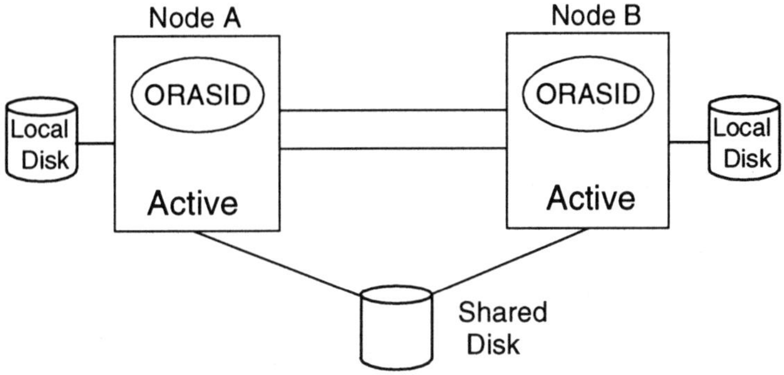

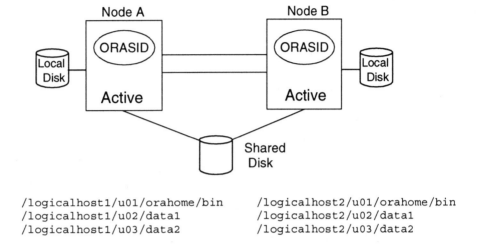

```
/logicalhost1/u01/orahome/bin        /logicalhost2/u01/orahome/bin
/logicalhost1/u02/data1              /logicalhost2/u02/data1
/logicalhost1/u03/data2              /logicalhost2/u03/data2
```

Figure 5-4 Symmetric Configuration with Database Software on the Logical Host

The configuration in Figure 5-4 shows that each node is hosting one instance bound to one logical host—in this situation, having the binaries on the logical hosts is acceptable. One copy of the database binaries will not be sufficient because a logical host can only be mastered by one node at a time. In this configuration, putting binaries on the logical or local disk would not make a difference.

When using multiple logical hosts in a symmetric configuration (Figure 5-5), one set of shared binaries per logical host only works for a physical failover (similar to the asymmetric configuration). For logical failures or maintenance functions, the database software has to be placed on the node's local disk to ensure the software is available for all instances residing on the node.

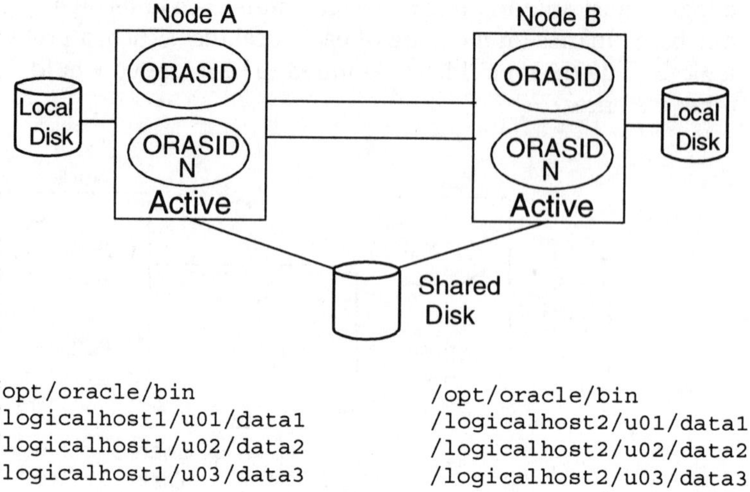

Figure 5-5 Symmetric Configuration with Database Software on Local Disks

Table 5-4 is a quick reference for database software placement:

Table 5-4 Database Software Placement

HA Mode	1 Logical Host, 1 DB Instance	1 Logical Host, Multiple DB Instances	Multiple Logical Hosts, Multiple Instances
Asymmetric	Logical Host	Local Disk	Local Disk
Symmetric	Logical Host	Local Disk	Local Disk

Configuring Highly Available Databases

Prior to configuring a database for high availability, the cluster software should be installed and configured for the appropriate topology. At some point during the installation process, the user is required to choose which data services should be installed. Oracle, Sybase, and Informix data service agents are supplied with the Sun Cluster 2.2 CD-ROM. For other database products (not on the CD-ROM), contact the database vendor.

Installation of the data service can be confirmed using the UNIX `pkginfo -l SUNWscora` command, or by viewing the data service directory structure in Table 5-5:

Table 5-5 Support File Location

Vendor	Directory	Support Files
Oracle	/etc/opt/SUNWscora	haoracle_support,haoracle_config_V1
Sybase	/etc/opt/SUWscsyb	hasybase_support,hasybase_config_V1
Informix	/etc/opt/SUNWscinf	hainformix_support,hainformix_config_V1

Note: Data service modules are sold separately. Ensure any required modules have been acquired and licensed.

The support file indicates to the cluster framework which versions of the vendor product are supported. In the following example, the file `/etc/opt/SUNWsor/haoracle_support` indicates only Oracle versions 7.3.x and 8.0.x are supported—no other version will work correctly. This file should be queried to ensure the database version to be made highly available is supported.

```
# @(#)haoracle_support 1.9 96/08/16 SMI
#
# Copyright 08/16/96 Sun Microsystems, Inc. All Rights Reserved.
#
# List of supported Oracle version for HA Oracle
7.3.[2-9]*     haoracle_fmon   haoracle_config_V1
8.0.*         haoracle_fmon   haoracle_config_V1
```

Note: Currently, only Oracle 8.1.x (8i) is supported in an HA configuration using Solaris 2.6 and 2.7 on SC2.2 software.

In the following boxes, the asterisk represents a wildcard character; therefore, 11.5* indicates Sybase version 11.5 and higher is supported. Likewise, versions of Oracle within the 7.3.x range are supported, i.e., 7.3.2.3.

The following box shows the contents of the hasybase_support file:

```
#ident "@(#)hasybase_support   1.5      96/08/16 SMI"
#
# Copyright 08/16/96 Sun Microsystems, Inc. All Rights Reserved.
#
# List of supported Sybase version for HA Sybase
11.0.[1-9]*     hasybase_fmon    hasybase_config_V1
11.5*           hasybase_fmon    hasybase_config_V1
```

The following codebox shows the contents of the hinformix_support file:

```
#ident "@(#)hainformix_support   1.3      96/08/16 SMI"
#
# Copyright 08/16/96 Sun Microsystems, Inc. All Rights Reserved.
#
# List of supported Informix version for HA Informix
7.[23][0-9].*   hainformix_fmon hainformix_config_V1
```

The support file is ASCII-based, making it easy to view and edit. It is strongly advised that you not edit this file to add a database version that does not exist.

Support files change from release to release and sometimes between patch level upgrades. Modifying a support file could cause the database agent to monitor the database incorrectly.

The database probe checks the support and configuration files during cluster startup (and during the probe cycle sequence). Database error conditions may change between patch level revisions; therefore, an error condition could be encountered without an appropriate action for the probe to take—potentially leaving the database probe in a unknown state.

The support file should be verified each time a software or patch level upgrade is applied to the cluster.

Caution: After the database version has been confirmed and the issue of binary placement has been addressed, creation of the logical host can begin. Due to its inherent complexity, configuring clusters is a time-consuming process that can be error-prone. Use the following checklist as a guide.

Items to be completed prior to creating the logical host:

- Hardware is installed and working according to specifications
- Cluster nodes have identical OS software and patches
- Cluster software is installed and configured for the appropriate topology
- The database data service module is installed with the correct database version to make it highly available

Where to locate database software was discussed in a previous section.

Database software placement is dependent on the cluster configuration. If the programs are to be placed on a local disk(s), it is recommended that a separate disk be used for the binaries and boot disk—also, they should be mirrored to enhance availability.

If the programs are to be placed on the logical host, the logical host must be created and configured prior to binary installation (see following section).

Creating Logical Hosts

In this example, the hardware configuration is a two-node cluster. Oracle is used as the database vendor with the binaries placed on the node of each local disk. Only database data will reside on the logical host.

Create the volume manager diskgroups or Solstice disk sets for the logical hosts and populate them with the required disks.

Note: When using a volume manager (SEVM, CVM, or VxVM), you cannot create diskgroups without a `root dg`. Likewise, with SDS, you cannot create meta sets without database replicas, see Chapter 4, "Sun Cluster 2.2 Administration."

A good practice to follow for data placement on logical hosts is to ensure all nodes within the cluster can see each array (with identical controller numbers). This helps ensure consistency when using storage for data placement.

For example, each node might have an array controller configured as `c5txdx`, with `c6txdx` configured on the other node. Data should only reside on disk array `c5` and be mirrored to `c6`. Using this standard helps ensure each disk on array `c5` is mirrored to each disk on array `c6`.

This practice makes administration easier and can speed disk replacement. For additional details, see Chapter 4, "Sun Cluster 2.2 Administration."

After the diskgroup (or disk set) has been set up and populated with disks to service the logical host, start the cluster software (on any node) — it makes no difference which node starts the cluster; however, it must be *only one*, see Chapter 4, "Sun Cluster 2.2 Administration."

After the cluster software finishes loading, join node B to the cluster using the following command:

```
clnode1> scadmin startnode
```

Verify cluster membership by running the following command on each node:

```
clnode0> scconf solarflare -p
Checking node status...
Current Configuration for Cluster solarflare
Hosts in cluster: clnode0 clnode1 <---- Note both nodes are members of the
cluster.
Private Network Interfaces for:
    clnode0: qe0 qe1
    clnode1: qe0 qe1
Quorum Device Information
Quorum device for hosts clnode0 and clnode1: 00000078C059.KHXL
Logical Host Timeout Value:
Step10:720
Step11:720
Logical Host:180
```

Edit the /etc/hosts file and define a name and IP address for the logical host. Next, create the logical host(s) necessary for the number of instances requiring HA services.

The following box contains the general syntax for creating a logical host(s):

```
scconf clustername -L <logical-host> -n <nodelist> -g <dglist> -i <iplist> [-m]
```

Logical Host Syntax

The syntax for creating a logical host(s) is as follows:

```
scconf solarflare -L lhost1 -n clnode0,clnode1 -g oradg -i hme0,hme0,lhost1 -m
```

Where:

`scconf` is the binary used to create or modify cluster configuration.

`solarflare` is the name of the cluster.

`-L` is the logical host (in this case, `lhost1`).

`-n` is a list of nodes that monitor the logical host (`clnode0` is the default master).

`-g` is the diskgroup associated with the logical host (in this case, `oradg`).

`-i` is a list of the network interfaces that will be used to service the logical IP address (in this case, `hme0` for both nodes).

`-m` is the automatic failback switch (in this case, automatic failback has been disabled).

The previous syntax creates a logical host called `lhost1` with `clnode0` being the default master, with a diskgroup called `oradg` assigned to it. The public network interface that services the logical IP address is `hme0` for both nodes.

Note: Creation of the logical host should be performed on one node only.

Using the `-m` argument will ensure the logical host does not automatically migrate back to the master node in the event of a failure. If the `-m` option is not used, the logical host automatically switches back to `clnode0` as soon as `clnode0` rejoins the cluster. For database systems, this is not normally a desirable action because most connections to database systems are not stateless. Therefore, if the application or database does not handle client connectivity, a logical host switch will cause the database to lose uncommitted transactions—any connected clients would need to re-establish their connections.

If transaction and session information is handled by a separate transaction processing monitor (TPM), excluding the -m option would be a desirable option because the TPM can be configured to handle client connection and transaction processing, thereby ensuring that transactions or sessions are not lost in a logical host switch. The cluster framework provides flexibility to configure a logical host for automatic or manual migration (to and from the master node).

The scconf command updates the CCD—this will enable all nodes within the cluster to know of the logical host's existence. After the logical host has been configured, the master node will take control of the disks and master the logical host.

Running the scconf command with the -p option will display logical host configuration as shown in the following box:

```
clnode0> scconf solarflare -p
Checking node status...
Current Configuration for Cluster solarflare
    Hosts in cluster: clnode0 clnode1
Private Network Interfaces for:
    clnode0: qe0 qe1
    clnode1: qe0 qe1
Quorum Device Information
Quorum device for hosts clnode0 and clnode1: 00000078C059.KHXL
Logical Host Timeout Value:
    Step10: 720
    Step11: 720
    Logical Host: 180
Logical Host: lhost1 <---- Definition of logical host
Node List: clnode0 clnode1 <---- clnode0 is the defined master of lhost1
Disk Groups: oradg
Logical Address: lhost1
Logical Interface: 1
Network Interface: hme0 (clnode0) hme0 (clnode1) Interfaces for logical host.
Automatic Switchover: no <---- M option used, fail back to master is not automatic
```

HA Status Volumes

After creating the logical host, the HA status (`hastat`) volumes should be created. The purpose of the `hastat` volume is to track the logical host.

Depending on the type of data service, the `hastat` volume could play a major role in the cluster, see Chapter 4, "Sun Cluster 2.2 Administration."

For database systems, the HA status volume tracks which node is the master and which node(s) is monitoring the logical host.

The syntax for creating the `hastat` volume is as follows:

```
scconf solarflare -F oradg
```

Note: After creating the `hastat` volume, ensure a corresponding mirror exists on a different array.

The first time the `scconf -F` command is invoked, it creates the `hastat` volume and a corresponding mirror in the `oradg` diskgroup (also a mount point for the logical host). In addition to creating the `hastat` volume, the `-F` option creates two other important files:

- `/etc/opt/SUNWcluster/conf/hanfs/vfstab.lhost1`
- `/etc/opt/SUNWcluster/conf/hanfs/dfstab.lhost1`

The `scconf solarflare -F oradg` command must be executed on *at least* one node; however, it is useful to run the command on every node monitoring the logical host—this ensures all slave nodes have the above files and a logical host mount point.

If the command is not run on each node, the files have to be manually copied to each node and the logical host mount points created.

In the previous example, the logical host is servicing a database; therefore, the `dfstab.logicalhost` file is not necessary and can be deleted. The `vfstab.logicalhost` file holds information necessary for mounting the volumes or meta devices for the database.

The semantics of the two files is similar to the `vfstab` file found in the UNIX `/etc` directory. Although these files look and work similarly, there are differences. The main difference is that mount points are not automatically mounted any time during or after the boot phase. Mounting is performed by means of the cluster framework (exclusively).

When viewing the contents of the vfstab.lhost1 file, the first entry is the mount point for the hastat volume. This line is important and must always be listed first; any subsequent mount points must follow the hastat volume entry, see Chapter 4, "Sun Cluster 2.2 Administration."

A typical vfstab.lhost1 file looks as follows:

```
/dev/vx/dsk/oradg/oradg-stat /dev/vx/rdsk/oradg/oradg-stat /lhost1 ufs 1 no -
```

Setting Up the Logical Host Mount Point

The ha-status volume must be the first mount point for SC2.2 software regardless of the data service being used—therefore, a directory used by the ha-status volume is required for mounting. The mount point should be created on the node for each local disk. After the ha-status volume is mounted, all subsequent mount points listed in the vfstab.logical host file will be mounted.

It is a good approach to mount all HA volumes under the logical host mount point. Although not technically necessary, it can make administration easier and is less error-prone. The advantage of using this approach is that only one set of mount points needs to be created on the local disk. If the logical host(s) migrates to other nodes, the subsequent mount points will move with it and will be mounted under a single mount point on the node mastering the logical host.

The contents of the following box display an example of a logical host mount point (and other mount points required):

```
/lhost1 <---- Logical Host mount point on each node's root disk
/lhost1/u01
/lhost1/u02
/lhost1/u03 <---- U01,U02,U03 are mounted under the logical host
```

The only system administration consideration is to ensure the logical host(s) mount point exists on the root disk of all nodes monitoring the logical host(s). Creating individual mount points on a local disk can lead to confusion, mistakes, and the potential of accidentally deleting or unmounting required mount points.

After the devices have been configured for data (volumes or meta devices), the vfstab.logical host file should be updated to indicate the required mount points for the logical host. Ensure all nodes configured to run on the logical host have *identical* vfstab.logical hosts files.

The following box displays the contents of a `vfstab.logical` hosts file (configured for Oracle to mount under the logical host mount point):

```
/dev/vx/dsk/oradg/oradg-stat /dev/vx/rdsk/oradg/oradg-stat /lhost1 ufs 1 no -
/dev/vx/dsk/oradg/u01 /dev/vx/rdsk/oradg/u01 /lhost1/u01 ufs 1 no -
/dev/vx/dsk/oradg/u02 /dev/vx/rdsk/oradg/u02 /lhost1/u02 ufs 1 no -
/dev/vx/dsk/oradg/u03 /dev/vx/rdsk/oradg/u03 /lhost1/u03 ufs 1 no -
/dev/vx/dsk/oradg/u04 /dev/vx/rdsk/oradg/u04 /lhost1/u04 ufs 1 no -
```

After all steps for defining a logical host are completed, the logical host should be tested prior to continuing. Use the `scadmin` command to force a switch of the logical host.

To test the logical host, use the following command:

```
clnode0> scadmin switch solarflare clnode1 lhost1
node A releases the logical host
clnode0> Dec 28 11:55:26 clnode0 ID[SUNWcluster.loghost.1010]: Giving up logical
host lhost1
Dec 28 11:55:28 clnode0 ID[SUNWcluster.loghost.1180]: deporting oradg
Dec 28 11:55:29 clnode0 ID[SUNWcluster.loghost.1020]: Give up of logical host
lhost1 succeeded
```

In the previous box, node A gave up the logical host.

In the following box, node B succeeds in mastering the logical host:

```
clnode1>Dec 28 11:56:15 clnode1 ID[SUNWcluster.loghost.1030]: Taking over logical
host lhost1
Dec 28 11:56:15 clnode1 ID[SUNWcluster.loghost.1170]: importing oradg
Dec 28 11:56:24 clnode1 ID[SUNWcluster.loghost.1040]: Take over of logical host
lhost1 succeeded
```

Confirm the logical host mount points to ensure all mount points identified in the `vfstab.logical` host file have been mounted:

```
clnode1> df -lk
/dev/vx/dsk/oradg/oradg-stat
                      1055      12      938     2%    /lhost1
/dev/vx/dsk/oradg/u01
                    191983       9   172776     1%    /lhost1/u01
/dev/vx/dsk/oradg/u02
                    191983       9   172776     1%    /lhost1/u02
/dev/vx/dsk/oradg/u03
                     95983       9    86376     1%    /lhost1/u03
```

Note: The mount points are located under the logical host `ha-status`.

Database Monitoring Setup

After the logical host has been created and tested, install the database software to suit your requirements. If a database is to be created during software installation, ensure the cluster is running and the node receiving the software is mastering the logical host.

Fault probes connect to the database by means of a user-defined ID and password. Each database instance set up for high availability requires a user account and password. The user account will query specific system views, create and drop tables, and insert and query records.

Oracle Database Monitoring

There are three main areas requiring modification to make an Oracle instance highly available using SC2.2 software:

- Fault probe user account setup.
- The host portion of the `LISTENER` file should address the logical host IP address (not the physical IP address).
- Any services listed within the `TNSNAMES.ORA` file required to be highly available should point to the logical host (not the physical host).

Fault Probe Account Setup

Create a tablespace for the database fault probe to use. It is recommended that you create a tablespace on a device that is easy to delete and re-create.

Use the following command to create the fault probe tablespace:

```
create tablespace dbmonitor datafile '/lhost1/u01/dbmonitor'size 10M;
```

This command syntax is a basic `create tablespace` command, which is used to create the tablespace named `dbmonitor` with an associated 10 Mbyte data file.

Note: This example highlights simplicity. Note the lack of other storage parameters which could be associated when creating tablespaces.

If the dbmonitor tablespace becomes fragmented due to heavy use from the fault probe, the tablespace can be administered without first having to stop the database (or taking any key tablespaces offline).

Note: Ensure the user ID set up for database monitoring is performed in a part of the database that can be taken offline without affecting database operations.

The following steps are required to administer the dbmonitor tablespace (if required):

- Stop database monitoring
- Drop the tablespace
- Create the tablespace
- Start database monitoring

Then, create a user ID with a password.

Note: For security reasons, do not use the default Oracle user ID example as used in the *Software Installation Guide*.

When creating a user ID, choose a meaningful name that indicates its function. Within the Oracle software, the fault probe user must have access to the V$SYSSTAT view.

Use the Oracle Server Manager (or equivalent) to create a user ID (assign appropriate permissions). See the following box for an example of creating of a user ID.

Use the following commands (in the Server Manager):

```
create user hamonitor identified by hamonitor default tablespace dbmonitor;
grant connect, resource to hamonitor;
grant select on v_$sysstat to hamonitor;
```

Configuring the LISTENER.ORA File

In the host entry of the LISTENER.ORA file, the *logical host* is referenced instead of the physical host. The logical host is referenced because a listener must run on every node capable of running the Oracle database.

One function of the failover process is to determine if the listener is running on the node; if not, the cluster framework will start the listener automatically.

Configuring the listener.ora file to accept requests for the logical host will ensure the Oracle listener is able to service requests from clients (regardless of which node is hosting the database instances).

The following codebox contains an example of the output from a simplified LISTENER file:

```
LISTENER-ora =
        (ADDRESS_LIST =
            (PROTOCOL = TCP)
            (HOST = lhost1)   <---Logical Host
        (PORT = 1530)))
SID_LIST_LISTENER-ora
    (SID_LIST =
        (SID_DESC =
            (SID_NAME = sunha)))
```

Configuring the TNSNAMES.ORA File

When configuring the TNSNAMES.ORA file, users will require access to the database instance (regardless of where it resides).

The TNSNAMES.ORA file host entry should correspond to the listener file host entries.

The following box shows a sample TNSNAMES.ORA file:

```
solarflare =
    (DESCRIPTION =
        (ADDRESS =
            (PROTOCOL =  TCP)
            (HOST = lhost1)    <----- Logical Host
            (PORT = 1530)))
    (CONNECT_DATA =
        (SID = sunha))
```

In this example, the TNSNAMES.ORA file is used by clients to access an Oracle instance. The remote node also requires a copy of the TNSNAMES.ORA file. The master node connects to the Oracle instance through inter-process communication (IPC), whereas the remote node communicates via SQLNET—therefore, there is a need for a TNSNAMES.ORA file to be included for all nodes monitoring an Oracle logical host, including the master for the logical host.

The default location for this file (unless otherwise specified) is the same location used for the oratab and LISTENER.ORA (/var/opt/oracle) files. The master node requires these files in the /var/opt/oracle directory because it could be the node monitoring the instance(s) that it masters—this could happen during a planned migration or during a failover of all logical hosts.

All options in the oratab file should use the N option for each instance—this ensures the instance will not start automatically.

After the database is installed and the `ora.tab`, `LISTENER.ORA`, and `TNSNAMES.ORA` files are configured, the CCD needs to be informed of the instance(s) required to be monitored. Setting up database instances for monitoring is performed using the SC2.2 `haoracle` binary supplied with the cluster software. This binary updates the CCD as to which database instance require monitoring.

After the Oracle software is installed on each node (and any required logical host is created), the HA-Oracle data service module should be configured and registered.

Registering the data service with the cluster framework is accomplished using the `hareg` command. This command enables the registering, monitoring, and starting/stopping of data service agent monitoring (and other functions).

The following box contains an example of using the `hareg` command:

```
hareg -s -r oracle -h lhost1
```

As discussed in Chapter 4, "Sun Cluster 2.2 Administration," the `-s` option indicates the data service agent is supplied by Sun Microsystems. The `-r` option registers the data service with the SC2.2 framework. The `-h` option indicates the logical hosts.

Switch on the data service module by using the `hareg` command:

```
clnode0> hareg -y oracle
```

In the preceding box, note the use of the lowercase y. Using a lowercase `y` will turn on the Oracle module only—using an uppercase `Y` will turn on *all* data services.

Use the following command to display the data services that are registered and switched on:

```
clnode0> hareg
oracle on
nfs    on

clnode1> hareg
oracle  on
nfs     on
```

After the Oracle module has been registered and switched on, instance monitoring can be set up. The cluster framework will be made aware of which instances require monitoring by using the `haoracle` command.

The following is a list of arguments for the haoracle command:

s = Silent mode option

instance = Name of database instance to monitor (as specified in the /var/opt/oracle file)

insert = Option to insert a new record into the CCD for this database

delete = Delete record from the CCD

update = Update the CCD with new information for an existing database entry.

start = Start instance monitoring

list = Provide status of all configured databases

stop = Stop instance monitoring

status = Display databases monitored by fault probe

host = Name of logical host

probe cycle time = A fault probe parameter

connectivity probe cycle count = A fault probe parameter

probe timeout = A fault probe parameter

restart delay = A fault probe parameter

DB login = Fault probe user ID and password

Parameter File = Database configuration file (init.ora)

listener = Name of Oracle V2 listener (LISTENER.ORA)

When using the SC2.2 haoracle command to set up the database monitoring of an Oracle instance, it is recommended that all nodes be cluster members when this command is used. Doing so ensures each node has the correct monitoring state for the instance. Use the following command to configure an instance for HA-Oracle monitoring with SC2.2 software:

```
clnode0> haoracle insert sunha lhost1 60 10 120 300 scott/tiger
/oracle/admin/sunha/pfile/initsunha.ora listener
```

After the Oracle data service module has been configured, bring the database online by using the haroacle start command as follows:

```
clnode0> haoracle start sunha
```

The haoracle command will start the database and begin the monitoring process. To stop monitoring the database, use the haoracle stop command.

Note: The stop command does not stop or shut down the database—it is the data service monitoring that is stopped. Any instance will have to be shut down manually by logging onto the database.

After monitoring of the database has started, use the UNIX ps command to confirm the monitoring processes are running.

Enter the following commands:

```
clnode1> ps -ef | grep haoracle
    root  4070  3163  0    Feb 04 ?        0:30 haoracle_fmon -r lhost1 sunha 60
10 120 300 /etc/opt/SUNWscor/haoracle_config_V
    root  3163     1  0    Feb 04 ?        0:04 haoracle_fmon -r lhost1 sunha 60
10 120 300 /etc/opt/SUNWscor/haoracle_config_V
    root 22755 22740  0 14:16:56 pts/0     0:00 grep haoracle
```

The output is the same for the backup node; however, there is an -r indicator associated with the process—this indicates the node is running the fault probe remotely.

In this example, by viewing the process output of node A, it can be seen that two haoracle_fmon (Oracle fault monitoring) processes are running. The child process connects to the database and runs the probe sequence. The parent checks the status of the child process and determines if any action is necessary. When the child process reports the results of the last probe to the parent, the results are evaluated. If the probe results are inconsistent, they will be compared to an action file to determine if action is required (such as a logical host switch or database restart).

To identify which node is being monitored, use the haoracle list command on both nodes as follows:

```
clnode0> haoracle list
on:sunha:lhost1:60:10:120:300:scott/tiger:/oracle/admin/sunha/pfile/initsunha.o
ra:
```

The output of the haoracle list command displays the number of instances registered for monitoring with the SC2.2 framework, how they are configured, and the current monitoring status.

The first parameter identifies monitoring on/off status. When queried, all nodes should return an identical monitoring status.

The last step to be performed is the activation of the db_check script via a cron job. By default, the db_check script runs (updates the cluster monitor) each minute. The CMM uses this information to update the GUI tool. The script is used only for informational purposes and is not part of the fault monitoring process; therefore, it does not require configuring.

To configure db_check, log on as root and edit the cron.tab file to include the following entry:

```
* * * * * [-x /opt/SUNWcluster/bin/db_check] && /opt/SUNWcluster/bin/db_check >
/dev/null  2>&1
```

The SC2.2 GUI (if used) displays the status of the database. The scope of this function is limited; however, a system operator can quickly determine if a database is up or down depending on the color status of the database indicator.

This is a convenient method of confirming database availability without using either the db_check or ps commands (or logging into the database by means of an SQL console).

Database Monitoring

A powerful attribute of a highly available database fault probe is its ability to distinguish between a failed and inactive database. If a failure is detected on a node, the database probe restarts the database or starts a listener process.

Restarting a database instance on a functioning node is a faster recovery process than a full logical host failover. However (if necessary), the database probe can begin a logical host failover process.

After the monitoring agent is activated, the database data service module runs two background processes for monitoring a database(s) on each node. The following is the ordered sequence used by the HA-Oracle monitoring agent:

1. The HA-Database module logs into the database by means of an assigned user ID/password.

2. The Oracle alert log file ($ORACLE_HOME/rdbms/log/alert_$ORALCE_SID.log) is scanned for problems or error conditions.

3. Database statistics are checked by means of a query against the current system. If the statistics indicate database activity, the probe takes no action. The process repeats each probe cycle time (as set when the logical host was created).

If the statistics show no activity, the following transactions are performed on the database:

- Create table
- Insert row
- Update row
- Delete row
- Drop table

The method of deciding whether a database is active or inactive depends on the vendor. Depending on which database fault probe is installed, the active and inactive databases are viewed differently.

Within Oracle, the `V$SYSSTAT` view is queried via the SQL statement `select name, value from v$sysstat`. If differences are detected in the statistics of two consecutive fault probe cycles, the instance is considered active. If the values do not change between consecutive fault probes, the instance is considered inactive and will result in the fault probe issuing the previous transaction into a table called `test`, which will be created in the user's default tablespace.

The following codebox displays the columns monitored within the `V$SYSSTAT` view:

```
"user commits", "user rollbacks", "session logical reads", "messages
sent", "messages received", "enqueue timeouts", "enqueue waits",
"enqueue deadlocks","enqueue requests", "enqueue conversions",
"enqueue releases", "global lock gets (non async)","global lock gets
(async)", "global lock get time", "global lock converts (non async)",
"global lock converts (async)", "global lock convert time", "global
lock releases (non async)", "global lock releases (async)", "global
lock release time", "db block gets", "consistent gets", "physical
reads", "physical writes", "write requests", "summed dirty queue
length", "db block changes", "change write time", "consistent changes",
"redo synch writes", "redo synch time", "exchange deadlocks", "free
buffer requested", "dirty buffers inspected", "free buffer inspected",
"DBWR make free requests", "DBWR free buffers found", "DBWR lru scans",
"DBWR summed scan depth", "DBWR buffers scanned", "DBWR checkpoints",
"remote instance undo block writes", "remote instance undo header
writes", "remote instance undo requests", "cross instance CR read",
"calls to kcmgcs", "calls to kcmgas", "redo entries linearized", "redo
buffer allocation retries", "redo wastage", "redo writes", "redo blocks
written", "redo write time", "redo log space requests", "redo log space
wait time", "redo ordering marks", "hash latch wait gets", "background
checkpoints started", "background checkpoints completed", "transaction
lock foreground requests", "transaction lock foreground wait time",
"transaction lock background gets", "transaction lock background get
time", "table scans (long tables)", "table scan rows gotten", "table
scan blocks gotten", "table fetch by rowid", "table fetch continued
row", "cluster key scans", "cluster key scan block gets", "sorts
(memory)", "sorts (disk)"
```

Note: Ensure the fault probe user ID does not use the system tablespace as a default tablespace.

If an error is encountered, the configuration file is parsed. Error messages are compared to the action configuration file—if an error message has an associated procedure (start, stop, restart, takeover, or none), the appropriate action will be performed; if an error message does not have an associated procedure, no action will be performed.

Under normal situations, the database being monitored will service user requests. The fault probe logs into and out of the database and checks for activity. If no activity is being performed, the fault probe issues transactions to test if the database is operating correctly.

Not every database error produces a failover. For example, if Oracle issues a `table space full` error message, this would not force a logical host failover because the same condition would persist on the backup node. The problem is wholly within the domain of the database.

However, if an error message such as `cannot allocate shared memory segment` is returned, a switchover would occur (only after attempts to restart the database have failed). A switchover of the logical host occurs because multiple restarts on the primary server may indicate hardware problems. Without access to shared memory, Oracle would not be able to continue operating correctly.

If errors are encountered during transactions made on the database, the error code is referenced to an action file (`haoracle_configV`)—if an error code matches, the fault monitor will perform the necessary action dictated by the action file. If no match is found, the fault probe logs a message in the `/var/opt/SUNWcluster/oracle` file through the `syslog` facility and no further action is taken.

Fault probes can log database messages with notice priority. If `*.notice` is switched on in the `/etc/syslog.conf` file, notice messages will be seen in the `syslog` file.

Note: The behavior of a data service is vendor-specific—the semantics discussed in this section may not apply to all third-party database fault probes. Consult with your database vendor for probe-specific functionality.

When viewing the Oracle action file, it can be seen how the fault probe behaves when faced with specific errors—each type of error condition has a pre-defined option. The options include switching the logical host, restarting the database, stopping the database, or doing nothing at all.

The following box displays an example of the code in an Oracle `action` file:

```
# State DBMS_er proc_dilog_msgtimeoutint_errnew_staactionmessage co****1*stop
Internal HA-DBMS Oracle error while connecting to database
# ORA-07265 shows up in the log file if there are semaphore problems. This
# entry needs to be before entries that key of Oracle error codes, because
# the error code returned to clients is usually just 3113 (not as severe)
*   *   *   .*ORA-07265.***ditakeoverSemaphore access problem
co  18  *   *   *   *   di  none Max. number of DBMS sessions exceeded
co  20  *   *   *   *   di   none Max. number of DBMS processes exceeded
on  28  *   *   *   *   di   none Session killed by DBA, will reconnect
*   50  *   *   *   *   di   takeover O/S error occurred while obtaining an enqueue.
See o/s error.
*   51  *   *   *   *   di   none timeout occurred while waiting for resource
*   55  *   *   *   *   *   none maximum number of DML locks in DBMS exceeded
*   62  *   *   *   *   di  stop Need to set DML_LOCKS in init.ora file to value
other than 0
*   107 *   *   *   *   di   restart failed to connect to ORACLE listener process
*   290 *   *   *   *   di   takeover Operating system archival error occurred. See
error below
*   447 *   *   *   *   di   takeoverfatal error in background process
*   448 *   *   *   *   di   restartnormal completion of background process
*   449 *   *   *   *   di   restartbackground process '%s' unexpectedly terminated
with error%s
*   47[0123567]*** *    di  takeoverOracle background process died
*   474 *   *   *   *   di   restartSMON died, warm start required
*   480 *   *   *   *   di   restartLCK* process terminated with error
*   481 *   *   *   *   di   restartLMON process terminated with error
*   482 *   *   *   *   di   restartLMD* process terminated with error
*   602 *   *   *   *   di   takeoverinternal programming exception
on  604 *   *   *   *   di   noneRecursive error
*   705 *   *   *   *   di   restartinconsistent state during start up
on  942 *   *   *   *   *    none Warning - V$SYSSTAT not accessible - check grant
on V_$SYSSTAT
on  1001*   *   *   *   di   noneLost connection to database
on  1002*   *   *   *   * noneInternal error in HA-DBMS Oracle
on  1003*   *   *   *   di   noneResetting database connection
on  1012*   *   *   *   di   none Not logged on
di  1012*   *   *   *   co  restart Not logged on
*   1014*   *   *   *   *    noneORACLE shutdown in progress
*   1017*   *   *   *   *    stopPlease correct login information in HA-DBMS Oracle
database configuration
on  1031*   *   *   *   *    noneInsufficient privileges to perform DBMS operations
- check Oracle user privileges
co  1033*   *   0   0   co   noneOracle is in the shutdown or initialization process
```

In the previous code example, the database `action` file contains nine parameters. The first six parameters determine the previous state of the database probe and the last three parameters determine the current state.

Before a failover occurs, the data service module determines how long the database has been up. If the database has been up for a minimum of 30 minutes, the fault probe will first try to restart the database (prior to moving the logical host(s) to a standby node). If the database has been started N number of times within a specified time interval, a switchover will be performed.

The time taken for a failure scenario to complete depends on several factors. The following configuration variables (Table 5-6) may impact recovery time. Each of these issues is database-independent.

Table 5-6 Issues Affecting Recovery Time (database-independent)

Configuration Issue	Failover Impact
Raw devices vs. file system for data	High
Using journal logging vs. no journal logging	High
Stripe size for disks	Moderate to High
Uncommitted transactions that need to be backed out	Low to High
Database binary startup time	Low
Database mount/open	Moderate to High
Migration of logical host from one node to another node	Low
Importing Volumes for logical host(s)	Low to High

Note: Issues other than those listed (Table 5-6) are database related.

Database-*dependent* issues that may impact failover recovery time include:

- Frequency of database checkpoints
- Database block buffers allocated
- Size of rollback segments
- Parallel recovery mode
- Using RAW data file vs. file system

By reviewing Table 5-6 and the database-*dependent* issues, it can be seen that failover time is dependent on several factors (relating to both configuration and hardware), while other factors are operational and vendor-specific.

There are best practices that can be applied to reduce overall failover time:

- Use journal logging whenever possible
- Use 0+1 stripes for I/O
- Keep the number of logical hosts to a minimum (not more than three)
- Use dirty region logging whenever possible
- Commit transactions as soon as possible. If long running transactions are a business requirement, invest in a TP monitor

Fine-Tuning Fault Probe Cycle Times

Fault probe parameters are initially set when a database instance is set up for monitoring. The values assigned to the fault probe timing characteristics determine timing behavior.

The following box displays the syntax of fault probe timing characteristics:

```
haoracle insert suntest solarflare 60 10 120 300 scott/tiger
/opt/u01/ora/dba/init$ORALCE_SID.ora LISTENER
```

Where:

- *Probe cycle time* (value set to `60`). This parameter determines the start time between two database probes. In this example, the fault monitor will probe the database every 60 seconds unless a probe is already running.
- *Connectivity probe cycle count* (value set to `10`). This parameter determines if a database connection will be left open for the next probe cycle. In this example where the value is set to 10, database connectivity is checked after every ten probe cycles. If the tenth probe is successful, the connection is left open for the next probe. The eleventh probe will disconnect from the database and reconnect again to ensure connections are still possible. Setting the value to 0 will disable the function.
- *Probe timeout* (value set to `120`). This is the time after which a database probe is aborted by the fault monitor—in this example, after 120 seconds.
- *Restart delay* (value set to `300`). This is the minimum time that must pass between database restart operations. If a restart must be performed before 300 seconds, the fault probe initiates a switchover.

The defaults for these values are 60, 10, 120, and 300. Parameter changes are performed using the modify option.

The following box shows an example of modified probe timing values:

```
haoracle sunha update solarflare 80 25 100 400
```

Database Failover

What happens during failover?

It is important to understand that failures with computer systems will happen. Even a *fault-tolerant* class of machine can fail; however, the recovery times with this type of machine can be so short it appears they never go down. Knowing what to expect during a failure is critical for two reasons:

- Did my environment recover?
- Is the environment able to provide services at a level that can be considered acceptable?

To answer the first question, it is helpful to understand the overall computing environment, see Chapter 2, "Sun Cluster 2.2 Architecture."

The following is the general sequence of events that can be expected. Assume a two-node asymmetric cluster; single Oracle database instance; one node completely fails:

1. The CMM detects a node has failed.
2. The cluster begins its reconfiguration sequence to determine cluster membership, failure fencing is applied, disk groups are imported, and file systems are checked.
3. The standby node does not need to start a listener because one is already running.
4. Oracle is started (if necessary, the Oracle recovery begins).
5. Oracle becomes available.
6. The monitoring of the instance begins.
7. Clients re-establish connections.

The time to perform the preceding steps is determined by the following:

- Number of and type of logical host(s)
- Speed of machines
- Total number of disks configured to the logical host
- Number of file system(s)
- Whether journal logging is used
- The number of uncommitted transactions (if any) Oracle must recover

The following are guidelines that can help to reduce recovery time:

- Is there sufficient RAM in the server(s)? It makes little sense to have 6 Gbyte of RAM for a 500 Mbyte database instance—at the other extreme, using 750 Mbyte of RAM for the same size database might not be sufficient. Take into consideration user sessions, the OS, and the backup software. If the server begins to page or swap memory, it will slow the system, thereby increasing failover time.

Note: When using a symmetric configuration, the amount of RAM per node should be doubled.

- Understand how available your environment really is—it makes no sense to construct an HA environment to protect a revenue stream only to overburden the computing infrastructure. For example, if running 10 Oracle instances on the main production server, all 10 instances may be production databases; however, only one is a revenue-generating instance. Keeping down the number of instances can decrease failover time.
- If file systems are the data storage choice, use logging file systems. This can decrease the time for file system checks.
- Limit the number of logical hosts. If every database instance is required to be highly available, add a node to an existing cluster or create a new cluster.
- Users have to reconnect to the database. It is important to note that the SC2.2 software does not include a mechanism for client session failover. Therefore, it would be of little value to make a database which recovers in five minutes highly available, only to find it takes two hours to reconnect all users.

Finally, it is important to measure success when dealing with HA environments. There is little value in implementing a high availability solution only to find after a recovery that the database system is too slow to be of any use.

No IT professional would commit to a computing solution without knowing if the environment meets the business requirement. The same analysis should be applied when implementing an HA environment for both normal operation and in a failure scenario.

Fault Probe Debugging

Sometimes it is useful to have additional information to determine a problem. Detailed fault probe information can be extracted from the fault monitors (`haoracle_fmon`).

To enable debugging, add the following variables to the beginning of the `/opt/SUNWcluster/ha/oracle/haoracle_fmon_start` file:

- `HA_DBMS_DEBUG`
- `HA_DBMS_VERBOSE`
- export `HA_DBMS_DEBUG HA_DBMS_VERBOSE`
- Add the following line to the `/etc/syslog. conf` file:

```
local.debug; /var/adm/haoracle_fmon.debug
```

Create an `haoracle_fmon.debug` log file as follows:

```
clnode0> touch /var/adm/haoracle_fmon.debug
```

Restart the `syslog` daemon.

After editing the `haoracle_fmon_start` file, restart the fault probe.

When these variables are included, additional information for the `haoracle` log file will be available.

Note: After debugging is finished, remove the variables and clear the log file.

Handling Client Failover

The SC2.2 framework does not provide a method of re-establishing connections for clients in the event of a logical host switch or takeover. Database vendors provide that function for their products. Most database protocols such as SQLNET are not stateless. This means the connection must be maintained—if broken, it cannot be re-established from its previous state; therefore, a new connection must be established.

Some vendors provide an application developer with a set of libraries to enhance the functionality of client connections, while other vendors rely on third parties to perform this function.

There are currently several ways to address the issue of client re-connectivity following database failover:

- Database vendors provide tools necessary within the database engine (or by means of an API) to manage the session.
- The client application is written in such a way to provide transaction processing within the client application. An example of this could take the form of the following pseudo code, which can be implemented in a 4GL or 3GL programming language. Ideally, the program should be thread-based.

The following box shows a pseudo client application algorithm:

```
#include <sql.h>
main()
{submit transaction
        transaction mytrack;
        mytrack=insert into table abc values(1,2,3);
    if (mytrack!= 0){
    check connection;
          if (conneciton!=0){
               wait 30 seconds and try again.
            else
                 connect to alternate server.}
         submit transaction again.}
```

- Use a third-party transaction processing (TP) monitor. This software can be configured to manage session and transaction information between clients and database instances.

Note: Some vendors provide the tools neccessary to manage client connections; for example, Oracle provides this functionality through its OCI libraries.

Summary

Database systems are a major component of the IS infrastructure. The importance of their availability becomes apparent when a database service is unavailable. The SC2.2 framework offers a robust, flexible environment for configuring today's popular high availability/parallel implementation database systems. Because the SC2.2 framework offers high availability and parallel implementation, the choice of which to use becomes a business issue and not a technical one.

CHAPTER 6

Sun Cluster 2.2 Application Notes

This chapter enables the reader to integrate the concepts presented in the previous chapters into a working cluster. Because the SC2.2 software is complex, it is fundamental to understand the function of the individual components and their relationship with other components.

The solution presented in this chapter details a lower end implementation of the SC2.2 software using a Sun Enterprise™ 220R server. This solution details the implementation of a highly available NFS Web server application that uses a second cluster node as a standby failover node.

The application notes detail installation and configuration for the following elements:

- Solaris OE
- Hardware and software volume managers
- File systems
- Applications
- SC2.2 software

Each configuration step is explained and includes detailed comments. Where applicable, the best practices are highlighted. Administrators with SC2.2 software installation and configuration experience will find it worthwhile to review this chapter to identify the associated best practices.

Hardware Connectivity

The hardware arrangement includes two Sun Enterprise 220R servers, each containing two 450 MHz UltraSPARC™-II processors, 512 Mbytes of memory, and two 9.1 Gbyte/7200 rpm internal SCSI drives. Each server has two quad fast Ethernet cards to meet the private interconnect and public network requirements, and two Ultra-SCSI differential controllers to provide access to an external Sun StorEdge™ D1000 array. Review the hardware option information in Table 6-1 and controller placement details in Figure 6-1.

Table 6-1 HA NFS Server Controller Options

Description	Sun P/N	PCI Slot Location	Controller Instances
Internal PCI 10/100 BaseT Quad Fast Ethernet Controller	X1034A	1	qfe4, qfe5, qfe6, qfe7
Internal PCI 10/100 BaseT Quad Fast Ethernet Controller	X1034A	2	qfe0, qfe1, qfe2, qfe3
Internal PCI Ultra-SCSI Differential Controller	X6541A	3	c1
Internal PCI Ultra-SCSI Differential Controller	X6541A	4	c2

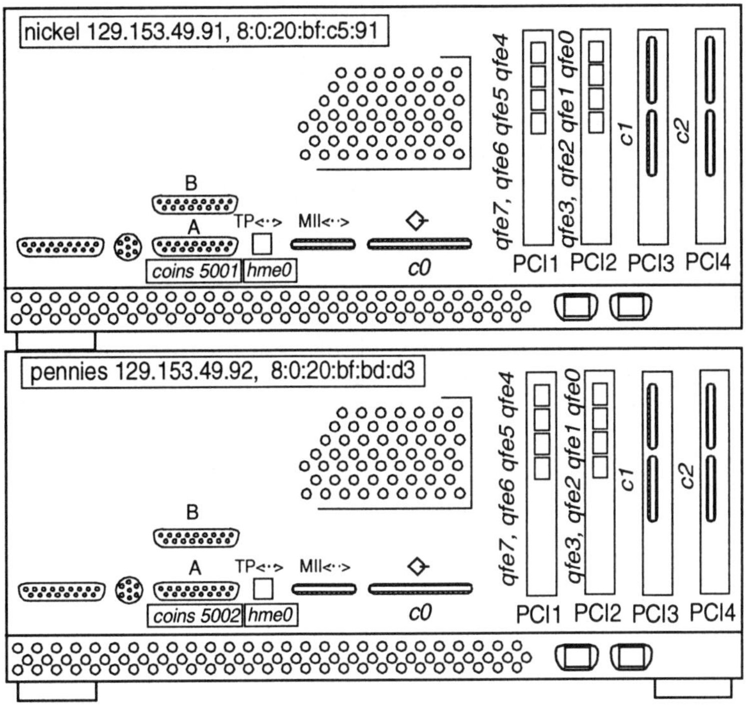

Figure 6-1 Server PCI Controller Placement (rear panel view)

The Sun StorEdge D1000 array contains two separate SCSI buses, each supporting four 9.1 Gbyte/7200 rpm SCSI drives. The production data resides on the first half of the array and is mirrored using the second half of the array. Each half of the D1000 is accessed by different controllers on each host (`c1`, `c2`) to increase availability.

Use separate disk trays to house the production and mirror data to avoid the disk tray becoming a single point of failure (SPOF).

Note: For the sake of expediency, we elected to use a single Sun StorEdge D1000 array—even though the single tray will be a SPOF.

In Figure 6-2 each node (*nickel* and *pennies*) in the two-node cluster has console access through a terminal concentrator (coins) and is managed by the cluster administrative workstation (`clusterclient00`).

All cluster components share the same production network subnet (`129.153.49.x`). The private interconnect for the cluster is connected across two separate controllers on each host (`qfe0`, `qfe4`) to increase availability. The dashed lines on the public network connections represent failover instances for the main network interfaces.

The network connections are connected to separate hubs to avoid a SPOF. Each hub connects its uplink ports (labeled *pu*) to highly available switches, see section, "Network Infrastructure" in Chapter 1, "High Availability Fundamentals."

The boot disk and its mirror should be attached to separate controllers to avoid making the controller a SPOF.

Note: In our example, the boot disk and its mirror are connected to the same controller, making the controller a SPOF. Although it is a best practice to avoid a SPOF, it may be impractical in some lower end solutions due to the reduced number of I/O slots.

Figure 6-2 Lower End Highly Available NFS Server Hardware Connectivity

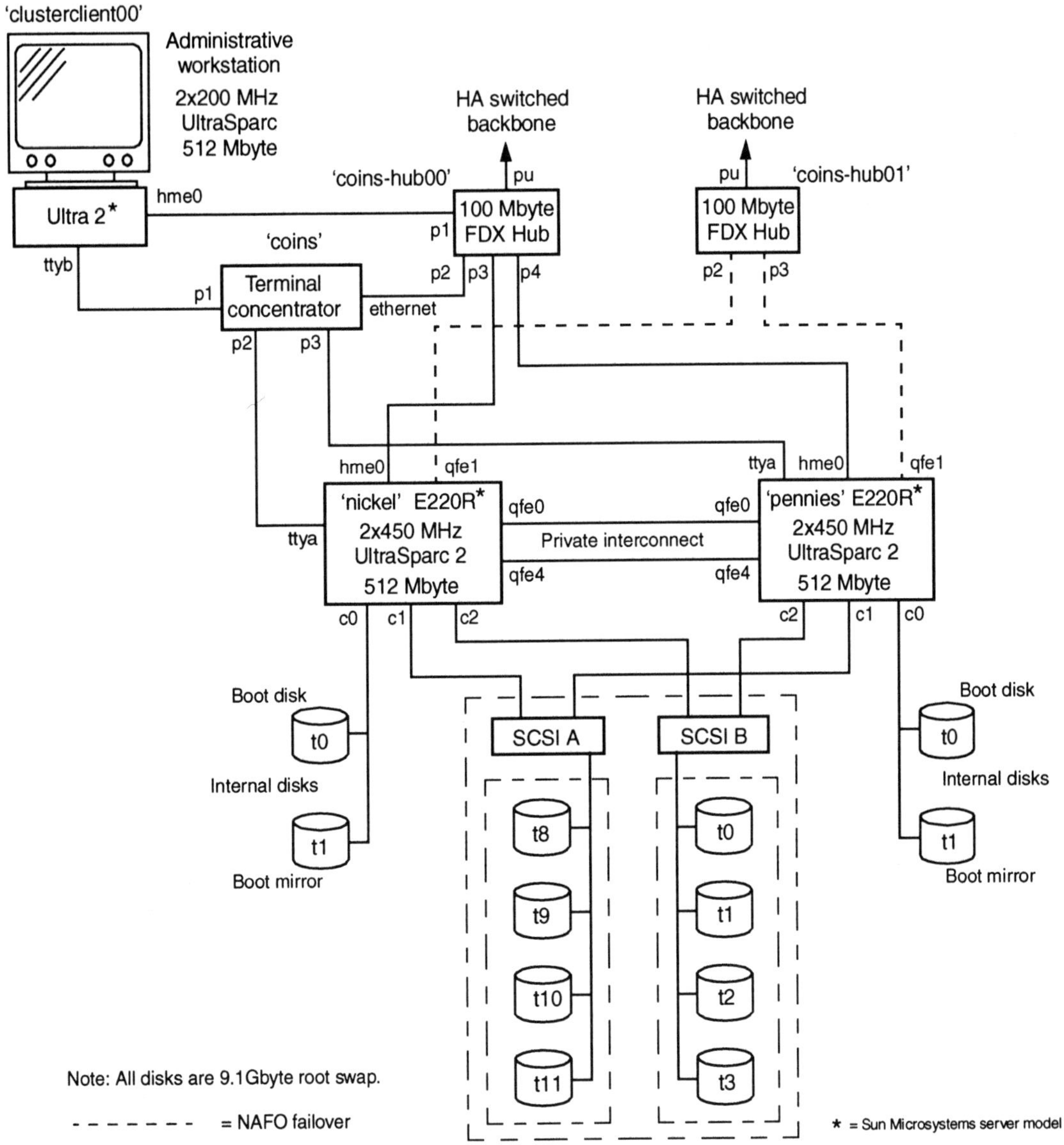

Software Connectivity

Setting up a cluster requires the integration of several software layers, see Figure 6-3.

Note: Each software layer should be installed and configured in the presented order. However, in this solution, the highly available application (in this case, NFS) is integrated into Solaris OE and does not need to be installed separately.

First Software Layer

The Solaris OE is where the network services are configured to comply with the SC2.2 network and host configuration requirements. If SCSI disks are shared between two cluster nodes, the SCSI-initiator ID for one of the nodes must be changed to avoid conflict.

Second Software Layer

The volume manager (SDS or VxVM) defines which disk groups are shared between cluster nodes—disk group ownership is negotiated by the SC2.2 infrastructure. Volume managers are also used to partition disk drives into RAID configurations.

Third Software Layer

The SC2.2 software provides the infrastructure to support a highly available application environment. The SC2.2 software includes the network adapter failover (NAFO) feature to provide higher availability by switching to an alternate network controller if a failure is detected.

Fourth Software Layer

The final software layer is the highly available application. The (standard) application and associated resources must be registered with a logical host to make them highly available, start the monitoring function, and implement a failover if a fault is detected.

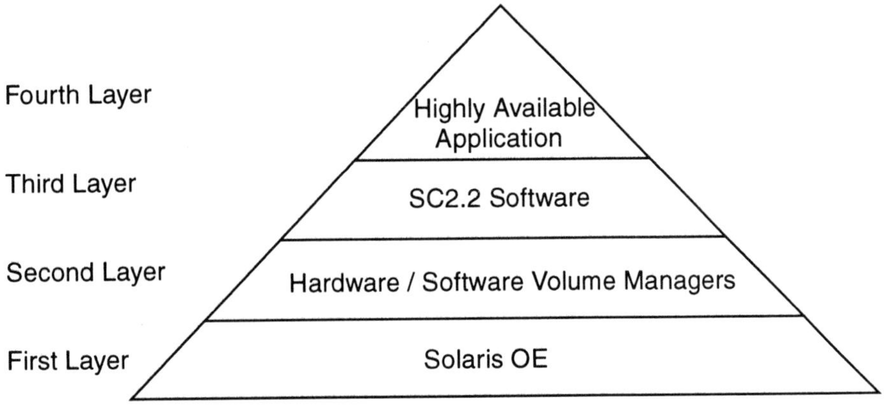

Figure 6-3 Software connectivity layers

Terminal Concentrator Setup

In the example illustrated in Figure 6-2, both cluster nodes require console access through a terminal concentrator. The nodes and terminal concentrator require configuring to integrate with the network. The SC2.2 software requires the Xylogics Micro Annex XL 8-port terminal concentrator (Sun Part No: 370-1434-02) to administer the console.

Configuration of the terminal concentrator (TC) requires a serial cable connection (Sun Part No: 530-2152) between port 1 of the TC and the ttyB port of the cluster administrative workstation.

Note: The administrative workstation requires the common desktop environment (CDE) terminal window for communication.

Start an interactive session by entering the `/usr/bin/tip` command into the terminal window (`dtterm` emulation) of the administrative workstation. The `tip(1)` command connects the administrative workstation terminal window (terminal window) to the TC to start an interactive session.

Note: Ensure the `hardwire` entry in the `/etc/remote` file includes the `/dev/term/b` device (associated with the ttyb port of the administrative workstation).

To configure the TC, power it on—and within 30 seconds—press, and hold the *TEST* button until the *POWER* LED starts blinking. After the *POWER* LED starts to blink, release the *TEST* button for at least six seconds and then briefly press the *TEST* button again.

The TC performs a series of diagnostics tests (displayed in binary format by the *STATUS* LEDs). These tests take approximately a minute to complete. At the end of the tests, the terminal window should display the following:

```
System Reset - Entering Monitor Mode
monitor::
```

Changing the Terminal Concentrator's IP Address

After the TC finishes the diagnostic tests, it enters monitoring mode. Modify the default IP address by entering the following commands:

```
monitor:: addr
 Enter Internet address [192.40.85.60]:: 129.153.49.79
 Internet address: 129.153.49.79
 Enter Subnet mask [255.255.0.0]:: 255.255.255.0
 Subnet mask: 255.255.255.0
 Enter Preferred load host Internet address [<any host>]:: 0.0.0.0
 Preferred load host address: <any host>0.0.0.0
 Enter Broadcast address [0.0.0.0]:: 129.153.49.255
 Broadcast address: 129.153.49.255
 Enter Preferred dump address [192.168.96.255]:: 0.0.0.0
 Preferred dump address: 0.0.0.0
 Select type of IP packet encapsulation (ieee802/ethernet)  [<ethernet>]:: ethernet
 Type of IP packet encapsulation: [<ethernet>]:: ethernet
 Load Broadcast Y/N [Y]:: N
 Load Broadcast: N
monitor::
```

Note: Provide the appropriate IP address, subnet mask, and broadcast address to suit your specific network environment.

Power cycle the TC to enable the IP address changes to be effected. Confirm that the TC responds to the new IP address by issuing the `ping coins` command from the administrative workstation.

Establishing a Default Route for the Terminal Concentrator

If the TC requires access from adjacent networks, the default router should be included in the terminal concentrator configuration. Enter the following commands:

```
# telnet coins
Trying 129.153.49.79...
Connected to coins.
Escape character is '^]'.
cli
Annex Command Line Interpreter   *   Copyright 1991 Xylogics, Inc.
annex: su
Password: 129.153.49.79 (password defaults to assigned IP address)
annex#  edit config.annex
```

Change the default TC password to avoid unnecessary security exposure.

After the edit config.annex command is used, the TC opens an editing session and displays (full-screen format) the contents of the config.annex file. The contents of the file are:

```
Ctrl-W: save and exit Ctrl-X: exit Ctrl-F: page down Ctrl-B: page up
# The following are definitions of gateway entries:
#
%gateway
net default gateway 129.153.49.254 metric 1 active
#
# The following are definitions of macro entries:
#
%macros
%include macros
#
# The following are definitions of rotary entries:
#
%rotary
%include rotaries
```

Because we are using a dtterm emulation to display the previous box, substitute your gateway IP address by using the appropriate editing keys (up-arrow, down-arrow, Backspace, and Delete). The keyboard should be set to insert mode—use the Backspace key to remove the old IP address. After the old address is removed, enter the new address. To end the session, use the <ctrl>w command to save changes to the config.annex file.

After the TC is configured and connected to the cluster node console ports, execute the banner Open Boot PROM (OBP) command on both nodes to extract the Ethernet address and system information and confirm connectivity.

Gain access to the *nickel* server by entering the following command sequence:

```
# telnet coins
Trying 129.153.49.79...
Connected to coins.
Escape character is '^]' <CR>

Rotaries Defined:
    cli

Enter Annex port name or number: . 1
{0} ok
```

After accessing the *nickel* server, extract the Ethernet address by entering the following command:

```
{0} ok banner
Sun Enterprise 220R (2 X UltraSPARC-II 450MHz), No Keyboard
OpenBoot 3.23, 512 MB memory installed, Serial #12565971.
Ethernet address 8:0:20:bf:bd:d3, Host ID: 80bfbdd3.
```

Gain access to the *pennies* server by entering the following command sequence:

```
# telnet coins
Trying 129.153.49.79...
Connected to coins.
Escape character is '^]' <CR>

Rotaries Defined:
    cli

Enter Annex port name or number: . 2
{0} ok
```

After accessing the *pennies* server, extract the Ethernet address by entering the following command:

```
{2} ok banner
Sun Enterprise 220R (2 X UltraSPARC-II 450MHz), No Keyboard
OpenBoot 3.23, 512 MB memory installed, Serial #12565971.
Ethernet address 8:0:20:bf:bd:d3, Host ID: 80bfbdd3.
```

Administrative Workstation Setup

The administrative workstation should be set up as an install server to simplify the software installation process on both cluster nodes. The administrative workstation requires the SC2.2 *client* software to be installed to enable cluster administrative functions.

Note: All commands discussed in this section should be entered into the administrative workstation unless otherwise directed.

To minimize operator error, use the Solaris Jumpstart™ software to fully automate installation of the Solaris OE and application packages.

Note: Although Jumpstart techniques are a best practice, they are not implemented in this chapter because it is important to identify the best practices associated with a manual installation. For additional information on Jumpstart techniques, refer to other Sun BluePrints publications at `http://www.sun.com/blueprints`.

SC2.2 Client Software Installation

Insert the SC2.2 software CD (Part No. 704-6374-10) into the CD-ROM drive. The `vold(1M)` daemon automatically mounts under the `/cdrom` directory.

Enter the following command sequence:

```
# cd /cdrom/Sun_Cluster_2_2/Sol_2.6/Tools
# ./scinstall
...
============ Main Menu =================
1) Install / Upgrade - Install or Upgrade Server
Packages or Install Client Packages.
2) Remove   - Remove Server or Client Packages.
3) Verify   - Verify installed package sets.
4) List     - List installed package sets.
5) Quit     - Quit this program.
6) Help     - The help screen for this menu.
```

```
Please choose one of the menu items: [6]:  1
 ==== Install/Upgrade Software Selection Menu =======================
Upgrade to the latest Sun Cluster Server packages, or select package
sets for installation. The list of package sets depends on the Sun
Cluster packages currently installed.
        Choose one:
        1) Upgrade                Upgrade to Sun Cluster 2.2 Server packages
        2) Server                 Install the Sun Cluster packages needed on a server
        3) Client                 Install the admin tools needed on an admin workstation
        4) Server and Client      Install both Client and Server packages
        5) Close                  Exit this Menu
        6) Quit                   Quit the Program
        Enter the number of the package set [6]:  3
What is the path to the CD-ROM image [/cdrom/cdrom0]:  /cdrom/Sun_Cluster_2_2
...
Install mode [manual automatic] [automatic]:  manual
...
Do you want to install these conflicting files [y,n,?,q] y
...
Install SUNWcsnmp? [yes no list close quit help] [yes]: yes
...
Do you want to install these conflicting files [y,n,?,q] y
...
Do you want to continue with the installation of <SUNWcsnmp> [y,n,?] y
...
Install SUNWscsdb? [yes no list close quit help] [yes]:  y
...
Do you want to continue with the installation of <SUNWscsdb> [y,n,?] y
...
============ Main Menu =================
1) Install/Upgrade - Install or Upgrade Server
```

```
Packages or Install Client Packages.
2) Remove   - Remove Server or Client Packages.
3) Verify   - Verify installed package sets.
4) List     - List installed package sets.
5) Quit     - Quit this program.
6) Help     - The help screen for this menu.
Please choose one of the menu items: [6]: 5
```

SC2.2 Client Software Configuration

Update the `/etc/clusters` file by inserting the following line:

```
low-end-cluster nickel pennies
```

Update the `/etc/serialports` file by inserting the following lines:

```
nickel coins 5001
pennies coins 5002
```

Update the `/etc/hosts` file by inserting the following lines:

```
129.153.49.91   nickel
129.153.49.92   pennies
```

The `/etc/nsswitch.conf` file should be modified to enable the administrative workstation to use local files ahead of any name services. The following is a sample line from the `/etc/hosts` file for an administrative workstation using NIS:

```
hosts: files nis xfn [NOTFOUND=return]
```

To access `man(1)` pages and binaries for the SC2.2 client packages, update the `MANPATH` and `PATH` variables. The following sample code lines illustrate a Bourne or Korn shell environment:

```
PATH=$PATH:/opt/SUNWcluster/bin;export PATH
MANPATH=$MANPATH:/opt/SUNWcluster/man;export MANPATH
```

Starting the Cluster Console

After the SC2.2 client software has been configured, start a *Cluster Console* window for both nodes using the `ccp(1)` command. The *Cluster Control Panel* window is displayed after the `/opt/SUNWcluster/bin/ccp` command is entered, see Figure 6-4.

Enter the following command:

```
# ccp&
```

Note: When using the `ccp(1)` command remotely, ensure the `DISPLAY` shell environment variable is set to the local hostname.

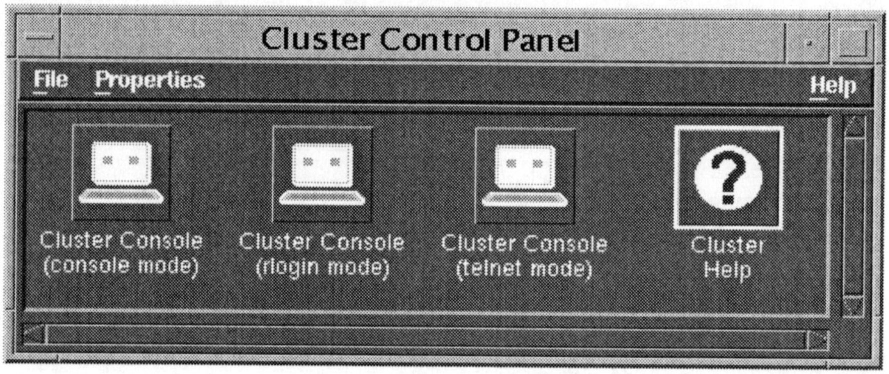

Figure 6-4 *Cluster Control Panel* Window

On the *Cluster Control Panel* window (Figure 6-4), double-click the *Cluster Console (console mode)* icon to display the *Cluster Console* window, see Figure 6-5.

On the *Cluster Console* window's menu (Figure 6-7), click *Hosts*, then choose the *Select Hosts* option to display the *Cluster Console: Select Hosts* window. For the *Hostname* option within the *Cluster Console: Select Hosts* window, enter the name "`low-end-cluster`" (as registered in the `/etc/clusters` file)—see Figure 6-5.

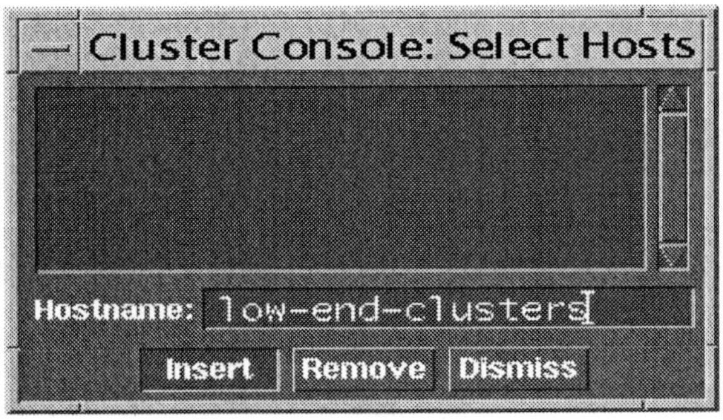

Figure 6-5 *Cluster Console: Select Hosts* window

Click the *Insert* button to display the console windows for both cluster nodes (*nickel* and *pennies)*—see Figure 6-6.

To enter text simultaneously into both node windows, click in the *Cluster Console* window (to activate the window) and enter the required text. The text is not displayed in the *Cluster Console* window, but is displayed in both node windows. For example, the `/etc/nsswitch.conf` file can be edited on both cluster nodes simultaneously using the *Cluster Console* window. This ensures both nodes end up with identical file modifications.

Note: Before using an editor within the *Cluster Console* window, ensure the `TERM` shell environment value is set and exported to a value of `vt220` (which is the terminal emulation being used).

Enter the `banner` command in the *Cluster Console* window to display system information for both nodes.

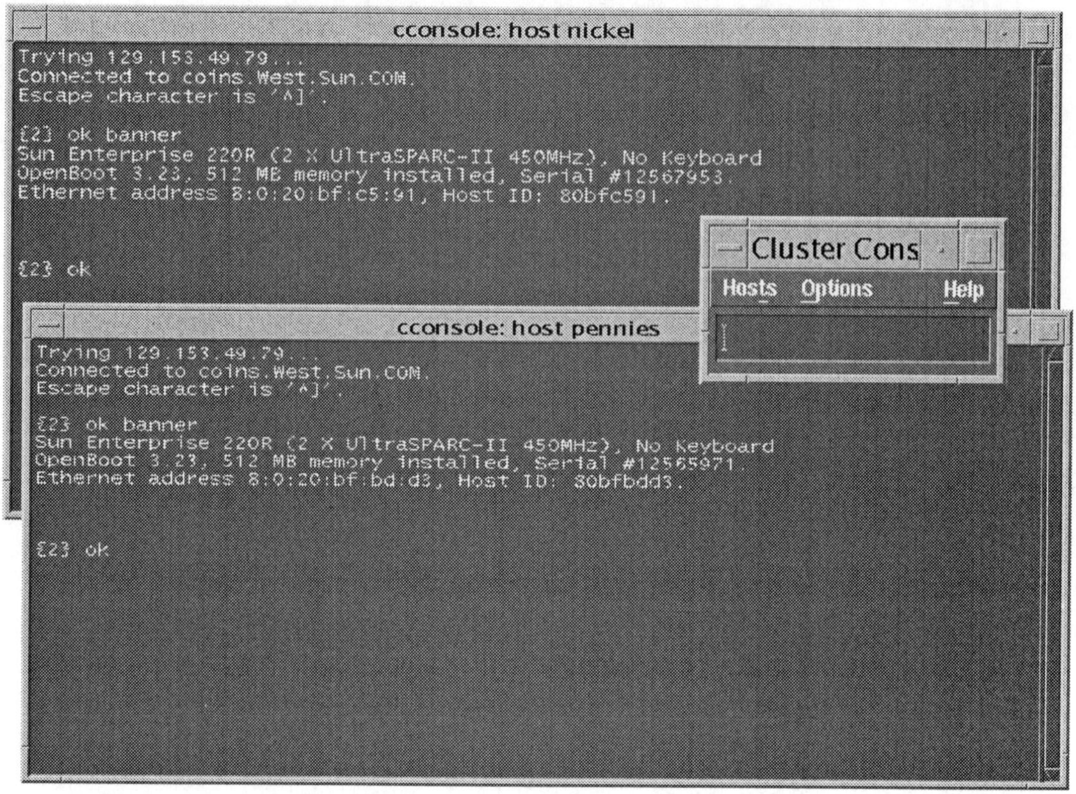

Figure 6-6 Node Console Windows

To issue a `Stop-A` command to the cluster nodes (to access the OBP prompt), position the cursor in the *Cluster Console* window and enter the `<ctrl>]` character to force access to the telnet prompt.

Enter the `Stop-A` command as follows:

```
> send brk
```

Note: The console windows for both cluster nodes are grouped; that is, the three windows move in unison (Figure 6-6). To ungroup the *Cluster Console* window from the cluster node console windows, select *Options* from the *Hosts* menu (Figure 6-7) and uncheck the *Group Term Windows* checkbox.

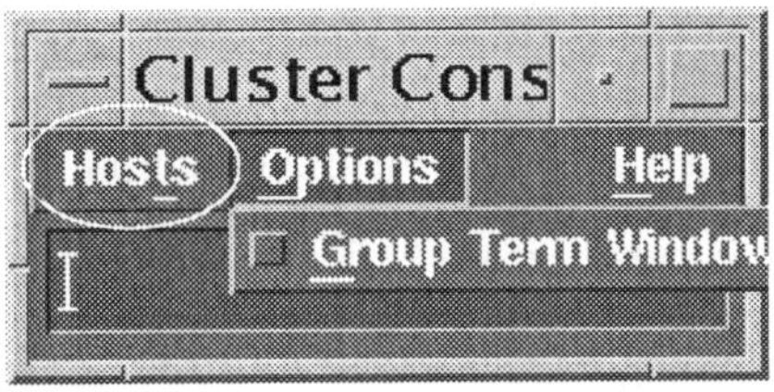

Figure 6-7 *Cluster Console* Window

Setting Up an Install Server

Insert the Solaris 2.6 CD in the CD-ROM drive. The `vold(1M)` daemon automatically mounts the CD under the `/cdrom` directory.

Create a directory to hold the contents of the OS CD (ensure the directory has enough space) by entering the following commands:

```
# mkdir -p /local/OS/Solaris2.6Hardware3
# cd /cdrom/sol_2_6_sparc_smcc_svr/s0/Solaris_2.6/Tools
# ./setup_install_server /local/OS/Solaris2.6Hardware3
Verifying target directory...
Calculating the required disk space for the Solaris_2.6 product
Copying the CD image to disk...
Copying of the Solaris image to disk is complete
```

The name of a created directory should indicate its contents. For example, `Solaris2.6Hardware3` denotes the OS version.

Ensure the OS image is available to install clients through NFS by inserting the following line in the `/etc/dfstab` file:

```
share -F nfs -o ro,anon=0 /local/OS/Solaris2.6Hardware3
```

Note: The `ro,anon=0` option provides install clients with root privileges and access to the installation directory. After the `/etc/dfstab` file is modified, make the installation directory available by using the `shareall(1M)` command.

Configuring the Install Server

After the operating system image is available locally, cluster nodes should be registered as install clients to enable installation of the OS software over a network.

To register the nodes as install clients, enter the following commands:

```
# cd /local/OS/Solaris2.6Hardware3/Solaris_2.6/Tools
# ./add_install_client -i 129.153.49.91  -e 8:0:20:bf:c5:91 nickel sun4u
# ./add_install_client -i 129.153.49.92  -e 8:0:20:bf:bd:d3 pennies sun4u
```

Cluster Nodes Software Installation and Configuration

From this point forward, the `ccp(1M)` command is used to invoke the *Cluster Console* window. The *Cluster Console* window is used to broadcast commands to both cluster nodes.

Confirm the presence of the installed hardware devices in both cluster nodes.

Confirm the installed hardware by entering the following command:

```
{0}ok show-devs
/SUNW,UltraSPARC-II@2,0 (System CPU 1)
/SUNW,UltraSPARC-II@0,0 (System CPU 1)
...
/pci@1f,2000/pci@1/SUNW,qfe@3,1 (qfe port 7)
...
/pci@1f,2000/pci@1/SUNW,qfe@2,1 (qfe port 6)
...
/pci@1f,2000/pci@1/SUNW,qfe@1,1 (qfe port 5)
...
/pci@1f,2000/pci@1/SUNW,qfe@0,1 (qfe port 4)
...
/pci@1f,4000/scsi@5,1 (PCI SCSI controller instance 2)
...
/pci@1f,4000/scsi@4,1 (PCI SCSI controller instance 1)
...
/pci@1f,4000/scsi@3,1 (mother board SCSI controller instance 0)
...
/pci@1f,4000/network@1,1 (motherboard hme instance 0)
...
/pci@1f,4000/pci@2/SUNW,qfe@3,1 (qfe port 3)
...
/pci@1f,4000/pci@2/SUNW,qfe@2,1 (qfe port 2)
...
/pci@1f,4000/pci@2/SUNW,qfe@1,1 (qfe port 1)
...
/pci@1f,4000/pci@2/SUNW,qfe@0,1 (qfe port 0)
...
```

Disable auto-booting on both servers at the OBP level until installation is complete. This prevents booting without the correct SCSI-initiator ID.

Disable auto-booting by entering the following command:

```
{0} ok setenv auto-boot? false
auto-boot? =           false
{0} ok
```

Disabling the Local MAC Address

The Solaris OE shares a common MAC (medium access control) address among all network interfaces. Although each network interface could have a unique MAC address by configuration of the `local-mac-address?` OBP environment variable, it is not supported by the SC2.2 infrastructure. Local MAC address support is disabled by using the following command:

```
{0} ok setenv local-mac-address? false
local-mac-address? =          false
{0} ok
```

Setting the SCSI-Initiator ID

When using SCSI devices for shared storage between nodes, the SCSI-ID of one of the cluster nodes should be changed from its default value to avoid conflicts on a shared SCSI bus. The host SCSI-ID should be changed globally by modifying the OBP `scsi-initiator-id` environment variable.

If the host SCSI-ID is modified globally to a value of "`6`," there will be a conflict with the internal CD-ROM device; therefore, the SCSI-initiator ID of the motherboard controller (`scsi-initiator-id`) should be changed back to its original value (of "`7`") using an `nvram` script. Refer to Appendix A, "SCSI-Initiator ID" for detailed information on setting the SCSI-initiator ID.

Assigning Global Values to SCSI-Initiator IDs

To modify the SCSI-initiator ID, enter the following command on the *pennies* host:

```
{0} ok setenv scsi-initiator-id 6

scsi-initiator-id =   6
```

Changing the Main System Board SCSI-Initiator ID

Before using the `nvedit` command, remember the `nvram` editor is in *insert* mode; use Table 6-2 as a guide to `nvram` editor keystrokes.

To create the nvram script to reset the main system board SCSI-initiator ID back to the default value, enter the following commands:

```
{0} ok nvedit
   0: probe-all
   1: cd /pci@1f,4000/scsi@3
   2: 7 " scsi-initiator-id" integer-property
   3: device-end
   4: install-console
   5: banner
   6: <CTRL-C>
{0} ok nvstore
{0} ok setenv use-nvramrc? true
use-nvramrc? =          true
{0} ok printenv nvramrc
nvramrc =               probe-all
                        cd /pci@1f,4000/scsi@3
                        7 " scsi-initiator-id" integer-property
                        device-end
                        install-console
                        banner
{0} ok
```

Note: There is a space after the first quotation mark in the "*scsi-initiator*-id" string.

Table 6-2 The nvram Editor Keystroke Commands

Keystroke	Function
<ctrl> b	Moves backward one character.
<ctrl> c	Exits the nvramrc editor and returns to the OBP command interpreter. The temporary buffer is preserved, but is not written back to the nvramrc (use nvstore to save changes).
Delete	Deletes previous character.
<ctrl> f	Moves forward one character.
<ctrl> k	Joins the next line to the current line (when the cursor is at the end of a line). Deletes all characters in a line when the cursor is at the beginning of the line.
<ctrl> l	Lists all lines.
<ctrl> n	Moves to the next line of the nvramrc editing buffer.
<ctrl> o	Inserts a new line at the cursor position (the cursor stays on the current line).
<ctrl> p	Moves to the previous line of the nvramrc editing buffer.
<CR>	Inserts a new line at the cursor position (the cursor advances to the next line).

Solaris 2.7 11/99 Software Installation

Use the ccp(1M) *Cluster Console* window to enter commands *into both nodes* simultaneously (unless otherwise stated). Start the software installation program by entering the following sequence of commands:

```
{0} ok boot net
-Select a Language
                0 (English)
        -Select a Locale
                0 (USA - English ASCII only)
        -Terminal type
                13 (Other)
                Terminal type: vt220
        -Solaris Installation program
                <Esc-2>
        -Identify This System
(set current time)
                <Esc-2>
        -Date and Time
                <Esc-2>
        -Solaris Interactive Installation
                <Esc-4>
        -Solaris Interactive Installation
                <Esc-2>
        -Allocate Client Services?
                <Esc-2>
        -Select Languages
                <Esc-2>
        -Select 64-bit
                <Esc-2>
        -Select Disks (Use up/down-arrow to move cursor and Spacebar to select the
following option:)
                 c0t0d0
                 <Esc-2>
        -Preserve Data?
                <Esc-2> (Continue)
        -Automatically Layout File Systems?
                <Esc-4> (Manual layout)
        -File System and Disk Layout
                <Esc-4> (Customize c0t0d0s2)
```

```
-Customize Disk: c0t0d0
              Slice    MountPoint      Size (MB)
              0            /              8000
              1           swap             615
              <Esc-2> (OK)
       -File System and Disk Layout
              <Esc-2> (Continue)
       -Mount Remote File Systems?
              <Esc-2> (Continue)
       -Profile
              <Esc-2> (Continue)
       -Warnings on unused disk space
              <Esc-2> (Continue)
 -Reboot After Installation?
              Manual Reboot  (Select with Spacebar)
           <Esc-2> (Begin installation)
```

Note: In the previous example, the warning message *unused disk space* should be ignored.

To enable VxVM root encapsulation, ensure partitions 3 and 4 are not used. There should be at least 16 MBytes of unallocated disk space at the end of the disk to implement VxVM's private region.

After installation is complete, review the `install_log` and `sysidtool.log` files in the `/a/var/sadm/system/logs` directory to confirm that all software packages were correctly installed.

When using the `/user/bin/vi` command to view the log files, set up terminal emulation using the following command:

```
# TERM=vt220;export TERM
```

After reviewing all installation log files, reboot the system by entering the following command:

```
# reboot
```

While the system is rebooting, enter the root password when prompted:

```
Root password:  abc
Re-enter Root password:  abc
```

Note: The password used in the above box is an example only. Select your own password to avoid security exposure.

Operating System—Post Installation and Configuration

After the Solaris OE has been installed, the hardware and network interfaces should be configured for a clustered environment.

Note: Use the `ccp(1M)` *Cluster Console* window to enter commands into both nodes simultaneously unless otherwise directed.

Note: In this section, we used the Solaris 7 OE version 11/99.

Establishing a Default Router Entry

Establish a default route (gateway) *before* the server solicits a router via the network.

Note: In this example, we use `129.153.49.254` as the default router.

A Sun Microsystems server with more than one network interface automatically becomes a router (and may be selected over an efficient hardware router). To circumvent this situation, establish a default route by entering the following commands:

```
# echo "129.153.49.254" > /etc/defaultrouter
# route flush (Clear routing tables of existing router entries)
# route add default 129.153.49.254 1
```

Disabling Solaris Software Routing

Disable the routing function for Solaris OE whenever more than one *active* network interface is detected in a server.

Software routing is less efficient than hardware routing; therefore, disable software routing on both cluster nodes by entering the following commands:

```
# touch /etc/notrouter (Disables routing upon booting)
# ndd -set /dev/ip ip_forwarding 0 (Disables routing already in progress)
```

Disabling Solaris IP Interface Groups

Following version 2.6, the Solaris OE IP driver was enhanced to enable multiple network controllers to host the same IP address (for load balancing). The IP driver enhancements included one *cache entry* per destination IP address which is based on a round-robin algorithm to identify outgoing network interfaces.

Solaris IP interface groups are disabled when the kernel variable `ip_enable_group_ifs` value is set to zero.

Confirm that the value has been set to zero by entering the following command:

```
# ndd -get /dev/ip ip_enable_group_ifs
0 (Returns a value of 1 when enabled)
```

The SC2.2 infrastructure does not support Solaris IP interface groups—they must be *permanently* disabled to prevent network anomalies during a logical host migration. Solaris IP interface groups can be disabled by entering the following commands:

```
# ndd -set /dev/ip ip_enable_groups_ifs 0 (Disables IP interface groups)
# echo "ndd -set /dev/ip ip_enable_groups_ifs 0" >> /etc/init.d/inetinit
(Appends command to rc file)
```

Configuring Local Directory Services

A clustered environment requires directory services to be supported by local files before making use of any naming services. This requirement can improve availability because it prevents dependency on external services.

Because we are using NIS in our environment, the following entries are included in the `/etc/nsswitch.conf` file:

```
hosts: files nis [NOTFOUND=return]
rpc: files nis [NOTFOUND=return]
ethers: files nis [NOTFOUND=return]
netmasks: files nis [NOTFOUND=return]
```

Configuring the Network Netmask

When using additional public networks that have different base addresses from the main network interface, include a netmask entry in the `/etc/netmasks` file. For example, if using subnet `129.2.xxx.xxx` in addition to the `129.153.xxx.xxx` network, append the following entry in the `/etc/netmasks` file:

```
129.212.0.0           255.255.255.0
```

Note: Obtain the appropriate netmask value from your network administrator.

Configuring the Local Hostnames File

A clustered environment uses physical and logical IP addresses that should be included in the `/etc/hosts` file. Append the following entries to the `/etc/hosts` file:

```
# Physical hosts (physical addresses):
129.153.49.79 coins #Terminal concentrator
129.153.49.91 nickel #Primary cluster node
129.153.49.92 pennies #Standby cluster node

# Cluster interconnect using two separate controllers for higher availability:
#nickel-qfe0 is patched to pennies-qfe0
#nickel-qfe4 is patched to pennies-qfe4

# Network Adapter Failover (NAFO) interfaces:
# qfe1 is a failover interface for hme0 (sustaining nickel, pennies & hanfs1)

# Unused interfaces: nickel and pennies
# qfe2, qfe3, qfe5, qfe6, qfe7

# Logical hosts (virtual hosts sustained by SC2.2 infrastructure)
129.153.49.85 hanfs1 #First highly available NFS server
```

Configuring Remote Execution

The cluster environment uses the `rsh(1)` and `rcp(1)` commands (with root privileges) to manage cluster nodes.

Append the following entries to the `/.rhosts` file:

```
nickel
pennies
ha-nfs1
```

Testing Remote Shell Capabilities

The root-privileged remote shell capabilities of both cluster nodes should be tested to ensure the infrastructure is functional before being used by the SC2.2 software.

Test the remote shell capability by entering the following command on the *nickel* node:

```
# rsh pennies netstat -i
```

Test the remote shell capability by entering the following command on the *pennies* node:

```
# rsh nickel netstat -i
```

Note: If the remote shell test fails, debugging should be performed. (Consultation with your service provider may be required.)

Testing Network Interfaces

Test existing network interfaces on both cluster nodes to ensure the infrastructure is functional prior to being used by the SC2.2 software.

Verify network connectivity between cluster nodes by entering the following command on the *nickel* node:

```
# ping pennies (System should return a "pennies is alive" message)
```

Verify network connectivity for the first private interconnect by entering the following commands on the *nickel* node:

```
# ifconfig qfe0 plumb (Activates first private interconnect interface)
# ifconfig qfe0 172.16.0.1 netmask + broadcast + up
# rsh pennies ifconfig qfe0 plumb (Activates first private interconnect interface)
# rsh pennies ifconfig qfe0 172.16.0.2 netmask + broadcast + up
# ping 172.16.0.2 (should return a "172.16.0.2 is alive" message)
# ifconfig qfe0 unplumb (Deactivates first private interconnect interface)
# rsh pennies ifconfig qfe0 unplumb (Deactivates first private interconnect
interface)
```

Verify network connectivity for the second private interconnect by entering the following commands on the *nickel* node:

```
# ifconfig qfe4 plumb (Activates second private interconnect interface)
# ifconfig qfe4 172.16.0.1 netmask + broadcast + up
# rsh pennies ifconfig qfe4 plumb (Activates second private interconnect
interface)
# rsh pennies ifconfig qfe4 172.16.0.2 netmask + broadcast + up
# ping 172.16.0.2 (should return a "172.16.0.2 is alive" message)
# ifconfig qfe4 unplumb (Deactivates second private interconnect interface)
# rsh pennies ifconfig qfe4 unplumb (Deactivates second private interconnect
interface)
```

Verify network connectivity for the NAFO failover of the main network interface (`hme0` on both nodes) by entering the following commands:

```
# ifconfig qfe1 plumb (Activates alternate interface for hme0)
# ifconfig qfe1 172.16.0.1 netmask + broadcast + up
# rsh pennies ifconfig qfe1 plumb (Activates alternate interface for hme0)
# rsh pennies ifconfig qfe1 172.16.0.2 netmask + broadcast + up
# ping 172.16.0.2 (Should return a "172.16.0.2 is alive" message)
# ifconfig qfe1 unplumb (Deactivates alternate interface for hme0)
# rsh pennies ifconfig qfe1 unplumb (Deactivates alternate interface for hme0)
```

Note: If the network interface test fails, debugging should be performed. (Consultation with your service provider may be required.)

Installing Recommended Solaris Operating Environment Patches

The method of downloading patches from the Sun service Web site may deviate from the following procedure. Check with your local Sun service provider.

To download patches, go to:

`http://sunsolve.sun.com`

Click the *Patches* option (left side of GUI). At the *Recommended and Security Solaris Patch Clusters* window, select the *Solaris 2.6* (not x86) cluster patch.

Create a `/PATCHES` directory on the install server in which to store all patches that have been applied since the OS was installed. The `/PATCHES` directory should be made available through NFS services.

Create a directory in which to store patches by entering the following command:

```
# mkdir -p  /PATCHES/Solaris2.6Cluster
```

Click the *Download FTP* button. Click the *GO* button, and when prompted, store the downloaded `2.6_Recommended.zip` file in the `/PATCHES/Solaris2.6Cluster` directory.

Unzip and install the patch files by entering the following commands:

```
# cd /PATCHES/Solaris2.6Cluster
# unzip 2.6_Recommended.zip
# cd /PATCHES/Solaris2.6Cluster/2.6_Recommended
# ./install_cluster
Are you ready to continue with install? [y/n]: y
Installing 106960-01...
Installing 107038-01...
...
Installing 108721-01...
...
For more installation messages refer to the installation logfile:
 /var/sadm/install_data/Solaris_2.6_Recommended_log
Use the /usr/bin/showrev -p command to verify installed patch-IDs.
Refer to individual patch README files for additional patch detail.
Rebooting the system is usually necessary after installation.
```

Note: Some patches included in the patch cluster will fail installation with a "`Return code 2`" error message because they were already included in the Solaris OE base software installation. Review the `/var/sadm/install_data/Solaris_2.6_Recommended_log` file to verify patch installation errors.

Reboot the system to activate the patches. Enter the following command:

```
# reboot
```

Veritas Volume Manager Version 3.0.2 Installation

We elected to use Veritas VxVM version 3.0.2 to create the file systems to take advantage of distributed spindles (in a mirrored striped configuration). Insert the Veritas 3.0.2 CD into the CD-ROM drive. The `vold(1M)` daemon automatically mounts the drive under the `/cdrom` directory.

Use the `ccp(1M)` *Cluster Console* window to enter commands simultaneously into both nodes.

Enter the following command sequence—respond to the prompts as appropriate:

```
# cd /cdrom/vm_3_0_2/pkgs

# pkgadd -d.

The following packages are available:

  1  VRTSvmdev      VERITAS Volume Manager, Header and Library Files

                    (sparc) 3.0.2,REV=08.30.1999.15.56

  2  VRTSvmdoc      VERITAS Volume Manager (user documentation)

                    (sparc) 3.0.2,REV=08.26.1999.22.51

  3  VRTSvmman      VERITAS Volume Manager, Manual Pages

                    (sparc) 3.0.2,REV=08.30.1999.15.55

  4  VRTSvmsa       VERITAS Volume Manager Storage Administrator

                    (sparc) 3.0.3,REV=08.27.1999.13.55

  5  VRTSvxvm       VERITAS Volume Manager, Binaries

                    (sparc) 3.0.2,REV=08.30.1999.15.56

Select package(s) you wish to process (or 'all' to process all packages). (default: all)
[?,??,q]: <CR>

...

Installation of <VRTSvmdev> was successful.

...

VERITAS Volume Manager (user documentation)

...

Select the document formats to be installed (default: all) [?,??,q]: 1 (Postscript)

...

Installation of <VRTSvmman> was successful.
```

```
...
VERITAS Volume Manager Storage Administrator
...
Where should this package be installed? (default: /opt]) [?,q] <CR>
Should the Apache HTTPD (Web Server) included in this package be installed?
(default: n) [y,n,?,q] <CR>
(The Volume Manager Storage Administrator Client will be installed regardless)
(default: y) [y,n,?,q] <CR>
...
Do you want to continue with the installation of <VRTSvmsa> [y,n,?]y
...
Do you want to continue with the installation of <VRTSvmsa> [y,n,?]y
...
Installation of <VRTSvmsa> was successful.
...
VERITAS Volume Manager, Binaries
...
Install for which version of Solaris?
        [7, 2.6, 2.5.1] (default: 7): 2.6
The following Sun patch(s) are required for Solaris 2.6.
  Sun patch(s):
        106541   (SPARC)
        106542   (x86)
Continue installation? [y,n,q,?] (default: n): y
...
The following Sun patch(s) are required for Solaris 2.6.
  Sun patch(s):
        106541   (SPARC)
        106542   (x86)
Continue installation? [y,n,q,?] (default: n):y
...
```

```
Do you want to install these as setuid/setgid files [y,n,?,q] y
...
Installation of <VRTSvxvm> was successful.
...
Select package(s) you wish to process (or 'all' to process all packages). (default: all)
[?,??,q]: q
```

Activate the patches by rebooting the system—use the following command:

```
# reboot
```

Installing Recommended VxVM 3.0.2 Patches

The method of downloading patches from the Sun Web site may deviate from the following procedure. Check with your local Sun service provider for the best method of acquiring patches for your currently installed application. To download the patches, go to:

`http://sunsolve.sun.com`

Select the *Patches* section (left side of page).

Enter the patch number (`106541`) in the *Patch Finder* text box, then click the *Find Patch* button to display the patch `README` file. At the top of the `README` file, click the *Download Patch* FTP link to download.

Store the downloaded `106541-xx.zip` file in the `/PATCHES/VxVM3.0.2` directory.

Create a directory in which to store the patches by entering the following command:

```
# mkdir -p /PATCHES/VxVM3.0.2
```

Unzip the file and install the patches by entering the following commands:

```
# cd /PATCHES/VxVM3.0.2
# unzip 106541-*.zip
# cd 106541-*
# patchadd .
```

To enable the patches, reboot the system by entering the following command:

```
# reboot
```

Veritas 3.0.2 Software Configuration

After the VxVM software is installed, it must be configured and all disk drives to be managed must be registered as part of the configuration. Enter separate license numbers when prompted (obtained from Veritas) to enable basic and RAID 5 functions.

Note: RAID 5 functionality is a less expensive alternative to disk mirroring; however, RAID 5 affects performance because calculations are computed on the host, which introduces latency. For additional information on RAID options, review Chapter 3, "Sun Cluster 2.2 Components."

To start the VxVM 3.0.2 configuration, enter the following command on both nodes—answer the prompts to suit your specific environment:

```
# /usr/sbin/vxinstall
...
No valid licenses found.
Are you prepared to enter a license key [y,n,q,?] (default: y) y
Please enter your key: XXXX XXXX XXXX XXXX XXXX XXXX
vrts:vxlicense: INFO: Feature name: CURRSET [95]
vrts:vxlicense: INFO: Number of licenses: 1 (non-floating)
vrts:vxlicense: INFO: Expiration date: Sun Apr 30 01:00:00 2000 (30.5 days from now)
vrts:vxlicense: INFO: Release Level: 20
vrts:vxlicense: INFO: Machine Class: All
vrts:vxlicense: INFO: Key successfully installed in /etc/vx/elm/95.
Do you wish to enter another license key [y,n,q,?] (default: n) y
Please enter your key: XXXX XXXX XXXX XXXX XXXX XXX
vrts:vxlicense: INFO: Feature name: RAID [96]
vrts:vxlicense: INFO: Number of licenses: 1 (non-floating)
vrts:vxlicense: INFO: Expiration date: Sun Apr 30 01:00:00 2000 (30.5 days from now)
```

```
vrts:vxlicense: INFO: Release Level: 20

vrts:vxlicense: INFO: Machine Class: All

vrts:vxlicense: INFO: Key successfully installed in /etc/vx/elm/96.
// continued on next page

Do you wish to enter another license key [y,n,q,?] (default: n) n

...

Volume Manager Installation Options

Menu: VolumeManager/Install

 1      Quick Installation

 2      Custom Installation

 ?      Display help about menu

 ??     Display help about the menuing system

 q      Exit from menus

Select an operation to perform: 2

...

Encapsulate Boot Disk [y,n,q,?] (default: n) y

Enter disk name for  [<name>,q,?] (default: rootdisk) bootdisk

The c0t0d0 disk has been configured for encapsulation.

Hit RETURN to continue.

...

Installation options for controller c0

Menu: VolumeManager/Install/Custom/c0

 1      Install all disks as pre-existing disks. (encapsulate)

 2      Install all disks as new disks. (discards data on disks!)

 3      Install one disk at a time.

 4      Leave these disks alone.

 ?      Display help about menu

 ??     Display help about the menuing system

 q      Exit from menus

Select an operation to perform: 3

...
```

```
Installation options for disk c0t1d0

Menu: VolumeManager/Install/Custom/c0/c0t1d0

 1       Install as a pre-existing disk. (encapsulate)

 2       Install as a new disk. (discards data on disk!)

 3       Leave this disk alone.

 ?       Display help about menu

 ??      Display help about the menuing system

 q       Exit from menus

Select an operation to perform: 2

Are you sure (destroys data on c0t1d0) [y,n,q,?] (default: n) y
// continued on next page

Enter disk name for c0t1d0 [<name>,q,?] (default: disk01) bootmirror

...

Installation options for controller c1

Menu: VolumeManager/Install/Custom/c1

 1       Install all disks as pre-existing disks. (encapsulate)

 2       Install all disks as new disks. (discards data on disks!)

 3       Install one disk at a time.

 4       Leave these disks alone.

 ?       Display help about menu

 ??      Display help about the menuing system

 q       Exit from menus

Select an operation to perform: 4

Note—All external disks are left alone to keep them from being a part of the rootdg
disk group. Configure them into separate disk groups to be used by the SC2.2
software.

...

Installation options for controller c2

Menu: VolumeManager/Install/Custom/c2

 1       Install all disks as pre-existing disks. (encapsulate)

 2       Install all disks as new disks. (discards data on disks!)

 3       Install one disk at a time.
```

```
 4       Leave these disks alone.

 ?       Display help about menu

 ??      Display help about the menuing system

 q       Exit from menus

Select an operation to perform: 4

...

 The following is a summary of your choices.

        c0t0d0  Encapsulate

        c0t1d0  New Disk

Is this correct [y,n,q,?] (default: y) y

The system now must be shut down and rebooted in order to continue

the reconfiguration.

Shutdown and reboot now [y,n,q,?] (default: n) y
```

Use the vxprint(1M) command after the system reboots to confirm that the boot disk, boot mirror, and swap volumes are active.

Veritas VxVM 3.0.2 Post-Configuration

After the VxVM 3.0.2 software is installed, the new disks must be registered with VxVM. Disk groups, volumes and file systems should be created to reflect the desired configuration. All volumes, including the boot- and swap-encapsulated volumes, should be mirrored to avoid a SPOF.

Mirroring Root and Swap

To mirror the root and swap partitions of the boot drive on both hosts, use the following commands:

```
# /etc/vx/bin/vxrootmir bootmirror
# /usr/sbin/vxassist -g rootdg mirror swapvol layout=nostripe bootmirror
```

Note: These VxVM commands produce a bit-by-bit copy of the root and swap partitions into their respective mirrors (mirror synchronization). The performance of the machine will be degraded until the copy operation is completed.

External Disk Initialization

Before VxVM can use the external disks (in this case, *coins-d1k00)* they must be registered by entering the following commands on the *nickel* host only:

```
# /etc/vx/bin/vxdisksetup -i c1t8d0
# /etc/vx/bin/vxdisksetup -i c1t9d0
# /etc/vx/bin/vxdisksetup -i c1t10d0
# /etc/vx/bin/vxdisksetup -i c1t11d0
# /etc/vx/bin/vxdisksetup -i c2t0d0
# /etc/vx/bin/vxdisksetup -i c2t1d0
# /etc/vx/bin/vxdisksetup -i c2t2d0
# /etc/vx/bin/vxdisksetup -i c2t3d0
```

Disk Group Initialization

Create a new VxVM disk group (`NFS1DG`) by entering the following command on the *nickel* host:

```
# /usr/sbin/vxdg init NFS1DG d1k00t8=c1t8d0s2
```

Populate the `NFS1DG` VxVM disk group with the rest of the available disks from *coins-d1k00* by entering the following commands on the *nickel* host:

```
# /usr/sbin/vxdg -g NFS1DG adddisk d1k00t9=c1t10d0s2
# /usr/sbin/vxdg -g NFS1DG adddisk d1k00t10=c1t10d0s2
# /usr/sbin/vxdg -g NFS1DG adddisk d1k00t11=c1t11d0s2
# /usr/sbin/vxdg -g NFS1DG adddisk d1k00t0=c2t0d0s2
# /usr/sbin/vxdg -g NFS1DG adddisk d1k00t1=c2t1d0s2
# /usr/sbin/vxdg -g NFS1DG adddisk d1k00t2=c2t2d0s2
# /usr/sbin/vxdg -g NFS1DG adddisk d1k00t3=c2t3d0s2
```

The VxVM disk name should indicate the name of the physical disk array it is associated with. This helps identify a physical location if an error occurs. For example, the `d1k00t10` VxVM disk name (from the previous box) indicates SCSI target `10` of the first Sun Enterprise D1000 array.

Confirmation of Disk Group Import and Deport Functions

After the NFS1DG disk group has been created, verify that the disk group *import* and *deport* functions can be migrated between hosts.

To migrate the NFS1DG disk group to the *pennies* host, enter the following command on the *nickel* host:

```
# /usr/sbin/vxdg -h pennies deport NFS1DG
```

Import the NFS1DG disk group by entering the following commands on the *pennies* host:

```
# /usr/sbin/vxdg import NFS1DG
# /usr/sbin/vxvol -g NFS1DG startall (this command ensures all volumes
in the disk group are enabled)
```

Note: After the NFS1DG disk group is imported into the *pennies* host, verify its presence using the vxprint(1M) command.

After it is been determined that the NFS1DG disk group can be migrated to the *pennies* host, export the disk group back to the *nickel* host by entering the following command on the *pennies* host:

```
# /usr/sbin/vxdg -h nickel deport NFS1DG
```

Import the *NFS1DG* disk group by entering the following commands on the *nickel* host:

```
# /usr/sbin/vxdg import NFS1DG
# /usr/sbin/vxvol -g NFS1DG startall
```

Creating the Administrative Volume and File System

The SC2.2 infrastructure requires the creation of an administrative file system for each logical host to manage the logical hosts and data services. Create the NFS1DG-stat file system (100 Mbyte), volume, and related mirror by entering the following commands on the *nickel* host:

```
# /usr/sbin/vxassist -g NFS1DG -U fsgen make NFS1DG-stat 100M layout=nolog d1k00t0
# /usr/sbin/vxassist -g NFS1DG mirror NFS1DG-stat layout=nostripe d1k00t9
```

After the NFS1DG-stat VxVM volume is mirrored, create the file system by entering the following command on the *nickel* host:

```
# /usr/sbin/newfs /dev/vx/rdsk/NFS1DG/NFS1DG-stat
newfs: construct a new file system /dev/vx/rdsk/NFS1DG/NFS1DG-stat: (y/n)? y
```

Although the SC2.2 software creates the administrative volume and file system with a single command, there is no control over disk selection. Therefore, build the administrative volume and file system ahead of the SC2.2 software to enable manual selection of the disks.

Creating the NFS Services Volume and File System

The remainder of the available disks in the *coins-d1k00* array are used for the highly available NFS data service. Create the HANFS mirrored volume by entering the following commands on the *nickel* host:

```
# /usr/sbin/vxassist -g NFS1DG -U fsgen -p maxsize layout=stripe,nolog \
nstripe=3 stripeunit=128 d1k00t0 d1k00t1 d1k00t2
52410368
# /usr/sbin/vxassist -g NFS1DG make HANFS1 52410368 layout=stripe,nolog \
nstripe=3 stripeunit=128 d1k00t0 d1k00t1 d1k00t2
# /usr/sbin/vxassist -g NFS1DG mirror HANFS1 layout=stripe,nolog nstripe \
stripeunit=128 d1k00t9 d1k00t10 d1k00t11
```

Note: The first command used in the preceding box returns the maximum possible size for the proposed configuration to be used in the following VxVM command.

After the HANFS1 volume is mirrored, create a file system by entering the following command on the *nickel* host:

```
# /usr/sbin/newfs /dev/vx/rdsk/NFS1DG/HANFS1
newfs: construct a new file system /dev/vx/rdsk/NFS1DG/HANFS1: (y/n)? y
```

After the HANFS1 file system has been created, establish a directory mount point by entering the following command on both the *nickel* and *pennies* hosts:

```
# mkdir /nfs-services
```

Sun Cluster 2.2 Installation

Insert the SC2.2 software CD (Part No. 704-6374-10) into the CD-ROM drive of each node. The vold(1M) daemon automatically mounts the CD under the /cdrom directory.

Use the ccp(1M) Cluster Console window to enter the following commands into both nodes simultaneously:

```
# cd /cdrom/Sun_Cluster_2_2/Sol_2.6/Tools
# ./scinstall
...
============ Main Menu =================
1) Install/Upgrade - Install or Upgrade Server
Packages or Install Client Packages.
2) Remove   - Remove Server or Client Packages.
3) Verify   - Verify installed package sets.
4) List     - List installed package sets.
5) Quit     - Quit this program.
6) Help     - The help screen for this menu.
Please choose one of the menu items: [6]:  1
  ==== Install/Upgrade Software Selection Menu ======================
Upgrade to the latest Sun Cluster Server packages or select package
sets for installation. The list of package sets depends on the Sun
Cluster packages that are currently installed.
       Choose one:
       1) Upgrade             Upgrade to Sun Cluster 2.2 Server packages
       2) Server              Install the Sun Cluster packages needed on a server
      3) Client             Install the admin tools needed on an admin workstation
       4) Server and Client  Install both Client and Server packages
       5) Close               Exit this Menu
       6) Quit                Quit the Program
       Enter the number of the package set [6]:  2
```

```
What is the path to the CD-ROM image [/cdrom/cdrom0]:  /cdrom/Sun_Cluster_2_2
...
Install mode [manual automatic] [automatic]:  manual
...
Install SUNWsclb? [yes no list close quit help] [yes]:  <CR>
...
Install SUNWsc? [yes no list close quit help] [yes]:  <CR>
...
Do you want to install these as setuid/setgid files [y,n,?,q] y
...
Do you want to continue with the installation of <SUNWsc> [y,n,?] y
...
Install SUNWccd? [yes no list close quit help] [yes]: <CR>
...
Do you want to continue with the installation of <SUNWccd> [y,n,?] y
...
Install SUNWcmm? [yes no list close quit help] [yes]:  <CR>
...
Install SUNWff? [yes no list close quit help] [yes]: <CR>
...
Do you want to continue with the installation of <SUNWff> [y,n,?] y
...
Install SUNWmond? [yes no list close quit help] [yes]:  <CR>
...
Do you want to continue with the installation of <SUNWmond> [y,n,?] y
...
Install SUNWpnm? [yes no list close quit help] [yes]:  <CR>
...
Do you want to continue with the installation of <SUNWpnm> [y,n,?] y
...
Install SUNWscman? [yes no list close quit help] [yes]:  <CR>
```

```
...
Install SUNWsccf? [yes no list close quit help] [yes]:  <CR>
...
Do you want to continue with the installation of <SUNWsccf> [y,n,?] y
...
Install SUNWscmgr? [yes no list close quit help] [yes]: <CR>
...
Do you want to continue with the installation of <SUNWscmgr> [y,n,?] y
...
Volume Manager Selection
Please choose the Volume Manager that will be used
on this node:
1) Cluster Volume Manager (CVM)
2) Sun StorEdge Volume Manager (SSVM)
3) Solstice DiskSuite (SDS)
Choose the Volume Manager: 2
What is the name of the cluster? coins
How many potential nodes will currency have [4]? 2
How many of the initially configured nodes will be active [2]? 2
What type of network interface will be used for this configuration (ether|SCI)
[SCI]? ether
What is the hostname of node 0 [node0]? nickel
What is nickel's first private network interface [hme0]? qfe0
What is nickel's second private network interface [hme1]? qfe4
...
What is nickel's ethernet address? 8:0:20:bf:c5:91
What is the hostname of node 0 [node0]? pennies
What is pennies's first private network interface [hme0]? qfe0
What is pennies's second private network interface [hme1]? qfe4
...
What is pennies's ethernet address?  8:0:20:bf:bd:d3
```

```
Will this cluster support any HA data services (yes/no) [yes]?  <CR>
Okay to set up the logical hosts for those HA services now (yes/no) [yes]?  <CR>
What is the primary public network controller for "nickel"? hme0
What is the primary public network controller for "pennies"? hme0
Does the cluster serve any secondary public subnets (yes/no) [no]?  <CR>
Re-initialize NAFO on "nickel" with one ctlr per group (yes/no)?  <CR>
Enter the list of logical hosts you want to add (one per line):
        Logical host (^D to finish):  hanfs1
        Logical host (^D to finish):  <ctrl>d
The list of logical hosts is:
        hanfs1
Is this list correct (yes/no) [yes]?  <CR>
What is the name of the default master for "hanfs1"?  nickel
Enable automatic failback for "hanfs1" (yes/no) [no]?  <CR>
Disk group name for logical host "hanfs1" [hanfs1]?  NFS1DG
Is it okay to add logical host "hanfs1" now (yes/no) [yes]?  <CR>
...
Select quorum device for nickel and pennies.
Type the number corresponding to the desired selection.
For example: 1
1) DISK:c1t8d0s2:0005b3b50000000f3891cf60
2) DISK:c1t9d0s2:0005b3b5000000113839 8f6a
3) DISK:c1t10d0s2:0005b3b50000001438983 4b7
4) DISK:c1t11d0s2:0005b3b500000014678 87a4f
5) DISK:c2t0d0s2:0006cd580000000a383c0feb
6) DISK:c2t1d0s2:0006cd5800000010389847cd
7) DISK:c2t2d0s2:0006cd5800000011389856bc
8) DISK:c2t3d0s2:0005b3b50000007472456ac5
Quorum device: 1
...
```

```
What is the path to the CD-ROM image [/cdrom/Sun_Cluster_2_2]:
/cdrom/Sun_Cluster_2_2

...

1) Sun Cluster HA for Oracle

        2) Sun Cluster HA for Informix

        3) Sun Cluster HA for Sybase

        4) Sun Cluster HA for Netscape

        5) Sun Cluster HA for Netscape LDAP

        6) Sun Cluster HA for Lotus

        7) Sun Cluster HA for Tivoli

        8) Sun Cluster HA for SAP

        9) Sun Cluster HA for DNS


INSTALL 10) No Data Services

        11) DONE


Choose a data service: 11

============ Main Menu =================

1) Install/Upgrade - Install or Upgrade Server

             Packages or Install Client Packages.

2) Remove  - Remove Server or Client Packages.

3) Change  - Modify cluster or data service configuration

4) Verify  - Verify installed package sets.

5) List    - List installed package sets.

6) Quit    - Quit this program.

7) Help    - The help screen for this menu.

Please choose one of the menu items: [7]:  6
```

Sun Cluster 2.2 Post-Installation and Configuration

Before making configuration changes, both cluster nodes must join the *coins* cluster environment. On the *nickel* host, enter the following command:

```
# /opt/SUNWcluster/bin/scadmin startcluster nickel coins
```

On the *pennies* host, enter the following command:

```
# /opt/SUNWcluster/bin/scadmin startnode
```

Configuring Network Adapter Failover (NAFO)

Configure the NAFO for the main public interface by entering the following command on both the *nickel* and *pennies* hosts:

```
/opt/SUNWpnm/bin/pnmset
do you want to continue ... [y/n]: y
How many NAFO backup groups on the host [1]: 1
Enter backup group number [0]: 0
Please enter all network adapters under nafo0
hme0 qfe1
```

Note: Using the `pnmset` command updates the `/etc/pnmconfig` file. Manually updating this file is not recommended.

Configuring SC2.2 Administrative Files

To support a logical host, the SC2.2 infrastructure requires the following elements:

- A 2 Mbyte administrative UFS file system that resides on the logical host disk group. Create this file system on a mirrored disk group `stat` volume; for example, the `NFS1DG-stat` volume on the `NFS1DG` disk group.
- The `/etc/opt/SUNWcluster/conf/hanfs/vfstab` file to mount the file systems associated with the logical host.
- The `/etc/opt/SUNWcluster/conf/hanfs/dfstab` file to share the NFS file systems associated with the logical host.

Enter the following command on the *nickel* and *pennies* hosts to create the administrative volume, file system, and the cluster vfstab, and dfstab files:

```
# /opt/SUNWcluster/bin/scconf coins -F hanfs1 NFS1DG
```

Note: Because the administrative volume and file system were previously created using VxVM commands, the SC2.2 software will not re-create them, see section, "Creating the Administrative Volume and File System" on page 270.

Configuring the Cluster vfstab and dfstab Files

After the vfstab and dfstab files are created, they require updating to include the file system to be used by the highly available NFS services.

Edit the /etc/opt/SUNWcluster/conf/hanfs/vfstab file on the *nickel* and *pennies* hosts to include the following lines:

```
/dev/vx/rdsk/NFS1DG/NFS1DG-stat /dev/vx/rdsk/NFS1DG/NFS1DG-stat /hanfs1 ufs 1 no -
/dev/vx/rdsk/NFS1DG/HANFS1 /dev/vx/rdsk/NFS1DG/HANFS1 /nfs-services ufs 1 no -
```

Edit the /etc/opt/SUNWcluster/conf/hanfs/dfstab file on the *nickel* and *pennies* hosts to include the following line:

```
share -F nfs-services
```

Registering NFS Data Services

A data service must be registered with the SC2.2 software to make an association with a logical host (see section, "Data Service Method Registration" in Chapter 7, the "Sun Cluster 2.2 Data Services").

Register and enable the NFS data services by entering the following commands on the *nickel* host only:

```
# hareg -s -r nfs -h hanfs1
# hareg -y nfs
```

Failover Function Confirmation

Before a cluster is used in a production environment, the failover attributes of the individual services should be tested. The following sections discuss the verification of network and node failover capabilities.

Cluster Node State Verification

To verify the status of each cluster node, enter the following command on the *nickel* and *pennies* hosts:

```
# hastat
```

NAFO Verification

Confirm that a failover from the main network interface to the standby NAFO interface is possible by executing the following steps on the *nickel* and *pennies* hosts:

1. Confirm that `hme0` is currently the main network interface by entering the following command:

```
# ifconfig -a
```

2. Disconnect the `hme0` interface by unplugging the RJ45 Ethernet cable from the `hme0` host port (this action simulates a failed interface).

3. Confirm that `qfe1` has replaced `hme0` as the main network interface by entering the following command:

```
# ifconfig -a
```

Non-responsive Node Failover Verification

Simulate a non-responsive cluster node (no response to heartbeat messages) by executing the following steps on the *nickel* host:

1. Position the cursor in the *Cluster Console* window `(ccp(1M))`. Enter the `<ctrl>]` character to access the telnet prompt.

```
>
```

2. Force the Solaris OE into the OBP prompt by sending a break character (`Stop-A`) to the console with the following command:

```
> send brk
{0} ok
```

3. Confirm the NFS data services have been successfully failed over to the *pennies* node by verifying NFS client access to files.

4. After confirming that the *pennies* node has ownership of the NFS data services, force the *nickel* node back into the Solaris OE by entering the following command:

```
{0} ok go
```

Note: After relinquishing ownership of the NFS data services, the SC2.2 software may invoke a shutdown on the *nickel* node. If this occurs, cluster membership should be re-established by running the `scadmin startnode` command after rebooting.

Switching Data Services to the Default Master

Move the data services back to the default master node (*nickel)* by entering the following command on the *pennies* node:

```
# haswitch nickel hanfs1
```

Summary

A good method of assimilating technical concepts is by reviewing the implementation details of the solution. This chapter provided a detailed description of the highly available NFS services solution. Reviewing this information can help the reader better understand the cluster concepts, the environment (software and hardware components), and associated best practices.

CHAPTER 7

Sun Cluster 2.2 Data Services

Data services sit at the core of your business application's availability because they sustain the highly available environment by means of high availability agents (HA-agents). The Sun Cluster 2.2 (SC2.2) HA-agents continually monitor the status of the application. If errors are detected, the application attempts to restart on the same node, or is restarted on the standby node (following a brief outage).

Note: A data service combines the functionality of a standard application (not highly available) and the monitoring functionality of an HA-agent.

It is important to understand the implementation of HA-agents to ensure *all* advertised application functionality is correctly verified and sampled within a reasonable time frame. Application functionality is generally described in a service level agreement (SLA).

Additionally, details of the *start* and *stop* functions within the HA-agents should be understood to ensure that mission-critical applications are started correctly (and are available to all users), and when stopped, appropriate housekeeping is performed.

This chapter discusses the components of the data services API to provide a comprehensive understanding of the architecture framework and requirements for creating an HA-agent. Appendix B provides templates to simplify the development of HA-agents. For those not interested in developing their own HA-agents, review Chapter 3, "Sun Cluster 2.2 Components."

Note: Contact your local Sun service provider to license the HA-agents developed by Sun Microsystems or third-party vendors.

Highly Available Data Services

The SC2.2 software was developed to enhance data and application availability for business-critical or mission-critical environments. The basic SC2.2 premise is to connect two or more servers by means of a private network, and have all servers access the same application data using multi-ported disk storage. Because each cluster node is allocated the same network resources and disk data, it is capable of *inheriting* an application after its primary server is unable to provide services.

Note: Cluster nodes are not restricted to symmetric configurations.

SC2.2 software provides the framework to coordinate membership and device ownership between all cluster nodes while managing macro-level events such as a node crash or network failure, see Chapter 2, "Sun Cluster 2.2 Architecture." To manage application failover, each data service is required to be highly available and must have specific software or *agents* that take advantage of the SC2.2 framework. Sun Microsystems bundles data services with the basic SC2.2 software. Other agents can be obtained from third-party vendors, for example, IBM DB2 database, Netscape Enterprise Server, etc.

Note: Sybase version 12 and higher is supported and developed by Sybase. Contact your Sun sales representative to obtain the latest information on supported SC2.2 HA-agents.

Although off-the-shelf software is available for an increasing range of products, many customers choose to develop their own applications that include similar HA functionality. For example, having a highly available back-end database is of little use if the front-end application (user access) is not highly available.

This section discusses the SC2.2 HA-agent API and describes how to make an application highly available. A set of Bourne shell templates are supplied in Appendix B to assist in the development of HA-agents.

Note: Although the SC2.2 HA-agent API provides a data service library of functions that supports C language software development, it is not covered in this book.

Read the *Sun Cluster 2.2 API Programmer's Guide* and SC2.2 online man pages for additional information.

Qualifying a Highly Available Application

Software development requires justification because it embraces time, people, and money. Before developing an HA-agent for an existing business application, the application should be qualified to ensure it complies with basic HA requirements. The following sections detail application functions that should be considered before a business application is made highly available using the SC2.2 API.

Client/Server Environment and Services

In a client/server environment, connectionless applications (i.e., Web services, NFS services, etc.) can easily be made highly available because there is no state associated with client transactions. Connection-oriented applications (i.e., telnet, FTP, etc.) require persistent links and are less suited to the HA model because a cluster failover does not preserve the in-memory state—continuation of a service requires a new user connection.

Connection-oriented clients can benefit from the fast application recovery provided by the SC2.2 framework when the lost connection is re-established after a failover; for example, an FTP client will automatically retry an aborted download.

Highly available applications should include automatic retry capabilities in the client software. If an automated client retry facility (for example, a transaction process monitor) is not feasible, end-users should be instructed to manually retry any failed queries (for example, database queries, `http` requests, etc.).

Crash Tolerance

Because the SC2.2 HA model simulates a fast reboot of a failed system, the highly available application must access disk storage rather than system memory (temporary storage) to create a permanent record of its last known state (to be used during startup). Depending on the application, it may be necessary to perform an automatic rollback or data consistency check each time the application is started—this ensures any partially completed transactions are reconciled.

Dual-Ported Data

Although cluster configuration information is stored on local disks, applications should store dynamic data using shared disk storage—this ensures consistency across cluster nodes. Although *it is not* a best practice, symbolic links may be used for hardwiring shared storage to local files.

Symbolic links pointing to shared disk files could revert to non-shared local disk files because some applications create new file images to implement modifications. A symbolic link becomes a local disk file when the modified new file assumes the original file name by using the `rename(2)` system call or the `mv(1)` command. For a detailed discussion on inappropriate use of symbolic links, review the *Sun Cluster 2.2 HA API Programmer's Guide.*

Good arguments can be made in support of application binaries installed on either a local disk or in shared disk storage. When application binaries are stored locally, it is possible to perform *rolling upgrades* of the application software version (for example, an upgrade is performed on the standby node and a failover is induced to activate the new software version). Local application binaries simplify software upgrades but have the potential of introducing file synchronization problems between cluster nodes.

Physical Hostname Independence

A basic requirement of the SC2.2 environment is for clients to use the logical host's IP address because it determines a virtual entity that can be hosted by any cluster node. The SC2.2 environment requires all application and client references to be made to the logical host because references to a physical host are unresolved after a failover occurs.

Multi-Homed Host Support

A multi-homed host is accessible over multiple network interfaces. Each physical and logical host in the SC2.2 cluster should be assigned at least one IP address for each public network, thereby enabling the cluster and its data services to be accessible on more than one network.

An application that binds to a host's IP address must have the ability to bind to all IP addresses associated with a logical host. A basic method of creating multi-homed host support is to have the application bind to the `INADDR_ANY` wildcard option—this enables the application to bind to *all* available IP addresses on the node.

In some cases, binding to multiple IP addresses may not be possible. For example, if two logical hosts provide a different service on the same IP port, binding to all possible IP addresses mastered by the same physical node would create a conflict. To overcome this problem, an application must provide a configuration file to specify which IP address it should bind to.

Handling Multiple IP Addresses on a Single Network Interface

Support of multiple IP addresses (IP aliasing) is part of the core functionality of the SC2.2 software and enables the dynamic addition or removal of logical hosts. For example, a physical host may have a public network interface simultaneously host its physical IP address and its logical IP address. Highly available applications should not be affected by the fact that a given physical interface can emulate more than one IP address. Binding the application to the `INADDR_ANY` option will work in most cases; however, some applications may try to manipulate network traffic in ways that make them unable to manage more than one IP address per interface.

The Failover Process

Failover is the transfer of the logical host from an active node to a standby node. A logical host has access to a subset of available machine resources, including IP addresses and disk groups (VxVM) or disk sets (SDS). Each logical host is configured with a unique name, and has information about which physical node is the *preferred master* and which physical node is a potential failover node, see Figure 7-1.

Failover requires binding a data service to a logical host to enable the service to be managed by the SC2.2 infrastructure—this provides an environment for an application to be made highly available. The term *data service* is used as a collective term to include:

- Programs that make up the application
- HA-agent routines that manage the application
- Application data and shared access between nodes

Assigned Name
Preferred Master
Secondary Master(s)
IP Address(es)
Disk Set(s) or Disk Group(s)
Registered Data Services
Manual Failover

Figure 7-1 Logical Host Attributes

A data service is configured with a unique name—this name is bound to specific routines known as *data service methods* (hereafter termed DSMs). DSMs are created to manage an application during various states (i.e., running, aborting, starting, etc.). "Data Service Methods" on page 290 discusses implementation of the DSM routines.

A data service registration with multiple logical hosts is best suited to applications where resources can be partitioned independently within the same node or across separate nodes. A common data service can then be hosted by multiple logical hosts to distribute the load. The ha-NFS agent is an example of a single data service that can be registered with multiple logical hosts. Each logical host provides the same NFS services for separate file systems located on different disk sets (SDS) or disk groups (VxVM).

The SC2.2 infrastructure enables more than one data service to be registered with a given logical host. Although rarely applied, data services can also be registered with more than one logical host. Figure 7-2 illustrates a data service (Data Service C) that is registered with two separate logical hosts.

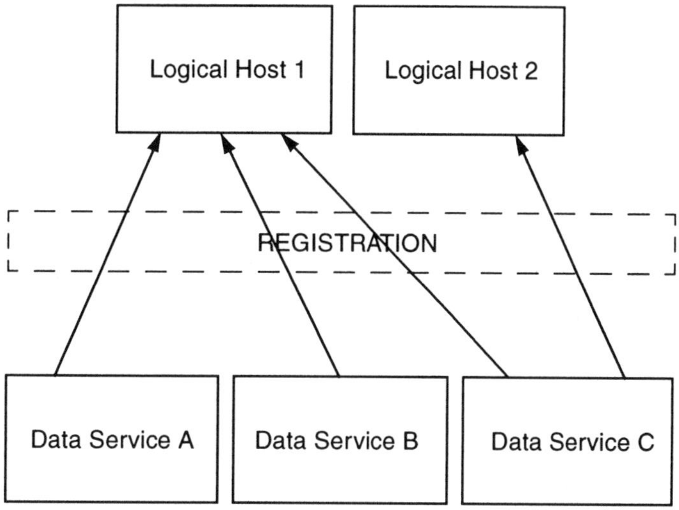

Figure 7-2 Data Service Registration

Dependent Data Services

Data services that are dependent on other data services must be registered to indicate their dependency, see section, "Data Service Method Registration" on page 292. Figure 7-2 illustrates dependent data services (A, B, and C) registered with Logical Host 1.

Dependent data services and their associated services should be members of the same logical host. A dependent data service will not start until the service it depends on has successfully started. Conversely, a data service will not stop until all dependent services are also stopped—that is, the last service started must be the first service stopped.

Note: SC2.2 software enables all data services to start and stop regardless of their dependencies on other data services. The `START` and `STOP` DSMs must include routines which verify availability of dependent data services.

Cluster Daemons and Reconfiguration

When logical hosts and data services are configured, a standby node is selected to fail over a highly available application. The `clustd(1M)` and `ccdd(1M)` daemon processes monitor the cluster to verify node membership and maintain consistency, see Chapter 2, Sun Cluster 2.2 Architecture." These two daemon processes run on each node and broadcast heartbeat information to other nodes on the private interconnect. The `cccd` daemon ensures that configuration commands performed on a node trigger a configuration database update on the remaining nodes. The `cccd` daemon preserves data integrity by locking each copy of the cluster configuration database (CCD) before modifications are committed, see Chapter 4, "Sun Cluster 2.2 Administration."

The `clustd` daemon establishes heartbeat communication between each node to verify the current state of the cluster membership. The SC2.2 infrastructure is associated with a *dead man's switch* mechanism (kernel resident) to enable the cluster node to abort from the cluster or panic into the OBP to avoid data corruption.

When the `clustd` daemon detects that cluster membership has changed, for example, a new cluster node has been added or removed or a cluster node does not respond to heartbeat queries, the daemon confirms the current cluster membership and initiates a *cluster reconfiguration*. A cluster reconfiguration involves launching a number of reconfiguration procedures on each node—these procedures are synchronized by the `clustd` daemon to ensure data integrity.

If a logical host is failed over to an alternate node, it relocates all data services associated with the failed node, see Figures 7-3 and 7-4. The logical host is the smallest resource set associated with a data service that can be transferred between nodes. This resource set is important to consider if a cluster provides multiple data services. It is advisable to register data services on different logical hosts to provide service independence.

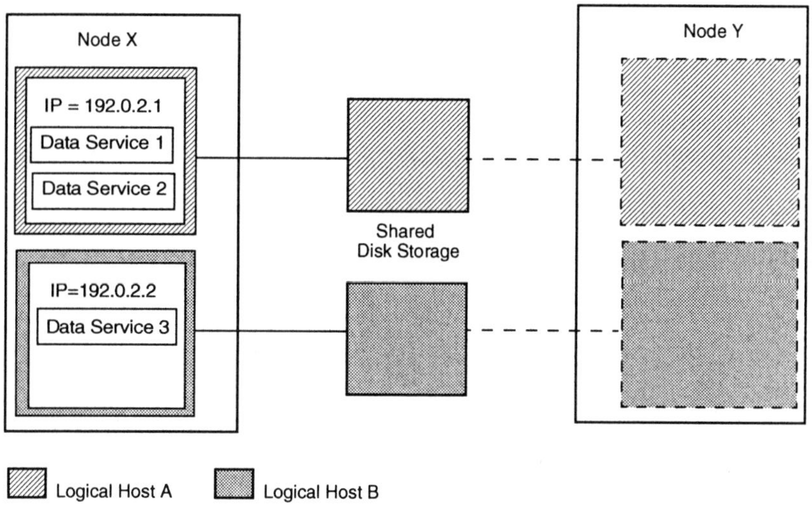

Figure 7-3 Cluster Nodes Before Failover of Logical Host B

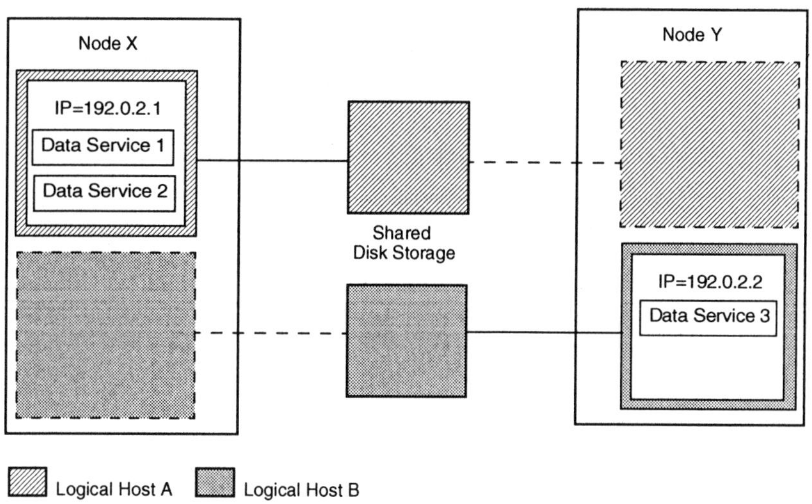

Figure 7-4 Cluster Nodes After Failover of Logical Host B

After the ownership of a logical host is determined, a set of routines (DSMs) are performed against each data service to ensure the highly available application is correctly stopped on the failed node and correctly started on the alternate node.

Data Service Methods

DSMs are a set of programs (C programs, shell scripts, Java programs, Perl scripts, etc.) developed to manage a highly available data service. These programs are automatically invoked by the SC2.2 data service framework when an application failure is detected, or when the application is started or stopped. A collection of DSMs make up what is known as a *data service agent*.

Note: SC2.2 DSMs are located in the `/opt/SUNWcluster/etc/reconf/conf.d` directory.

All DSMs supported by the SC2.2 framework address the specific needs of different applications. Some DSMs may not be applicable to specific applications; therefore, registration of these DSMs is not required. However, the `START` (or `START_NET`) and `STOP` (or `STOP_NET`) DSMs are mandatory, see section, "Data Service Method Registration," on page 292.

The core DSMs are as follows:

- `START` – Starts a data service before the logical host's network interfaces are configured (plumbed and activated).
- `START_NET` – Starts a data service after the logical host's network interfaces are configured (plumbed and activated).
- `STOP` – Stops a data service and removes unwanted processes (and their child processes) *after* the logical host network interface(s) has been brought down.
- `STOP_NET` – Stops a data service and removes unwanted processes (and their child processes) *before* the logical host network interface(s) has been brought down.
- `ABORT` – Used when a cluster node terminates abnormally. Any open files or processes will be cleaned *after* the logical host network interface(s) has been brought down.
- `ABORT_NET` – Used when a cluster node terminates abnormally. Any open files or processes will be cleaned *before* the logical host network interface(s) has been brought down.

Note: At least one `START` (or `START_NET`) and one `STOP` (or `STOP_NET`) DSM must be defined, configured, and registered with a data service before it can be activated.

The use of the ABORT and ABORT_NET DSMs is not mandatory but can be useful for saving temporary data files or killing application-related processes to ensure data integrity.

The following fault-monitoring DSMs can be registered to monitor the health of a data service. These DSMs have been designed to either report errors and/or perform specific actions as required:

- FM_INIT – Used on all cluster nodes registered with the data service to initialize the environment before a monitoring process is started.
- FM_START – Used on all cluster nodes registered with the data service to start the data service monitoring processes. This DSM enables monitoring of the data service from an external node.
- FM_STOP – Used on all cluster nodes registered with the data service to stop the fault-monitoring processes for the data service.
- FM_CHECK – Used to provide information to the hactl(1M) command before a failover is induced. This routine must return a value of zero on exit to indicate the host is functioning correctly (a non-zero value indicates a problem).

None of the previous fault monitoring DSMs are mandatory; however, if the FM_START DSM is registered, a corresponding FM_STOP DSM must also be registered.

Generally, fault monitoring requires a sound understanding of the application to be managed, including its protocol and possible states. Most cluster reconfiguration events encountered by an active node (node failure, network failure, etc.) can be managed directly by the SC2.2 framework using the START, START_NET, STOP, and STOP_NET DSMs. Fault-monitoring DSMs can be used to provide fine-grained failover control and application status reporting (as required).

Data Service Method Registration

Each DSM developed for an application is used to manage a specific application state. DSMs must be registered with a specific data service using the hareg(1M) command. The following box shows an example of DSM registration:

Note: The data service is managed by a specific logical host.

```
# hareg -r myDataService \
  -m START=/opt/myDataService/bin/myDataService_start \
  -h myLogicalHost
```

This example registers a newly developed data service called myDataService that is managed by the logical host designated myLogicalHost. Note how the START DSM is associated with the /opt/myDataService/bin/myStartScript.sh script.

Note: Each DSM only needs to be registered on a single node because the ccdd(1M) daemon will distribute the configuration information to all nodes. It is essential that the DSM's executable files are located in the same local disk location on each node; for example, /opt/myDataService/bin/myStartScript.sh.

The following box shows an example of how a *dependent* DSM is registered:

```
# hareg -r myNewDataService -d myDataService \
  -m START=/opt/myDataService/bin/myNewDataService_start \
  -h myLogicalHost
```

This example registers a newly developed data service called myNewDataService that is managed by the logical host designated myLogicalHost. This data service is dependent on a previously registered data service called myDataService. *Both* data services *must* run on the same logical host designated myLogicalHost.

Note how the START DSM is associated with the /opt/myNewDataService/bin/myNewStartScript.sh script.

Data Service Method Execution Order

As previously discussed, each DSM is created to manage various data service states (running, aborting, starting, etc.). The following list shows the sequence of events for a logical host failover. Each action in the list is not started until the preceding step is successfully completed.

Note: For ease of readability, the term "SC2.2" will be used in place of "SC2.2 software" in the following lists.

---

1. `FM_STOP`
2. `STOP_NET`
3. SC2.2 brings down all network interfaces associated with the logical host on the active node.
4. `STOP`
5. SC2.2 unmounts all file systems associated with the logical host on the active node.
6. SC2.2 deports all disk sets (SDS) or disk groups (VxVM) associated with the logical host on the active node.
7. SC2.2 switches the logical host to an alternate node.
8. SC2.2 imports all disk sets (SDS) or disk groups (VxVM) associated with the logical host on the alternate node.
9. SC2.2 mounts all file systems associated with the logical host on the alternate node.
10. `START`
11. SC2.2 brings up the network interfaces associated with the logical host on the alternate node.
12. `START_NET`
13. `FM_INIT`
14. `FM_START`

The following list shows the sequence of events for a logical host failover when Data Service A is dependent on Data Service B.

Each action in the list is not started until the preceding step has successfully completed.

1. FM_STOP for Data Service A.
2. FM_STOP for Data Service B.
3. STOP_NET for Data Service A.
4. STOP_NET for Data Service B.
5. SC2.2 brings down all network interfaces associated with the logical host on the active node.
6. STOP for Data Service A.
7. STOP for Data Service B.
8. SC2.2 unmounts all file systems associated with the logical host on the active node.
9. SC2.2 deports all disk sets (SDS) or disk groups (VxVM) associated with the logical host on the active node.
10. SC2.2 switches the logical host to an alternate node.
11. SC2.2 imports all disk sets (SDS) or disk groups (VxVM) associated with the logical host on the alternate node.
12. SC2.2 mounts all file systems associated with the logical host on the alternate node.
13. START for Data Service B.
14. START for Data Service A.
15. SC2.2 brings up the network interfaces associated with the logical host on the alternate node.
16. START_NET for Data Service B.
17. START_NET for Data Service A.
18. FM_INIT for Data Service B.
19. FM_INIT for Data Service A.
20. FM_START for Data Service B.
21. FM_START for Data Service A.

As previously discussed, the ABORT and ABORT_NET DSMs are not called during the reconfiguration process, but rather are called when the cluster determines that a data service must be brought down due to a serious problem.

When the clustd (1M) daemon is sent a TERM signal, it invokes the ABORT and ABORT_NET DSMs and triggers the following sequence of events:

1. ABORT_NET

2. SC2.2 brings down all network interfaces associated with the logical host.

3. ABORT

The content of the ABORT and ABORT_NET DSM routines should be similar to that of the STOP and STOP_NET DSMs. For many highly available applications, it may be possible to use slightly modified versions of the STOP and STOP_NET DSMs in place of the ABORT and ABORT_NET DSMs.

The ABORT and ABORT_NET DSMs are asynchronous routines that can be called at any time (including when the START or STOP DSMs are running). The code routines associated with the ABORT DSMs should be designed to check for and kill any existing START or STOP process.

Note: The ABORT DSMs are cleanup programs that should be designed efficiently because they may not have much time to run.

Data Service Method Program Arguments

When the routines associated with any of the START, STOP, or ABORT DSMs are invoked by the SC2.2 software, they are passed three arguments equivalent to variables $1, $2, and $3 in a shell script (or argc and argv in a C program). The definitions of these arguments are:

- The first argument is a comma-separated list of logical hosts the physical host is required to master.
- The second argument is a comma-separated list of logical hosts the physical host executing the DSM is not required to master.
- The third argument is the time (in seconds) the DSM is set to run before being timed out. The timeout value is set when the data service is registered (using the hareg(1M) command).

Data Service Method Argument Mechanics

This section discusses the DSM argument concept with an example that shows how the argument values are modified when there is a change to the state of the cluster environment. The *first state* of the cluster represents the environment after the cluster is started. Table 7-1 illustrates this first state, where logical hosts `logical-A` and `logical-B` are mastered by the `physical-A` node.

The following tables show a cluster environment named *mycluster* that is formed by two physical nodes, `physical-A` and `physical-B`, and two logical hosts, `logical-A` and `logical-B`. The highly available `dataservice-A` is registered with `logical-A`, and `dataservice-B` is registered with `logical-B`.

Table 7-1 First State: `logical-A` and `logical-B` mastered by `physical-A`

Function	**`physical-A`**	**`physical-B`**
Supposed to master	`logical-A` `logical-B`	none
Not supposed to master	None	`logical-A` `logical-B`
Data services running	`dataservice_A` `dataservice_B`	None
Administrative file systems mounted	`logical-A` `logical-B`	None
Disk sets/disk groups owned	`logical-A` `logical-B`	None

Table 7-2 shows the second state of the cluster after the use of the `scadmin(1M)` command (`scadmin switch mycluster physical-B logical-A`). The `scadmin` command is used to switch logical host `logical-A` from the node `physical-A` to `physical-B`.

Table 7-2 Second State: STOP and STOP_NET DSMs Are Invoked on All Cluster Nodes

Function	physical-A	physical-B
Supposed to master	logical-B	logical-A
Not supposed to master	logical-A	logical-B
Data services running	dataservice_A dataservice_B	None
Administrative file systems mounted	logical-A logical-B	None
Disk sets/disk groups owned	logical-A logical-B	None

Table 7-3 shows the third state of the cluster following the use of the STOP and STOP_NET DSMs on both nodes. Notice how the logical-A file system resources have been unmounted from the physical-A node and mounted on the physical-B node.

Table 7-3 Third State: START and START_NET DSMs Are Invoked on All Cluster Nodes

Function	physical-A	physical-B
Supposed to master	logical-B	logical-A
Not supposed to master	logical-A	logical-B
Data services running	dataservice_B	None
Administrative file systems mounted	logical-B	logical-A
Disk sets/disk groups owned	logical-B	logical-A

Table 7-4 shows the cluster state following the use of the START and START_NET DSMs on both nodes. Notice how the file system resources have been unmounted from the physical-A node and mounted on the physical-B node.

Table 7-4 Fourth State: START and START_NET DSMs Have Completed on Both Cluster Nodes

Function	physical-A	physical-B
Supposed to master	logical-B	logical-A
Not supposed to master	logical-A	logical-B
Data services running	dataservice_B	dataservice_A
Administrative file systems mounted	logical-B	logical-A
Disk sets/disk groups owned	logical-B	logical-A

The tables presented in this section demonstrate that when the same DSMs are executed on different nodes, they are assigned unique arguments during a cluster reconfiguration. The tasks required to be performed by a DSM are based on the arguments passed to it. The state of the data services and disk sets or disk groups should be determined to establish which additional tasks are to be performed by each DSM. For example, a physical host must not attempt to start a highly available application if the node is not the master of the logical host managing the data service. There is little point in having a physical host stop a data service if the data service is not running on the node.

Examples of how to implement code that tests the current state of a node, logical host, and data services are provided in Appendix B, "SC2.2 Data Service Templates."

Developing HA-Agents

As discussed previously, the development of an HA-agent for an application involves the creation of DSMs (and their registration with the SC2.2 infrastructure) to automatically start, stop, and monitor a highly available application. The following sections discuss some of tools provided with the SC2.2 software which can be useful for developing a DSM. Appendix B contains shell script templates with sample code for all supported DSMs. These templates can be used to reinforce the concepts presented in this chapter, and to simplify the development of an HA-agent.

SC2.2 Monitoring Tools

The primary task to be performed by each DSM is to determine the *exact* state of a cluster node. Because DSMs are run on all physical nodes capable of mastering a logical host, it may be necessary for a DSM to be aborted to avoid data corruption (i.e., avoid starting a data service on the wrong cluster node). As discussed in "Data Service Methods" on page 290, the state of a cluster node is available to DSM routines by means of the command arguments.

The SC2.2 framework provides tools for monitoring the cluster, see Chapter 4, Sun Cluster 2.2 Administration." The `haget(1M)` command should be included in a shell script to extract cluster configuration information and status. The `haget` command is included in the templates provided in Appendix B. C programs should make use of the `ha_get_calls(3HA)` call provided with the `/opt/SUNWcluster/liblibhads.so` data services library to extract cluster configuration information and state.

Note: All C functions supported by the `liblibhads.so` library are listed in the `ha_get_calls(3HA)` man pages.

The SC2.2 software includes the `pmfadm(1M)` command, which is a process-monitoring utility that manages the DSMs and their child processes. Because no C library calls include the `pmfadm(1M)` function, C programs must use the `exec(2)` facility to invoke the `pmfadm(1M)` command.

The `pmfadm(1M)` command was created to monitor DSMs and restart them if needed. Only a specified number of restarts are allowed within a time window. The monitoring of DSMs and their child processes can be stopped with the `-s` option of the `pmfadm(1M)` command.

The following command line provides an example of how the `pmfadm(1M)` command is used to restrict application restarts:

```
# pmfadm -c myproc -n 10 -t 60 \

-a /opt/ds/bin/failureprog /opt/ds/bin/myprog
```

The preceding example will start a monitoring process associated with the string identifier `myproc`; if the string identifier already exists, the `pmfadm` process will exit. The monitoring process will execute the `/opt/ds/bin/myprog` routine, which will be restarted if the program fails. The invocation of the routine is restricted to 10 restarts within the same 60-minute window.

If the /opt/ds/bin/myprog routine exits more than 10 times within the same 60-minute window, the program /opt/ds/bin/failureprog is invoked with the failed and myproc arguments. The /opt/ds/bin/failureprog program can include functions that remove any partially processed data, alert system administrators, and force a failover to an alternate node.

At certain times during the monitoring of a data service, it may be necessary to force a switchover of a logical host (or all logical hosts sustained by a physical node). The switchover can be performed using the hactl(1M) command, which executes system status checks prior to starting the failover. The FM_CHECK DSM will be invoked if it is registered with the data service.

Summary

High availability of business applications is important to guarantee expected service levels to external and internal customers and prevent losses in productivity, business, and market share. The SC2.2 data services, or HA-agents, manage business applications to provide highly available services. This chapter introduced qualification requirements for making existing applications highly available, see section, "Qualifying a Highly Available Application" on page 283. The elements involved in an application failover using the SC2.2 data services architecture were explained in detail.

Data service methods (DSMs) are the routines that manage a business application to make it highly available. All DSMs supported by the SC2.2 software, their suggested content, and their invocation sequence within SC2.2 reconfiguration events were also discussed in detail. Appendix B enhances the concepts presented in this chapter by providing sample code templates to assist in the development of an HA-agent.

CHAPTER 8

Beyond Sun Cluster 2.2

This chapter describes the architecture of the next product release in Sun Microsystems' cluster strategy—Sun Cluster 3.0 (SC3.0) software. SC3.0 software was designed as a general-purpose cluster solution. In the evolution of the cluster product line, SC3.0 software represents a major milestone. Sun Microsystems views clusters as a strategically critical technology and has made, and will continue to make, a commitment to this technology in terms of resources and research. As this book went to print, SC3.0 was released for general availability.

As with the SC2.2 software, the fundamental design criteria for SC3.0 software are data integrity and application availability. Although the design parameters are the same, the method of implementing the technology is completely different. The SC2.2 software provides a platform for availability and affords limited scalability;[1] however, SC3.0 is designed for continuous availability and unlimited scalability.

During the early development of the cluster products, a Sun Labs engineering team led by Dr. Yousef A. Khalidi began a research initiative to investigate important areas of future cluster technology. The research included (but was not limited to) global file systems, high-performance I/O, high availability, and networking. With the valuable experience gained by this project, the cluster engineering team developed a powerful cluster solution in conjunction with the SC2.2 development. Many of the technologies and techniques (but not all) developed and tested in this project eventually made their way into the SC3.0 product line.

The SC3.0 software is an expandable, robust, scalable, and highly available computing environment built around a new object-oriented framework designed for mission-critical applications operating in the Internet, intranet, and datacenter environments. SC3.0 software provides a unified image of file systems, global networking, and global device access, ensuring an environment that is scalable and easier to administer.

1 Scalability within SC2.2 is limited to parallel database-aware applications such as Oracle Parallel Server, Informix Extended Server, and IBM DB2 EEE.

Not all features of the SC3.0 software are covered in this chapter. A forthcoming Sun BluePrints book will detail the SC3.x product. This chapter presents a high-level overview of some the main areas of this important and exciting technology.

Main Features of the Sun Cluster 3.0 Software

- Continuous availability
- Scalable applications support
- Robust availability for hardware and software
- Single management view of resources
- Global device access
- Global IP services
- Global file services
- Full integration with the Solaris OE
- 64-bit API for developing HA- and scalable agents
- Support for up to eight nodes
- Support for a wide range of applications from leading vendors, including Web servers, database servers, e-mail, NFS, DNS, LDAP, and TP monitors[1]
- Built-in support for future high-speed, memory-to-memory interconnects
- Network adapter failover (NAFO)
- Support for Network Time Protocol (NTP)
- Enhanced cluster management tools

1 This is only a partial list—changes to the list occur frequently.

Continuous Availability

SC2.2 applications are highly available; that is, in the event of hardware or software failure, a correctly configured logical host(s) will migrate to a surviving node. The time required for a logical host to be ready for client requests depends on several variables (some of which are out of the control of system administrators), for example, the amount of time it takes for disk groups to be exported, then imported, and (if necessary) perform a file system check. The problem is compounded when there are a large number of disks.

When using global file services, the time required for the importing and deporting of disk groups is significantly reduced. With SC3.0 software, continuous availability has been built into the framework. Any detected failures when using the SC3.0 product will be isolated to hardware or software, thereby increasing availability and minimizing system interruptions.

Clustering within the Solaris Operating Environment

SC3.0 software is the first version in the Sun Cluster product line to implement clustering as an integral part of the Solaris OE. After the SC3.0 software is installed and a node is fully configured (including OS, cluster software, services, storage, file systems, etc.), it will automatically join a cluster if one is available. Conversely, if no cluster is available, the software will create a new cluster without user intervention.

Note: Although the Solaris OE currently supports clustering, SC3.0 is not a standard component of the OS and requires its own user license.

After a node becomes a member of a cluster, it is not permitted to drop out of the cluster environment (as with the SC2.2 software). Cluster nodes can boot in non-cluster mode; however, in a standard boot sequence (simple `boot` command at the `ok` prompt), nodes will either join or form a cluster and respond to cluster messages and heartbeats.[1] No further actions or processes need to be invoked for nodes to participate in or form a cluster.

Not requiring a system administrator to start or bring nodes into a cluster has advantages when a cluster is used in a lights-out datacenter. Additionally, this feature can be advantageous when used in combination with hardware that is able to blacklist or isolate failed components (failure fencing) by means of built-in RAS capabilities.

1 A node can form a new cluster only if a cluster did not exist, or if the node was the last node to leave a current cluster.

For example, if a cluster node has built-in RAS capabilities and experiences a faulty hardware component, the node can isolate the faulty component and reboot around it—effectively fencing off the component from the rest of the hardware.

Note: Some older architectures may not have RAS capabilities. Also, RAS features have limitations, see Chapter 4, "Sun Cluster 2.2 Administration" for further discussion of RAS and its capabilities.

After rebooting, the node automatically joins the cluster, thereby increasing application availability.

Operating System Clustering Advantages of SC3.0 Software

Performance – Core cluster software runs at the kernel level, thereby improving performance and minimizing resource contention.

Reliability – Clusters implemented at the OS level have increased reliability. This reliability is due to extensive testing of the OS kernel modules.

Ease-of-use – When clustering is integrated into the OS function, it becomes a case of set-and-forget. After the semantics and syntax of the product are fully understood, functionality becomes similar to that of any other integral OS process.

Security – Less reliance on user-level programs to run the framework enables a system administrator to further tighten OS security.

Maintainability – The OS patch management maintains critical cluster patches, thereby reducing maintenance costs and decreasing the time cycle for cluster software maintenance releases.

Topology

The physical architecture of a cluster implemented with SC3.0 software is similar to a cluster implemented with SC2.2 software, in that all nodes must have the same version of the Solaris OE and all nodes must be connected to a private network of redundant high-speed interconnects. However, unlike SC2.2, not every cluster node needs to have physical access to shared storage.

Topologies Supported by SC3.0 Software

- Clustered pairs
- N+1
- Pair + N (new to SC3.0)

Network Adapter Failover

SC3.0 software has the option to make network interfaces highly available. If a node is to be available via a public network, it will require a network interface. If redundancy is required, interfaces can be configured in a redundant group. Also, if a node hosts a service, even if this service is going to be accessed via a global IP, it will require a network adapter to reply to requests (i.e., outbound traffic).

Cluster Interconnects

As with SC2.2 software, the interconnects pass cluster membership information, cluster heartbeats, and in some configurations, application data between nodes. SC3.0 software also uses the interconnects to pass new data types for global file services traffic, global devices traffic, metadata, and redirected IP traffic. Also, as with SC2.2 software, the interconnects must be made redundant using Ethernet, SCI, or Gigabit Ethernet. Each cluster node must be configured with a minimum of two interconnect interfaces (with a maximum of six). However, unlike SC2.2 software, all private network interfaces are used in parallel for data transport and cluster messages.

As discussed in Chapter 2, "Sun Cluster 2.2 Architecture," SC2.2 software uses only one interconnect for data and heartbeats, while the other is used as a fault-tolerant redundant link (managed by the switch management agent [SMA]). However, with SC3.0 software, all interconnect interfaces are used simultaneously. Data on the interconnect is striped across all interconnect interfaces for increased throughput. Individual I/O is transported via a single interface—these interfaces are used in a round-robin process. Another performance benefit developed for the SC3.0 interconnect is a true zero copy optimization algorithm. Data is moved from the network adapters directly to the session layers of the protocol stack, thereby speeding packet transfers dramatically.

Adding adapters to the interconnect topology increases the available bandwidth used for message passing, scalable services, and disk I/O—at the same time, increasing availability of the interconnect. Losing one or more of the interconnects does not affect cluster operation (assuming enough redundancy) because the cluster will continue using the remaining interconnects (at a lower aggregate bandwidth). For example, if a cluster is configured with five adapters for the interconnect, all five adapters will be used simultaneously; if one adapter fails, the remaining four will be used.

Although SC3.0 software will continue to work with a failure of an interconnect adapter, interconnect performance will decrease. As with SC2.2 software, if a cluster contains more than two nodes, switches will have to be used for the cluster interconnects; however, in a two-node cluster, a direct point-to-point connection is sufficient.

Local Storage (Boot Disks) for SC3.0 Software

The boot disk should be large enough to hold the following:

- Solaris OE
- Cluster software
- Volume manager software
- Backup software
- System management software
- Administration logs
- Web or database server software (if required)
- 100 Mbyte disk partition required for global devices

Note: Although not required, boot disks should be mirrored for availability. Shared boot devices are not supported by SC3.0 software (including the `/usr` and `/etc/` directories).

Shared Storage

Unless dual-attached devices (such as a Sun StorEdge™ A3500) are being used, shared storage must be dual-ported and mirrored for availability. A minimum of two nodes should be connected to shared storage devices. If one node leaves the cluster, all I/O is routed to another node that has access to the storage device (see Figure 8-1). This behavior is important, because with SC3.0 software, only one path at a time is permitted to be the active path to a disk.

Note: A single active path is not applicable when OPS is used with SC3.0

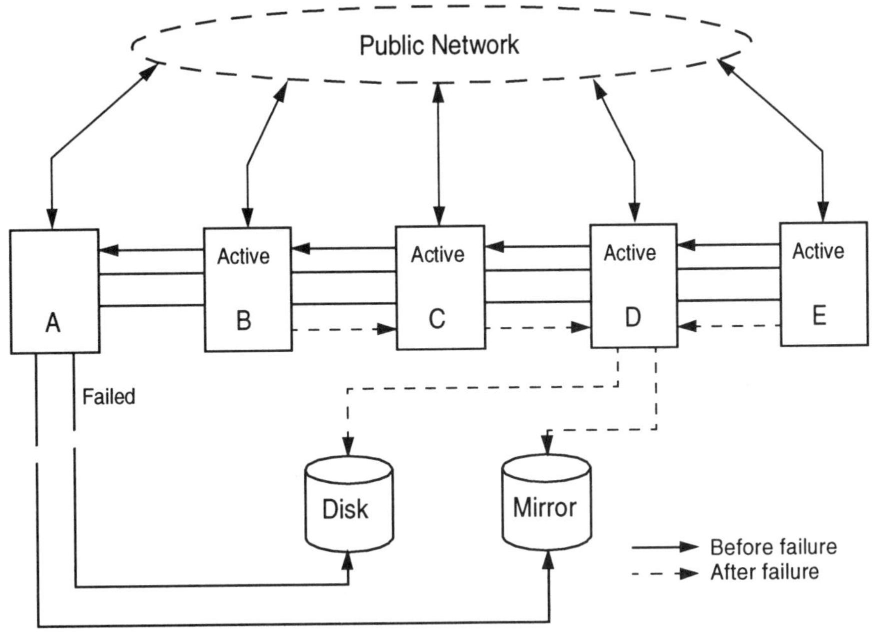

/data1 globally mounted on node B is made available to all nodes
/data2 globally mounted on node E is made available to all nodes

Figure 8-1 Shared Storage

Global Devices

A major difference between SC2.2 and SC3.0 software is the capability of SC3.0 software to make all storage hardware resources available across a cluster without regard to where a device is (physically). A storage device attached to any node can be made into a global device. These devices include:

- Local disks
- Storage arrays
- Tape drives
- CD-ROM drives

For example, a CD-ROM drive on node A can be made into a global device that is accessible to all nodes in the cluster. Storage devices are referenced with a global disk ID (DID) that is supplied to node hardware by means of a DID driver. If a failure occurs, SC3.0 will automatically redirect device access to another I/O path (only applicable for dual- and multi-ported storage devices).

Access to devices (not directly attached to the node) is gained by means of the cluster interconnect. The DID driver automatically probes all nodes within a cluster and builds a list of available devices. Each device is assigned a unique ID which includes major and minor numbers. Global devices are accessed using the DID device number rather than the standard c(x) t(y) d(z) notation. For example, `d10s7` translates to device `d10` slice `7`). Each node maintains its own copy of the global namespace located in the `/dev/global` directory. Device files are stored in the `/dev/global/rdsk` directory for blocks, the `/dev/global/dsk` directory for disks, and the `/dev/global/rmt` directory for tape devices. Assigning a global access naming convention ensures device consistency across the cluster.

Global device access enables the use of dual-ported devices in a four-node cluster. Additionally, system administration is simplified when the storage capacity of the cluster is increased. For example, when a new array is added to the cluster, all nodes connected to the array should be reconfigured using the Solaris `drvconfig`, `disks`, and `devlinks` commands. The DID driver will update the `/dev/global` directory on the local node and will then issue updates to all nodes in the cluster. The new array will now be visible to all nodes. Global device access enables the creation of a cluster storage environment that is easy to scale and manage.

Resource Group Manager

Within SC2.2, logical hosts are an abstraction of connectivity, storage, and application (logical IP address, disk group or metaset, and data service agent). These components must exist before a logical host can be created. This approach is relatively easy to configure and manage; however, its main drawback is flexibility. Storage has to be assigned to a logical host (a logical host cannot be created without a storage component). The SC3.0 framework enables greater flexibility when creating logical hosts (including creating new, different types of services). Additionally, each of these layers (storage, network, service) can now be managed separately.

The resource group manager (RGM) is a software mechanism within the SC3.0 framework that enables the creation of cluster resources that provide applications with failover or scalable services. The RGM can automatically or manually start and stop resources according to pre-configured policies for software or hardware failures.

The following is the hierarchy of resources created and managed using the RGM:

- Resources groups – Act as a container for a resource.
- Resources – Instantiations of the resources group.
- Resource types – A template for the creation of resources.

Data Services and Resource Types

Data services and resource types are supplied by Sun Microsystems and third-party vendors, or can be custom created with the Version 2.0 cluster API. Types of resources include:

- *High availability* – HA resources that provide failover capabilities.
- *Scalable resources* – Enables applications to take advantage of cluster scalability and failover. Application workload can be load-balanced across cluster nodes, helping to take advantage of natural resiliency and redundancy.

The SC3.0 API has a generic resource type that enables system administrators to quickly implement data services for proprietary applications with little or no programming. This generic resource has the same basic failover functions as the SC3.0 software, and the same method to start and stop an application. Although the generic resource does not have a monitoring method, the generic data services enable custom applications to take advantage of HA without writing custom data services, for example, an application running background processes (data collection, backup agent, or monitoring agent).

New Cluster API

SC3.0 software has a new cluster (Version 2) API (SC2.2 uses Version 1). The Version 2 API is not compatible with Version 1; therefore, data services written for SC2.2 do not work with the SC3.0 API. To circumvent this incompatibility, the SC3.0 product contains utilities to migrate custom data services written with Version 1 into Version 2 (with little or no modification).

Object-based

SC3.0 software is object based (unlike the SC2.2 framework). The interface definition language (IDL) for SC3.0 software is C++; however, new IDLs can be created for other object-oriented languages such as Java™ and Enterprise Java Beans™ (EJB™). Object-oriented programming enables the expansion of existing code without the need to rewrite the code. Although an inheritance model for the RGM will not be available, the software structure is in place; as market conditions warrant, the inheritance model can be made readily available.

Single System Image for Standard Applications

A fundamental attribute of cluster technology is to provide a framework that gives programmers the tools necessary for the creation of applications to provide a single system image (SSI). The SSI environment offers scalability, HA, global data storage, and enhanced management capability. For additional information on SSIs, see Chapter 2, "Sun Cluster 2.2 Architecture."

A cluster that provides an SSI must provide a mechanism to ensure data integrity by means of locking semantics robust enough to handle a wide range of failure and recovery scenarios without impacting system performance.

The SC3.0 product supports cluster-aware parallel databases (as does the SC2.2 product), for example, Oracle Parallel Server (OPS), Informix XPS, and IBM DB2/EEE. Using any of these database products with a cluster enables clients to access the same database from any node, thereby providing a single system image of the database.

The strength of these applications is that they enable each participating node to process information and write to a common persistent datastore simultaneously. For non-database applications to achieve the benefits of an SSI, the cluster framework must provide semantics for a common persistent datastore with simultaneous access. SC3.0 software achieves this function by means of a global file system, thereby providing a mechanism for horizontal scalability.

Global File System (GFS)

SC3.0 software introduces an enhanced method of using file systems with the Solaris OE. An advantage of a GFS is that each node within a cluster can mount files simultaneously, thereby providing a cluster-wide persistent data store. The SC3.0 kernel interface enables the export of a valid UNIX file system globally to all cluster members. The cluster file system semantics are implemented under the virtual file system (VFS) within the operating system kernel, which acts as a proxy layer between the kernel and storage, see Figure 8-2.

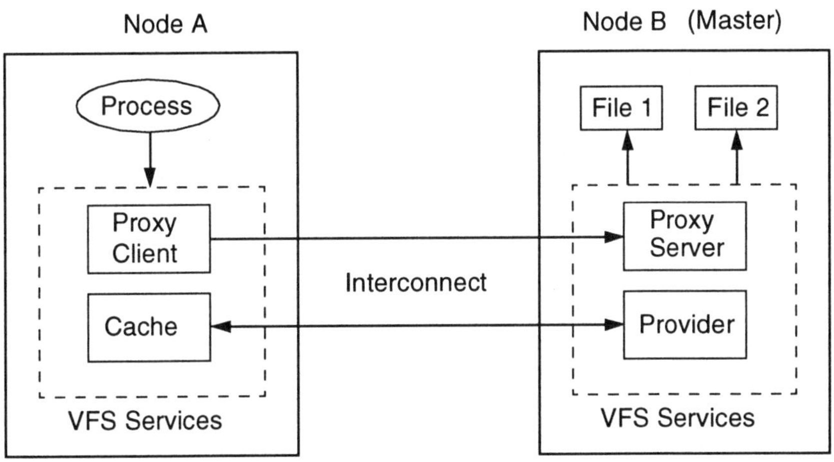

Figure 8-2 Global File Service Proxy Layer

By applying identical semantics to the UNIX file system, implementation of the cluster file system structure is performed under the VFS layer. Therefore, file formats such as UNIX File System (UFS), Veritas File System (VxFS), and High Sierra File System (HSFS) can be created and exported globally. Implementing a cluster file system under the vnode layers insulates users and applications from the underlying workings. Applications do not need to be rewritten to take advantage of GFS because the internal locking mechanism manages cache coherency and concurrent access. Like traditional UNIX file systems, cluster file systems are independent of the underlying volume manager, thereby giving system administrators a choice of using SDS or VxVM software.

A globally mounted file system can be manipulated using identical Solaris OE file system semantics (mount/unmount) as a non-GFS file system, and is transparent to applications and end-users. File systems designated for global access are mounted using the new `mount` command (`mount -g`). Although every node could have a GFS entry in its `/etc/vfstab` file, only one node does the actual mounting of the file system—it is then mounted on every node (using the same mount point).

A GFS has the added flexibility of being mounted by multiple nodes for simultaneous read/write access. Read/write access is not limited to different areas of the file system (as with NFS), but is limited to the same files. Global file services use caching extensively on local nodes, see Figure 8-3.

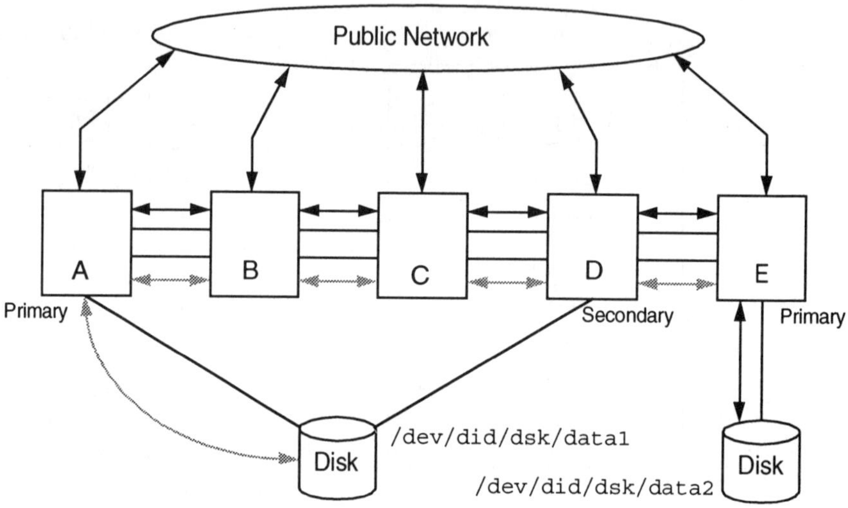

Node A Masters `/dev/did/dsk/data1`, all I/O to this file system goes through A
Node E Masters `/dev/did/dsk/data2`, all I/O to this file system goes through E

Figure 8-3 SC3.0 Global File Systems

Before any read operation is requested, the node checks its own local cache (Figure 8-2). If the requested data is not available in the local cache, the requesting node contacts the file system master for the required request. This caching system works the same as a file buffer cache; that is, if two nodes hold data in their caches and one node performs an update, then the other node needing to make an update issues a request for an update, the old page is invalidated, and a new page is sent.

Each GFS has a primary master and (if necessary) can have a secondary master. The primary master issues I/O requests to the underlying storage from all nodes having access to the file system. All reads/writes pass through the master node, even though other nodes have direct access to the storage system. The master node, in turn, issues the I/O request for each node. The secondary node acts as a backup in case the primary node is no longer available.

All data, including disk access, is passed via the interconnect. The primary node(s) controls I/O to the file system; that is, all reads/writes are passed through the primary node. If the primary node becomes unavailable, a secondary node becomes the primary. Implementing primary and secondary nodes ensures that global file systems are always available even if the primary node fails. A powerful attribute of GFS is its capability to transparently retry file system transactions; users or applications will not see an I/O error, only a delay. If there is a path to the storage device, the GFS associated with that storage device will always be available.

Global file systems can be configured with a primary node and no secondary. File systems configured in this way are not highly available—that is, if the primary node fails, applications accessing the file system will generate access errors. This configuration should be used only if the overall cluster design allows for such configurations; for example, creating a GFS on a local disk. Because no other node has physical access to the disk, there is no secondary node. If the master node fails, nodes will not have access to that file system. With the intelligent use of caching, data striping, and the aggregate of available bandwidth of the interconnect, latency is limited by the throughput of the disk subsystem.[1]

Highly Available, Scalable Data Services

Scalability is a term that describes how a machine or application performs when new hardware or software is introduced. As discussed in Chapter 5, '"Highly Available Databases," scalability with SC2.2 software is only achieved with application software that is cluster-aware, for example, Oracle OPS, Informix XPS, or IBM DB2/EEE (parallel database applications). Applications not written specifically to take advantage of clustering would not benefit by adding nodes. However, adding nodes to a cluster does offer higher application availability, see Chapter 1, "High Availability Fundamentals"). The SC3.0 framework offers expansive application configurations that can maximize HA.

1 High bandwidth interconnects must be used.

In addition to HA data services, SC3.0 software provides scalable data resources that load-balance the application workload across cluster nodes (scalability). For example, adding a third node to a two-node cluster enables the cluster framework to use the new node as a resource for increased throughput. By contrast, SC2.2 software can use an additional node only as an application or standby node.

Types of Scalability

As previously discussed in Chapter 2, "Sun Cluster 2.2 Architecture," there are two types of scalability: *vertical* (adding more CPUs to a node) and *horizontal* (adding more nodes to a cluster).

Vertical Scalability

Vertical scalability is limited within the domain of a single machine. Adding CPU capacity increases the scalability potential. Vertical scalability is useful for long-running database queries or complex computing-intensive jobs (such as finite element analysis) requiring large amounts of CPU power. Using twice the number of CPUs should theoretically decrease processing time by half.

Horizontal Scalability

Horizontal scalability is not limited to a single machine. Data or processes are spread across several machines in a horizontal configuration (such as a cluster environment). An example of application horizontal scalability is numerous small jobs benefiting from multiple machines accessing the same data store. If a single node can manage 100 users, then two nodes should (theoretically) be able to manage 200 users, thereby doubling application scalability.

The Addition of CPUs to an Existing Machine

Adding CPUs is easy and cost-effective; however, even the largest server has physical limitations with respect to memory, network bandwidth, I/O processing capability, and the number of CPUs that can be installed.

Note: Even if an application is CPU-bound, adding more CPUs does not guarantee linear scalability. Eventually, other limitations will be revealed.

The Addition of Nodes to an Existing Cluster

Another approach to achieve scalability is by using a cluster, adding nodes to the cluster, and spreading the application workload over the nodes (load-balancing). SC3.0 software provides a new resource to assist in creating scalable resources for applications.

An example of using scalable resources is the shared address resource (basic resource type supplied with SC3.0 software). The shared address resource load-balances IP requests across all nodes. Web servers use the IP protocol as the underling delivery method. A Web user connects to a Web server through an HTTP connection. This address is then converted to the Web server's IP address.

In Figure 8-4, all nodes (with the exception of E) are configured as Web servers. Node A is configured as the global IP node. Node A accepts requests for specific IP addresses and distributes those requests via the interconnect to nodes B, C, and D. After receiving a request, each node responds directly to the client making the request. Node E is configured as a database server. Requests to node E do not come through node A—instead, clients make requests directly to node E; likewise, node E responds directly to the requestor.

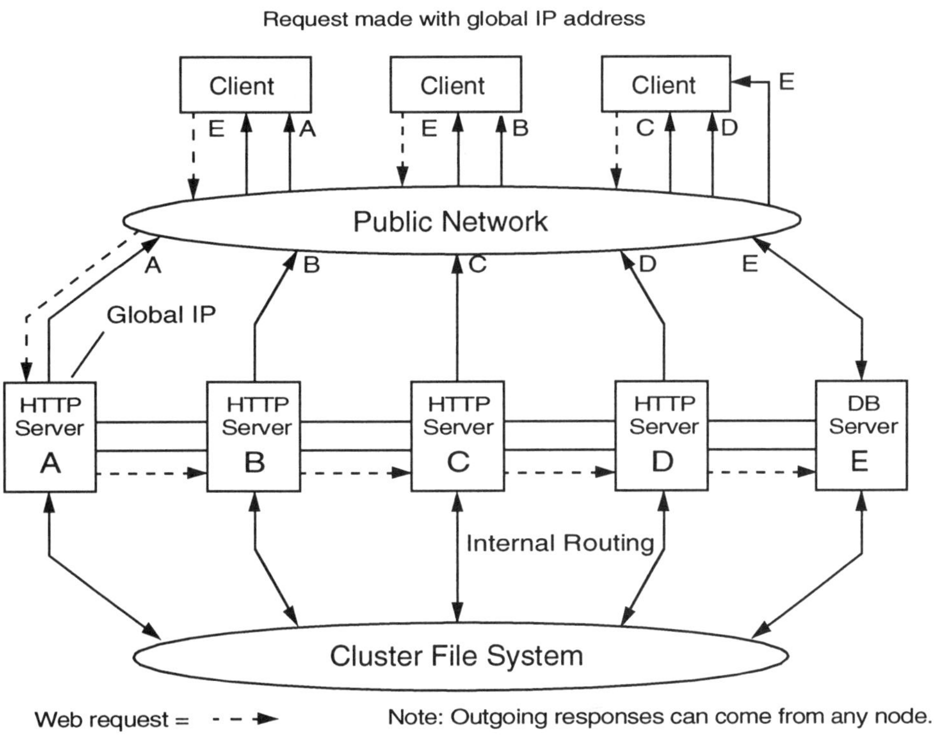

Figure 8-4 Load-Balancing Using Global Networking

Note: Node A is highly available; if node A fails, any other node can pick up the global IP requests and function as node A. Shared address resources are not bound to any storage or GFS. Therefore, in the event of failure, a shared resource can be quickly mastered by any node within the cluster.

Additionally, the scalable address resource can be configured to distribute IP requests with either of the following pre-determined algorithms:

- *Round-robin* – Requests are sent in round-robin fashion to nodes configured as a shared address resource.
- *Weighted IP* – Each node is given a weighted value out of 100. The shared address resource can be configured to use this weighting. This algorithm is useful for a heterogeneous mix of cluster nodes because it fine-tunes the load balance; for example:
  - Node A—10 responds to 10 requests for every 100.
  - Node B—30 responds to 30 requests for every 100.
  - Node C—30 responds to 30 requests for every 100.
  - Node D—30 responds to 30 requests for every 100.

Both algorithms can be configured to use sticky IP, where requests are sent to specific nodes. This approach can be useful for shopping basket e-commerce applications, or other applications where clients need to maintain connectivity to the same server during the entire transaction.

Communications Framework

The SC3.0 communications framework was written using an object request broker (ORB) framework. Security is not an issue because the ORB implementation is internal to the cluster framework. Cluster messages are not passed on the public network, only on the interconnect. Similarly, only cluster members receive ORB messages. Using a message-passing model creates a cluster with a framework that is more resilient to fault conditions because object isolation cluster recovery is isolated to the location at which a fault occurred. With object orientation, the ORB is easily expandable, thereby opening the framework to technologies such as EJB components and servlets.

Cluster Management

Cluster management tools have been enhanced in SC3.0 software. Both the command-line tool and graphical tools are available for cluster-wide management. A comprehensive set of command-line tools is available for node configuration, diagnostics, and cluster status information. Management tools are cluster-aware, so commands can be used from any node, incorporated into UNIX shell scripts, and run from `cron` jobs.

SC3.0 software has modules that can implement Sun Management Center™ resources to monitor cluster activities, including nodes, storage, logs, configurations, and cluster messages. Cluster-aware agents enable system administrators to view, monitor, and log cluster activity from a central GUI.

Summary

The SC3.0 framework has undergone extensive testing during its development. The features discussed in this chapter are accurate at the time of publication.

The SC3.0 software offers extensive capability and potential; therefore, a forthcoming Sun BluePrints book will be devoted to the SC3.0 environment.

Because of the benefits clustering offers, clustering technology will continue to evolve. Sun Microsystems is dedicated and committed to the future of cluster technology.

Appendix A: SCSI-Initiator ID

Setting up a cluster is a complex task involving detailed configuration changes. Many of the changes involve the OS, the volume manager, and sometimes high availability data services. These types of configuration changes are routinely made by system administrators and are commonplace; however, when a clustered system employs a shared SCSI chain, there are additional configuration requirements that are performed using Open Boot PROM (OBP) commands.

Because OBP commands are unfamiliar to many system administrators, implementing changes can be complicated. This appendix provides all necessary information for using OBP commands to change a host's SCSI-initiator ID.

Changing the SCSI-initiator ID is necessary for configurations using shared SCSI devices to enable them to function correctly when connected to multiple hosts. Each SCSI ID on the chain *must* be unique, including the SCSI-initiator ID. Although there are numerous ways of configuring shared SCSI chains, the procedure described in this appendix can eliminate many potential problems faced when using other methods.

SCSI Issues in Clusters

When connecting multiple SCSI devices in a chain, it is important to ensure the SCSI IDs do not conflict. Each SCSI device requires a unique ID because the ID identifies a physical address on the SCSI bus.

To prevent conflict problems, the SCSI device ID should be uniquely set. However, the methods used to set the SCSI ID will vary, depending on whether the device is a disk or host. For example, with disks, the ID can be set on the hardware.

Note: The ID of a Sun storage enclosure is generally hardwired to a drive position within the enclosure. This method ensures that each position has a unique SCSI ID associated with the position.

Setting the SCSI ID for a host that is a SCSI-initiator is more complex.

The SCSI protocol supports two classes of devices:

Initiator

An initiator is generally a host device that can initiate a SCSI command. The default SCSI-initiator ID is 7.

Target

A target is a device that will respond to SCSI commands.

Note: A target is generally a storage device, although it could be a printer, scanner, or any other device on the SCSI chain.

Because target devices generally require an initiator to function, they should not use ID 7. Other available IDs fall within the ranges of 0-6 and 8-15. Narrow SCSI target devices have IDs available in the 0-6 range, with wide SCSI devices having IDs available in the range of 0-15.

Note: If only one system is connected to a SCSI chain, the SCSI-initiator ID (the SCSI ID of the system) will not generally require changing.

Each SCSI chain attached to a system is associated with a single SCSI controller. Each controller is the connection point of the system to a specific SCSI chain. The host can have a different address on each SCSI chain; therefore, it can be useful to think of the SCSI address as belonging to a specific controller (the host's connection to a specific chain) itself, rather than to the host. The SCSI-initiator ID represents the system's address on a specific chain and can be set environment-wide for all controllers on the system (or individually for each SCSI controller). An environment-wide ID sets the default value for all controllers not having an ID explicitly set.

Clustered configurations are more complex to configure than a single machine because there could be multiple initiators on the SCSI chain. If only one initiator is on a chain, all targets will be local to the initiator—that is, they can only receive requests from that initiator. In a single non-clustered system configuration, there can be several SCSI chains—each with its own set of SCSI IDs. However, each chain will still be local to the single initiator.

A clustered configuration could be made up of a combination of local and global chains. Any local chains will have connections from a specific host to target devices only, whereas any global chains will contain connections to target devices and other initiators.

On local chains, each host must retain the default SCSI ID of 7 to prevent local chain conflicts—however, on global chains, the default ID for one of the initiators must be changed. If the ID is not changed, both initiators will share the same ID, and therefore, the same address. Figure A-1 illustrates a SCSI address conflict.

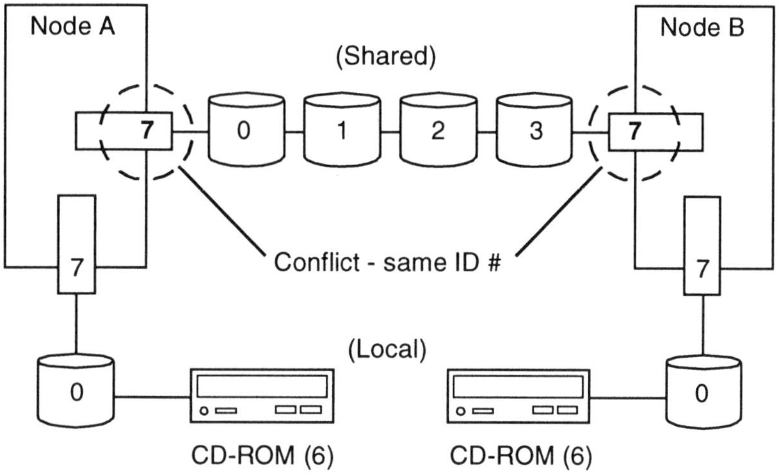

Figure A-1 Conflicting SCSI-initiator IDs

On local chains, the SCSI-initiator ID should be kept at the default value of 7—thereby preventing SCSI ID conflicts with devices such as the boot disk or CD-ROM (and any internal devices to be installed in the future).

On shared chains, one of the hosts should have its SCSI ID set to 6—this will prevent conflict problems, see Figure A-2. The SCSI ID for the other host should be left at the default value.

Note: Setting the SCSI ID to 6 prevents a drive with a higher priority from hijacking the bus. Although changing the global SCSI-initiator ID of a device to 8 (or another unique ID on the chain) could solve a SCSI-initiator conflict and avoids the necessity of writing an `nvram` script, there could be a precedence problem because ID 8 has a precedence below that of other targets. A SCSI ID of 7 has the highest precedence—followed by 6, decreasing down to 0. IDs 8 to 15 have a precedence below ID 0.

When changing the SCSI-initiator ID, ensure none of the drives (or other devices) in the chain have the same ID. This holds true for global and local chains—that is, on any given chain, ensure each SCSI address is only used once. For example, with some Sun servers, the internal drives exist at IDs 0 and 1, with the internal CD-ROM being set to ID 6. Therefore, the SCSI-initiator ID should not be set to 0, 1, or 6 on the internal SCSI chain.

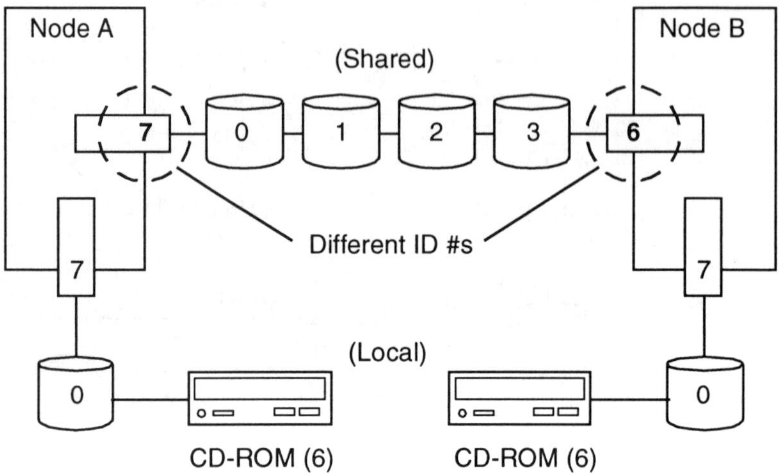

Figure A-2 Non-conflicting SCSI-initiator IDs

Changing the SCSI-initiator ID Overview

Any changes made to the SCSI-initiator ID should be made before connecting the host to the affected SCSI chain.

The procedure for changing the SCSI-initiator ID requires modifying some OBP variables and setting up a script that will run as part of the OBP initialization. This can be performed using shell commands or by working directly at the OBP level (the ok prompt). Changes made to an OBP environment variable are non-volatile—all changes are retained even when the system is rebooted or the OS is reinstalled.

The procedure should only be performed on one node of a two-node cluster—a similar procedure could be followed for clusters with more than two nodes; however, the SCSI chains have to be mapped, and a decision must be made as to which controllers on specific chains are to be changed. It is a good idea to make changes on as few machines as possible. For example, in a four-node ring topology cluster, two nodes should remain unchanged, while the other two nodes should have the SCSI ID of the external controllers set to 6. The nodes with their IDs set to 7 would only share disks with nodes that have their IDs set to 6. Remember, all IDs on a chain must be unique.

If you administer multiple clusters, you should have a standard procedure for determining which device node will have the SCSI ID changed. For example, changing the initiator ID of the node with the highest Ethernet address, or the node with the highest suffix in the hostname (if node names are the cluster name affixed with a number), makes it easier to remember which node has a non-default SCSI-initiator ID.

All changes made to the SCSI-initiator ID at the OBP level should be documented to assist in future troubleshooting.

Changing an environment-wide SCSI ID on one node of a two-node cluster and explicitly setting the local chains back to 7 eliminates conflicts on the shared chains and is transparent to devices on the local chains. A cluster environment usually has only one local SCSI chain (but could have several shared chains). This method reduces the number of controllers that require the SCSI IDs to be explicitly changed. Additionally, most cluster configurations will not require extra work to add a new shared chain—any new controllers automatically have their SCSI IDs set to the default.

Note: Ensure the host SCSI IDs do not interfere with each other, and also that target IDs do not interfere with the host IDs. Each SCSI ID on the chain must be unique, regardless of whether used by a target or initiator device. This could mean leaving an empty slot in a storage enclosure if the SCSI ID for the slot conflicts with the modified SCSI-initiator ID.

Note: Setting the SCSI ID for individual controllers is more complex than setting an environment-wide default. Both require using the OBP prompt or the Solaris OE `eeprom` command. Veritas Volume Manager (and other programs) store information in the `NVRAM`; therefore, it is important to check the `NVRAM` contents before making changes. This is performed using the `printenv nvramrc` OBP command, or the `eeprom nvramrc` command at the Solaris OE shell prompt. In most cases, existing `NVRAM` contents can be appended to the `nvram` script that sets the initiator ID. Some firmware upgrades will modify the OBP variables, see section, "Maintaining Changes to `NVRAM`" on page 337.

The nvram script consists of OBP commands run in sequence. The script is called after system initialization (but before the device tree is built). However, because a device tree must *already* exist for some OBP commands to work correctly, the nvram script must first run the probe-all command (which creates an OBP device tree). Because the probe-all command is also run independently during the startup procedure, two OBP device trees would be created (only one will be seen by the OS). The nvramrc changes are effected in the tree that is not seen by the OS. To prevent this, a process to stop the second probe-all operation from starting needs to be invoked. The system startup procedure has a work-around to prevent two sets of trees from being created. This work-around will enable running the probe-all command in the nvram script, and will prevent the probe-all command from running during the standard system startup procedure (as listed in Table A-1).

Table A-1 System Startup Process

Order	Procedure	Description
1	POST	Power on self-test
2	System initialization	
3	Evaluate nvramrc	Evaluates the nvramrc script (if the use-nvramrc? Open Boot environment variable is true)
4	Run probe-all command*	Builds the device tree and initializes the devices
5	Run install-console command*	Sets up the console (keyboard or terminal port)
6	Run banner command*	Prints system information to the console
7	Secondary diagnostics	
8	Boot	Boots the system

* Only runs if the banner command is not called during the nvramrc script evaluation.

The work-around script uses the banner command (which displays system configuration information) in the nvram script to signal that the part of the standard system startup that runs the probe-all, install-console, and banner commands is being executed by the nvram script. If the banner command appears *anywhere* in the nvram script, the banner command will not run outside of the script (neither will the install-console or probe-all commands).

Note: Instead of using the `banner` command to signal the `probe-all` and `install-console` commands to run within the `nvram` script, the `suppress banner` command can be used (anywhere in the nvramrc script). However, the `suppress-banner` command does not display system information.

The device node properties (including the SCSI ID) can be changed after the `probe-all` command has created the device node tree. The Open Boot directory structure lists devices in a manner similar to the UNIX environment—each device node represents a level in the hardware hierarchy.

The peripheral bus (sbus or PCI) is a primary node under the root. All peripheral devices branch off this node—each device has a unique name which comprises the following parts:

Device Identifier

The first part of the name identifies the device; however, the naming convention may vary for each type of device node. The device identifier is followed by the @ symbol.

Note: Device identifiers for peripheral cards are generally identified by the manufacturers symbol, followed by a comma, then the device type abbreviation (for example, SUNW,qfe@2,8c00000 identifies a quad fast Ethernet device manufactured by Sun Microsystems).

Device Address and Offset

After the @ symbol, the device address and offset identifier are listed—the address is listed first, followed by a comma, then the offset. These identifiers generally reflect a connector or slot location. For example, the `sbus@f,0` and `sbus@e,0` entries in Figure A-3 shows two different sbus hardware slots.

This identifier/address/offset combination enables multiple devices (of the same type) to be uniquely identified using the address and offset. Figures A-3 and A-4 show examples of OBP device trees. Some devices in the OBP device tree do not represent actual devices—these are termed pseudodevices. Other OBP devices represent hardware components unrelated to the peripheral cards; for example, in Figure A-4, the CPU is represented by the name `SUNW,UltraSPARC™-II`.

Although an understanding of the OBP device tree is beneficial for comprehending the architecture of the machine, it is not essential for changing the SCSI-initiator ID.

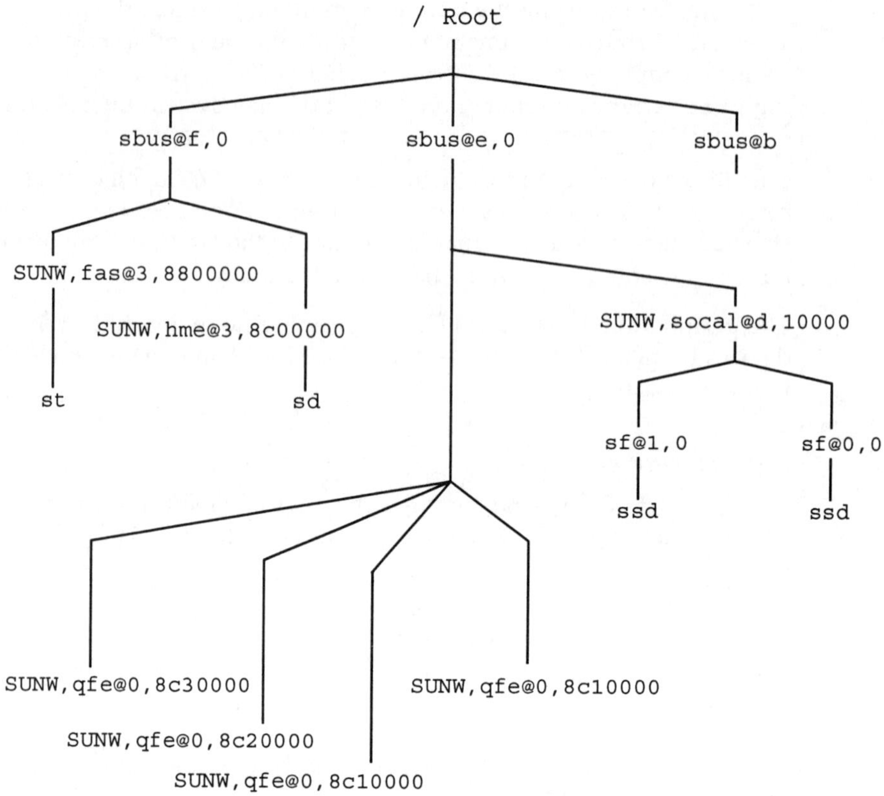

Figure A-3 Example of sbus OBP Device Tree (incomplete)

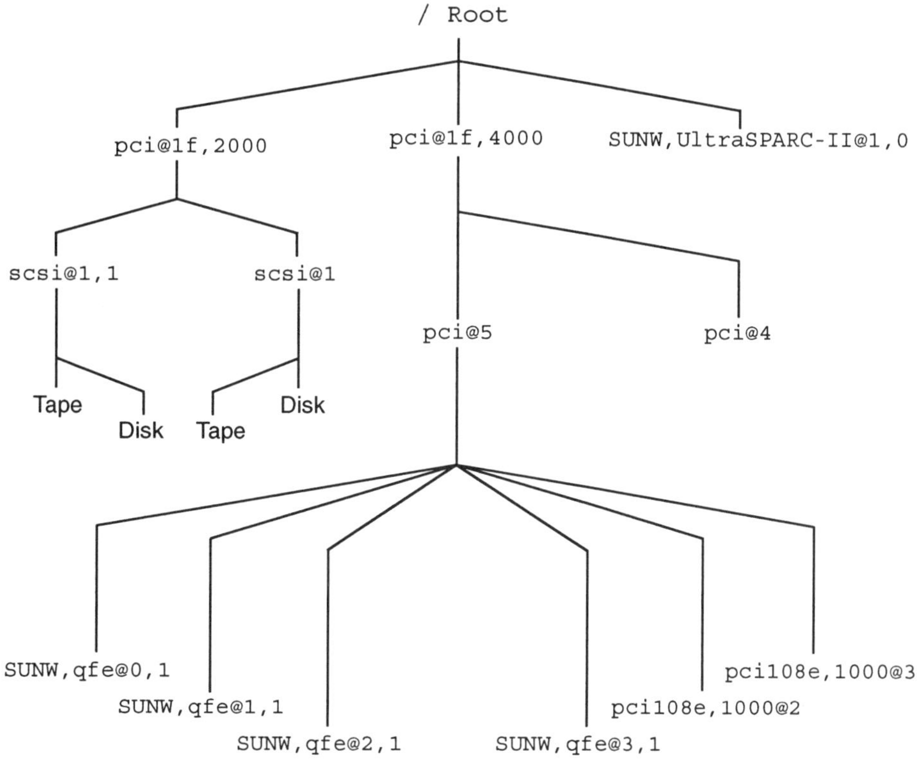

Figure A-4 Example of PCI OBP Device Tree—Sun Enterprise 250 (incomplete)

Mapping an OBP address to a physical card location can be difficult. To map a hardware location to an OBP node, use the following tables: A-2, A-3, A-4, and A-5. These tables display the mapping of device slots to OBP device nodes across several product families for the current generation of Sun systems. Additional platform-specific information about OBP nodes can be found in the appropriate service manuals. The variable *devname* represents the name of the device in a given slot. Figure A-5 shows the physical device slots referred to in Table A-2.

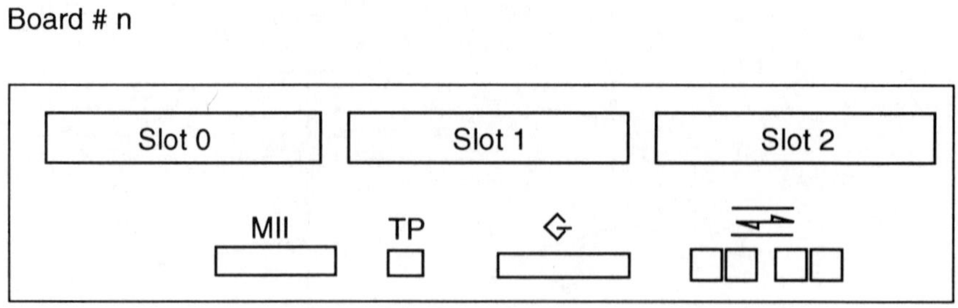

Figure A-5 I/O Board Interfaces in the Sun Enterprise xx00 Series

Table A-2 Sun Enterprise *xx*00: Relationships of Physical Locations to OBP Nodes

Hardware Slot on Board # n	OBP Device Tree Node
2	`/sbus@(2n)/`*devname*`@2`
1	`/sbus@(2n)/`*devname*`@1`
0	`/sbus@(2n+1)/`*devname*`@0`
Ethernet (TP)	`/sbus@(2n+1)/hme@3`
SCSI	`/sbus@(2n+1)/fas@3`
Fiber	`/sbus@(2n)/socal@d`

Table A-3 Sun Enterprise 450: Relationships of Physical Locations to OBP Nodes

PCI Slot Number (labeled)	OBP Device Tree Node
10	`pci@1f,4000/`*devname*`@4`
9	`pci@4,4000/`*devname*`@2`
8	`pci@4,4000/`*devname*`@3`
7	`pci@4,4000/`*devname*`@4`
6	`pci@4,2000/`*devname*`@1`
5	`pci@1f,2000/`*devname*`@1`
4	`pci@6,2000/`*devname*`@1`
3	`pci@6,4000/`*devname*`@2`
2	`pci@6,4000/`*devname*`@3`
1	`pci@6,4000/`*devname*`@4`

Table A-4 Sun Enterprise 420R or Netra™ t 1400/1405: Relationships of Physical Locations to OBP Nodes

PCI Slot Number (labeled)	OBP Device Tree Node
4	`pci@1f,4000/`*devname*`@5`
3	`pci@1f,4000/`*devname*`@2`
2	`pci@1f,4000/`*devname*`@4`
1	`pci@1f,2000/`*devname*`@1`

Table A-5 Sun Enterprise 250/220R or Netra t 1120/1125: Relationships of Physical Locations to OBP Nodes

PCI Slot Number (labeled)	OBP Device Tree Node
4	`pci@1f,4000/`*devname*`@5`
3	`pci@1f,4000/`*devname*`@4`
2	`pci@1f,4000/`*devname*`@2`
1	`pci@1f,2000/`*devname*`@1`

Navigating through the device tree is performed in a manner similar to the UNIX environment (using the `cd` and `ls` commands). However, when working at the OBP prompt, you begin outside the device tree. To gain access to the device tree, the `dev` command or an absolute path (one beginning with the root slash) must be used. To exit the device tree, use the `device-end` command.

The `.properties` command displays the properties of the current device node and can be useful for debugging problems when setting the SCSI-initiator ID. The following example shows an output from the `.properties` command run from a device node that represents a SCSI controller:

```
ok pwd
/sbus@1f,0/SUNW,fas@e,8800000
ok .properties
scsi-initiator-id         00000007
hm-rev                    00 00 00 22
device_type               scsi
clock-frequency           02625a00
intr                      00000020 00000000
interrupts                00000020
reg                       0000000e 08800000 00000010
                          0000000e 08810000 00000040
name                      SUNW,fas
```

In this example, the current SCSI-initiator ID for the controller is listed in the `scsi-initiator-id` field. Unless the value of the `scsi-initiator-id` field is set explicitly, it will default to the value of the `scsi-initiator-id` OBP environment variable.

Changing a SCSI-initiator ID is discussed in the following sections.

Changing the SCSI-initiator ID

The `nvram` script can be edited from either a Solaris OE shell or from the OBP prompt. The shell method is easier to use if the OS is operational. Additionally, the shell method can be scripted and is easier to document than working at the OBP level. However, if the OS is down, it will be easier to implement changes using the OBP method. In either case, the machine has to be rebooted for changes to take effect.

This procedure is intended for a two-node cluster. Some of the issues involved in modifying this procedure to work with more than two nodes were discussed earlier in this appendix.

Shell Command Prompt Method

Set the environment-wide SCSI-initiator ID to 6 using the `eeprom` command. This command must be run at the shell prompt as the root user.

```
# eeprom scsi-initiator-id=6
```

The `eeprom` command enables changes to the eeprom (which is visible from the OBP level). Because the preceding command made a change to the EEPROM, the change becomes permanent (even if the OS is reinstalled). To ensure a change does not interfere with local SCSI chains (including the CD-ROM and boot devices), write a script that resets the local chain controller IDs back to 7.

An easy way to create an `nvram` script at the shell prompt is to make a file that contains a script of OBP commands (*not* shell commands). Then, store the script in NVRAM using the `eeprom` command. Create this file using a text editor and store it where it can be retrieved at a later date. The following is a step-by-step description of the commands required in the script.

The first command required is the `probe-all` command. This command is the first action taken by the `nvram` script—it will probe the devices and create a device tree. The file should look as follows:

```
probe-all
```

Next, change the SCSI-initiator ID back to 7 on the local chains (which are not connected to other initiators). For each controller connected to a local chain, the script should enter the device node that represents the controller (using the `cd` command) and change the SCSI-initiator ID value. For example, if the internal/local controller represented by the device node `SUNW,fas@e,8800000` is connected to the sbus card at address `1f` (as with Ultra 1 and Ultra 2 systems), the following command would be added to the file:

```
cd /sbus@1f,0/SUNW,fas@e,8800000
```

Note: The device node path used is only an example. In a situation where there are multiple local chains, the script is required to execute commands to enter each device node representing a local controller and explicitly change its initiator ID.

After entering the device node, change the SCSI-initiator ID to 7 by inserting the following line in the file:

```
7 " scsi-initiator-id" integer-property
```

Note: There should be a space before and after the first quotation mark. The quotation mark is a special OBP command that tells the tokenizer to treat the next word (which must be immediately followed by a quotation mark) as a string of characters. Therefore, the quote mark is separated from the string by a space because it is a command that operates on the string (not a syntactic marker as would be the case in UNIX).

The file should now look similar to the following:

```
probe-all
cd /sbus@1f,0/SUNW,fas@e,8800000
7 " scsi-initiator-id" integer-property
```

Change the SCSI-initiator ID for any other local chains to 7 (using the method described previously).

After the local chain SCSI-initiator IDs have been changed, insert the `device-end` command into the file. Inserting this command will enable the script to exit the device tree. The file should now look similar to the following:

```
probe-all
cd /sbus@1f,0/SUNW,fas@e,8800000
7 " scsi-initiator-id" integer-property
device-end
```

As discussed previously, when the `probe-all` command is used in an `nvram` script, include the `banner` command in the file as a flag to keep the `probe-all` command from running again when the script has completed. Because the `banner` command also prevents the `install-console` command from running automatically, you must include the `install-console` command in the script as well. At the end of the file, include the `install-console` and `banner` commands. The file should now look similar to the following:

```
probe-all
cd /sbus@1f,0/SUNW,fas@e,8800000
7 " scsi-initiator-id" integer-property
device-end
install-console
banner
```

The next step is to store the contents of the file in NVRAM. Before doing so, review the existing contents of NVRAM (if any) to ensure they are preserved. The `eeprom nvramrc` command displays the (current) contents of the `nvramrc` variable. The contents of the `nvramrc` variable should be prepended to the file to ensure no NVRAM information is overwritten. To store the file contents in NVRAM, run the `eeprom` command. The actual command to be run is dependent on the filename. For example, if your file is named `/var/adm/scripts/nvram_file`, the command to use would be as follows (for Bourne and Korn shells):

```
# eeprom nvramrc="`cat /var/adm/scripts/nvram_file`"
```

In the previous command, the *backtics* (`) signal the shell to interpret the `cat` command. If the quotation marks are not included, only the first line will make it into the `nvramrc` variable. If the backtics are not included, the `nvramrc` variable will contain the unevaluated string `cat /var/adm/scripts/nvarm_file`. Because different shells treat backtics and quotes differently, check the values of the variables when finished.

The `nvramrc` environment variable should now be configured; however, the `nvram` script will not be run at initialization unless the `use-nvramrc?` environment variable is set to `true` using the following command:

```
# eeprom use-nvramrc?=true
```

Confirm all modified NVRAM values by using the `eeprom` command. The `eeprom` command displays the value corresponding to a specific variable if run with that variable as an argument (without specifying a new value with the equals sign). Enter the following commands to confirm the appropriate OBP variables:

```
# eeprom scsi-initiator-id
scsi-initiator-id=6
# eeprom nvramrc
nvramrc=probe-all
cd /sbus@1f,0/SUNW,fas@e,8800000
7 " scsi-initiator-id" integer-property
device-end
install-console
banner
# eeprom use-nvramrc?
use-nvramrc?=true
```

Using the Open Boot PROM (OBP) Prompt Method

All steps performed in the previous section may be implemented at the OBP prompt; however, the process differs slightly.

Note: The steps discussed in this section are for an OBP prompt only and are not suitable for running at the shell command prompt.

Set the environment-wide SCSI-initiator ID to 6 using the `setenv` command. Enter the following command into the OBP prompt:

```
ok setenv scsi-initiator-id 6
```

Because the preceding command sets an OBP environment variable (stored in NVRAM), the change becomes permanent automatically. Therefore, a script should be created to reset the local chain controller IDs back to 7. Create the script using the `nvedit` command.

The `nvedit` command starts a basic editor that operates in insert mode only and uses keystrokes similar to EMACS (see Table A-6). The `nvedit` editor displays a line number at the beginning of each line (which is the only way to know which line you are on).

The editor begins with line zero; the line you are currently editing is always displayed at the bottom of the screen. Pressing Return at the end of any line will create a new line. If there are additional lines after a newly added line, they will have their line numbers adjusted to account for the new line.

Note: It is easy to unintentionally press Return and move existing lines down without realizing it; therefore, it is a good idea to review the finished file using the `<ctrl> p` or `<ctrl> n` keystrokes.

To start the `nvedit` editor, enter the following command at the OBP prompt:

```
ok nvedit
   0:
```

Note: In the preceding codebox, `0` is the first line number.

Table A-6 The nvedit Commands

Keystrokes	Action
`<ctrl> c`	Exits the nvramrc editor and returns to the OBP command interpreter. The temporary buffer is preserved, but is not written back to the nvramrc variable. (Use nvstore to write back.)
`<ctrl> l`	List all lines.
`<ctrl> p`	Move to previous line.
`<ctrl> n`	Move to next line.
`<ctrl> b`	Move back one character.
`<ctrl> f`	Move forward one character.
Delete	Delete a character.
Enter/Return or `<ctrl> o`	Start a new line.
`<ctrl> k`	Delete (kill) all characters from the cursor to the end of the line (including the next carriage return). If used at the end of a line, it will join the current line with the next line. If used at the beginning of a line, it will delete the entire line.

On line zero, enter the probe-all command (followed by pressing Return). This will cause the nvram script to probe the devices and create the device tree. The nvram script should look as follows:

```
0:  probe-all
```

After pressing Return, line 0 will move up the page and the cursor will be on line 1.

For each controller connected to a local chain, use the cd command to enter the device node (that represents the controller) and reset the SCSI-initiator ID value to 7. For example, if the internal/local controller is represented by the device node SUNW,fas@e (connected to the sbus card at address 1f), enter the device node by inserting the following command:

```
cd /sbus@1f,0/SUNW,fas@e,8800000
```

The SCSI-initiator ID value is changed by entering the following line:

```
7 " scsi-initiator-id" integer-property
```

Note: In the previous box, there should be a space before and after the first quotation mark.

In this example, the SCSI-initiator ID for the controller can be set in NVRAM when the previous two commands are added to lines 1 and 2 of the `nvram` script—as shown:

```
1: cd /sbus@1f,0/SUNW,fas@e,8800000
2: 7 " scsi-initiator-id" integer-property
```

The previous lines should be repeated for each local chain. After the IDs have been changed for all local devices, add the following commands to the end of the script (the line numbers used in the following codebox are examples only):

```
3: device-end
4: install-console
5: banner
6:
```

The Return following the `banner` command (line 5) will create a new line (6). Because the script is now completed, press `<ctrl> c` to exit the `nvedit` editor. Although the script is completed, it is not yet committed to NVRAM. To save the changes, use the `nvstore` command to move the `nvedit` buffer into NVRAM. Enter the following command at the OBP prompt:

```
ok nvstore
```

The `nvramrc` script should now be configured; however, it will not be run unless the `use-nvramrc?` environment variable is set to `true` by using the `setenv` command. Enter the following command at the OBP prompt (note the output):

```
ok setenv use-nvramrc? true
use-nvramrc? =          true
```

Verify the contents of the nvramrc variable using the printenv nvramrc command. The command and output should look as follows:

```
ok printenv nvramrc
nvramrc =    probe-all
   cd /sbus@1f,0/SUNW,fas@e,8800000
   7 " scsi-initiator-id" integer-property
   device-end
   install-console
   banner
```

If there are errors, use the nvedit editor again and make the required changes. Move to the line(s) to be edited using the <ctrl> p or <ctrl> n keystrokes—edit the line, or delete it using the <ctrl> k keystrokes.

After making changes, run the nvstore command again. When the nvramrc script is correct, restart the machine for changes to take effect by entering the following command:

```
ok reset-all
```

Maintaining Changes to NVRAM

Some patches or system upgrades may alter the NVRAM or disable the use-nvramrc? environment variable, and could erase the nvram script. For example, the Solaris OE version 7 software includes a firmware patch to enable some older Sun Enterprise Ultra-1 and Ultra-2 servers to use 64-bit addressing. Although using this patch is optional, it will reset the use-nvramrc? environment variable and prevent the nvram script from running. After applying patches or making changes that involve server firmware or the EEPROM, check the value of any non-default OBP variables.

To confirm the nvram variables, run the following UNIX commands:

```
eeprom use-nvramrc?
eeprom nvramrc
eeprom scsi-initiator-id
```

As a precaution against errors or poor configurations, the contents of the NVRAM should be regularly backed up. This can be performed using a `cron` script in combination with the `eeprom` command. As with any system configuration documentation, it is a good idea to print a hard copy and store it in a secure location. The following command can be used in the `cron` script to create a dated backup file:

```
eeprom > /var/adm/doc/`date +%Y%m%d`.eeprom.out
```

If a cluster node is decommissioned or needs to be returned to a pristine state, the `set-defaults` command can be used at the OBP prompt to reset all `nvram` variables to their default values.

Summary

Changing the SCSI-initiator ID on a cluster node enables two nodes to share SCSI storage devices on a single SCSI chain. This procedure is essential for correct operation of a shared SCSI chain. Changing SCSI IDs requires either direct or indirect modification of the `nvramrc` script. Changes are permanent (even after re-installation of the OS).

Because some firmware upgrades can modify OBP variables, it is critical to check the variables after any firmware changes. Regular backups of the EEPROM settings are also crucial.

Appendix B: SC2.2 Data Service Templates

The following Bourne shell script templates are provided as examples of data service methods (DSMs) required by the SC2.2 software to convert standard applications into highly available applications.

Each template is targeted to a basic (non-complex) data service. The templates include a flow diagram and supporting documentation. If these templates are to be used for complex data services, the error checking component of the scripts must be enhanced.

The DSM code presented in this appendix provides building blocks for developing HA-agents (those not currently provided by Sun Microsystems).

Sun Microsystems, Inc. is not responsible for the use of this code. The DSM script templates presented here are for illustrative purposes only and are not supported by Sun Microsystems, Inc. or any of its subsidiaries.

The following DSM script templates have been designed using the following assumptions:

- The data service has a *unique* name.
- The configuration file and DSM scripts are located in the same directory.
- The data service name is used as a prefix for the configuration file and DSM scripts. For example, the `START_NET` DSM script for the `ha_webserver` data service should be named `ha_webserver_start_net`, with its corresponding configuration file named `ha_webserver.config`.
- The process monitoring facility (PMF) is required for use inside the template scripts for starting and monitoring the data service—the PMF will use the data service name as its identifier.

Each DSM template script uses a configuration file. This file is a text file containing attributes and values that can be imported into the Bourne shell (for example, `ATTRIBUTE=VALUE`).

An important reason for having a configuration file is to store variable modifications required by a new application, rather than modifying the DSM template script itself.

It is recommended that the `STOP_NET` DSM script include additional code to ensure a data service or highly available application is correctly stopped.

The following two variables *must* be included in the global configuration file:

1. SERVICE_NAME

The name of the data service registered with the SC2.2 infrastructure. The `SERVICE_NAME` is used as the prefix for the configuration file, for example, `SERVICE_NAME.config`.

Note: To access the global configuration file, the DSM script templates need to extract the `SERVICE_NAME` variable by stripping off the first part of the program name; for example, the `ha_webserver` is stripped from the `ha_webserver_stop_net` string. The `SERVICE_NAME` variable *must* still be included in the configuration file (to accurately reflect the data service name), which prevents the DSM script templates from failing.

---

2. START_PROGRAM

An executable file invoked by the `pmfadm(1m)` command within the `START_NET` DSM script, which is responsible for starting an application hosted by the data service. For example, the `START_PROGRAM` executable starts a Web server application (with appropriate arguments) associated with the `ha_webserver` data service.

The following variables can be (optionally) included in the global configuration file:

- REQUIRED_FILESYSTEMS

A shell list of additional file system mount points required by the data service. If this variable exists, the DSM script templates will check for availability of these file systems, and will fail if the file systems are not mounted.

Note: The SC2.2 infrastructure manages disk groups (VxVM) and disk sets (SDS), administrative file systems, data service file system ownership, and availability of each logical host.

- PMF_RETRIES

The maximum number of times a failed data service can be restarted (the pmfadm -n option).

- PMF_PERIOD

Time period (in minutes) after which a failed data service is restarted (the pmfadm -t option).

- PMF_ACTION

The executable file invoked when a data service fails more than PMF_RETRIES times within a PMF_PERIOD interval (the pmfadm -a option).

- PMF_WAIT

Time period (in seconds) allocated to complete data service processes (the pmfadm -w option).

- PMF_SIGNAL

The type of process signal submitted to data service processes when a process is to be stopped. The PMF_SIGNAL value is commonly set to KILL or TERM signals.

- STOP_PROGRAM

Executable file used to stop a data service. This routine is used when sending TERM or KILL process signals to a data service to produce a clean shutdown.

- ABORT_PROGRAM

Executable file used to abort the data service. This routine is used when sending TERM or KILL process signals to a data service is not sufficient to produce a clean abort.

- FAULT_PROBE

Executable file used to perform fault monitoring on the data service.

Starting, Stopping, and Aborting Data Services

The first three DSM script templates presented are basic methods to start, stop, and abort a data service, and are intended to aid in the development of the START_NET, STOP_NET, and ABORT_NET DSMs (refer to Figures B-1, B-2, and B-3). The START DSM was left out because its functionality (establishing the application environment before network connectivity is enabled) can be included in the START_NET DSM—prior to the START_PROGRAM being started by the pmfadm(1M) utility.

The start of each DSM script involves setting up variables and reading the configuration file. The remainder of the script determines what course of action is to be taken (based on the routine arguments and current state of the cluster).

Each DSM script has a *debug* function that can be turned on to send information to the cluster's standard debug facility (usually the `syslog local0.debug` file). Because the DSM templates are invoked by the Sun Cluster framework, no output will be sent to `STDERR` or `STDOUT`. Similarly, the `doerror` function included in each DSM script will send error messages to the cluster's error logging facility (usually the `syslog local0.err` file).

Note: DSM script debugging can be turned on by setting the variable `kDEBUG` to 1, and turned off by setting the variable to 0.

Figure B-1 `START_NET` DSM Flow Control Diagram

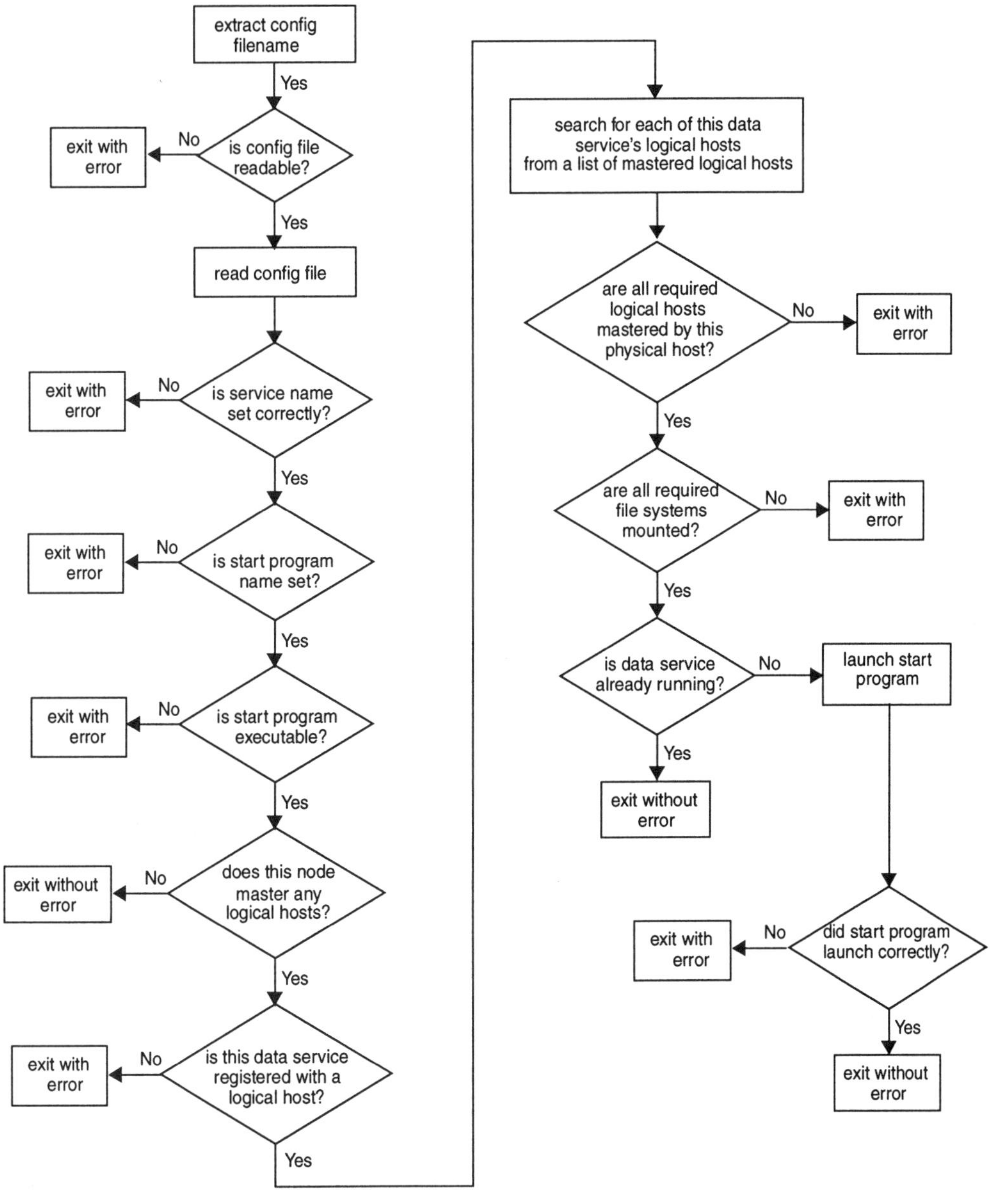

Code Example B-1 Shell Script Code for START_NET DSM:

```
#!/bin/sh#
# generic START_NET script for HA data services Version 1.3
# Copyright 1999 Sun Microsystems, Inc. All rights reserved.
# This script can be used as a template for developing a START_NET
# DSM for SunCluster 2.2 data services. The intention is to help reduce the
# amount of "boilerplate" work before a production script is developed.
# START_NET is called by clustd as part of the cluster reconfiguration
# process. This script can be invoked several times during a cluster
# reconfiguration process by the same node, and it should be written to
# manage a wide range of cluster states.
# When the START_NET script is launched, it is called with the
# following arguments:
#           $1 = comma-separated list of the logical hosts which should be
#                mastered by this physical node
#           $2 = comma-separated list of the logical hosts which should NOT
#                be mastered by this physical node
#           $3 = time in seconds until clustd will time out the process.
# This script makes the following assumptions:
#           - the script is named <dataservice>_start_net, where <dataservice>
#             is the unique data service name
#           - the file <dataservice>.config exists in the same directory as this
#             script and it defines at the very least the variables SERVICE_NAME
#             and START_PROGRAM
#           - the data service program can be started, stopped, and queried
#             using pmfadm
# If your data service does not support the above assumptions, then this script
# should be modified appropriately.
###########################################################################
#  debug function
debug()
  {
  if [ "$kDEBUG" = "1" ] ; then
    logger -p ${SYSLOG}.debug "${PROG} [$$]: $1"
  fi
  }
###########################################################################
# error function
doerror()
  {
```

```
  debug $1
  logger -p ${SYSLOG}.err "${PROG} [$$]: $1"
  }
##########################################################################
# The following variable should be set to 0 to turn debugging off
kDEBUG=1
PATH=/usr/sbin:/usr/bin:/opt/SUNWcluster/bin
PROG=`basename $0`
BASEDIR=`dirname $0`
SYSLOG=`haget -f syslog_facility`
MASTERED=$1
NOT_MASTERED=$2
TIMEOUT=$3
##########################################################################
debug "called as ${PROG} \"${MASTERED}\" \"${NOT_MASTERED}\" ${TIMEOUT}"
# Strip the DSM suffix from the program name to build the config file name,
# then extract its contents to build required variables.
CONFIG_FILE=`echo ${PROG} | sed s/_start_net/.config/`
if [ ! -r "${BASEDIR}/${CONFIG_FILE}" ] ; then
  doerror "cannot read config file ${BASEDIR}/${CONFIG_FILE}"
  exit 1
fi
debug "reading config file ${BASEDIR}/${CONFIG_FILE}"
. ${BASEDIR}/${CONFIG_FILE}
# fail if service name does not exist
if [ -z "${SERVICE_NAME}" ] ; then
  doerror "cannot determine service name"
  exit 1
fi
# fail if start program name does not exist
if [ -z "${START_PROGRAM}" ] ; then
  doerror "cannot determine start program name"
  exit 1
fi
# fail if start program cannot be found or it's not executable
executable=`echo ${START_PROGRAM} | awk -e '{print $1}'`
if [ ! -x "${executable}" ] ; then
  doerror "cannot find executable start program ${executable}"
  exit 1
fi
```

```
# exit peacefully if no logical hosts are mastered on this node
if [ -z "${MASTERED}" ] ; then
  debug "no logical hosts mastered by this node"
  exit 0
fi
# fail if there are no logical hosts assigned to this service
SERVICE_HOSTS=`hareg -q  ${SERVICE_NAME} -H | xargs echo `
if [ -z "${SERVICE_HOSTS}" ] ; then
  doerror "no logical hosts assigned to ${SERVICE_NAME}"
  exit 1
fi
########################################################################
# At this point the trivial cases of failure have been managed and
# we can start verifying appropriate node resource allocation, e.g.,
# logical host mastering.
debug "trivial failure cases passed OK"
# Now loop through all logical hosts required by this data service,
# and compare against the list of hosts mastered by this node. Yield
# a failure if no mastered logical hosts are found.
MASTERED_HOSTS=`echo ${MASTERED} | tr ',' ' '`
for required_host in ${SERVICE_HOSTS} ; do
  foundHost=0
  debug "searching for ${required_host}"
  for mastered_host in ${MASTERED_HOSTS} ; do
    debug "  - considering ${mastered_host}"
    if [ "${mastered_host}" = "${required_host}" ] ; then
      debug "  - found ${required_host} = ${mastered_host}"
      foundHost=1
    fi
  done
# fail if no mastered host matches the required host
  if [ ${foundHost} -ne 1 ] ; then
    doerror "node does not master required logical host \
${required_host}"
    exit 1
  fi
done
########################################################################
# At this point we know the set of mastered hosts contains the set
# of required hosts.
```

```
debug "logical hosts mastered OK"

# Check that the administrative file system of each required logical host
# is mounted correctly. Yield failure if required file system is not mounted.
CURRENT_MOUNTS=`mount | awk -e '{print $1}' | xargs echo `
for required_host in ${SERVICE_HOSTS} ; do
  neededMount=`haget -f pathprefix -h ${required_host}`
  foundMount=0
  debug "searching for filesystem on ${neededMount}"
  for mountPoint in ${CURRENT_MOUNTS} ; do
    debug "  - considering ${mountPoint}"
    if [ "${mountPoint}" = "${neededMount}" ] ; then
      debug "  - found ${mountPoint}"
      foundMount=1
    fi
  done
# Fail if no mounted file system matches a required file system
  if [ ${foundMount} -ne 1 ] ; then
    doerror "administrative filesystem ${neededMount} for logical \
host ${required_host} is not mounted"
    exit 1
  fi
done
# Check that additional file systems, if defined, are mounted and available
# to this physical node. Required file systems are defined as a word list in the
# config file
if [ -n "${REQUIRED_FILESYSTEMS}" ] ; then
  for neededMount in ${REQUIRED_FILESYSTEMS} ; do
    foundMount=0
    debug "searching for filesystem on ${neededMount}"
    for mountPoint in ${CURRENT_MOUNTS} ; do
      debug "  - considering ${mountPoint}"
      if [ "${mountPoint}" = "${neededMount}" ] ; then
        debug "  - found ${mountPoint}"
        foundMount=1
      fi
    done
# Yield failure if no mounted file system matches requirements
    if [ ${foundMount} -ne 1 ] ; then
      doerror "required extra filesystem ${neededMount} is not mounted"
```

```
      exit 1
    fi
  done
fi
##########################################################################
# At this point we know that the file systems are mounted and the logical
# hosts are mastered by this node.
debug "required filesystems mounted OK"

# Any extra checking,e.g.,testing to see if an additional config file is accessible,
# should be placed in this section. After verifying that additional testing is
# successful we can proceed to verify if a data service is already running.
debug "additional checking passed OK"
# Check and exit if data service has already been started.
if `pmfadm -q ${SERVICE_NAME}` ; then
  debug "${SERVICE_NAME} is already running on this node"
  exit 0
fi
##########################################################################
# At this point we can ensure the data service is not already running and
# it can be started.
debug "data service ${SERVICE_NAME} is not already running"
# Ensure that the START program can actually be executed; otherwise,
# complain and attempt to use the default TERM on the pmfadm process.
if [ -n "${START_PROGRAM}" ] ; then
  executable=`echo ${START_PROGRAM} | awk -e '{print $1}'`
  if [ ! -x "${executable}" ] ; then
    doerror "cannot execute ${executable} "
    exit 1
  fi
fi
# Parse any arguments that were set by the config file. Exit if data service
# cannot be started.
retries=""
period=""
action=""
if [ -n "${PMF_RETRIES}" ] ; then
  retries="-n ${PMF_RETRIES}"
  if [ -n "${PMF_PERIOD}" ] ; then
    period="-t ${PMF_PERIOD}"
```

```
  fi
  if [ -n "${PMF_ACTION}" ] ; then
    action="-a \"${PMF_ACTION}\""
  fi
fi
# Start the data service & verify successful startup
pmfadm -c ${SERVICE_NAME} ${retries} ${period} ${action} \
          ${START_PROGRAM}
if [ $? -ne 0 ] ; then
  doerror "couldn't start \"${START_PROGRAM}\". error was $?"
  exit 1
fi
########################################################################
# At this point the start program is running
debug "data service has started"
exit 0
```

Figure B-2 `STOP_NET` DSM Script Flow Diagram

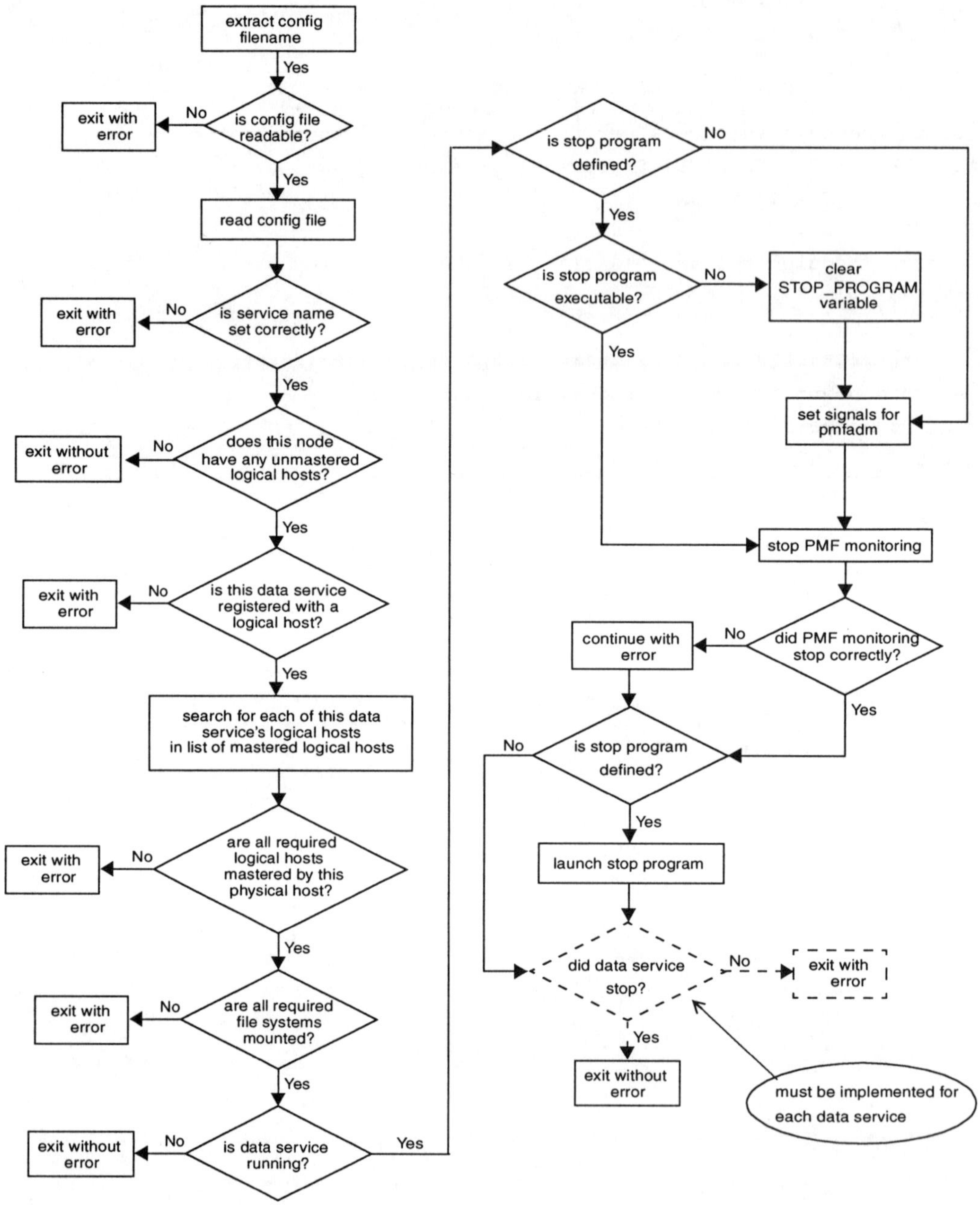

Code Example B-2 Shell Script Code for STOP_NET DSM

```
#!/bin/sh
# generic STOP_NET script for HA data services Version 1.3
# Copyright 1999 Sun Microsystems, Inc. All rights reserved.
# This script can be used as a template for developing a STOP_NET
# DSM for SunCluster 2.2 data services. The intention is to help reduce the
# amount of "boilerplate" work before a production script is developed.
# STOP_NET is called by clustd as part of the cluster reconfiguration
# process. This script can be invoked several times during a cluster
# reconfiguration process by the same node, and it should be written to
# manage a wide range of cluster states.
# When the STOP_NET script is launched, it is called with the
# following arguments:
#           $1 = comma-separated list of the logical hosts which should be
#                mastered by this physical node
#           $2 = comma-separated list of the logical hosts which should NOT
#                be mastered by this physical node
#           $3 = time in seconds until clustd will time out the process.
# This script makes the following assumptions:
#           - the script is named <dataservice>_stop_net, where <dataservice>
#             is the unique data service name
#           - the file <dataservice>.config exists in the same directory as this
#             script and it defines at the very least the variables SERVICE_NAME
#             and START_PROGRAM
#           - the data service program can be started, stopped, and queried
#             using pmfadm
# If your data service does not support the above assumptions, then this script
# should be modified appropriately.
##########################################################################
#  debug function
debug()
  {
  if [ "$kDEBUG" = "1" ] ; then
    logger -p ${SYSLOG}.debug "${PROG} [$$]: $1"
  fi
  }
##########################################################################
# error function
doerror()
  {
  debug $1
  logger -p ${SYSLOG}.err "${PROG} [$$]: $1"
  }
##########################################################################
# The following variable should be set to 0 to turn debugging off
kDEBUG=1
```

```
PATH=/usr/sbin:/usr/bin:/opt/SUNWcluster/bin
PROG=`basename $0`
BASEDIR=`dirname $0`
SYSLOG=`haget -f syslog_facility`
MASTERED=$1
NOT_MASTERED=$2
TIMEOUT=$3
##########################################################################
debug "called as ${PROG} \"${MASTERED}\" \"${NOT_MASTERED}\" ${TIMEOUT}"
# Strip the DSM suffix from the program name to build the config file name,
# then extract its contents to build required variables.
CONFIG_FILE=`echo ${PROG} | sed s/_stop_net/.config/`
if [ ! -r "${BASEDIR}/${CONFIG_FILE}" ] ; then
  doerror "cannot read config file ${BASEDIR}/${CONFIG_FILE}"
  exit 1
fi
debug "reading config file ${BASEDIR}/${CONFIG_FILE}"
. ${BASEDIR}/${CONFIG_FILE}
# fail if service name does not exist
if [ -z "${SERVICE_NAME}" ] ; then
  doerror "cannot determine service name"
  exit 1
fi
# fail if stop program name does not exist
if [ -z "${STOP_PROGRAM}" ] ; then
  doerror "cannot determine stop program name"
  exit 1
fi
# fail if stop program cannot be found or it's not executable
executable=`echo ${START_PROGRAM} | awk -e '{print $1}'`
if [ ! -x "${executable}" ] ; then
  doerror "cannot find executable start program ${executable}"
  exit 1
fi
# exit peacefully if no logical hosts are mastered on this node
if [ -z "${MASTERED}" ] ; then
  debug "no logical hosts mastered by this node"
  exit 0
fi
# fail if there are no logical hosts assigned to this service
SERVICE_HOSTS=`hareg -q  ${SERVICE_NAME} -H | xargs echo `
if [ -z "${SERVICE_HOSTS}" ] ; then
  doerror "no logical hosts assigned to ${SERVICE_NAME}"
  exit 1
fi
##########################################################################
# At this point the trivial cases of failure have been managed and
# we can start verifying appropriate node resource allocation, e.g.,
```

```
# logical host mastering.
debug "trivial failure cases passed OK"

# Now loop through all logical hosts required by this data service,
# and compare against the list of hosts not mastered by this node. Yield
# a failure if no logical hosts are found in the list of host not mastered.
NOT_MASTERED_HOSTS=`echo ${NOT_MASTERED} | tr ',' ' '`
for required_host in ${SERVICE_HOSTS} ; do
  foundHost=0
  debug "searching for ${required_host}"
  for not_mastered_host in ${NOT_MASTERED_HOSTS} ; do
    debug "  - considering ${not_mastered_host}"
    if [ "${not_mastered_host}" = "${required_host}" ] ; then
      debug "  - found ${required_host} = ${not_mastered_host}"
      foundHost=1
    fi
  done
# fail if no NOT mastered host matched up with the required host
  if [ ${foundHost} -ne 1 ] ; then
    doerror "node does not deny mastering required logical host \
${required_host}"
    exit 1
  fi
done
##############################################################################
# At this point we know the set of NOT mastered hosts contains the set
# of required hosts.
debug "logical hosts mastered OK"
# Check that the administrative file system of each required logical
# host is mounted. Yield failure if a file system is not mounted.
# This section is required since to STOP a data service, access to
# the data service's shared files is probably required.
CURRENT_MOUNTS=`mount | awk -e '{print $1}' | xargs echo `
for required_host in ${SERVICE_HOSTS} ; do
  neededMount=`haget -f pathprefix -h ${required_host}`
  foundMount=0
  debug "searching for filesystem on ${neededMount}"
  for mountPoint in ${CURRENT_MOUNTS} ; do
    debug "  - considering ${mountPoint}"
    if [ "${mountPoint}" = "${neededMount}" ] ; then
      debug "  - found ${mountPoint}"
      foundMount=1
    fi
  done
# Fail if no mounted file system matches target file system
  if [ ${foundMount} -ne 1 ] ; then
    doerror "administrative filesystem ${neededMount} for logical host \
${required_host} is not mounted"
```

```
    exit 1
  fi
done
# Check that additional file systems, if defined, are mounted and available
# to this physical node. Required file systems are defined as a word list in the
# config file.
if [ -n "${REQUIRED_FILESYSTEMS}" ] ; then
  for neededMount in ${REQUIRED_FILESYSTEMS} ; do
    foundMount=0
    debug "searching for filesystem on ${neededMount}"
    for mountPoint in ${CURRENT_MOUNTS} ; do
      debug "  - considering ${mountPoint}"
      if [ "${mountPoint}" = "${neededMount}" ] ; then
        debug "  - found ${mountPoint}"
        foundMount=1
      fi
    done

# Yield failure if no mounted file system matches requirements
    if [ ${foundMount} -ne 1 ] ; then
      doerror "required extra filesystem ${neededMount} is not mounted"
      exit 1
    fi
  done
fi
########################################################################
# At this point we know that the file systems are mounted and the logical
# hosts are mastered by this node.
debug "required filesystems mounted OK"
# Any extra checking, e.g., testing to see if an additional config file is
accessible,
# should be placed in this section. After verifying that additional testing is
# successful, we can proceed to verify if a data service is already running.
debug "additional checking passed OK"
# Exit if the service has already been stopped
pmfadm -q ${SERVICE_NAME}
if [ $? -eq 1 ] ; then
  debug "${SERVICE_NAME} is not running on this node"
  exit 0
fi
########################################################################
# At this point we can be sure that the data service is already running
# and can be stopped.
debug "dataservice is currently running"
# If the STOP_PROGRAM variable is defined, ensure that the program is executable;
# otherwise, complain and attempt to use the default TERM on the pmfadm process.
if [ -n "${STOP_PROGRAM}" ] ; then
  executable=`echo ${STOP_PROGRAM} | awk -e '{print $1}'`
```

```
  if [ ! -x "${executable}" ] ; then
    doerror "cannot execute ${executable} \
- will try to terminate START program using pmfadm"
  STOP_PROGRAM=""
  fi
fi
# Parse any arguments which were set by the config file. If a STOP_PROGRAM
# is specified, then only stop monitoring using pmfadm.
wait_time=""
signal=""
if [ -z "${STOP_PROGRAM}" ] ; then
  if [ -n "${PMF_WAIT}" ] ; then
    wait_time=${PMF_WAIT}
  fi

  if [ -n "${PMF_SIGNAL}" ] ; then
    signal=${PMF_SIGNAL}
  else
    signal="TERM"
  fi
fi
# Stop monitoring the data service and ensure it did work.
pmfadm -s ${SERVICE_NAME} ${wait_time} ${signal}
if [ $? -ne 0 ] ; then
  doerror "couldn't stop monitoring \"${START_PROGRAM}\". \
error was $? continuing anyway"
fi
if [ -n "${STOP_PROGRAM}" ] ; then
  ${STOP_PROGRAM}
fi
########################################################################
# At this point the data service has been instructed to stop.
debug "data service has been instructed to stop through the ${STOP_PROGRAM}"

# If the STOP_PROGRAM variable is not defined in the config file, this
# section must include code to ensure that the data
# service has come to a proper stop, and that any leftover files, etc.,
# have been cleaned up. There is no simple way to generalize this.
########################################################################
# at this point the data service has stopped
debug "data service has stopped"
exit 0
```

Figure B-3 ABORT_NET DSM Flow Control Diagram

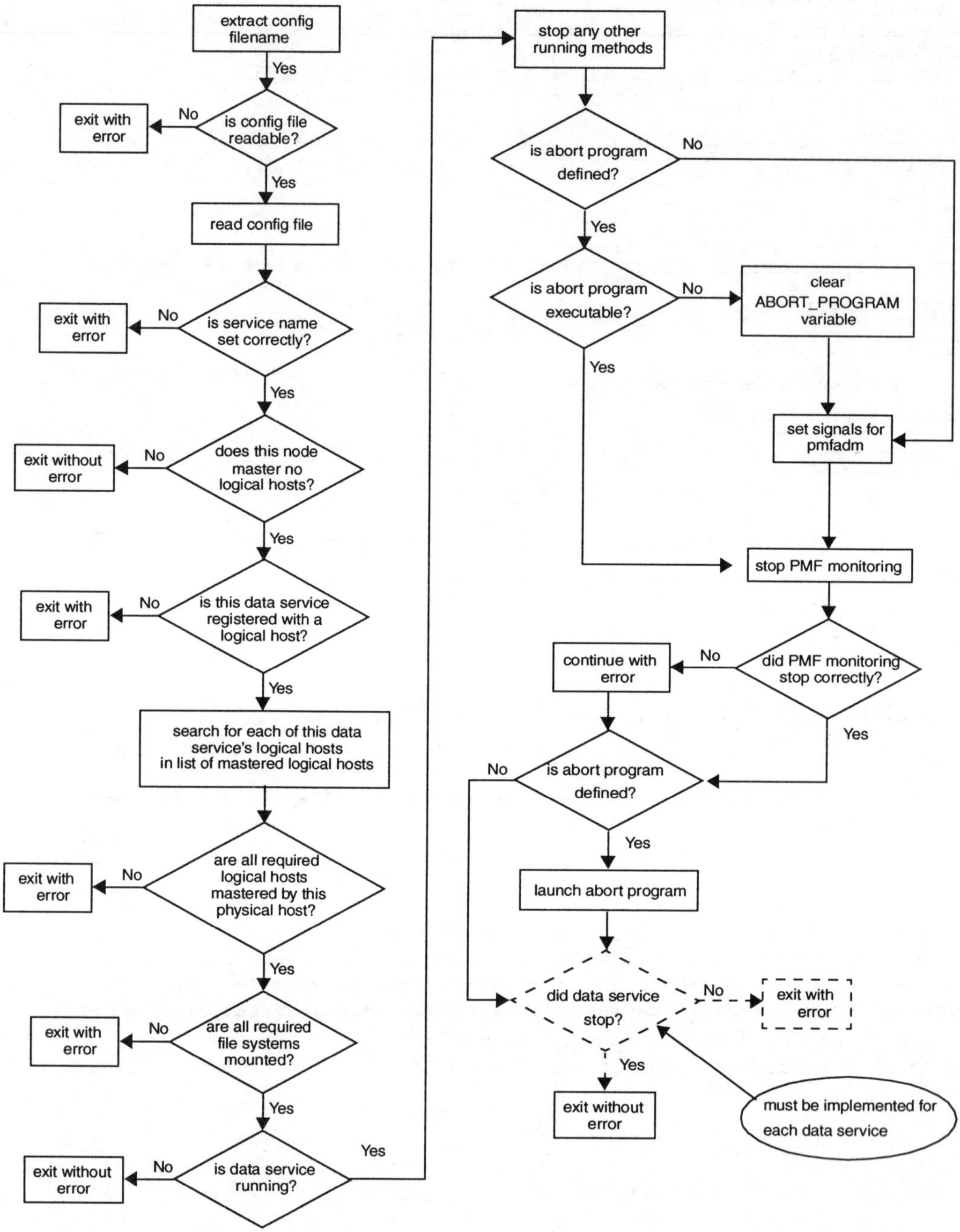

Code Example B-3 Shell Script Code for ABORT_NET DSM

```
#!/bin/sh#
# generic ABORT_NET script for HA data services Version 1.3
# Copyright 1999 Sun Microsystems, Inc. All rights reserved.
# This script can be used as a template for developing an ABORT_NET
# DSM for SunCluster 2.2 data services. The intention is to help reduce the
# amount of "boilerplate" work before a production script is developed.
# ABORT_NET is called by clustd when the node encounters certain problems.
# This script can be invoked at any time, including midway processing for the
# START and STOP DSM processing. ABORT_NET is only called on the physical
# node invoking the routine.
# When the ABORT_NET script is launched, it is called with the
# following arguments:
#           $1 = comma-separated list of the logical hosts which should be
#                mastered by this physical node
#           $2 = comma-separated list of the logical hosts which should NOT
#                be mastered by this physical node
#           $3 = time in seconds until clustd will time out the process.
# This script makes the following assumptions:
#           - the script is named <dataservice>_abort_net, where <dataservice>
#             is the unique data service name
#          - the file <dataservice>.config exists in the same directory as this
#            script and it defines at the very least the variables SERVICE_NAME
#             and START_PROGRAM
#           - the data service program can be started, stopped, and queried
#             using pmfadm
# If your data service does not support the above assumptions, then this script
# should be modified appropriately.
#########################################################################
#  debug function
debug()
  {
  if [ "$kDEBUG" = "1" ] ; then
    logger -p ${SYSLOG}.debug "${PROG} [$$]: $1"
  fi
  }
#########################################################################
# error function
doerror()
  {
  debug $1
  logger -p ${SYSLOG}.err "${PROG} [$$]: $1"
  }
#########################################################################
# The following variable should be set to 0 to turn debugging off
kDEBUG=1
PATH=/usr/sbin:/usr/bin:/opt/SUNWcluster/bin
```

```
PROG=`basename $0`
BASEDIR=`dirname $0`
SYSLOG=`haget -f syslog_facility`
MASTERED=$1
NOT_MASTERED=$2
TIMEOUT=$3
########################################################################
debug "called as ${PROG} \"${MASTERED}\" \"${NOT_MASTERED}\" ${TIMEOUT}"
# Strip the DSM suffix from the program name to build the config file name
# then extract its contents to build required variables.
CONFIG_FILE=`echo ${PROG} | sed s/_abort_net/.config/`
if [ ! -r "${BASEDIR}/${CONFIG_FILE}" ] ; then
  doerror "cannot read config file ${BASEDIR}/${CONFIG_FILE}"
  exit 1
fi
debug "reading config file ${BASEDIR}/${CONFIG_FILE}"
. ${BASEDIR}/${CONFIG_FILE}
# fail if service name does not exist
if [ -z "${SERVICE_NAME}" ] ; then
  doerror "cannot determine service name"
  exit 1
fi
# exit peacefully if all logical hosts are mastered by this node
if [ -z "${NOT_MASTERED}" ] ; then
  debug "all logical hosts are mastered by this node"
  exit 0
fi
# fail if there are no logical hosts assigned to this service
SERVICE_HOSTS=`hareg -q  ${SERVICE_NAME} -H | xargs echo `
if [ -z "${SERVICE_HOSTS}" ] ; then
  doerror "no logical hosts assigned to ${SERVICE_NAME}"
  exit 1
fi
########################################################################
# At this point the trivial cases of failure have been managed and
# we can start verifying appropriate node resource allocation, e.g.,
# logical host mastering.
debug "trivial failure cases passed OK"
# Now loop through all logical hosts required by this data service,
# and compare against the list of hosts not mastered by this node. Yield
# a failure if a required logical host is not found in the list of hosts
# not mastered by this node.
NOT_MASTERED_HOSTS=`echo ${NOT_MASTERED} | tr ',' ' '`
for required_host in ${SERVICE_HOSTS} ; do
  foundHost=0
  debug "searching for ${required_host}"
  for not_mastered_host in ${NOT_MASTERED_HOSTS} ; do
    debug "  - considering ${not_mastered_host}"
```

```
    if [ "${not_mastered_host}" = "${required_host}" ] ; then
      debug "  - found ${required_host} = ${not_mastered_host}"
      foundHost=1
    fi
  done
# fail if no NOT mastered host matches the required host *** Deleted extra "not"
***
  if [ ${foundHost} -ne 1 ] ; then
    doerror "node does not deny mastering required logical host \
${required_host}"
    exit 1
  fi
done
#########################################################################
# At this point we know the set of mastered hosts contains the set
# of required hosts.
debug "logical hosts mastered OK"
# Check for any running instances of STOP or START DSMs and kill them
for method in "START" "START_NET" "STOP" "STOP_NET" ; do
  progName=`hareg -q ${SERVICE_NAME} -M ${method}`
  if [ -n "${progName}" ] ; then
    debug "looking for ${progName}"
    pid=`ps -e -o tty,pid,args  | grep ${progName} | awk -e '{print $2}'`
    if [ -n "${pid}" ] ; then
      debug "killing ${progName}"
      kill -9 ${pid}
    fi
  fi
done
#########################################################################
# At this point we are guaranteed no other STOP or START DSMs are running.
debug "no stop or start methods should be running"
# Check that the administrative file system of each required logical host
# is mounted properly. Yield failure if required file system is not mounted.
# This section is necessary since data service file system access may be required
# in the cleanup process.
CURRENT_MOUNTS=`mount | awk -e '{print $1}' | xargs echo `
for required_host in ${SERVICE_HOSTS} ; do
  neededMount=`haget -f pathprefix -h ${required_host}`
  foundMount=0
  debug "searching for filesystem on ${neededMount}"
  for mountPoint in ${CURRENT_MOUNTS} ; do
    debug "  - considering ${mountPoint}"
    if [ "${mountPoint}" = "${neededMount}" ] ; then
      debug "  - found ${mountPoint}"
      foundMount=1
    fi
  done
```

```
# Fail if no mounted file system matches a required file system
  if [ ${foundMount} -ne 1 ] ; then
    doerror "administrative filesystem ${neededMount} for logical host \
${required_host} is not mounted"
    exit 1
  fi
done
# Check that additional file systems, if defined, are mounted and available
# to this physical node. Required file systems are defined as a word list in the
# config file
if [ -n "${REQUIRED_FILESYSTEMS}" ] ; then
  for neededMount in ${REQUIRED_FILESYSTEMS} ; do
    foundMount=0
    debug "searching for filesystem on ${neededMount}"
    for mountPoint in ${CURRENT_MOUNTS} ; do
      debug "  - considering ${mountPoint}"
      if [ "${mountPoint}" = "${neededMount}" ] ; then
        debug "  - found ${mountPoint}"
        foundMount=1
      fi
    done
# Yield failure if no mounted file system matches requirements
    if [ ${foundMount} -ne 1 ] ; then
      doerror "required extra filesystem ${neededMount} is not mounted"
      exit 1
    fi
  done
fi
########################################################################
# At this point we know that the file systems are mounted and the logical
# hosts are mastered by this node.
debug "required filesystems mounted OK"
# Any extra checking, e.g., testing to see if an additional config file is
accessible,
# should be placed in this section. After verifying that additional testing is
# successful, we can proceed to verify if a data service is already stopped.
# Check to see if the data service has already been stopped
pmfadm -q ${SERVICE_NAME}
if [ $? -eq 1 ] ; then
  debug "${SERVICE_NAME} is not running on this node"
  exit 0
fi
########################################################################
# At this point we can ensure the data service is running and can be stopped.
debug "dataservice is currently running"
# If the ABORT_PROGRAM variable is not defined by the config file, then all
# code that ensures appropriate cleanup of the data service must be included
# here. Ensure that the ABORT program can actually be executed; otherwise,
```

```
# complain and attempt to use the default TERM on the pmfadm process.
if [ -n "${ABORT_PROGRAM}" ] ; then
  executable=`echo ${ABORT_PROGRAM} | awk -e '{print $1}'`
  if [ ! -x "${executable}" ] ; then
    doerror "cannot execute ${executable} \
- will try to terminate START program using pmfadm"
  ABORT_PROGRAM=""
  fi
fi
# Parse options to pmfadm, if any were supplied in the config file
# If an ABORT_PROGRAM is specified, then only stop monitoring using
# pmfadm
wait_time=""
signal=""
if [ -z "${ABORT_PROGRAM}" ] ; then
  if [ -n "${PMF_WAIT}" ] ; then
    wait_time=${PMF_WAIT}
  fi

  if [ -n "${PMF_SIGNAL}" ] ; then
    signal=${PMF_SIGNAL}
  else
    signal="KILL"
  fi
fi
# Stop monitoring the data service and verify it worked
pmfadm -s ${SERVICE_NAME} ${wait_time} ${signal}
if [ $? -ne 0 ] ; then
  doerror "couldn't stop monitoring \"${START_PROGRAM}\". \
error was $? continuing anyway"
fi
if [ -n "${ABORT_PROGRAM}" ] ; then
  ${ABORT_PROGRAM}
fi
########################################################################
# At this point the data service has been instructed to stop.
debug "data service has been instructed to stop"
# This section should be extended with code to ensure that the data
# service has come to a proper stop and that any leftover files have
# been cleaned up. There is no simple way to generalize this and you need
# to resort to application expertise to make sure an appropriate cleanup
# has taken place.
########################################################################
# at this point the data service has stopped
debug "data service has stopped"
exit 0
```

The START_NET, STOP_NET, and ABORT_NET DSM scripts described previously could be used *as-is*, provided the DSM routines comply with the naming convention used, and the configuration file is correctly structured. However, it is advisable to insert code in the STOP_NET and ABORT_NET DSMs to ensure the application is correctly stopped prior to exiting—adding code to a DSM requires expert knowledge of the application covered by the data service and is not covered in this publication.

Fault Monitoring

The START_NET, STOP_NET, and ABORT_NET DSM template scripts previously discussed provide the basic functions required to start, stop, and abort applications associated with a data service. The following section provides a basic DSM script used for application monitoring and management using the Sun Cluster process monitoring facility (PMF).

Note: When running an application or associated children, if they die, they can be restarted by the PMF framework.

Implementation of application fault monitoring (and management) requires the creation and registration of fault monitoring programs. The FM_INIT, FM_START, FM_STOP, and FM_CHECK DSMs must be registered with the SC2.2 software. This section introduces basic FM_START and FM_STOP DSM script templates to implement application fault probing (refer to Figures B-4 and B-5).

Note: This section assumes the fault monitor process is executed on the same physical node as the data service.

Figure B-4 `FM_START` DSM Flow Control Diagram

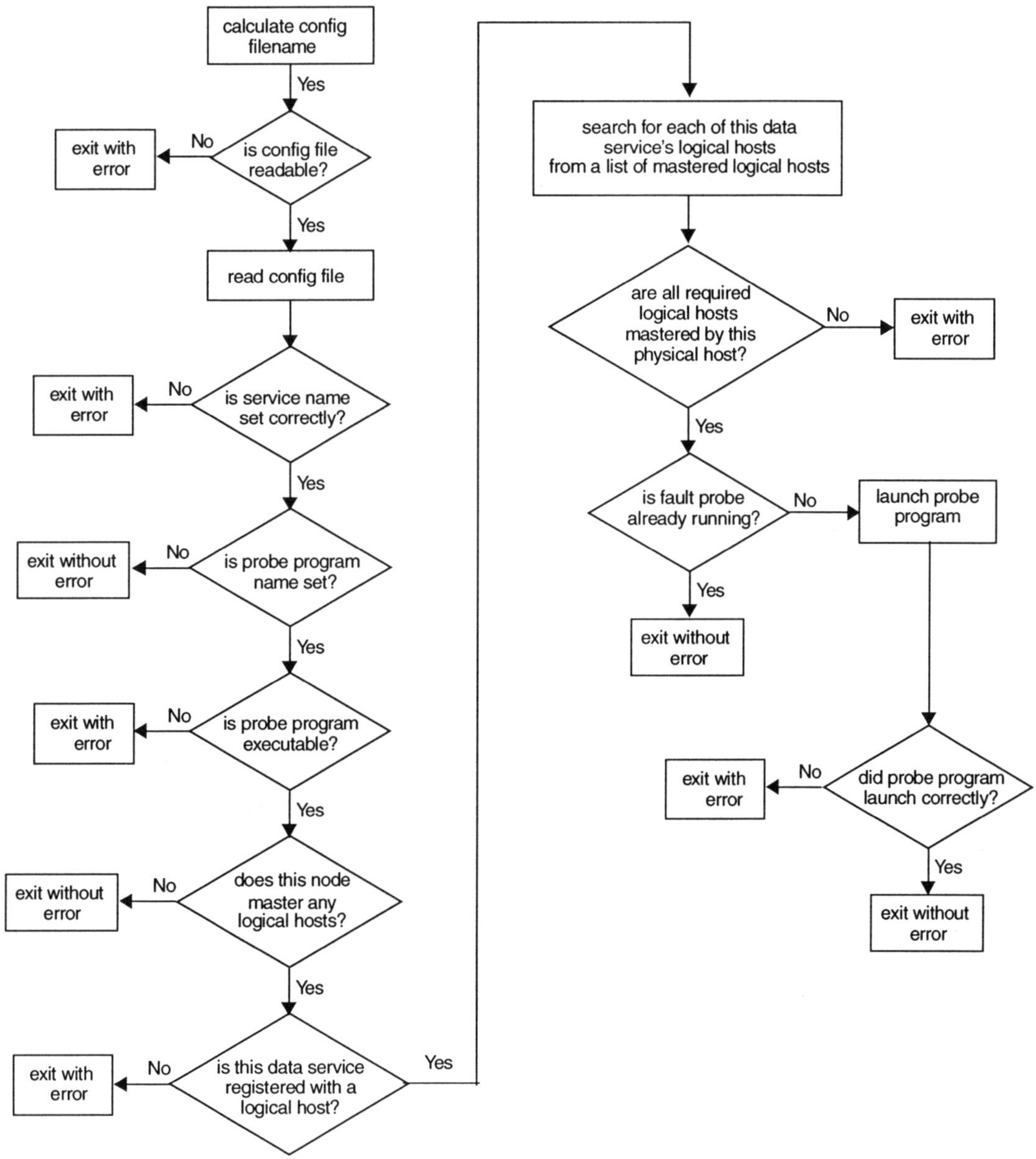

Code Example B-4 Shell Script Code for FM_START DSM

```
#!/bin/sh
# generic FM_START script for HA data services Version 1.3
# Copyright 1999 Sun Microsystems, Inc. All rights reserved.
# This script can be used as a template for developing an FM_START
# DSM for SunCluster 2.2 data services. The intention is to help reduce the
# amount of "boilerplate" work before a production script is developed.
# FM_START is called by clustd as part of the cluster reconfiguration
# process. This script can be invoked several times during a cluster
# reconfiguration process by the same node, and it should be written to
# manage a wide range of cluster states.
# When the START_NET script is launched, it is called with the
# following arguments:
#           $1 = comma-separated list of the logical hosts which should be
#                mastered by this physical node
#           $2 = comma-separated list of the logical hosts which should NOT
#                be mastered by this physical node
#           $3 = time in seconds until clustd will timeout the process.
# This script makes the following assumptions:
#           - the script is named <dataservice>_fm_start, where <dataservice>
#             is the unique data service name
#          - the file <dataservice>.config exists in the same directory as this
#            script and it defines at the very least the variables SERVICE_NAME
#            and START_PROGRAM
#           - the data service program can be started, stopped and queried
#             using pmfadm
#         - this FM_START DSM will execute on the same physical system where the
#             data service is running.
# If your data service does not support the above assumptions, then this script
# should be modified appropriately. For this script to perform any useful action,
a
# fault probe program must be developed, and registered in the configuration file
as
# FAULT_PROBE=fault_probe_program
##########################################################################
#  debug function
debug()
  {
  if [ "$kDEBUG" = "1" ] ; then
    logger -p ${SYSLOG}.debug "${PROG} [$$]: $1"
  fi
  }
##########################################################################
# error function
doerror()
  {
  debug $1
```

```
  logger -p ${SYSLOG}.err "${PROG} [$$]: $1"
  }
########################################################################
# The following variable should be set to 0 to turn debugging off
kDEBUG=1
PATH=/usr/sbin:/usr/bin:/opt/SUNWcluster/bin
PROG=`basename $0`
BASEDIR=`dirname $0`
SYSLOG=`haget -f syslog_facility`
MASTERED=$1
NOT_MASTERED=$2
TIMEOUT=$3
########################################################################
debug "called as ${PROG} \"${MASTERED}\" \"${NOT_MASTERED}\" ${TIMEOUT}"
# Strip the DSM suffix from the program name to build the config file name,
# then extract its contents to build required variables.
CONFIG_FILE=`echo ${PROG} | sed s/_fm_start/.config/`
if [ ! -r "${BASEDIR}/${CONFIG_FILE}" ] ; then
  doerror "cannot read config file ${BASEDIR}/${CONFIG_FILE}"
  exit 1
fi
debug "reading config file ${BASEDIR}/${CONFIG_FILE}"
. ${BASEDIR}/${CONFIG_FILE}
# Fail if service name does not exist
if [ -z "${SERVICE_NAME}" ] ; then
  doerror "cannot determine service name"
  exit 1
fi
# set the fault monitoring name
FM_NAME="${SERVICE_NAME}_FM"
# Exit if fault probe program name is unknown
if [ -z "${FAULT_PROBE}" ] ; then
  doerror "cannot determine fault program name"
  exit 0
fi
# Fail if the fault probe program cannot be found or is not executable
executable=`echo ${FAULT_PROBE} | awk -e '{print $1}'`
if [ ! -x "${executable}" ] ; then
  doerror "cannot find executable start program ${executable}"
  exit 1
fi
# exit peacefully if no logical hosts are mastered on this node
if [ -z "${MASTERED}" ] ; then
  debug "no logical hosts mastered by this node"
  exit 0
fi
# fail if there are no logical hosts assigned to this service
SERVICE_HOSTS=`hareg -q  ${SERVICE_NAME} -H | xargs echo `
```

```
if [ -z "${SERVICE_HOSTS}" ] ; then
  doerror "no logical hosts assigned to ${SERVICE_NAME}"
  exit 1
fi
#########################################################################
# At this point the trivial cases of failure have been managed and
# we can start verifying appropriate node resource allocation, e.g.,
# logical host mastering.
debug "trivial failure cases passed OK"
# Now loop through all logical hosts required by this data service,
# and compare against the list of hosts mastered by this node. Yield
# a failure if no mastered logical hosts are found.
MASTERED_HOSTS=`echo ${MASTERED} | tr ',' ' '`
for required_host in ${SERVICE_HOSTS} ; do
  foundHost=0
  debug "searching for ${required_host}"
  for mastered_host in ${MASTERED_HOSTS} ; do
    debug "  - considering ${mastered_host}"
    if [ "${mastered_host}" = "${required_host}" ] ; then
      debug "  - found ${required_host} = ${mastered_host}"
      foundHost=1
    fi
  done
# fail if no mastered host matches the required host
  if [ ${foundHost} -ne 1 ] ; then
    doerror "node does not master required logical host \
${required_host}"
    exit 1
  fi
done
#########################################################################
# At this point we know the set of mastered hosts contains the set
# of required hosts.
debug "logical hosts mastered OK"
# exit if the fault probe has already been started
if `pmfadm -q ${FM_NAME}` ; then
  debug "fault probe ${FM_NAME} is already running on this node"
  exit 0
fi
#########################################################################
# At this point we can be sure that the data service fault probing is not
# already running and it can be started.
debug "fault probe ${FM_NAME} is not already running"
# start the fault probe & check it started
pmfadm -c ${FM_NAME} ${FAULT_PROBE}
if [ $? -ne 0 ] ; then
  doerror "couldn't start \"${FAULT_PROBE}\". error was $?"
  exit 1
```

```
fi
##########################################################################
# At this point the fault probing program is running
debug "fault monitoring ${FM_NAME} has started"
exit 0
```

Figure B-5 FM_STOP DSM Flow Control Diagram

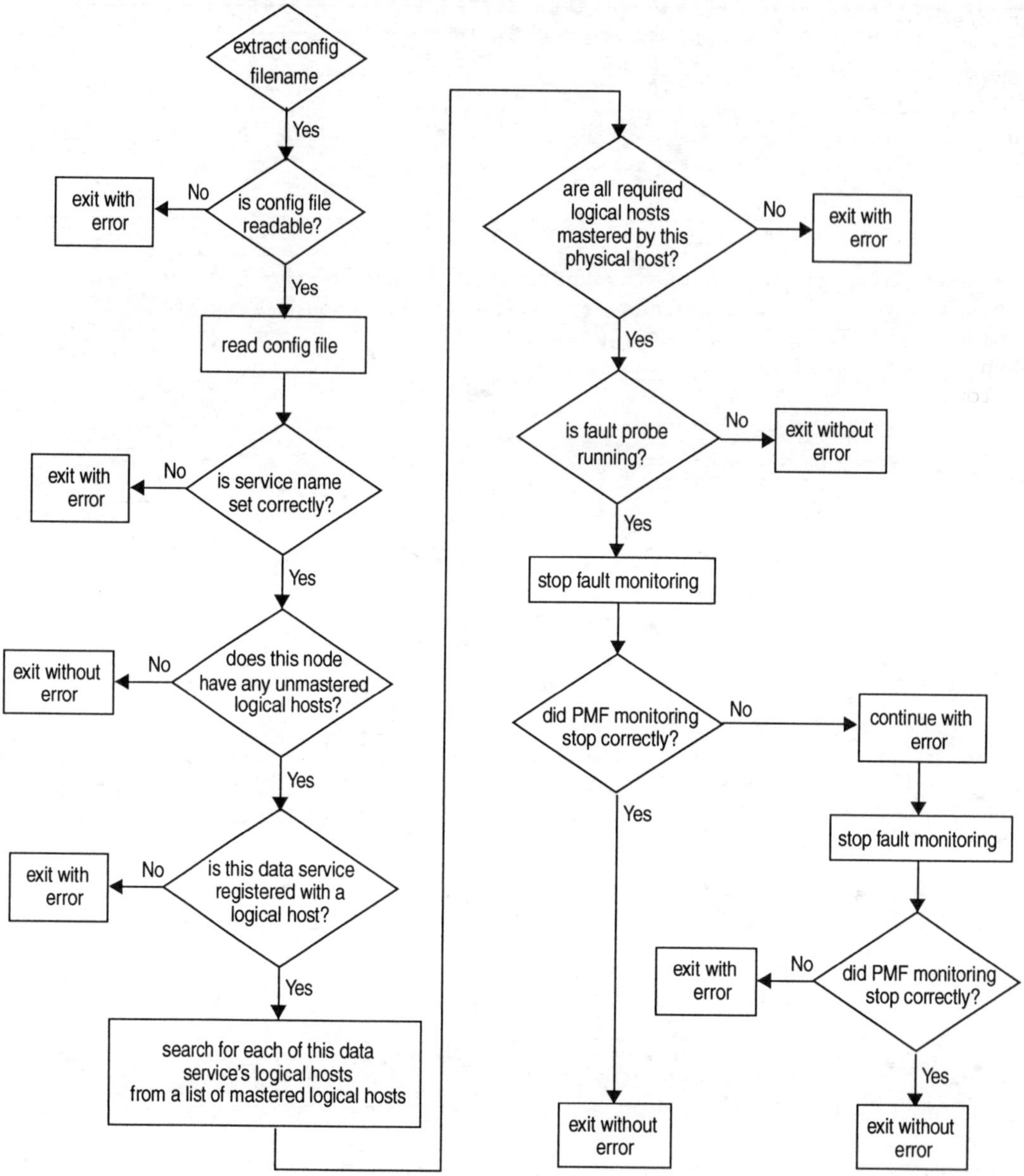

Code Example B-5 Shell Script Code for FM_STOP DSM

```
#!/bin/sh#
# generic FM_STOP script for HA data services Version 1.0
# Copyright 1999 Sun Microsystems, Inc. All rights reserved.
#
# This script can be used as a template for developing an FM_STOP
# DSM for SunCluster 2.2 data services. The intention is to help reduce the
# amount of "boilerplate" work before a production script is developed.
#
# FM_STOP is called by clustd as part of the cluster reconfiguration
# process. This script can be invoked several times during a cluster
# reconfiguration process by the same node, and it should be written to
# manage a wide range of cluster states.
# When the FM_STOP script is launched, it is called with the
# following arguments:
#            $1 = comma-separated list of the logical hosts which should be
#                 mastered by this physical node
#            $2 = comma-separated list of the logical hosts which should NOT
#                 be mastered by this physical node
#            $3 = time in seconds until clustd will time out the process.
# This script makes the following assumptions:
#            - the script is named <dataservice>_fm_stop, where <dataservice>
#              is the unique data service name
#            - the file <dataservice>.config exists in the same directory as this
#              script and it defines at the very least the variables SERVICE_NAME
#              and START_PROGRAM
#            - the data service program can be started, stopped and queried
#              using pmfadm
# If your data service does not support the above assumptions, then this script
# should be modified appropriately.
##########################################################################
#  debug function
debug()
  {
  if [ "$kDEBUG" = "1" ] ; then
    logger -p ${SYSLOG}.debug "${PROG} [$$]: $1"
  fi
  }
##########################################################################
# error function
doerror()
  {
  debug $1
  logger -p ${SYSLOG}.err "${PROG} [$$]: $1"
  }
##########################################################################
# The following variable should be set to 0 to turn debugging off
```

```
kDEBUG=1

PATH=/usr/sbin:/usr/bin:/opt/SUNWcluster/bin

PROG=`basename $0`
BASEDIR=`dirname $0`
SYSLOG=`haget -f syslog_facility`

MASTERED=$1
NOT_MASTERED=$2
TIMEOUT=$3
########################################################################
debug "called as ${PROG} \"${MASTERED}\" \"${NOT_MASTERED}\" ${TIMEOUT}"

## Strip the DSM suffix from the program name to build the config file name,
# then extract its contents to build required variables.
CONFIG_FILE=`echo ${PROG} | sed s/_fm_stop/.config/`

if [ ! -r "${BASEDIR}/${CONFIG_FILE}" ] ; then
  doerror "cannot read config file ${BASEDIR}/${CONFIG_FILE}"
  exit 1
fi
debug "reading config file ${BASEDIR}/${CONFIG_FILE}"
. ${BASEDIR}/${CONFIG_FILE}
# fail if service name does not exist
if [ -z "${SERVICE_NAME}" ] ; then
  doerror "cannot determine service name"
  exit 1
fi
FM_NAME="${SERVICE_NAME}_FM"
# exit peacefully if no logical hosts are mastered on this node
if [ -z "${NOT_MASTERED}" ] ; then
  debug "all logical hosts are mastered by this node"
  exit 0
fi
# fail if there are no logical hosts assigned to this service
SERVICE_HOSTS=`hareg -q  ${SERVICE_NAME} -H | xargs echo `
if [ -z "${SERVICE_HOSTS}" ] ; then
  doerror "no logical hosts assigned to ${SERVICE_NAME}"
  exit 1
fi
########################################################################
# At this point the trivial cases of failure have been managed and
# we can start verifying appropriate node resource allocation, e.g.,
# logical host mastering
debug "trivial failure cases passed OK"

# Now loop through all logical hosts required by this data service,
```

```
# and compare against the list of hosts mastered by this node. Yield
# a failure if no mastered logical hosts are found.
MASTERED_HOSTS=`echo ${MASTERED} | tr ',' ' '`
for required_host in ${SERVICE_HOSTS} ; do
  foundHost=0
  debug "searching for ${required_host}"
  for not_mastered_host in ${NOT_MASTERED_HOSTS} ; do
    debug "  - considering ${not_mastered_host}"
    if [ "${not_mastered_host}" = "${required_host}" ] ; then
      debug "  - found ${required_host} = ${not_mastered_host}"
      foundHost=1
    fi
  done
# fail if no mastered host matches the required host
  if [ ${foundHost} -ne 1 ] ; then
    doerror "node does not deny mastering required logical host \
${required_host}"
    exit 1
  fi
done
##########################################################################
# At this point we know the set of mastered hosts contains the set
# of required hosts.
debug "logical hosts mastered OK"
# Exit if the fault probe has already been stopped
pmfadm -q ${FM_NAME}
if [ $? -eq 1 ] ; then
  debug "${FM_NAME} is not running on this node"
  exit 0
fi
##########################################################################
# At this point we can be sure that the fault probe is running and can
# be stopped
debug "fault probe is currently running"
# Stop the fault probe and ensure stop worked
pmfadm -s ${FM_NAME} TERM
if [ $? -ne 0 ] ; then
  doerror "couldn't stop fault probe \"${FAULT_PROBE}\". \
error was $? trying KILL"
  pmfadm -s ${FM_NAME} KILL
  if [ $? -ne 0 ] ; then
    doerror "couldn't kill fault probe \"${FAULT_PROBE}\". error was $?"
    exit 1
  fi
fi
##########################################################################
```

```
# At this point the fault probe has been stopped
debug "fault probe has stopped"
exit 0
```

Correct implementation of a fault probe program requires in-depth knowledge of the application associated with the data service *and* the data service environment /protocols. In general, a fault probe program is kept in an infinite loop, testing the data service periodically.

An example of a fault probe script for the `in.named` data service is provided in the *Sun Cluster™ 2.2 API Programmer's Guide,* and is recommended reading.

Summary

If an HA-agent for a specific application is not available from Sun Microsystems or third-party partners, the Sun Cluster 2.2 HA API enables any application (after being qualified) to be managed within the highly available SC2.2 framework. This functionality is a useful resource when business-critical and mission-critical applications are bound to HA requirements.

The approach of associating a data service to a particular logical host (which in turn is bound to a pre-defined set of IP addresses and disk resources) could produce an out-of-control situation if the underlying DSMs managing the application are complex. The purpose of this Appendix, and the "Sun Cluster 2.2 Data Services" chapter is to familiarize the reader with the processes involved in managing a data service and to assist in planning a customized data service infrastructure.

Glossary

bus (1) A circuit over which data or power is transmitted; often acts as a common connection among a number of locations. (2) A set of parallel communication lines that connects major components of a computer system including CPU, memory, and device controllers.

cache A buffer of high-speed memory filled at medium speed from main memory, often with instructions. A cache increases effective memory transfer rates and processor speed.

CLI Command-line interface.

DoS Denial of service.

Ethernet A type of local area network that enables real-time communication between machines connected directly together through cables. Ethernet was originally developed by Xerox in 1976, for linking minicomputers at the Palo Alto Research Center. A widely implemented network from which the IEEE 802.3 standard for contention networks was developed, Ethernet uses a bus topology (configuration) and relies on the form of access known as CSMA/CD to regulate traffic on the main communication line. Network nodes are connected by coaxial cable (with two variations) or by twisted-pair wiring.

export To write data from a database into a transportable operating system file. An *import* instruction reads data from this file back into the database.

failure rate The inverse of either the hardware or system mean time between failures.

FC-AL See **fiber channel arbitrated loop.**

FDDI Fiber distributed data interface. A high-speed networking standard whose underlying medium is fiber optics, and the topology is a dual-attached, counter-rotating token ring. FDDI networks can be identified by the orange fiber "cable."

fibre channel arbitrated loop (FCAL) Also known as an FC-AL. A high bandwidth, serial communication technology that supports 100 Mbyte/sec per loop. Most systems support dual-loop connections, which enable a total bandwidth of 200 Mbyte/sec.

Gbyte One billion bytes. In reference to computers, bytes are often expressed in multiples of powers of two. Therefore, a Gbyte can also be 1024 Mbytes, where a Mbyte is considered to be 2^20 (or 1,048,576) bytes.

Gigabit Ethernet A networking technology (Ethernet) that provides 1 Gbit/sec bandwidth for campus networks at a lower cost than other technologies of comparable speed.

import To read data from an operating system file into a database. The operating system file is originally created by performing an *export* on the database.

infant mortality A component exhibits a high failure rate during the early stages of its life.

instantaneous availability The probability of a system performing its intended function at any instant in time, *t*.

Internet A collection of networks interconnected by a set of routers that enables them to function as a single, large virtual network.

I/O Input/output. Refers to equipment used to communicate with a computer, the data involved in the communication, the media carrying the data, and the process of communicating the information.

kernel The core of the operating system software. The kernel manages the hardware (for example, processor cycles and memory) and enables fundamental services such as filing.

local area network Also known as LAN. A group of computer systems in close proximity that can communicate with one another via connecting hardware and software.

local host The CPU or computer on which a software application is running; the workstation.

mean time between failures The length of time between consecutive failures in the life of an item (under stated conditions).

mean time between interruptions A temporary system outage where repairs are not required.

MTBF See **mean time between failures**.

Network file system (NFS) A technology developed by Sun Microsystems designed to give users high-performance, transparent access to server file systems on global networks.

Point-to-point protocol Also known as PPP. The successor to SLIP, PPP provides router-to-router and host-to-network connections over both synchronous and asynchronous circuits.

RAID Redundant array of inexpensive disks. A subsystem for expanding disk storage.

RAS Reliability, accessibility, and serviceability.

remote procedure call Also known as RPC. A common paradigm for implementing the client/server model of distributed computing. A request sent to a remote system to execute a designated procedure using supplied arguments, with the results being returned to the caller. There are many variations of RPC, which have resulted in a variety of different protocols.

SAN See **storage area network**.

SCSI Small computer systems interface. An industry-standard bus used to connect disk and tape devices to a workstation.

serviceability The probability of a service action being completed in a given time period, *t*.

service level agreement Also known as an SLA. A formalized agreement between an IT department and one of its customers that defines services provided, such as level of availability of computing resources.

SPOF Single point of failure.

SLA See **service level agreement**.

SMP See **symmetric multiprocessing**.

Solaris Operating Environment Also known as Solaris OE. An operating environment from Sun Microsystems, Inc.

Starfire The Sun Enterprise 10000, a high-end SMP server that scales to 64 processors and supports dynamic system domains for system partitioning.

storage area network Also known as a SAN. A high-speed dedicated network with a direct connection between storage devices and servers. This approach enables storage and tape subsystems to be connected remotely from a server. Tape SANs enable efficient sharing of tape resources. Both the backup and restore tool and the tape library require SAN support to make this sharing possible.

Sun Enterprise 10000 Sun Enterprise 10000 server, also known as the *Starfire*.

Sun-Netscape Alliance A business alliance between Sun Microsystems, Inc. and the Netscape division of AOL. See `http://www.iplanet.com`.

swap To write the active pages of a job to external storage (swap space) and to read pages of another job from external page storage into real storage.

symmetric multiprocessing Also known as SMP. A method of using multiple processors in computer systems to deliver performance levels more predictable than MPP systems. SMP is efficient, and does not require specialized techniques for implementation.

Wide Area Network Also known as WAN. A network consisting of many systems providing file transfer services. This type of network can cover a large physical area, sometimes spanning the globe.

Index

Symbols

D

E

F

G

H

I

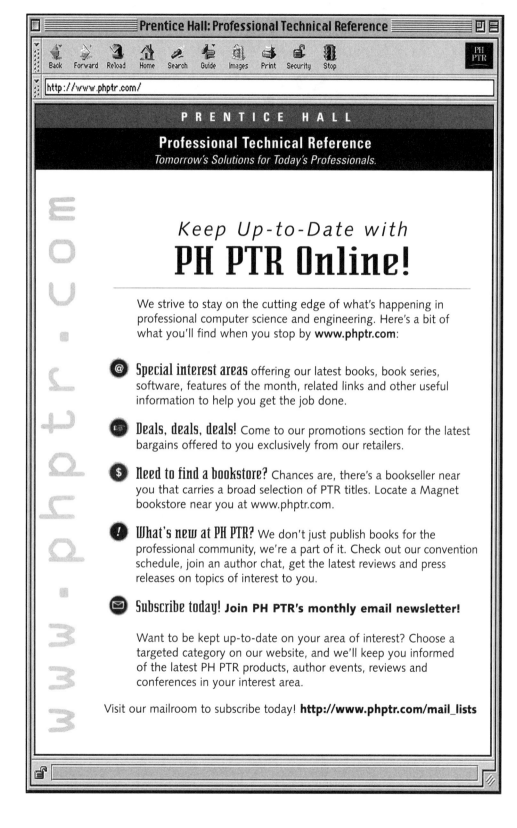

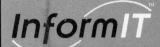

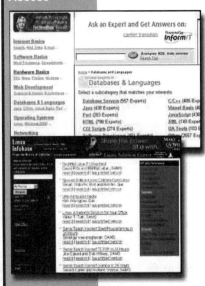